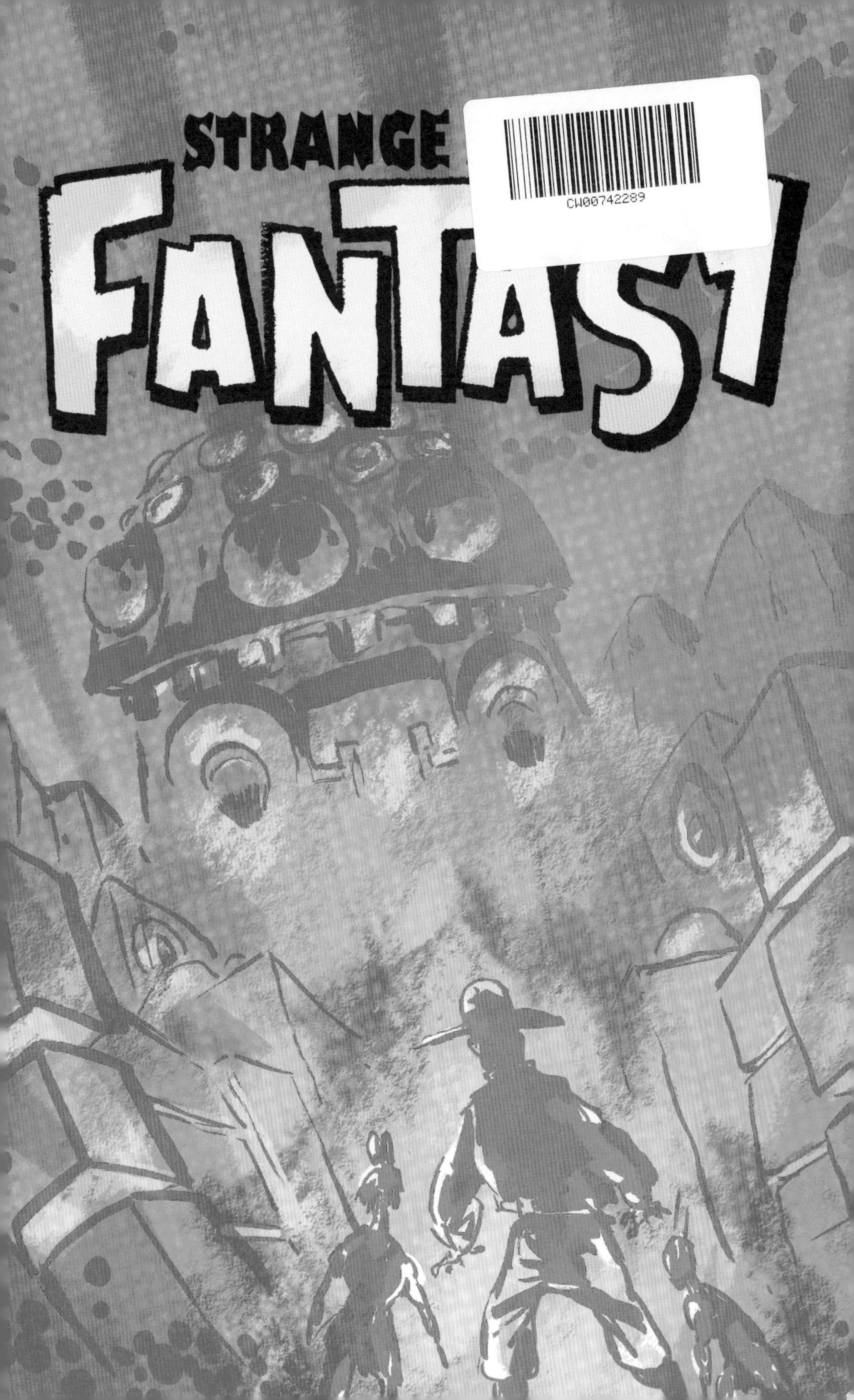
STRANGE
FANTASY

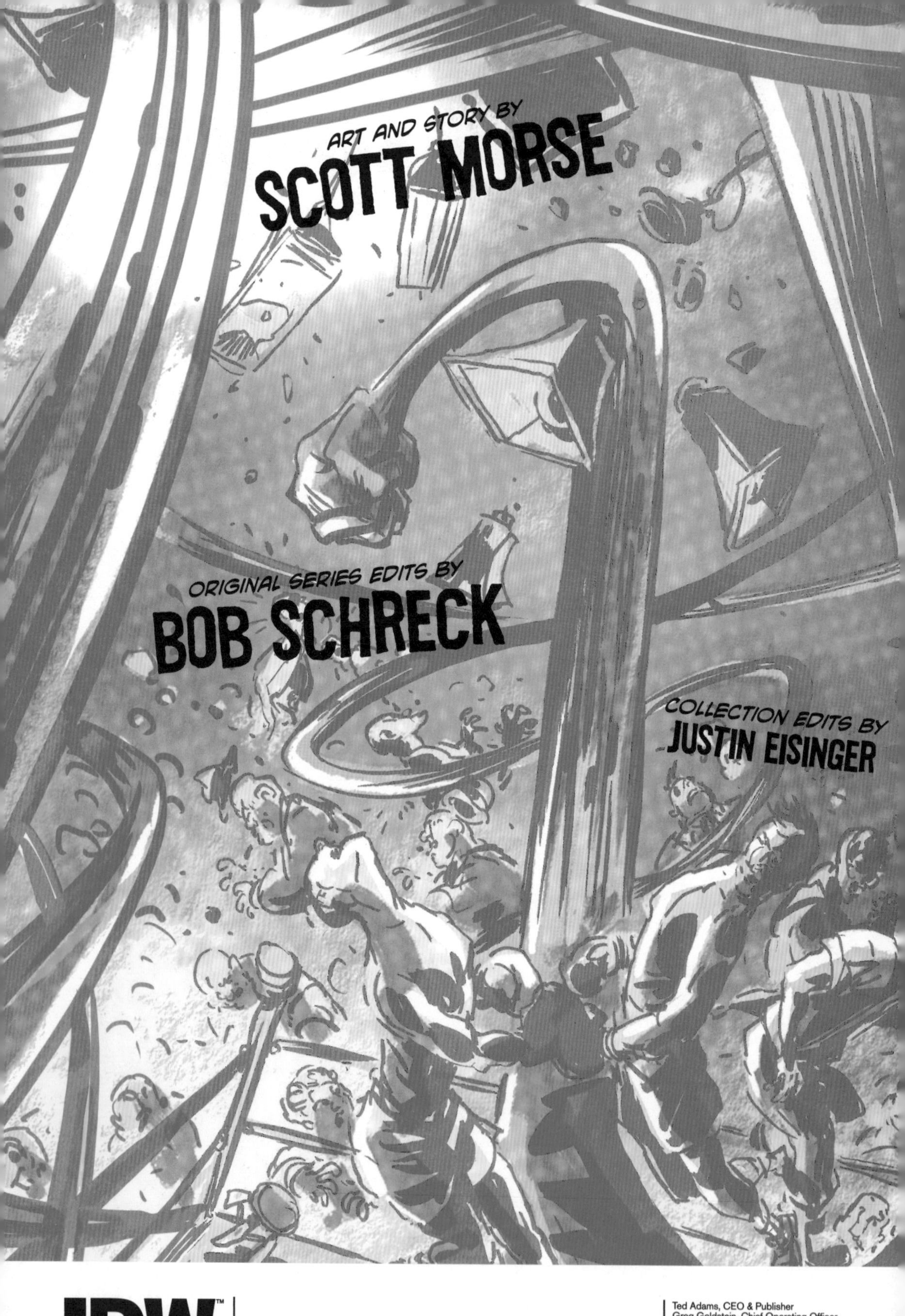
ART AND STORY BY
SCOTT MORSE
ORIGINAL SERIES EDITS BY
BOB SCHRECK
COLLECTION EDITS BY
JUSTIN EISINGER

IDW™

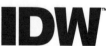

ISBN: 978-1-60010-888-4 14 13 12 11 1 2 3 4
www.IDWPUBLISHING.com

Originally published as STRANGE SCIENCE FANTASY Issues #1–6.

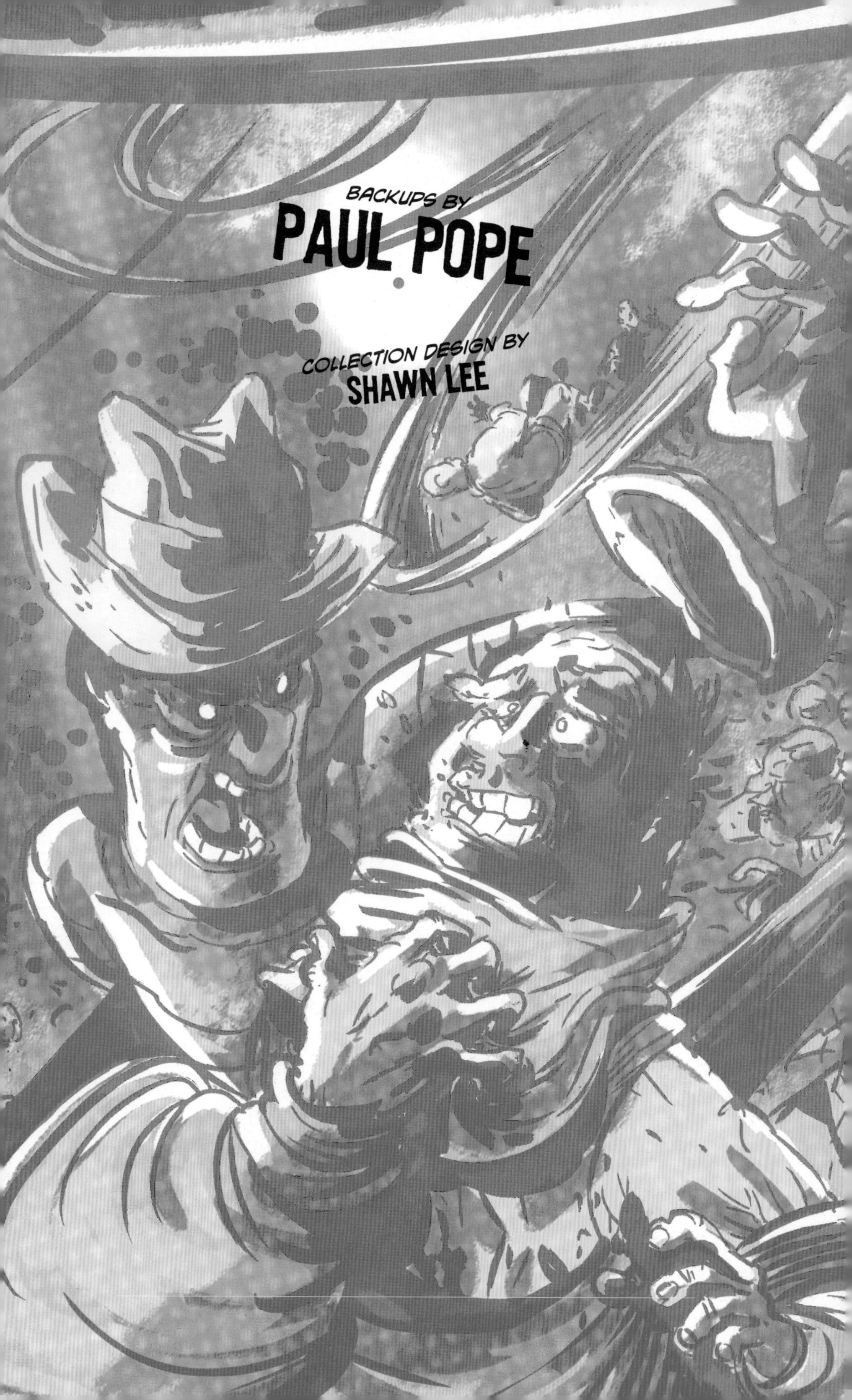
BACKUPS BY
PAUL POPE
COLLECTION DESIGN BY
SHAWN LEE

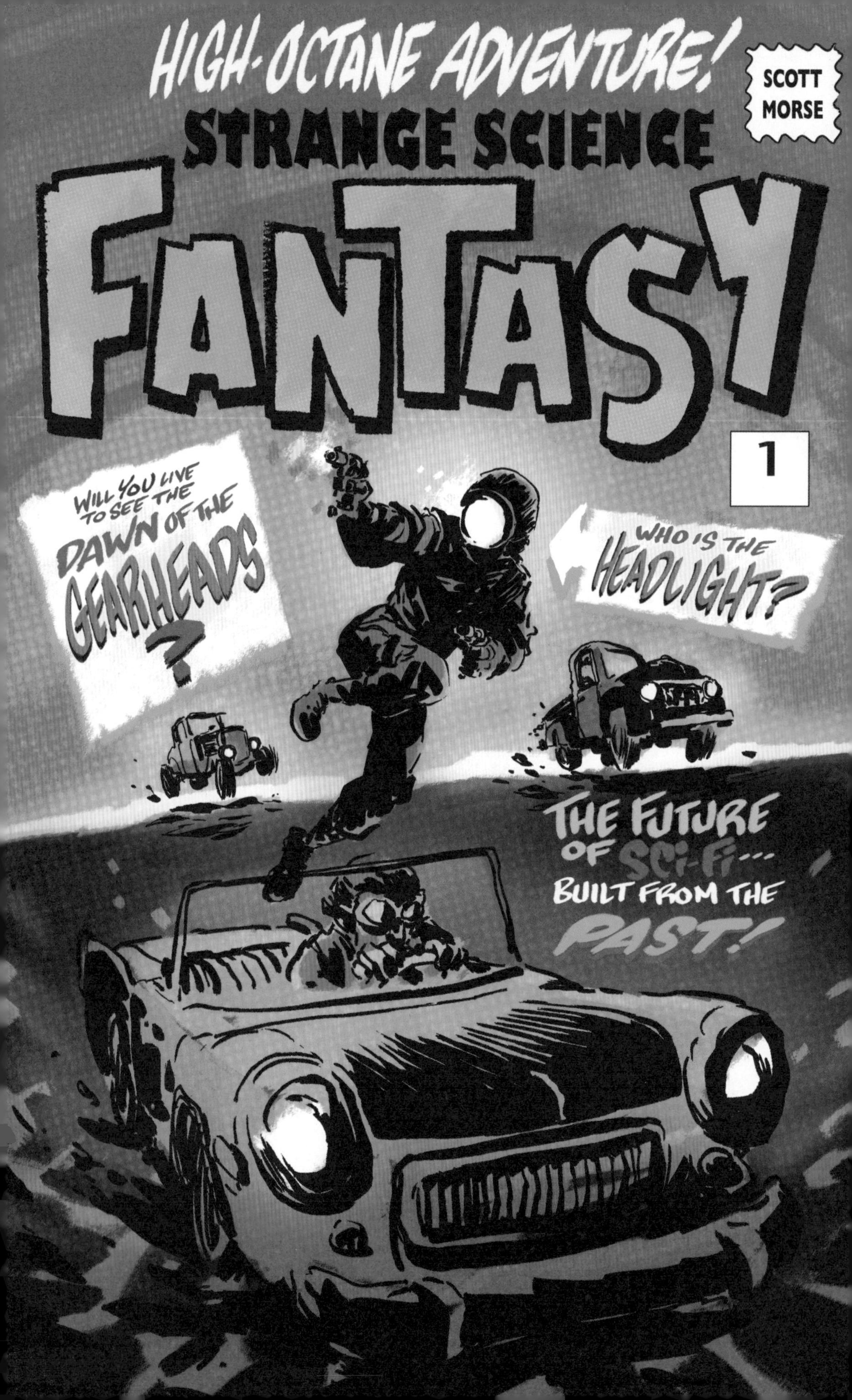
HIGH-OCTANE ADVENTURE!
SCOTT MORSE
STRANGE SCIENCE
FANTASY
1
WILL YOU LIVE TO SEE THE DAWN OF THE GEARHEADS?
WHO IS THE HEADLIGHT?
THE FUTURE OF SCI-FI... BUILT FROM THE PAST!

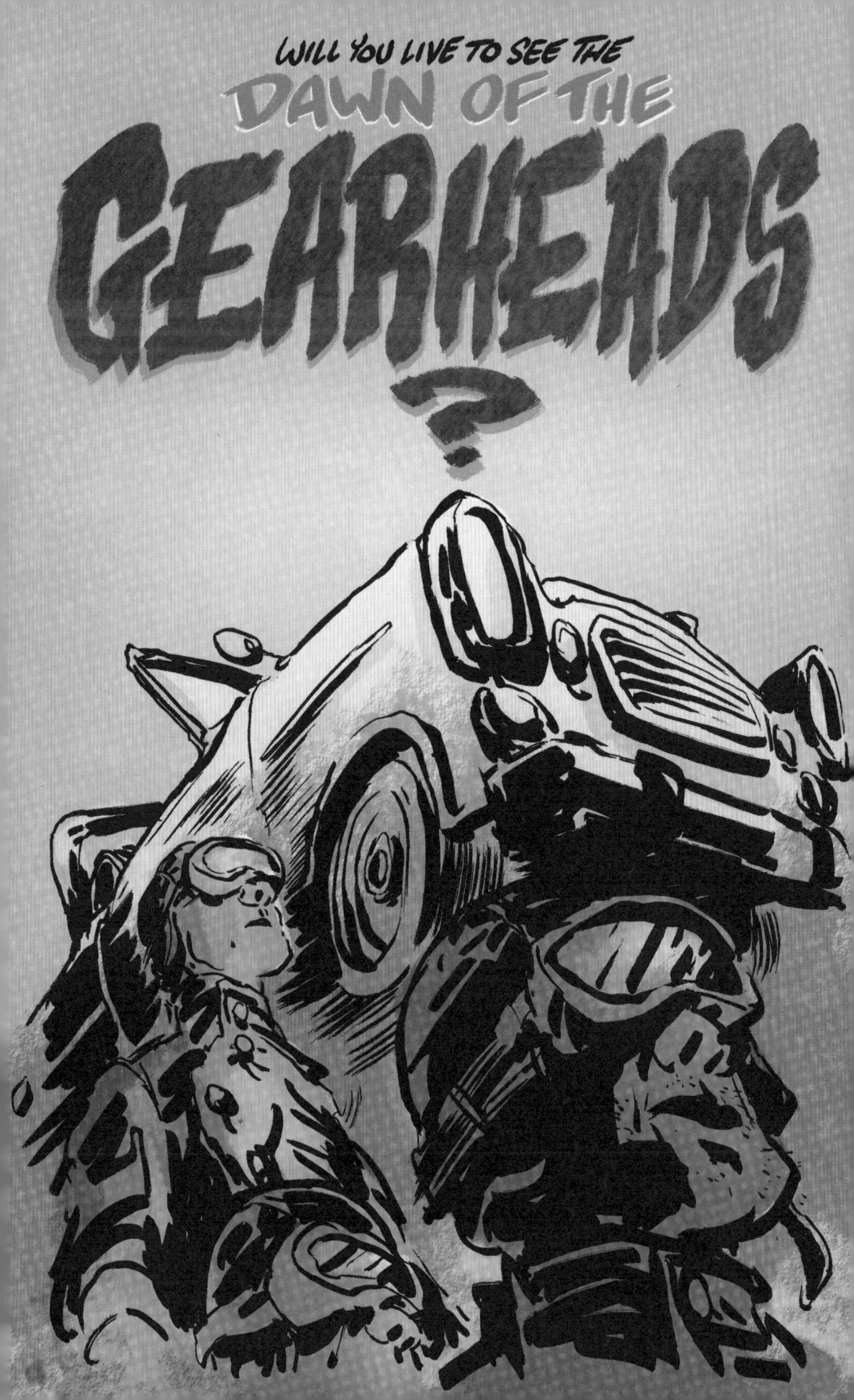
WILL YOU LIVE TO SEE THE
DAWN OF THE
GEARHEADS
?

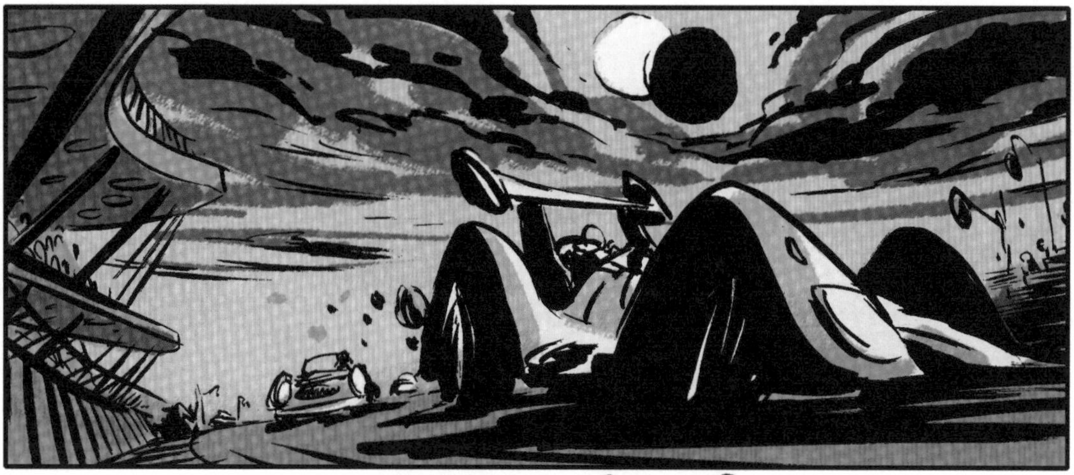

THE TIME: SOON!
THE PLACE: THE ASPHALT!

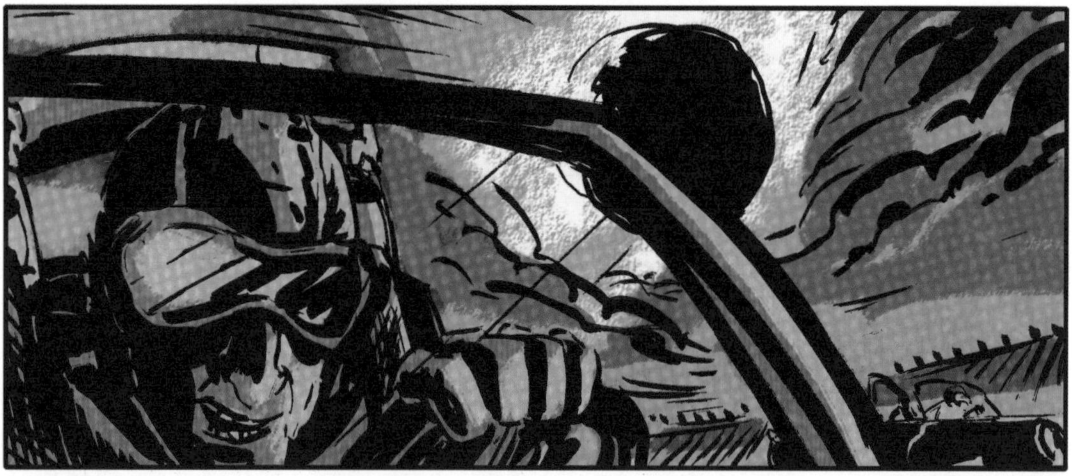

THE WORLD OF SPEED-DEMONS WOULD COMPLETE
THEIR FINAL LAP ON A CRASH-COURSE...

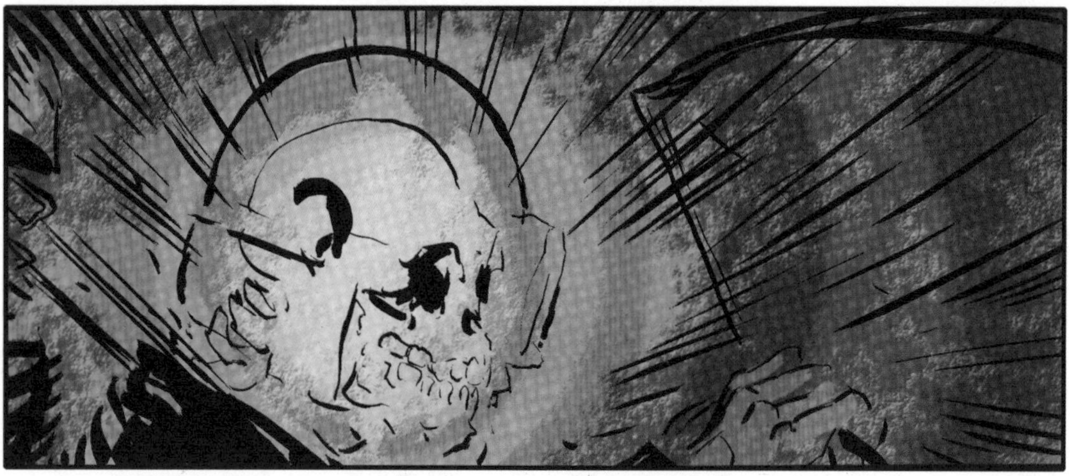

...WITH DESTINY!

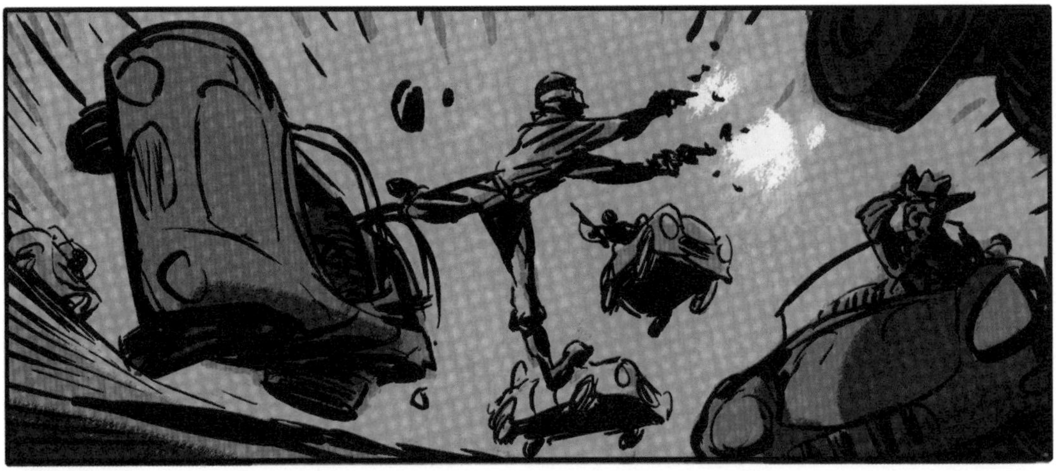

RACING SUDDENLY HAD NEW *MEANING* FOR THEM.

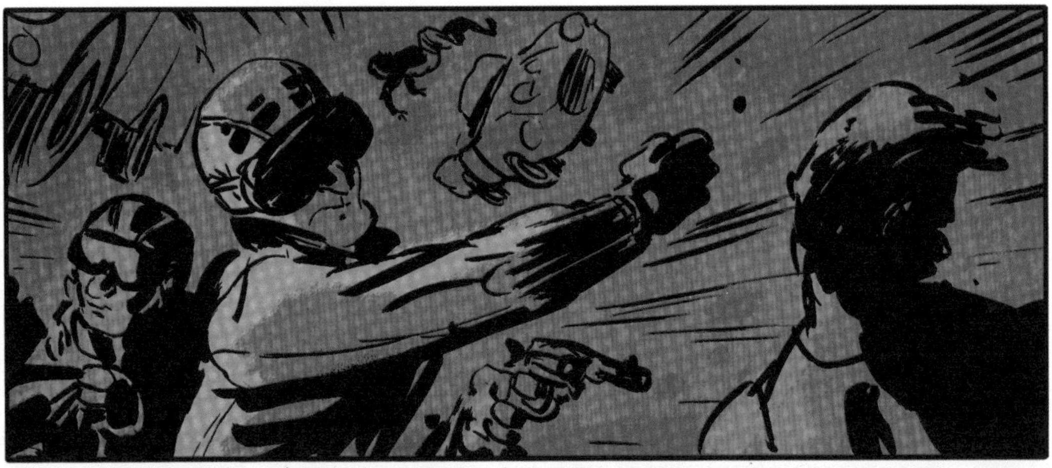

NO *LONGER* WOULD THEY GAUGE THEIR COURAGE
WITH PIT STOPS AND TIRE PRESSURE.

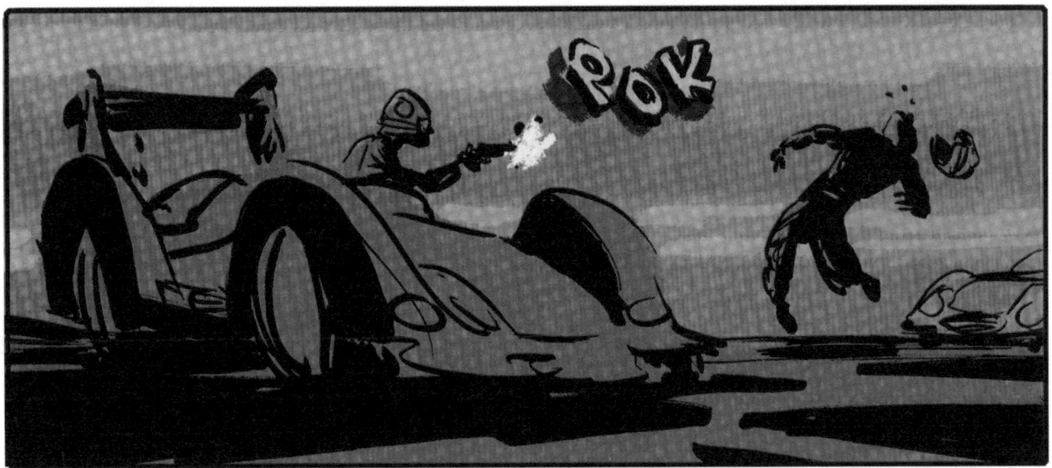
POK

A *NEW AGE* OF GEAR HEADS HAD CLAWED
THEIR WAY ONTO THE *TRACK*.

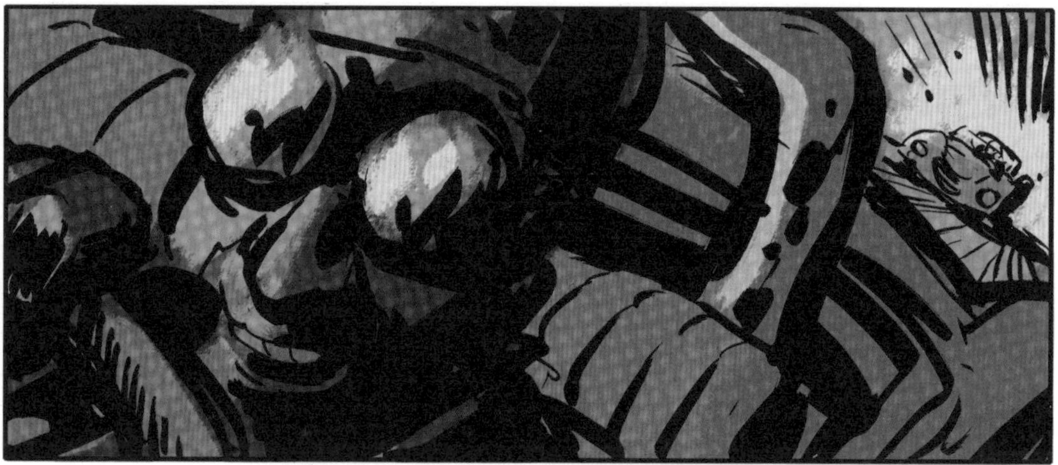

THIS WAS FOR *KEEPS* NOW.
NO *TROPHIES.* NO SPONSORS.

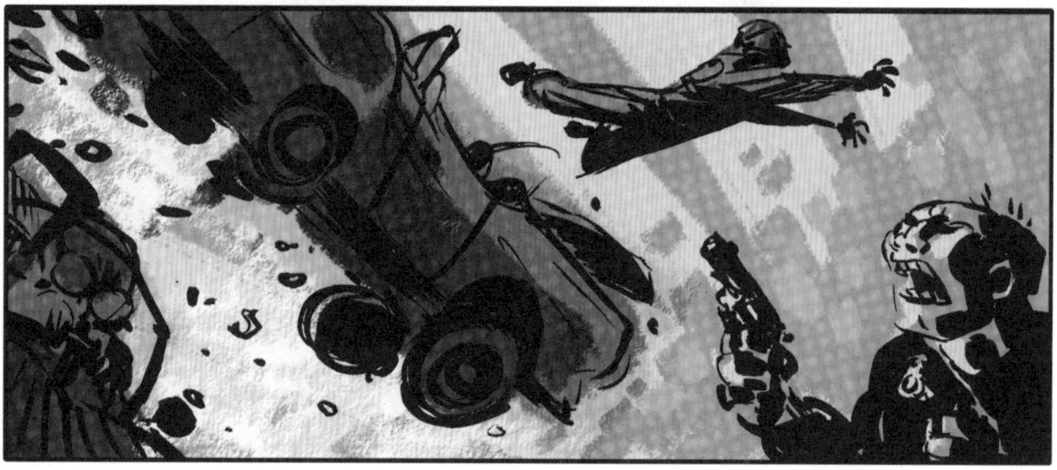

NO *TELECAST* TO ANSWER TO.

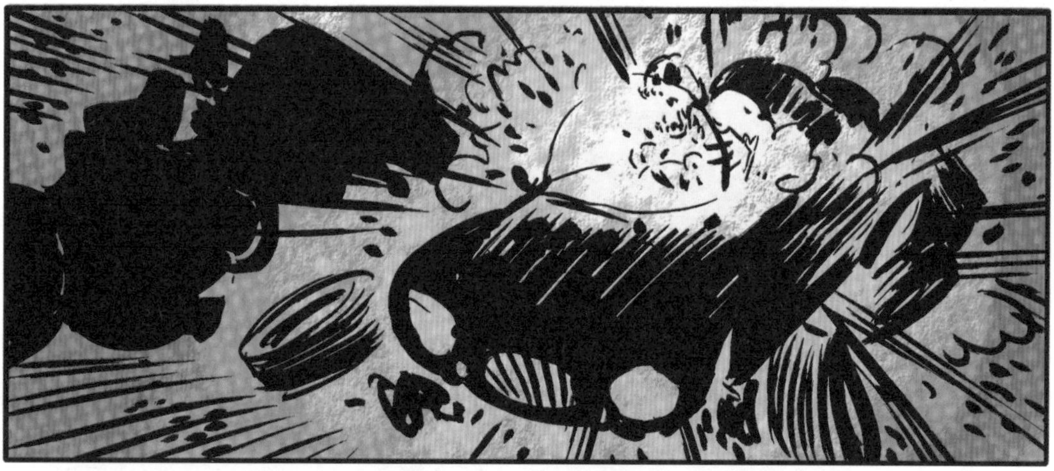

THE WORLD WOULD *WATCH*--
AND *CHEER.*

THESE WERE THE CONDITIONS BY WHICH IT CAME TO BE.

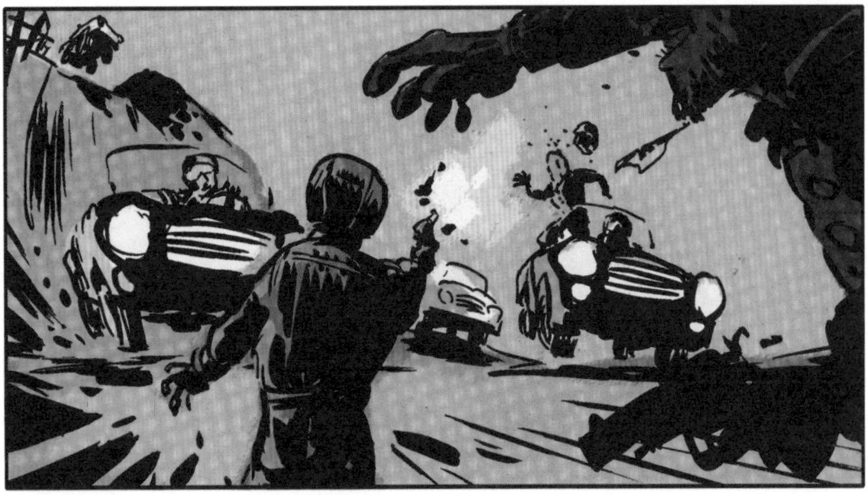

THEIR LEADER STOOD STOICALLY ON THE RACEWAY OF THE WORLD, PISTONS FIRING.

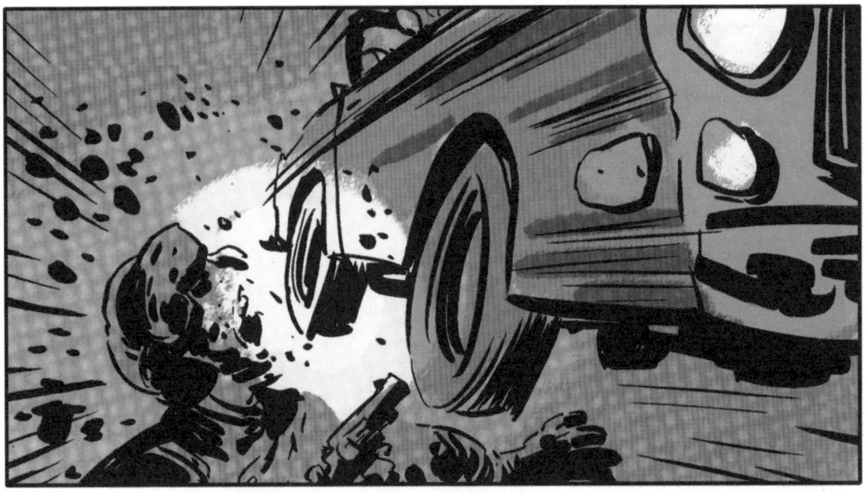

THE ENEMY DARED TO TREAD ON HIM.

MONTHS OF TOIL... SPARE PARTS AND ELBOW GREASE...

THE BRIGHTEST GEARHEADS WORKED MAGIC AND MECHANICAL ALCHEMY.

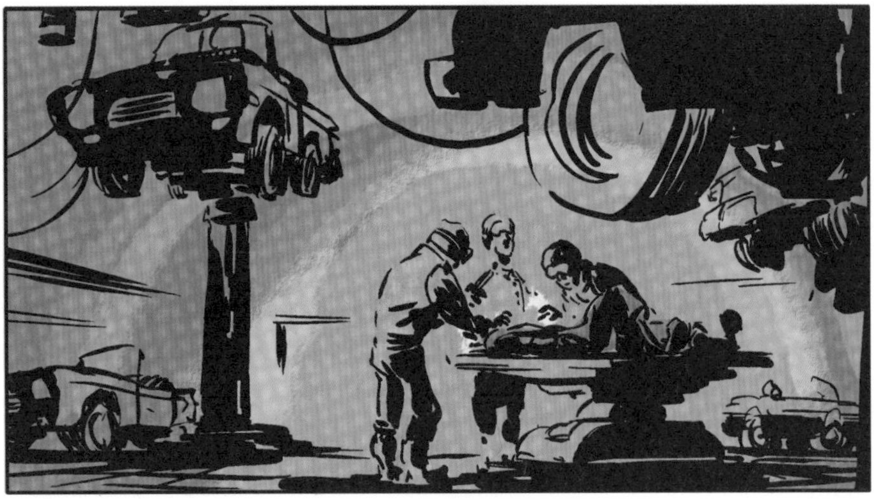

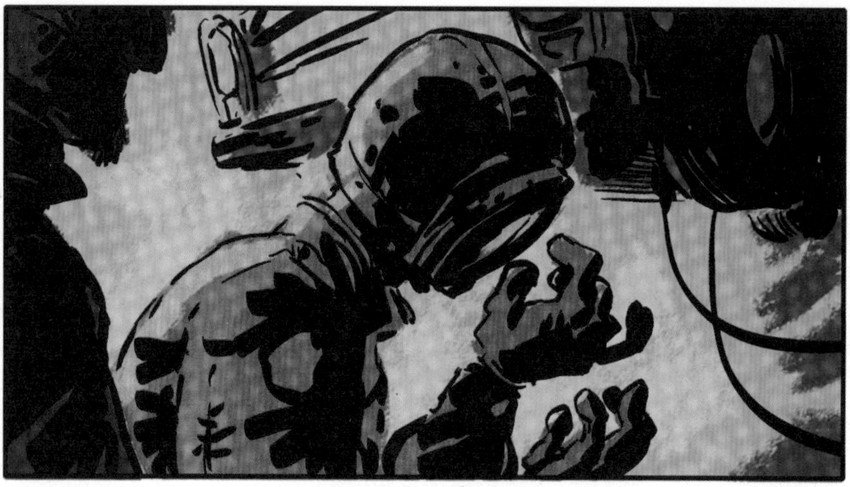

WHEN HE CAME TO, HE WEPT.

HIS TEARS OF JOY WERE BEAMS OF LIGHT.

LASER LIGHT. STRAIGHT FROM HIS SOUL.

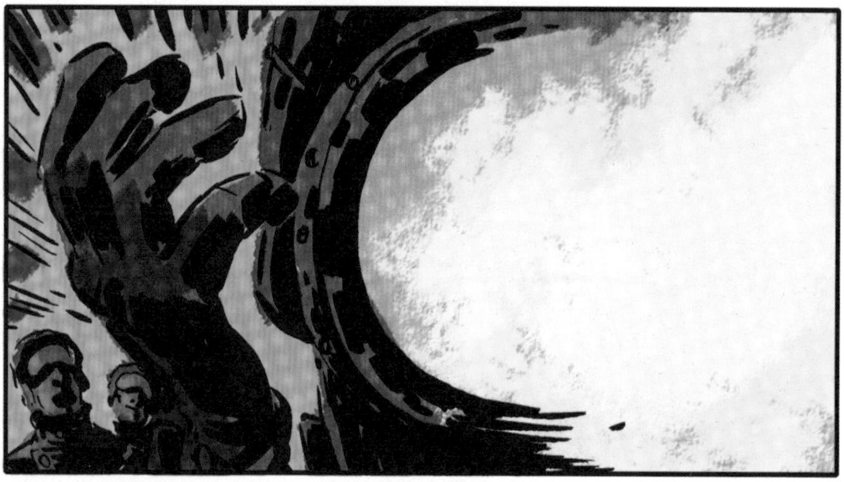

A NEW FACE FOR THEIR FUTURE.
A NEW NAME FOR THEIR LEADER.

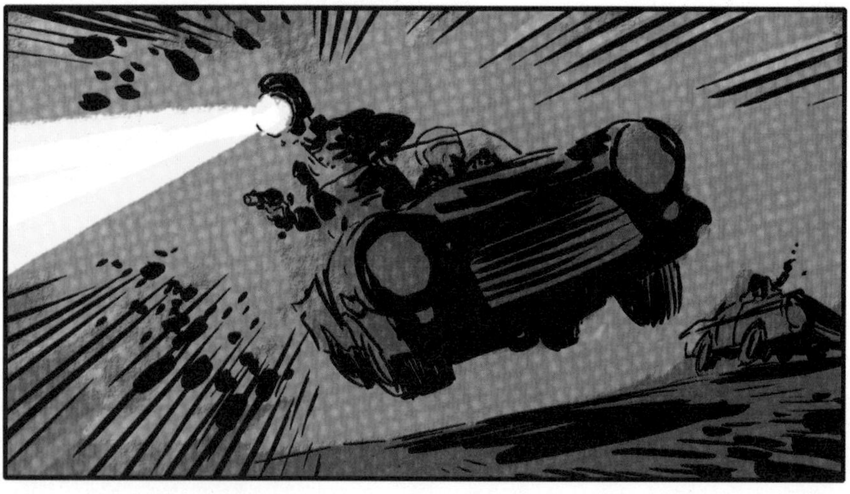

BRIGHT. FOCUSED.

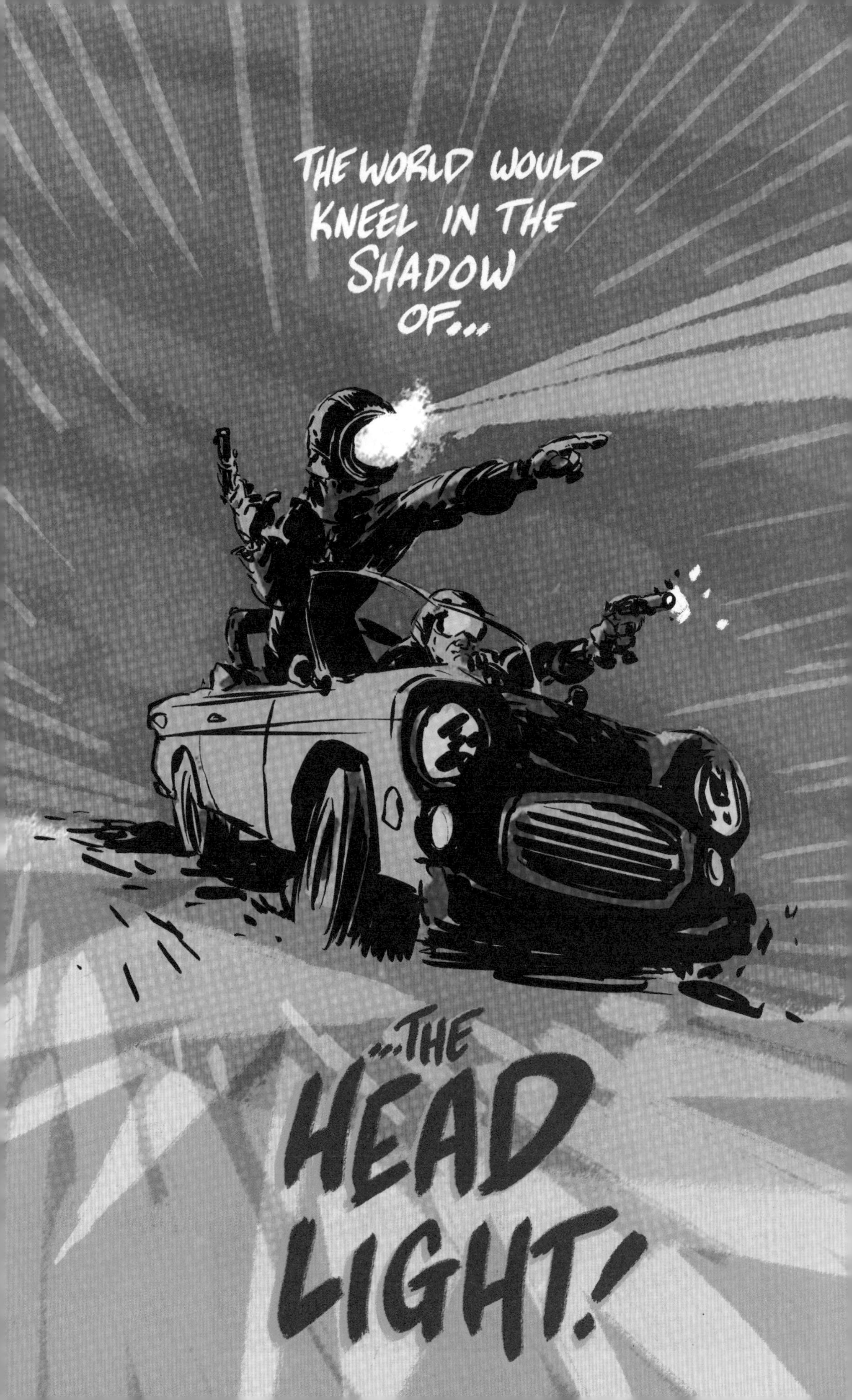
THE WORLD WOULD KNEEL IN THE SHADOW OF...
...THE HEAD LIGHT!

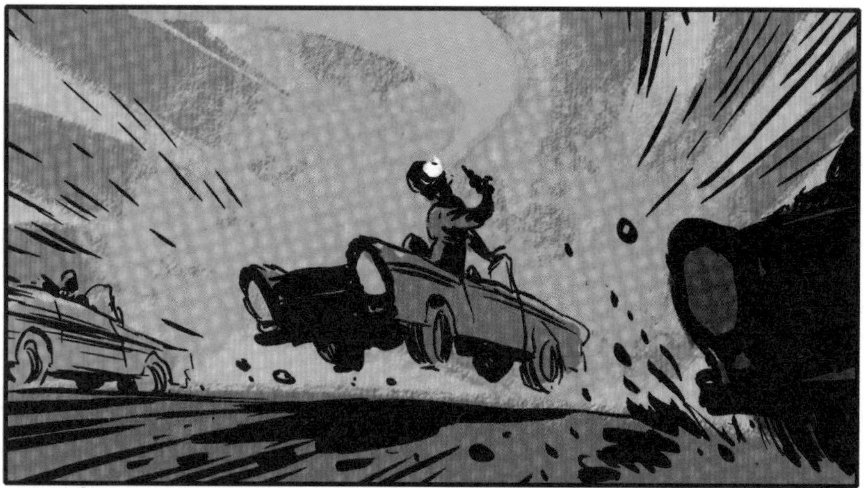

THE HEADLIGHT... FROM WHOM THE NEW-WORLD-ORDER WOULD BEAM LIKE A BEACON OF POSSIBILITY.

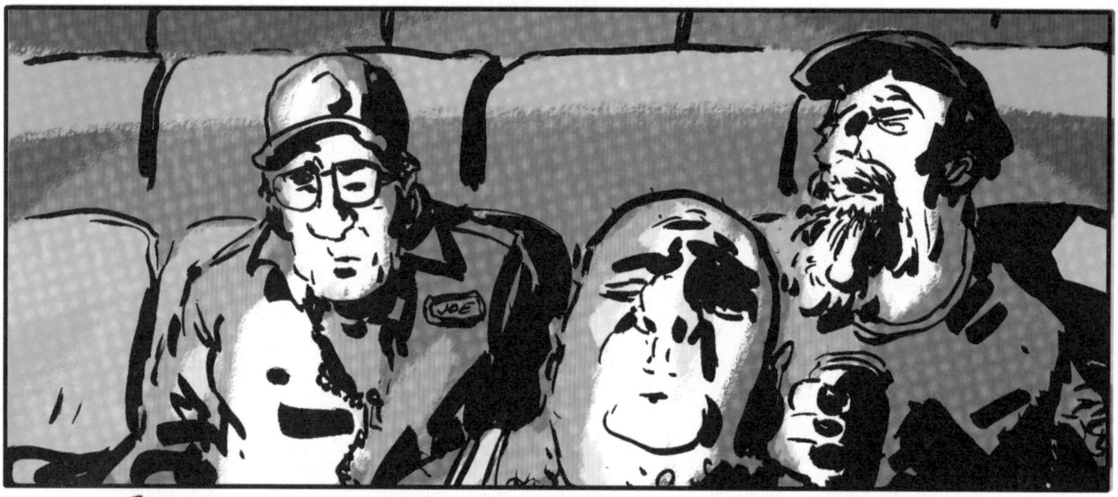
JOE

FOR THE OLD REGIME OF FANS, HOWEVER...

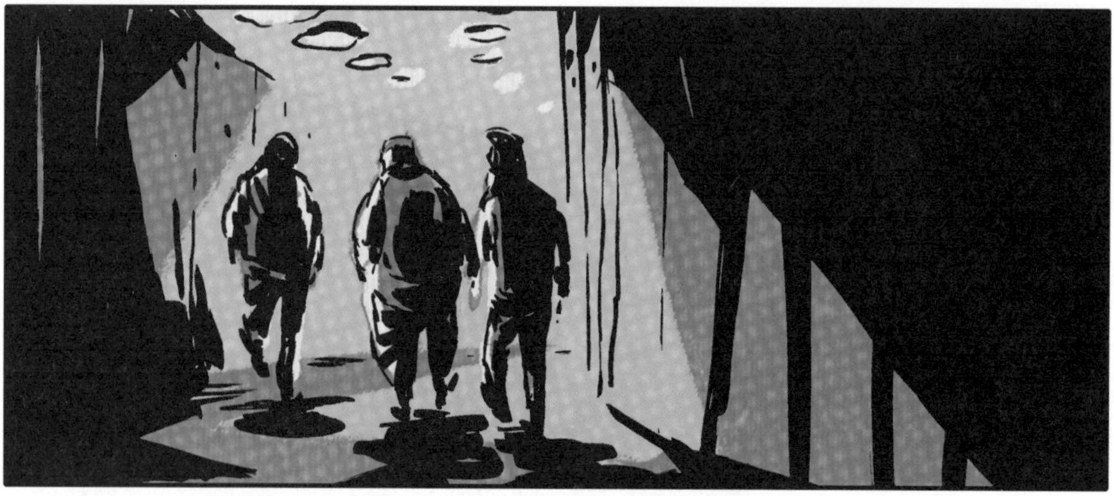

...THE JURY WOULD REMAIN OUT.

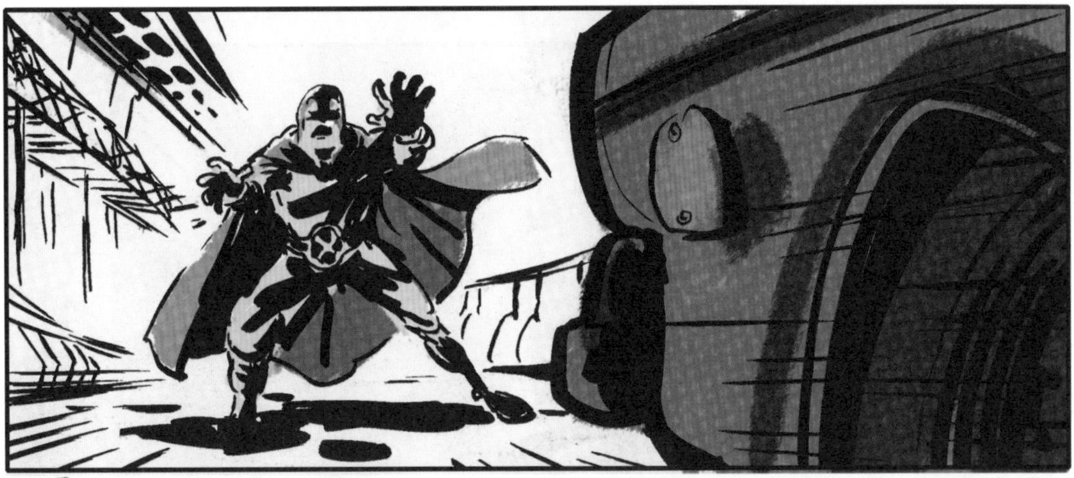

OTHER FANS FROM MORE ECCENTRIC WALKS OF LIFE WOULD ATTEMPT DIRECT CONTACT.

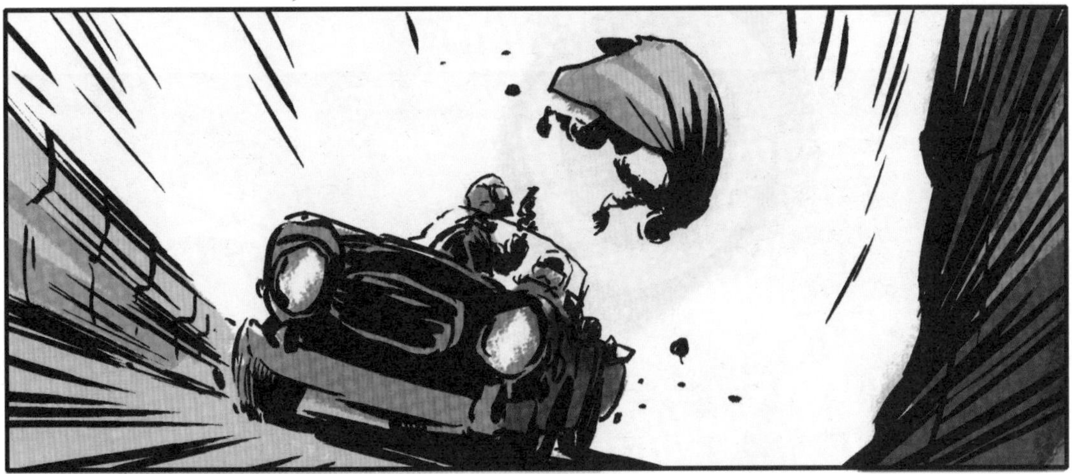

FOR THESE, EVEN, THERE WOULD BE NO UNIQUE AFFECTION.

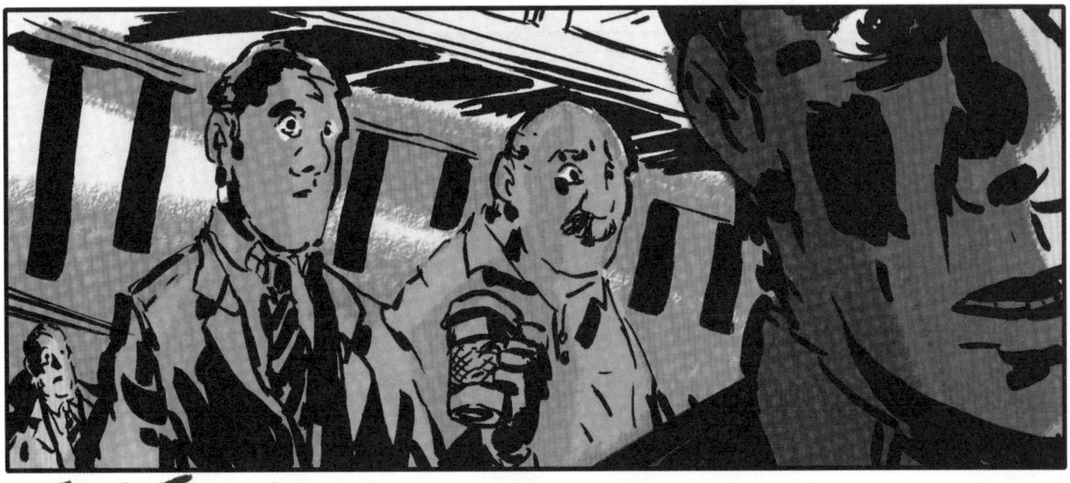

THE FAT CATS, THOSE WHO DINED ON THE MUSCLE OF THE DREAMERS...

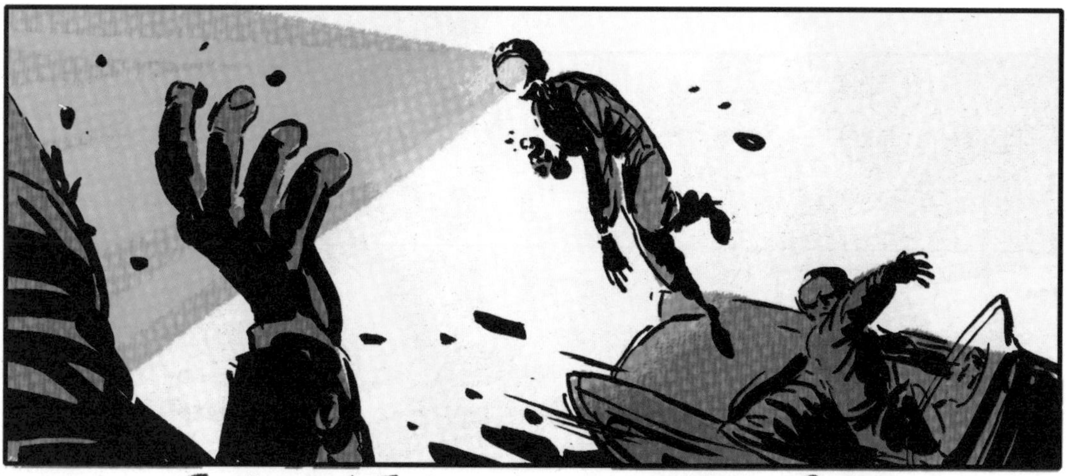

...FOR THEM, THE LIGHT SHINED BRIGHTEST.

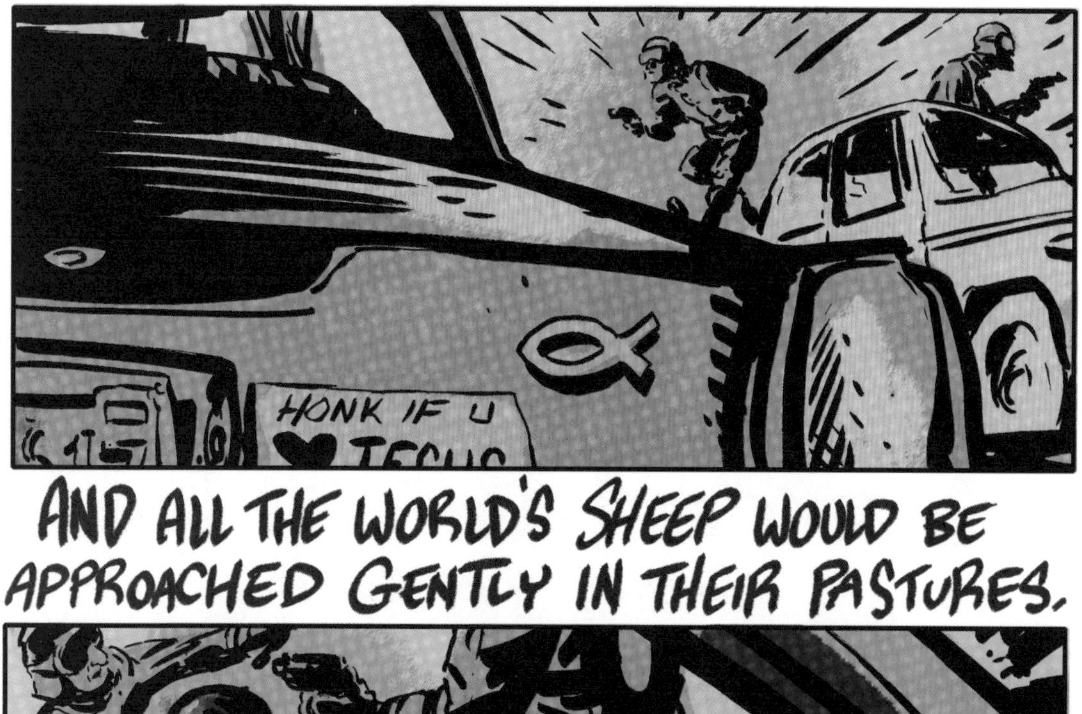
HONK IF U

AND ALL THE WORLD'S SHEEP WOULD BE APPROACHED GENTLY IN THEIR PASTURES.

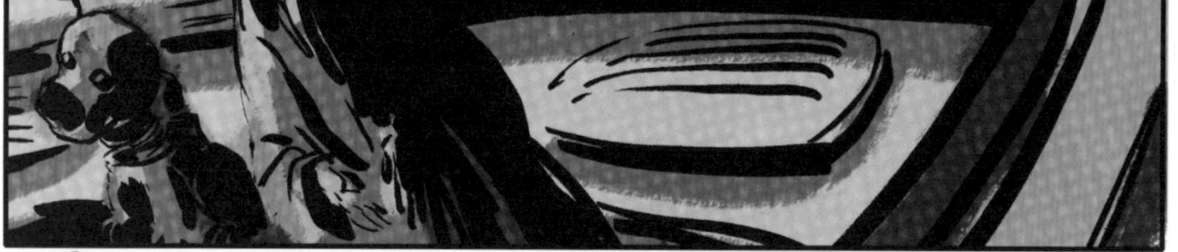

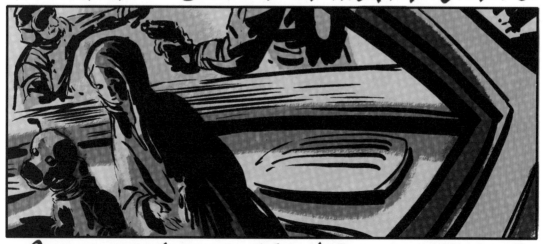

SOFT WORDS OF A NEW HOPE, OF A BETTER TOMORROW, WOULD BE WHISPERED.

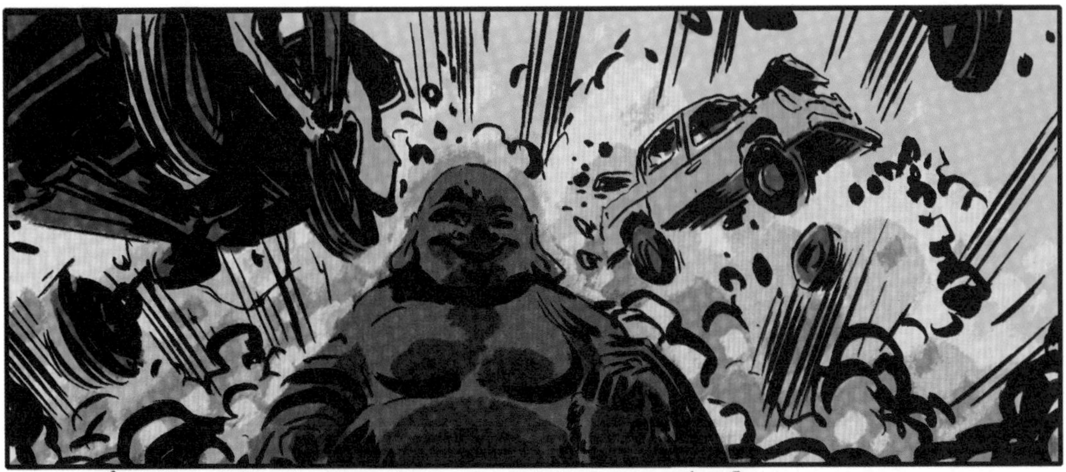

AND FOR THOSE WITH NO EAR TO LISTEN...
...GENTLE SLEEP.

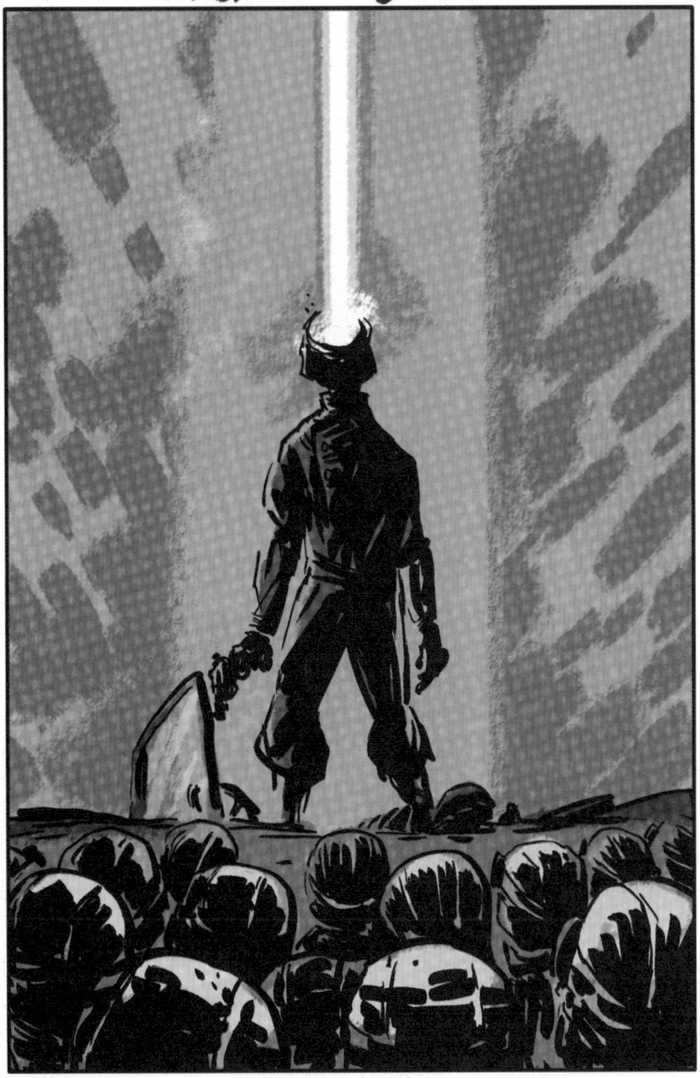

THERE COULD BE BUT *ONE* LIGHT TO FOLLOW
NOW.

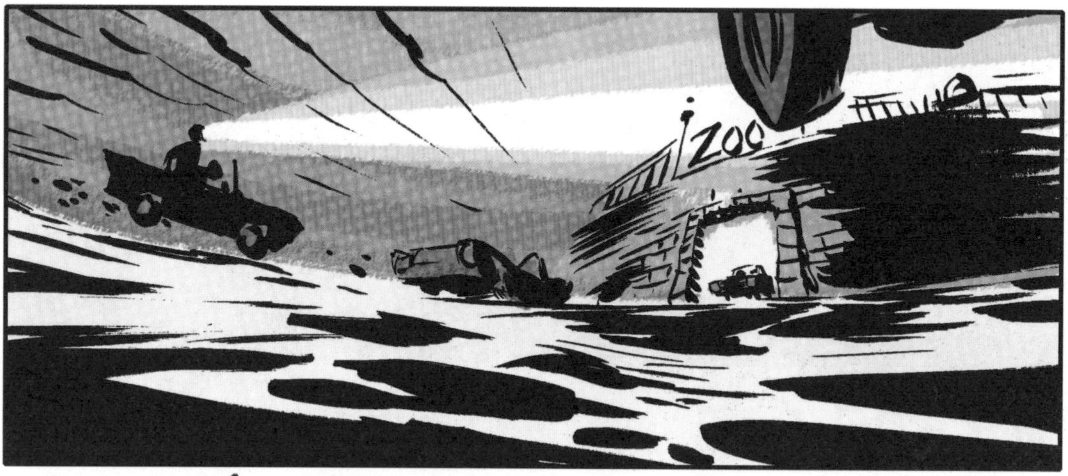
ZOO

A LIVING ARK WOULD BE BUILT FOR THE COMING DELUGE OF DELUSION.

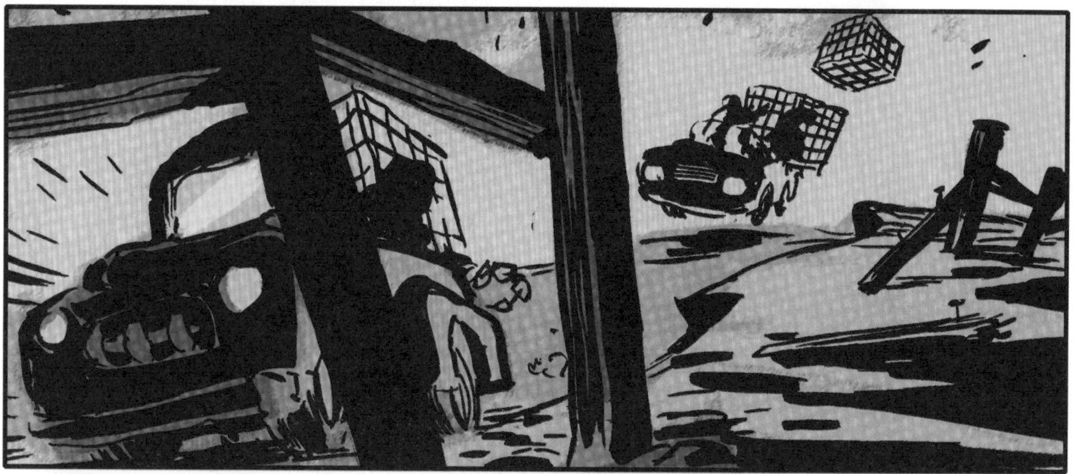

THE CAPTIVE CHILDREN OF CURIOUSITY WOULD BE GRANTED PARDON.

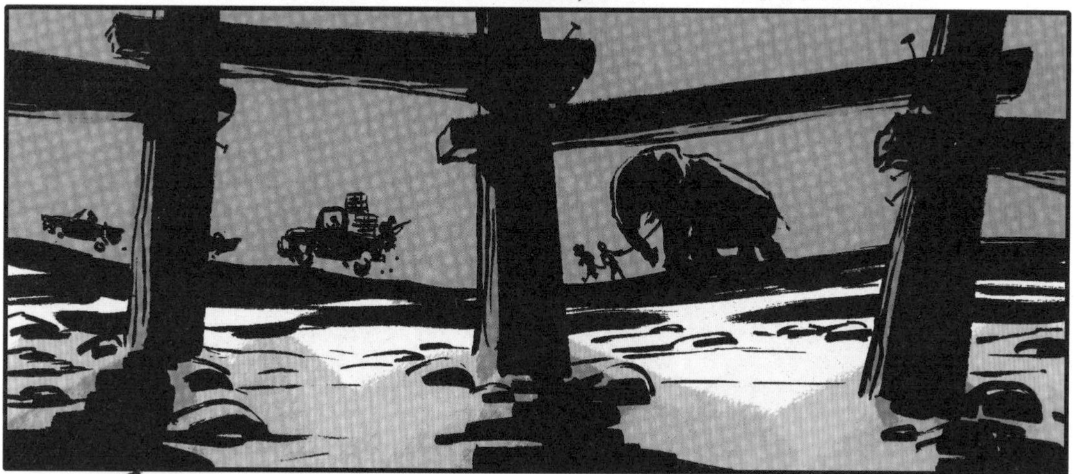

THEIR LIBERATORS WOULD LEAD THEM IN NEW PURPOSE.

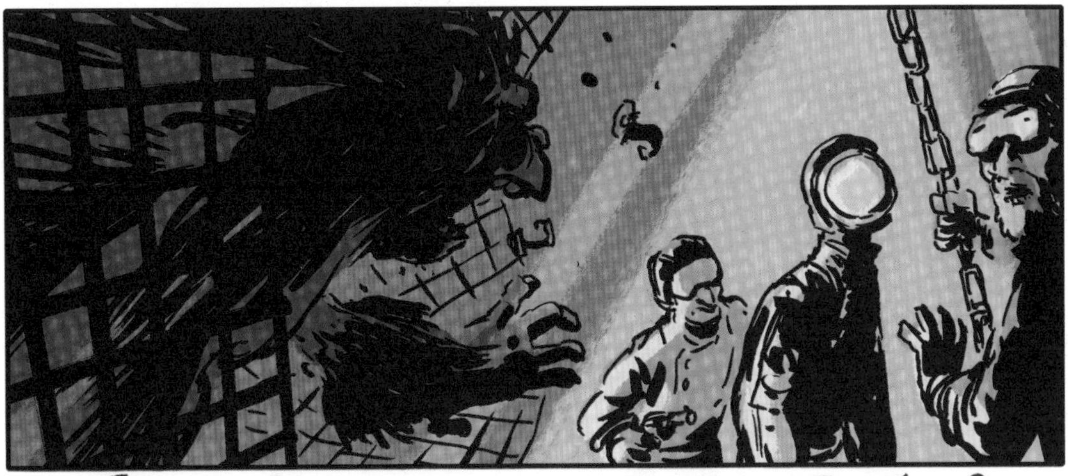

THEIR SEETHING ANGER AT THEIR WASTED LIVES...

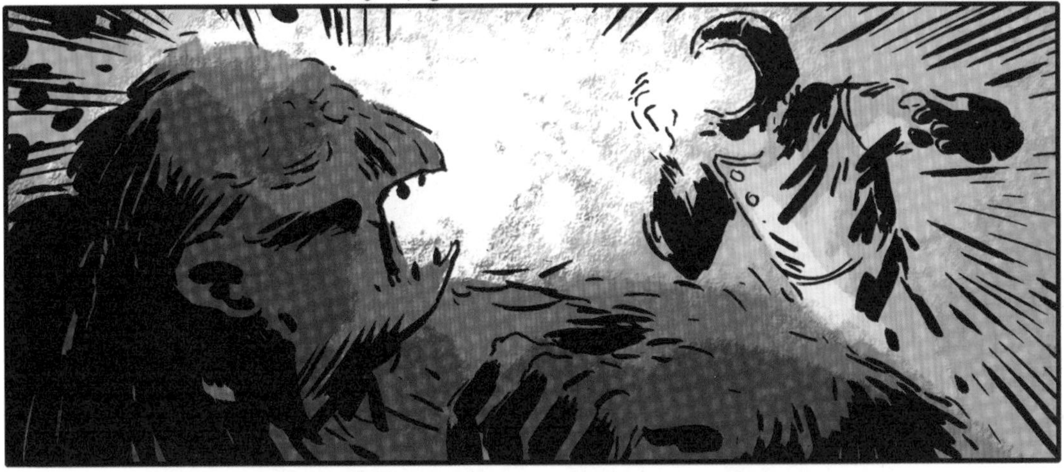

...PURGED BY THE LIGHT.

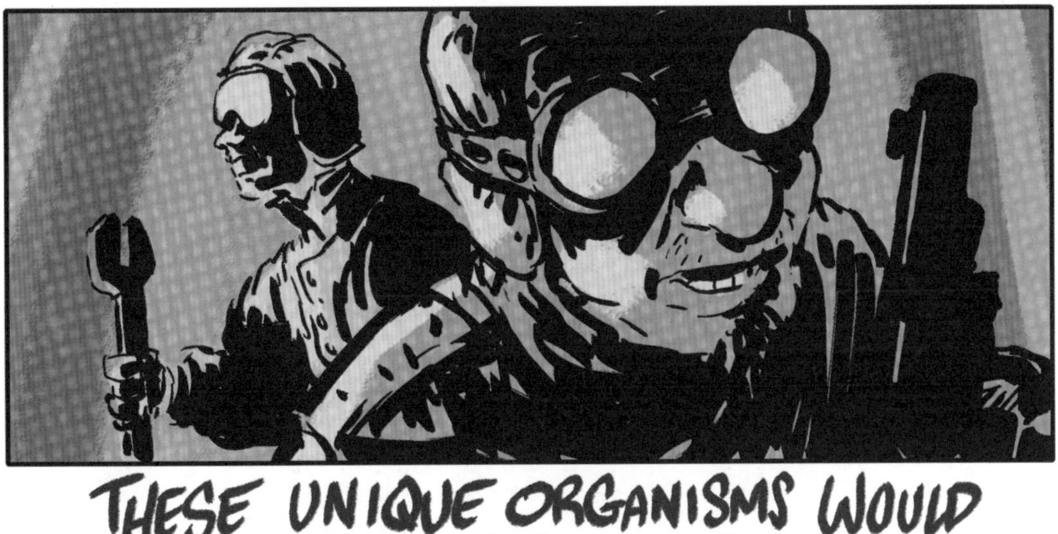

THESE UNIQUE ORGANISMS WOULD SERVE HARMONIOUSLY...

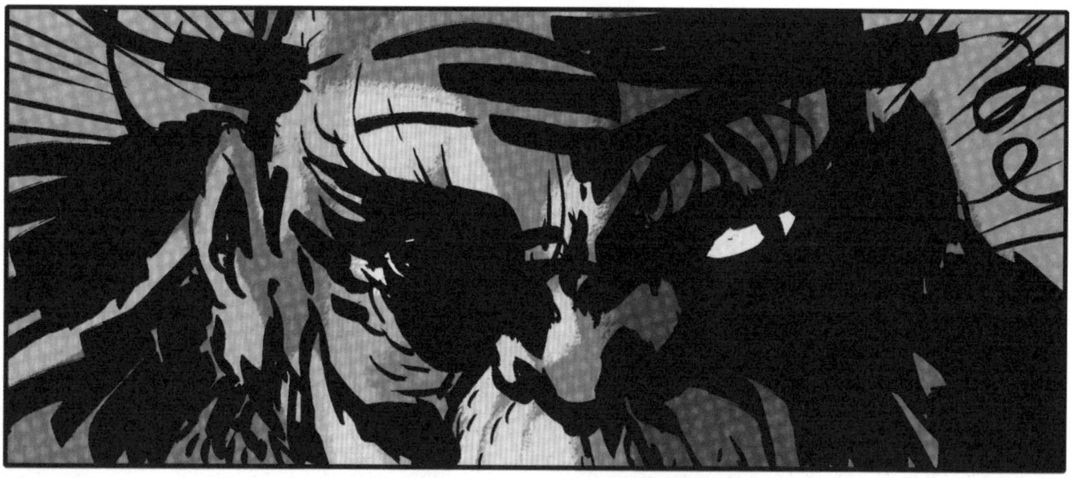

...HARMONIOUSLY.

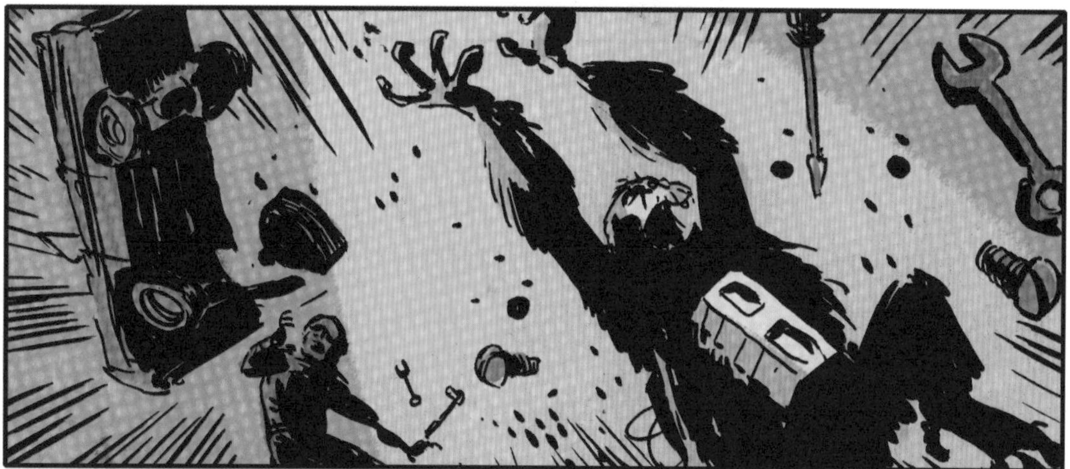

AND IF THEIR ANGER AT THE OLD WORLD PERSISTED...

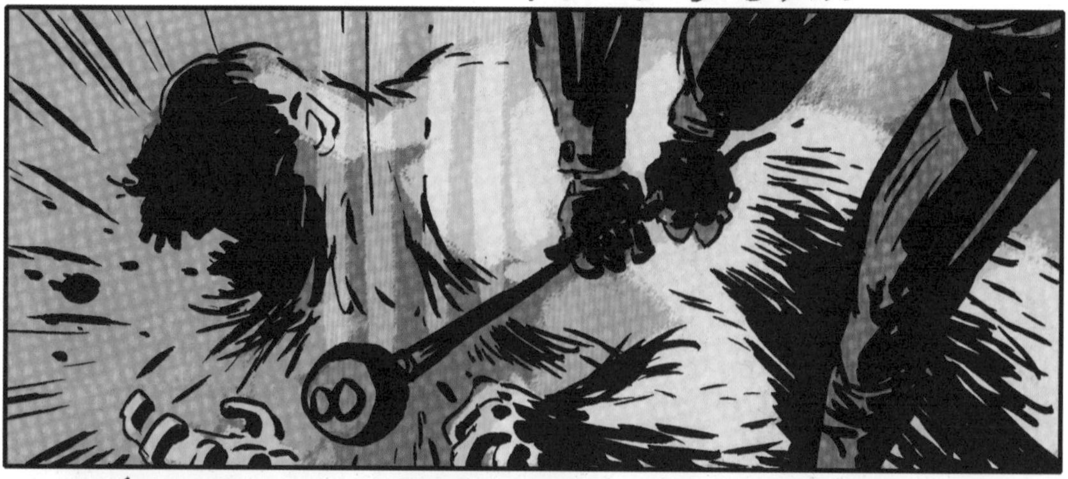

...HARMONY... AND THE TENENTS OF GLORIOUS MEMBERSHIP IN SOCIETY...

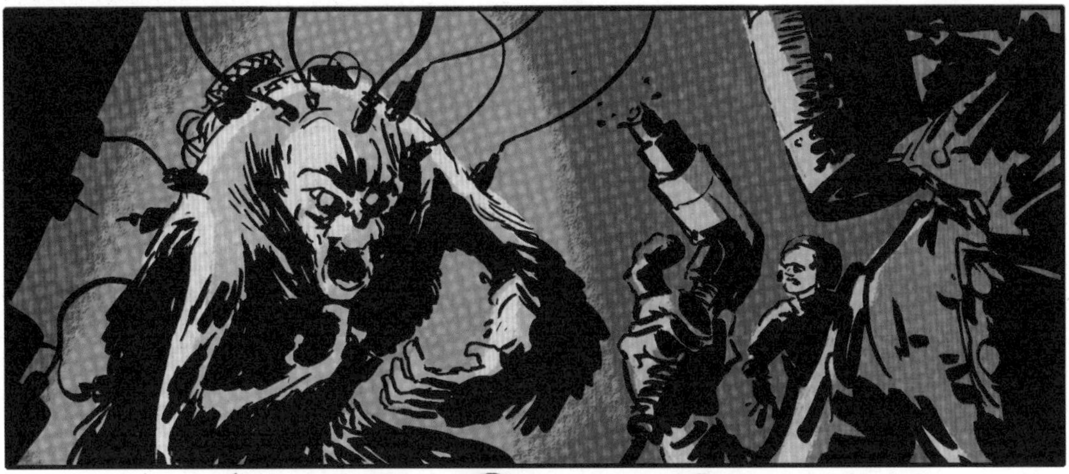

...WOULD BE INSTALLED MANUALLY.

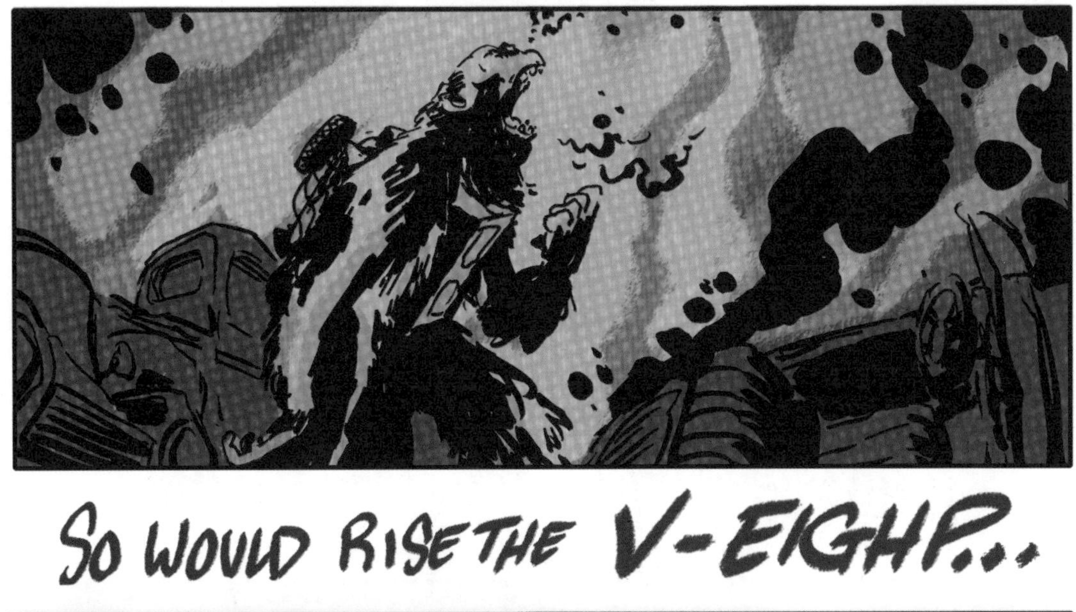

SO WOULD RISE THE V-EIGHT...

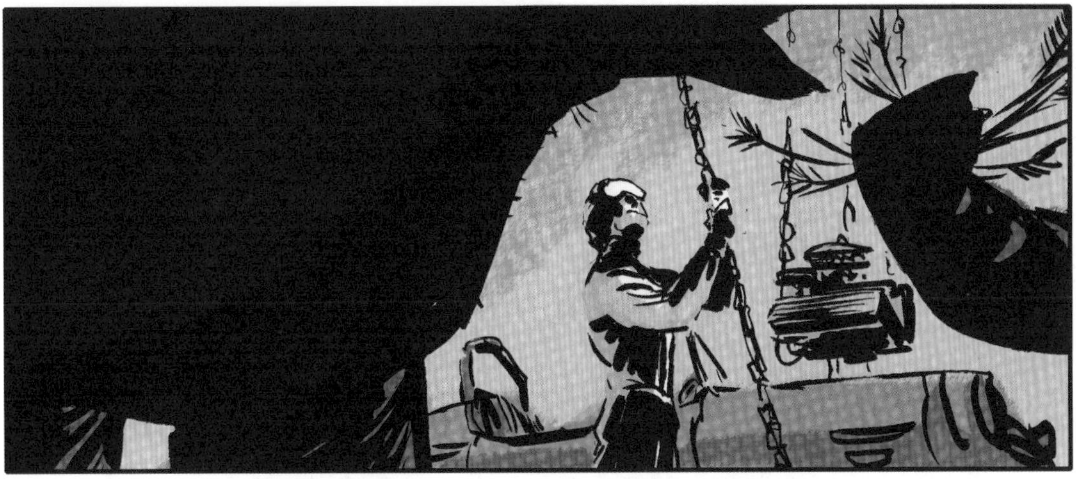

...AND OTHERS...

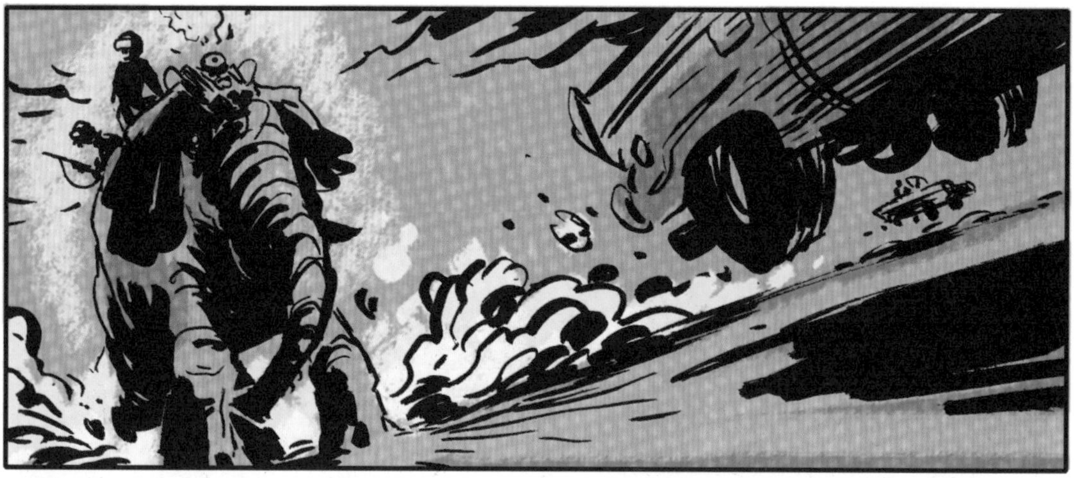

THIS MOTORCADE OF THE ANIMAL KINGDOM WOULD CHARGE SIDE-BY-SIDE WITH THE GEARHEADS.

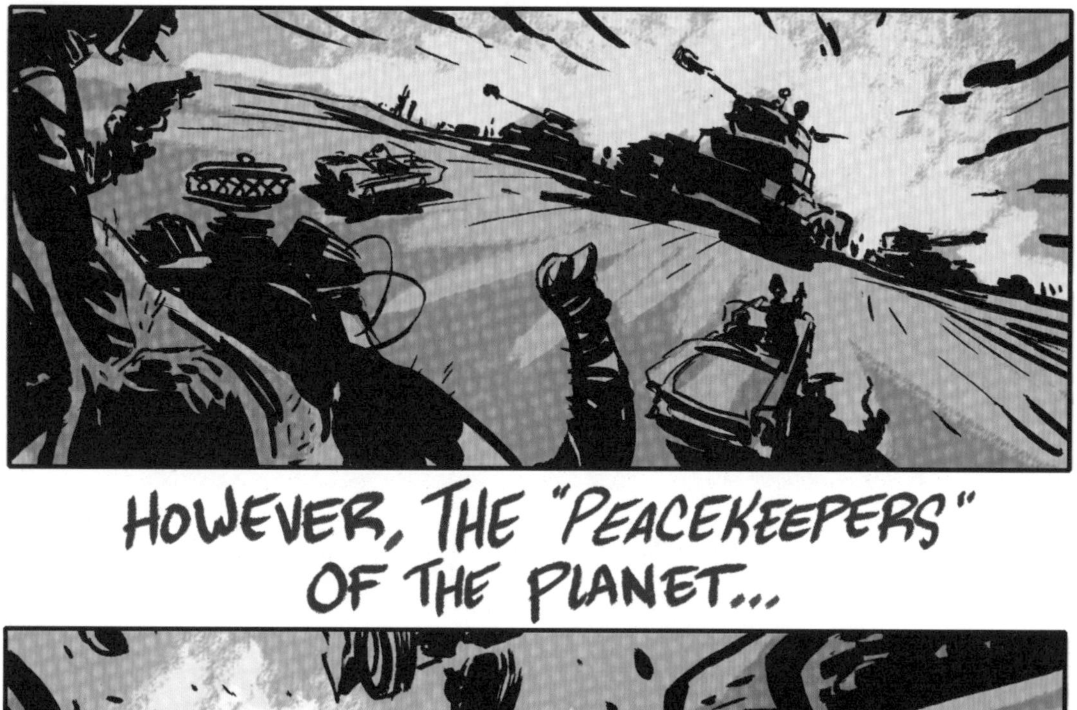

HOWEVER, THE "PEACEKEEPERS" OF THE PLANET...

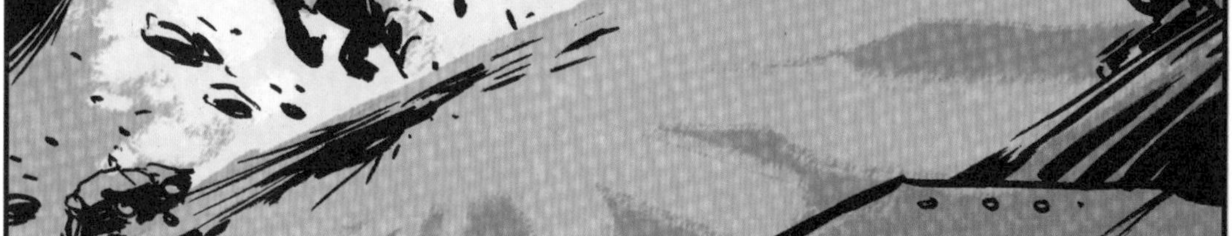

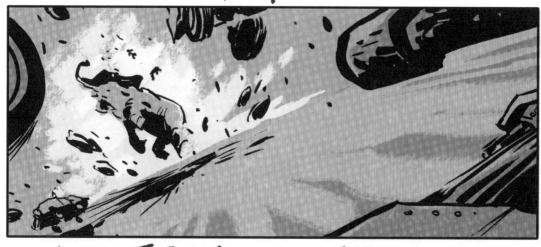

...WOULD TURN A DEAF EAR TO THE TRUMPETS OF CHANGE.

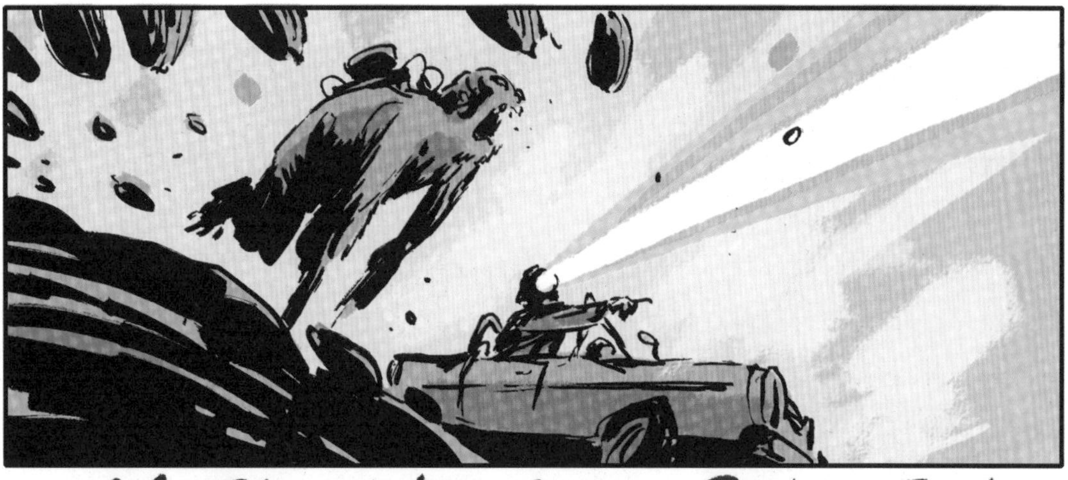

AS THE WHEELS OF REVOLUTION
TURNED, HOWLING...

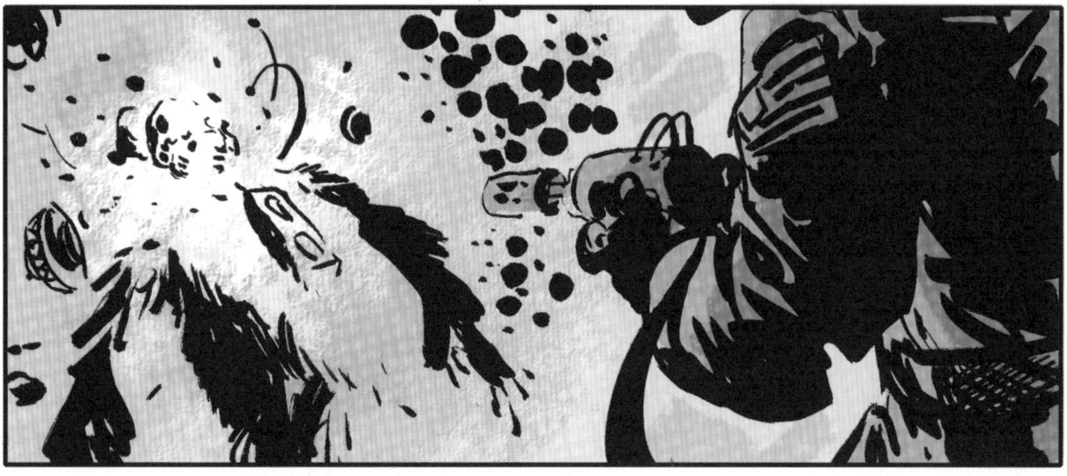

...THE ROADBLOCK WOULD STAND STRONG.

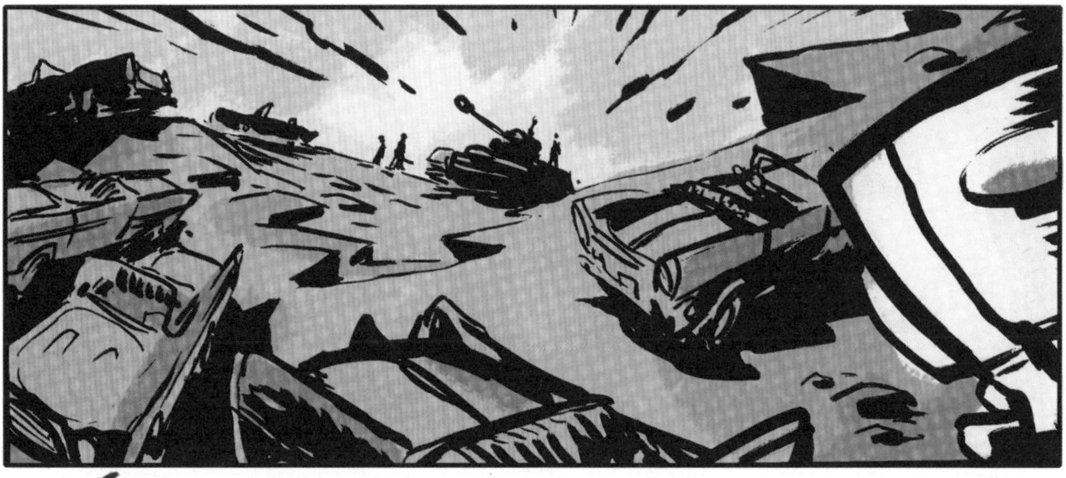

FOR A MOMENT, THE ENGINES OF THE
NEW-WORLD-ORDER WOULD FALL IDLE.

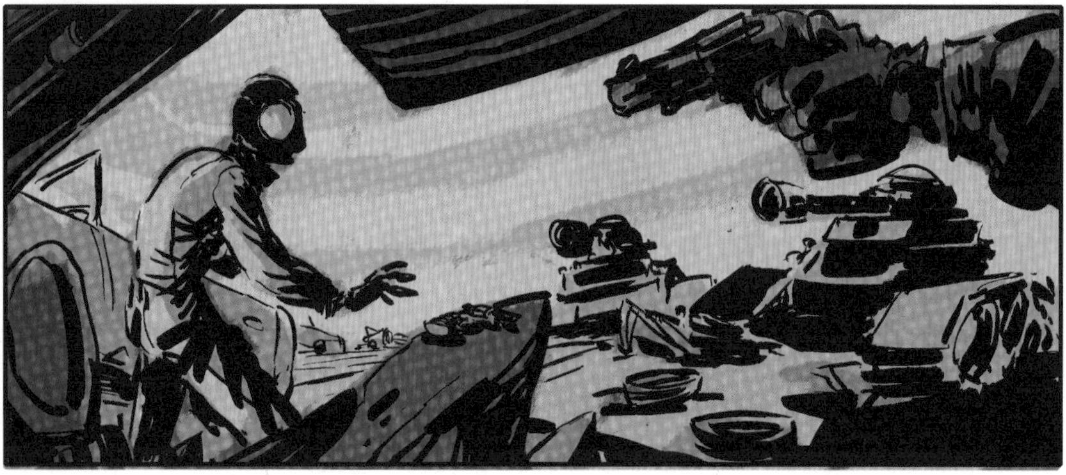

THE LIGHT WOULD *FLICKER* AND *DIM.*

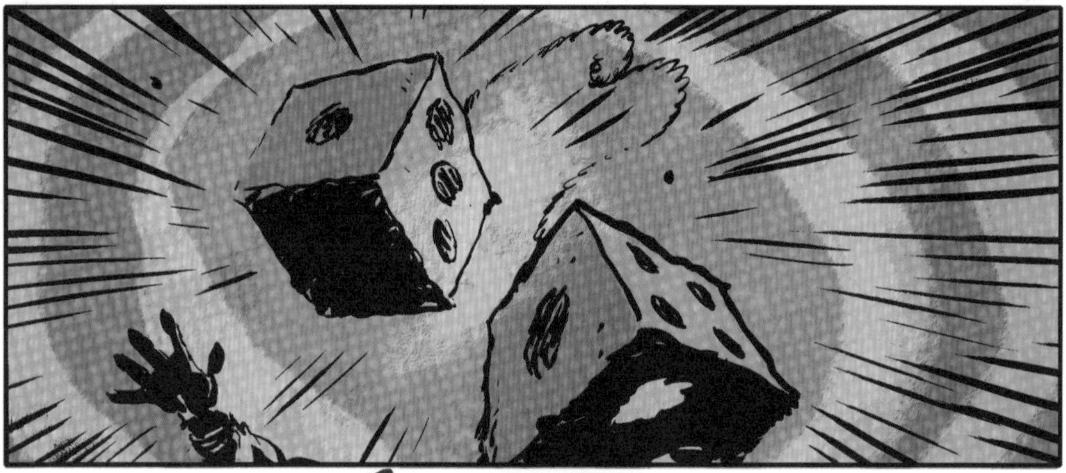

BUT *THEN...*

...A *NEW HOPE* WOULD BE GAMBLED UPON!

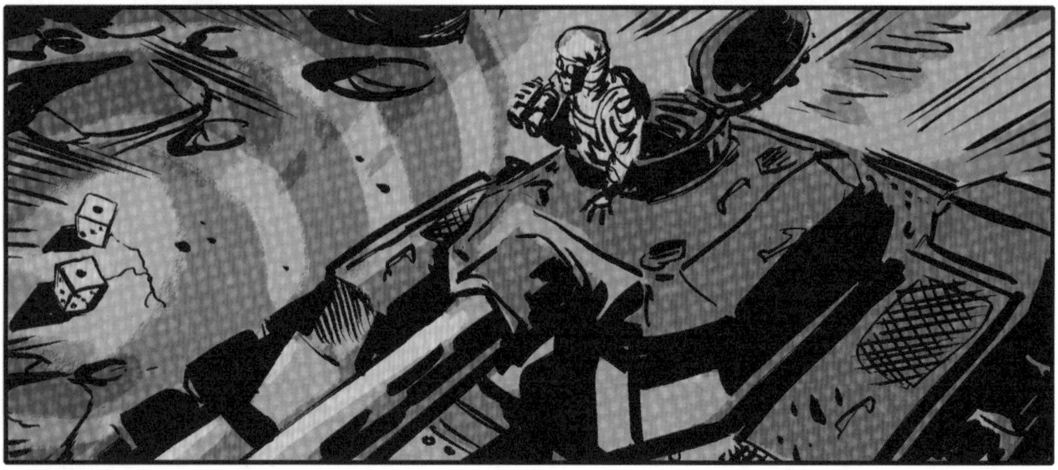

WHO WOULD *TOSS* SUCH A HAND AS *THIS?*

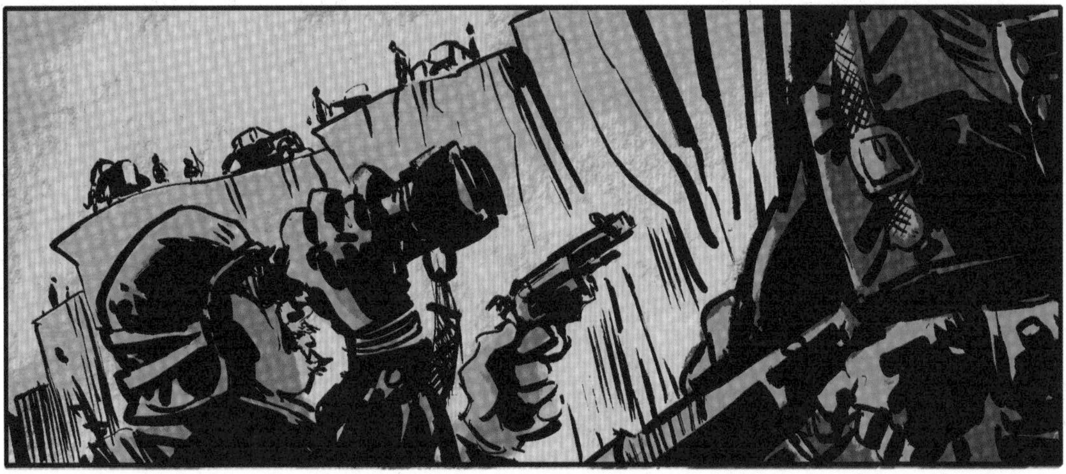

WHO?

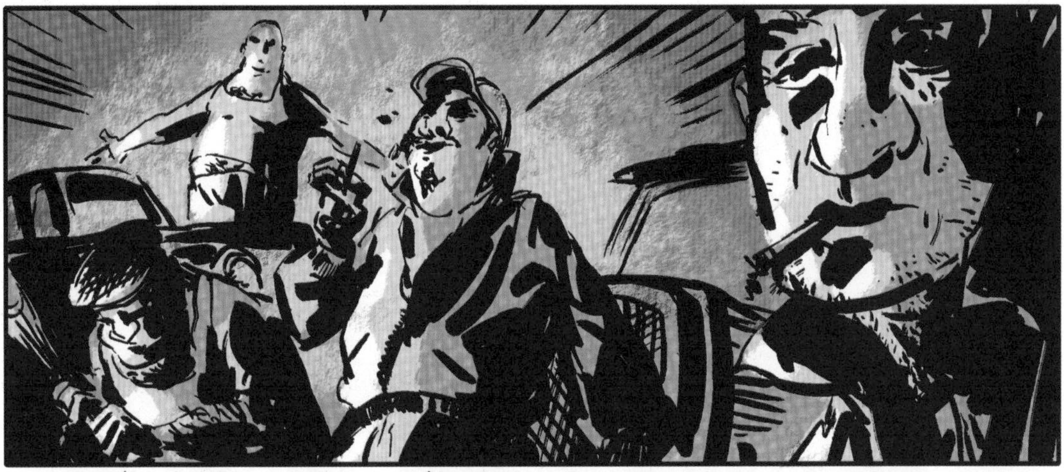

AHH, YES... THE HOPPED-UP GREASERS OF YESTERYEAR. THE GEARHEADS OF OLD.

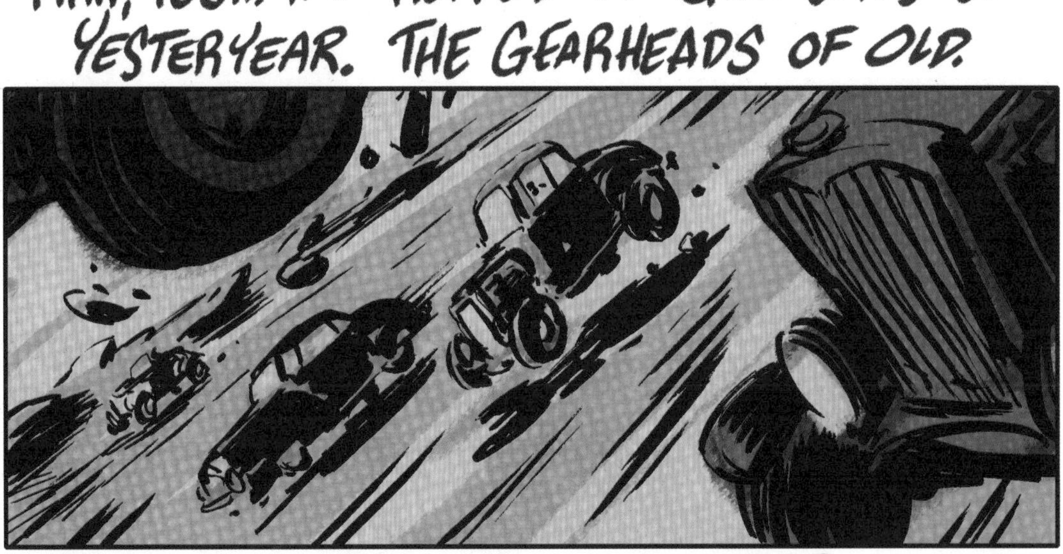

DIGNITY LACED THE OIL IN THEIR VEINS. HONOR FOR THE ASPHALT.

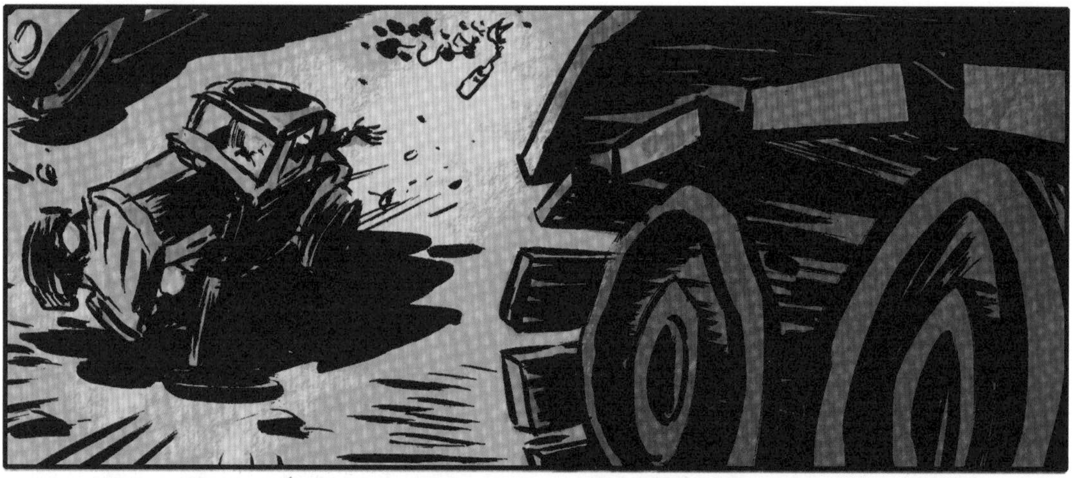

THERE WOULD BE NO QUARTER FOR THE OPPRESSORS.

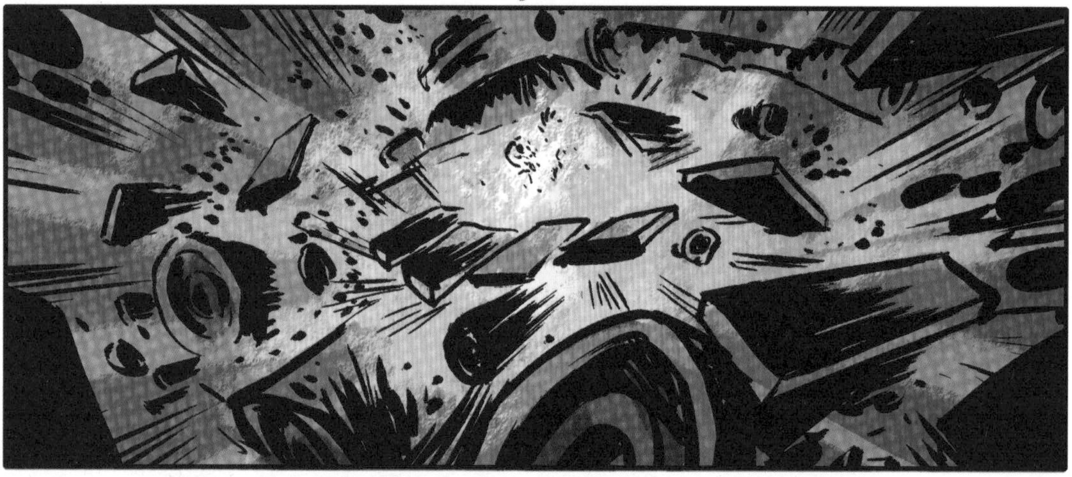

THE OLD SKOOL PLAYED FOR KEEPS, DADDY-O A' DADDY-O.

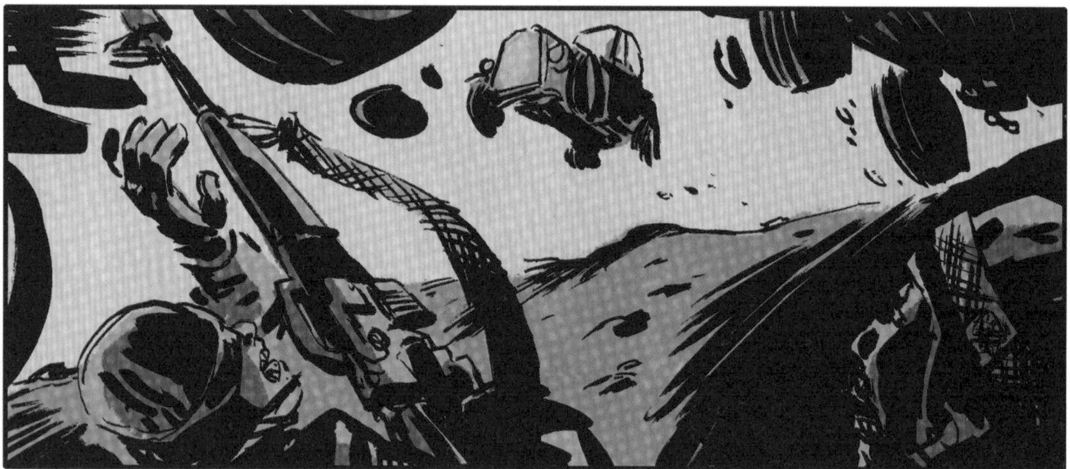

GEARHEADS OF ALL WALKS OF LIFE WOULD STICK TOGETHER, IT SEEMED.

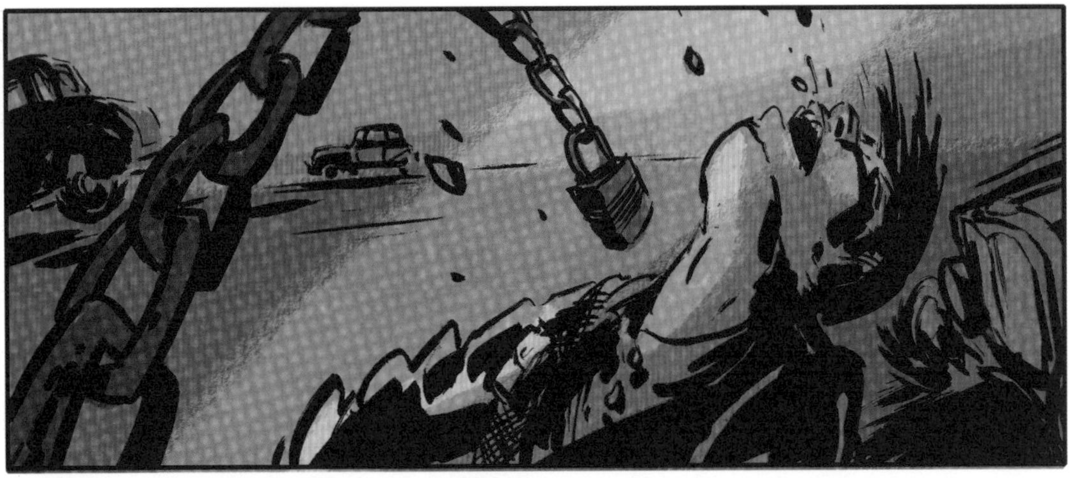

THE HIGH-TECH WEAPONS OF TOMORROW
WOULD TAKE A BACK SEAT.

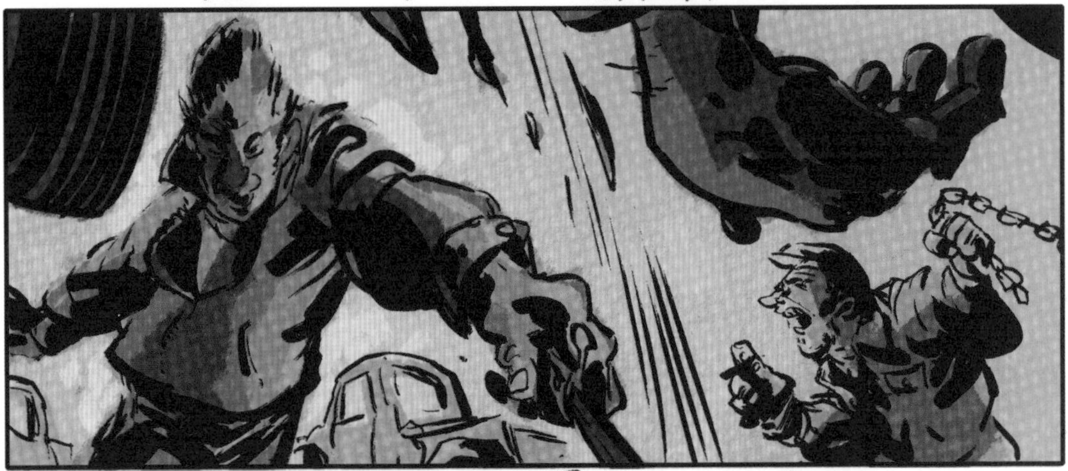

THE ART OF THE SWITCHBLADE...
...OF THE CHAIN...
...COULD STILL PAINT A PICTURE...

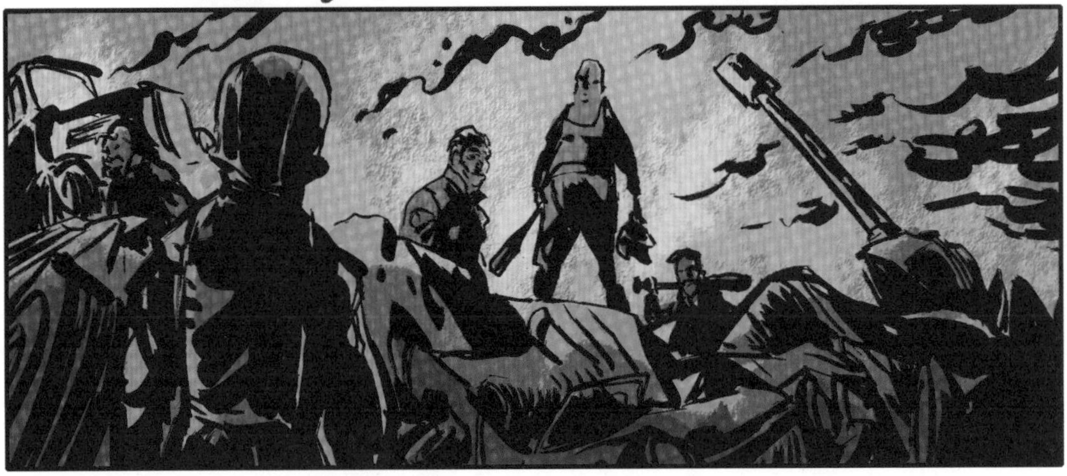

...BUT THE PORTRAIT OF A LEADER...?

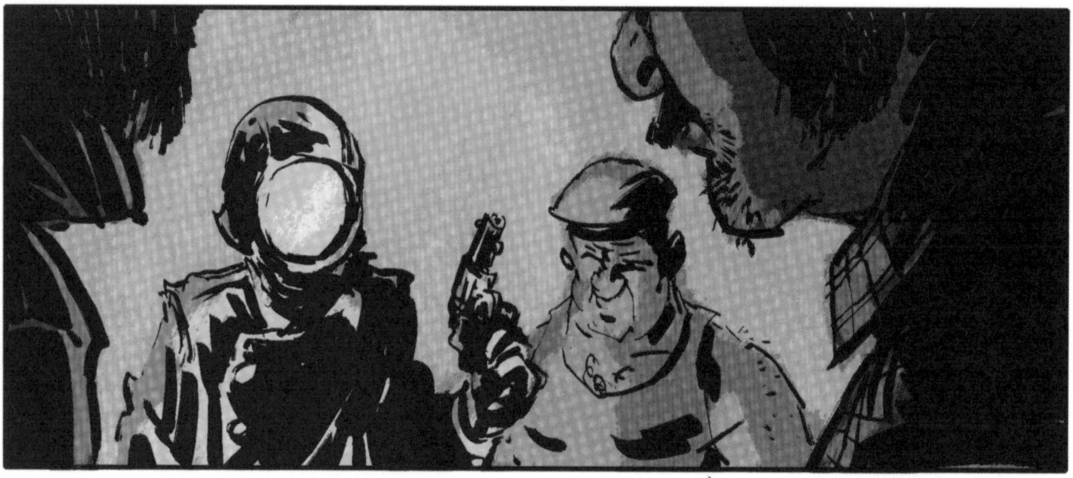

THAT PORTRAIT WAS YET TO BE
RENDERED.

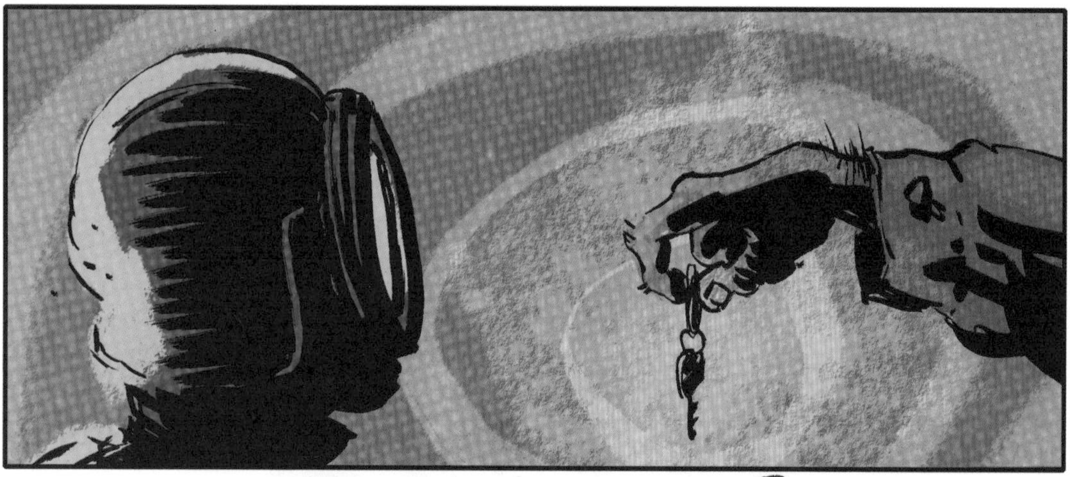

OLD SKOOL OR NEW?
WHICH LIGHT WOULD SHINE *BRIGHTER?*

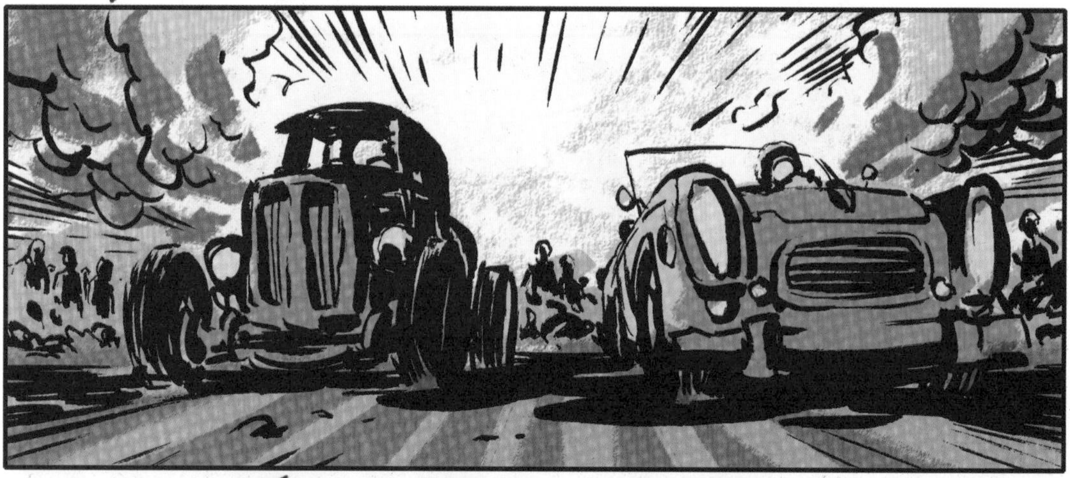

THE COURSE WAS SET,
AND THE PEDALS PRESSED!

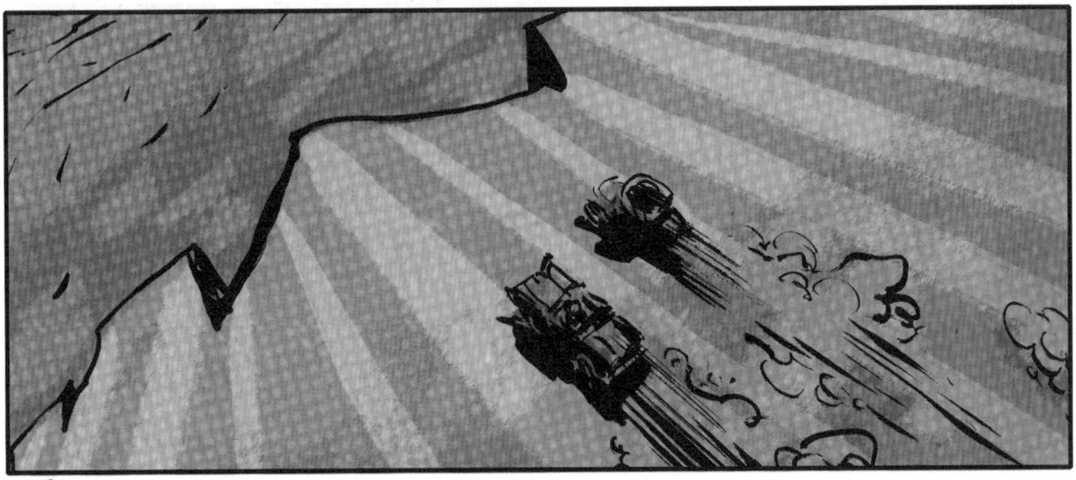

REBELS WITH NO TRUE CAUSE WOULD PLOW TOWARDS THE FINISH...

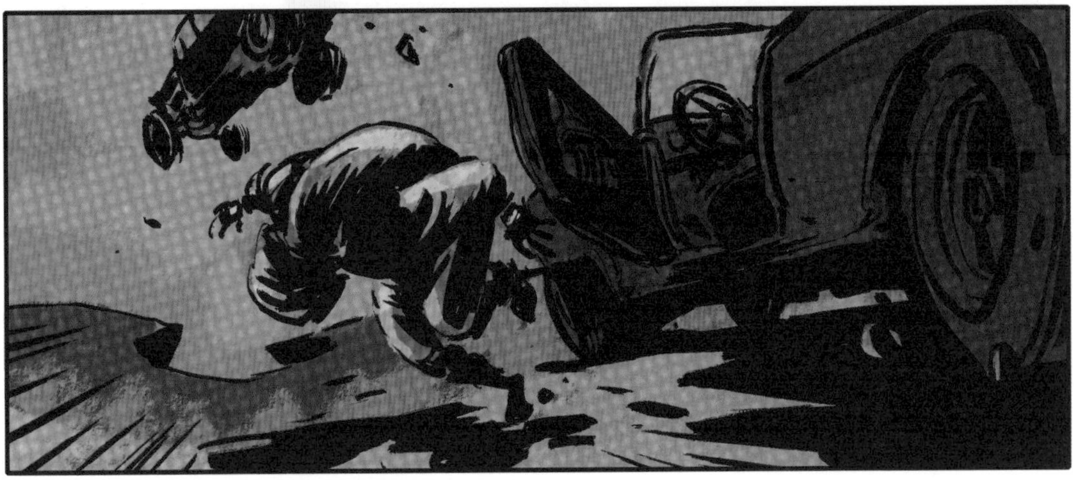

...AND BE THEY MAN OR CHICKEN...

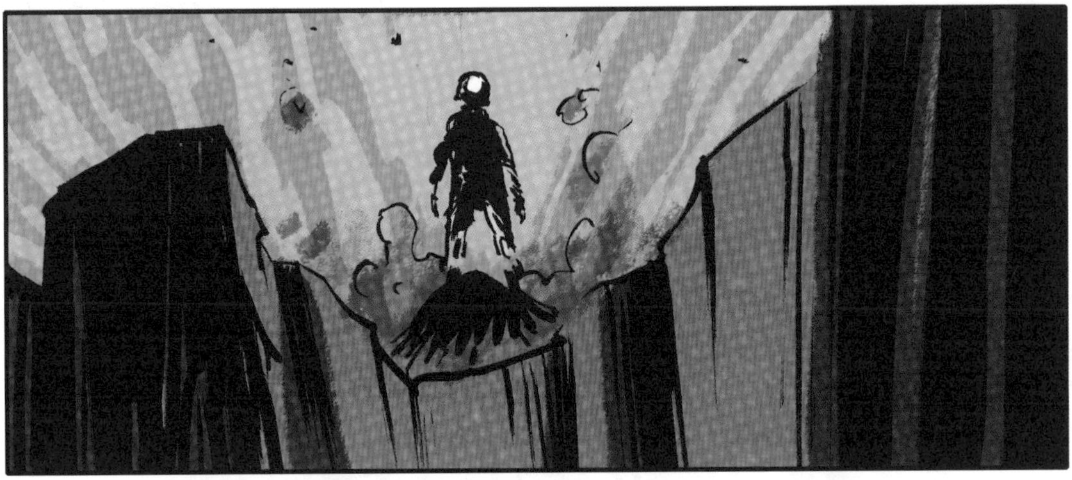

...ONLY ONE WOULD STAND TALL.

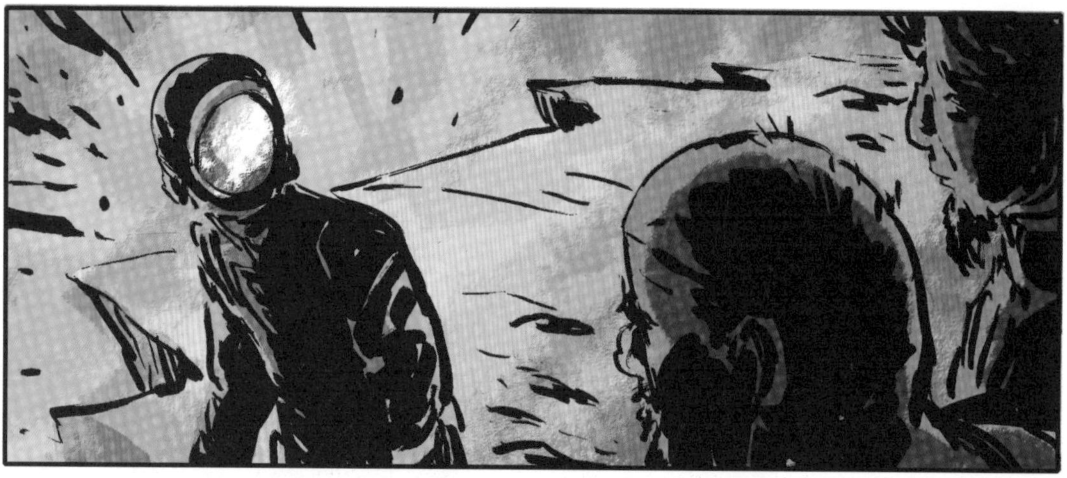

ONLY ONE TRULY HAD THE BRIGHT SCOPE OF A LEADER...

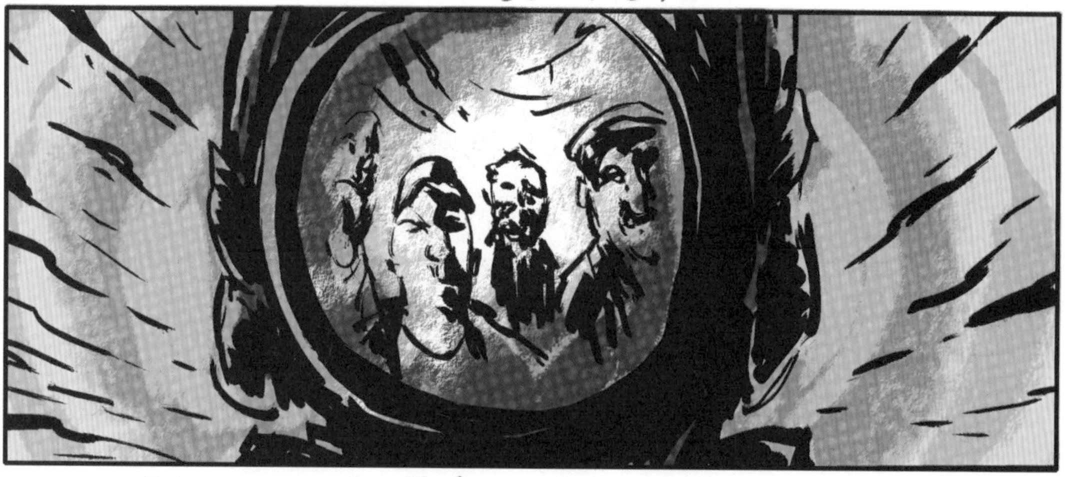

...THE KEEN EYE TO ILLUMINATE A NEW BEGINNING.

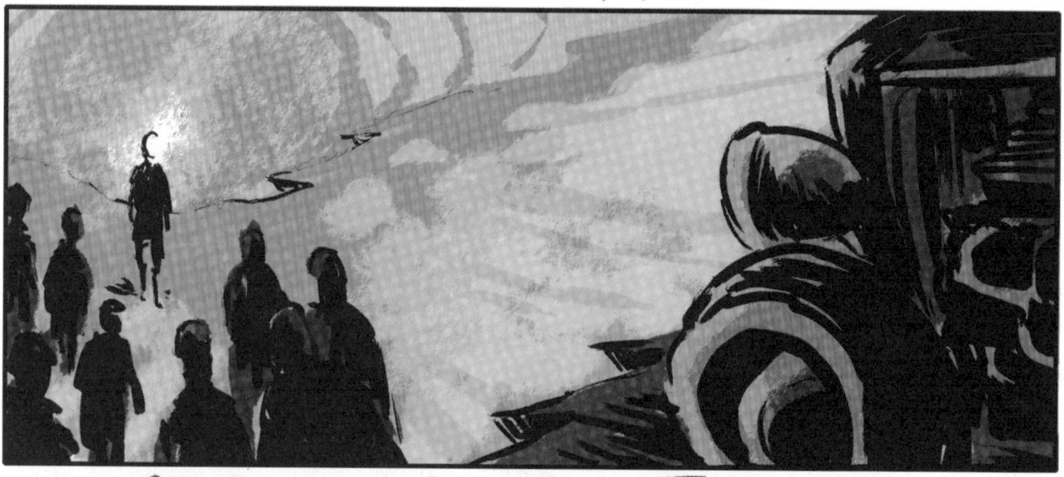

THEIR LANDSCAPE, DOTTED WITH METALLIC SCRAPS OF HOPE...

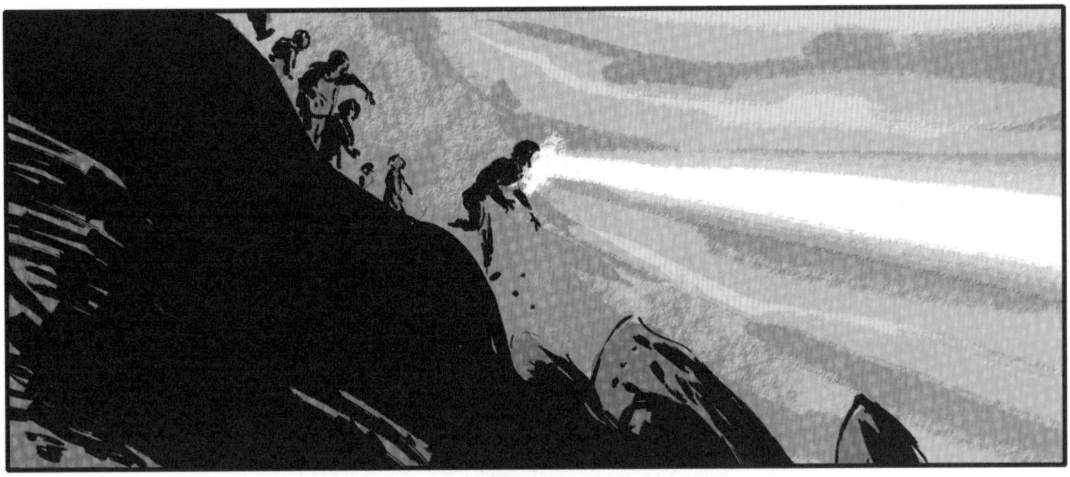

...WOULD SERVE AS A
ROADMAP OF EXPERIENCE.

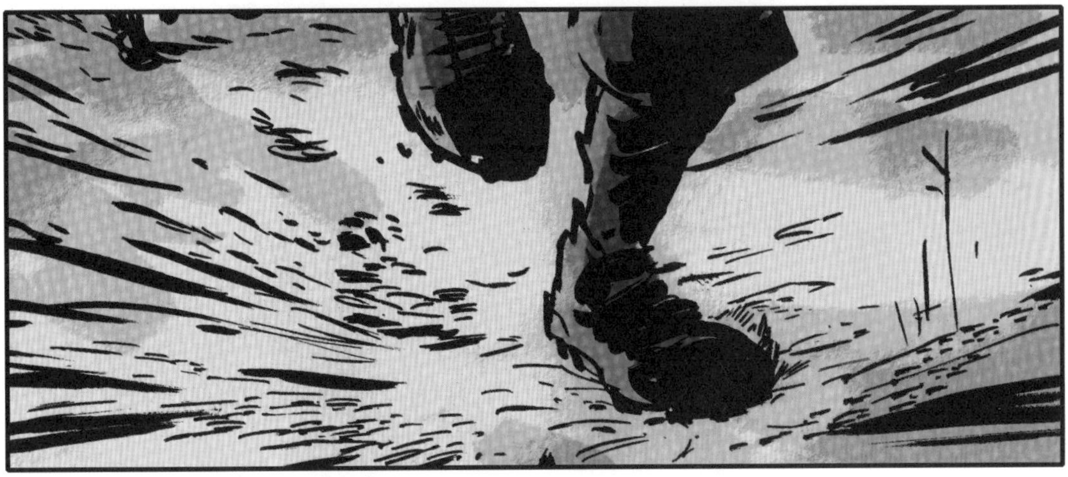

TIRE TREADS AND
SHOE LEATHER.

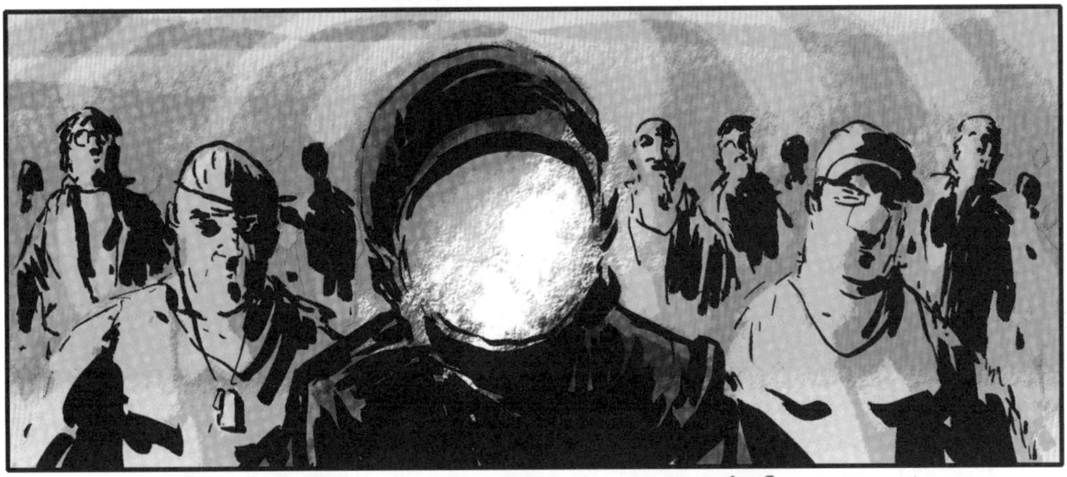

FLESH, BONE, GREASE, AND GRIME WOULD
TAKE A ROAD UNPAVED...

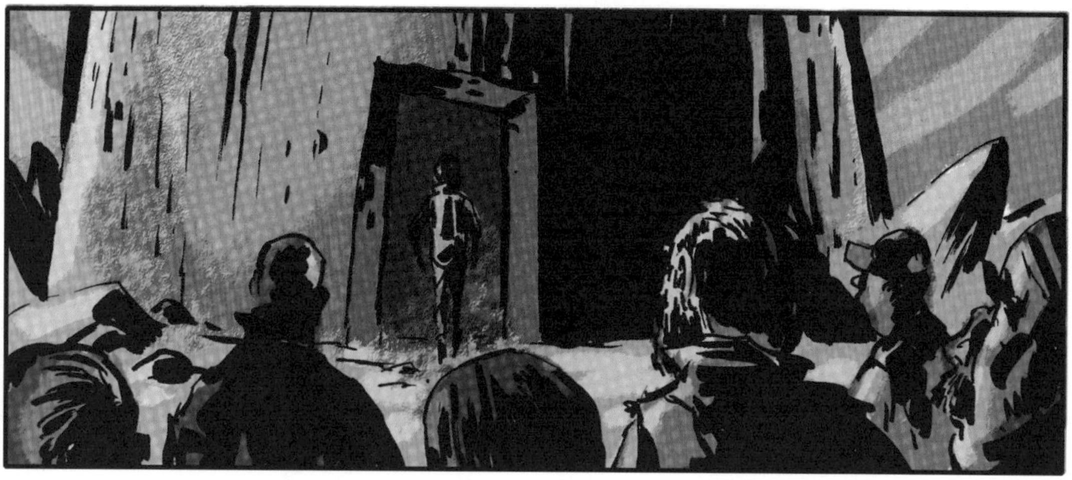

...UNPAVED AND UNTRAVELED.

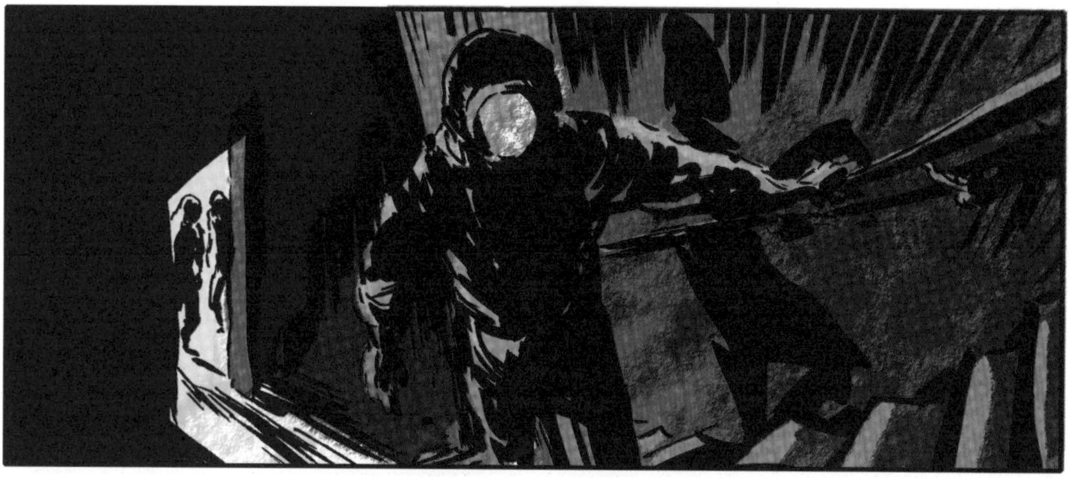

UNTIL NOW.

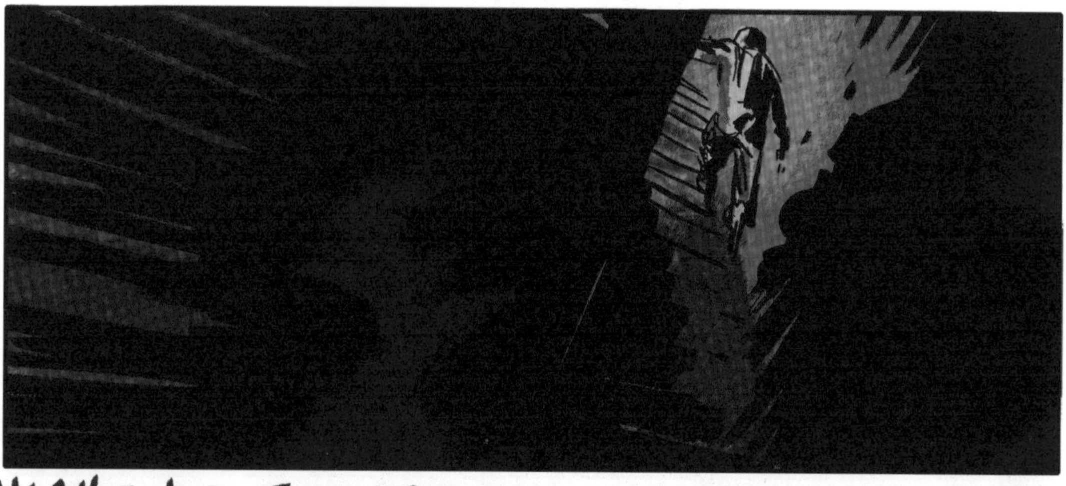

NIGHT HAD FOREVER SET ON THEIR HIGHWAYS.
IT WAS TIME TO ASCEND.

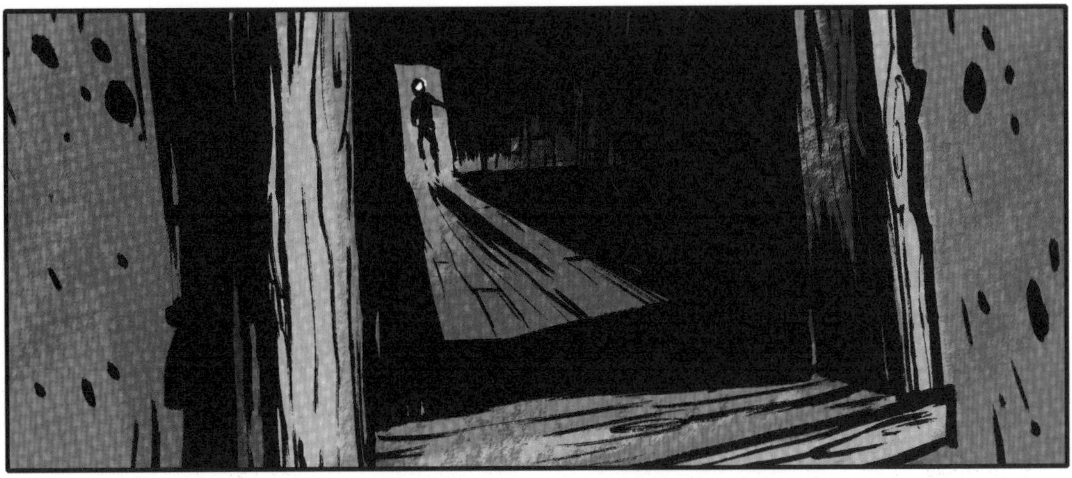

TIME TO RISE ANEW.

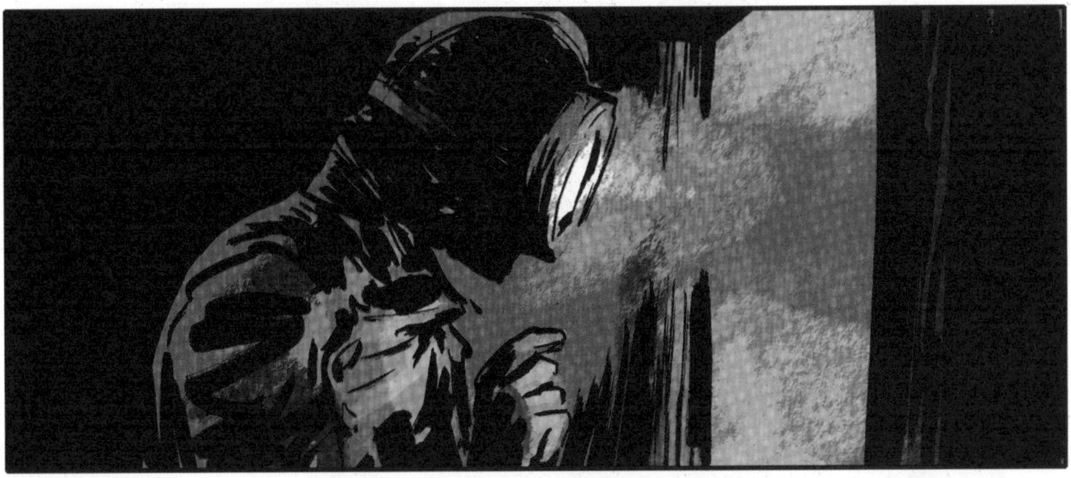

THE WINTER OF THEIR DISCONTENT HAD FALLEN ASIDE.
SPRING WAS AFOOT...

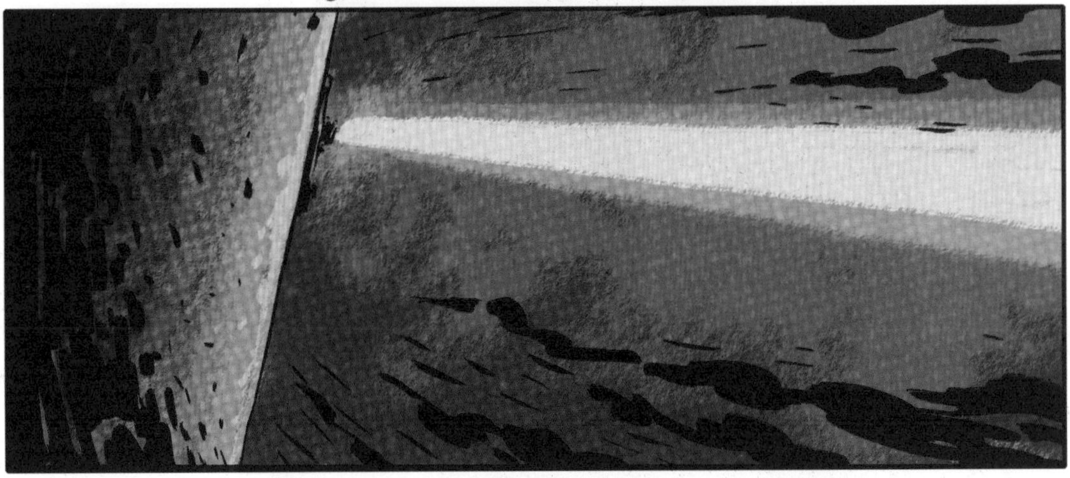

...AND AN ENDLESS SUMMER.

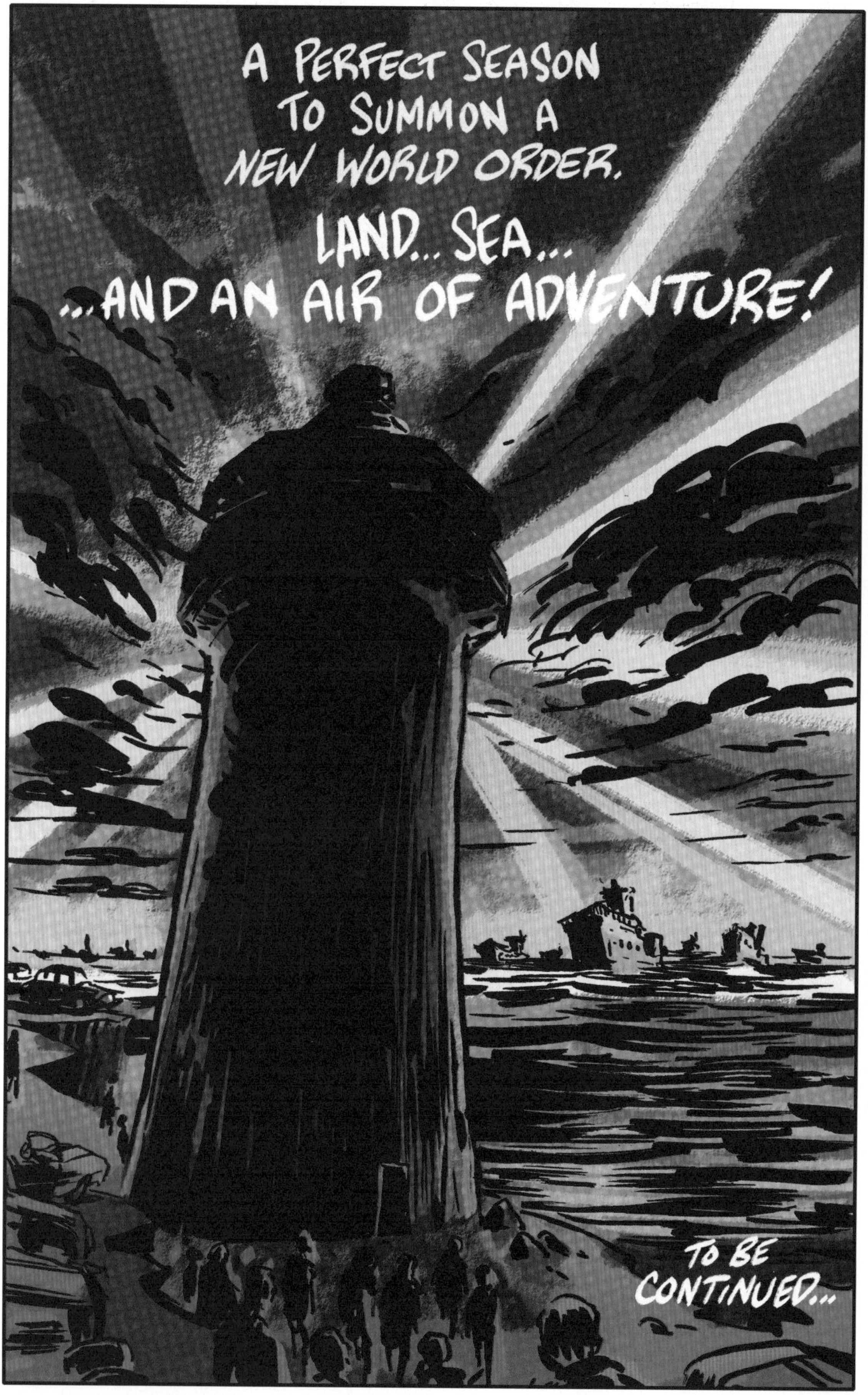
A PERFECT SEASON TO SUMMON A NEW WORLD ORDER.
LAND... SEA...
...AND AN AIR OF ADVENTURE!
TO BE CONTINUED...

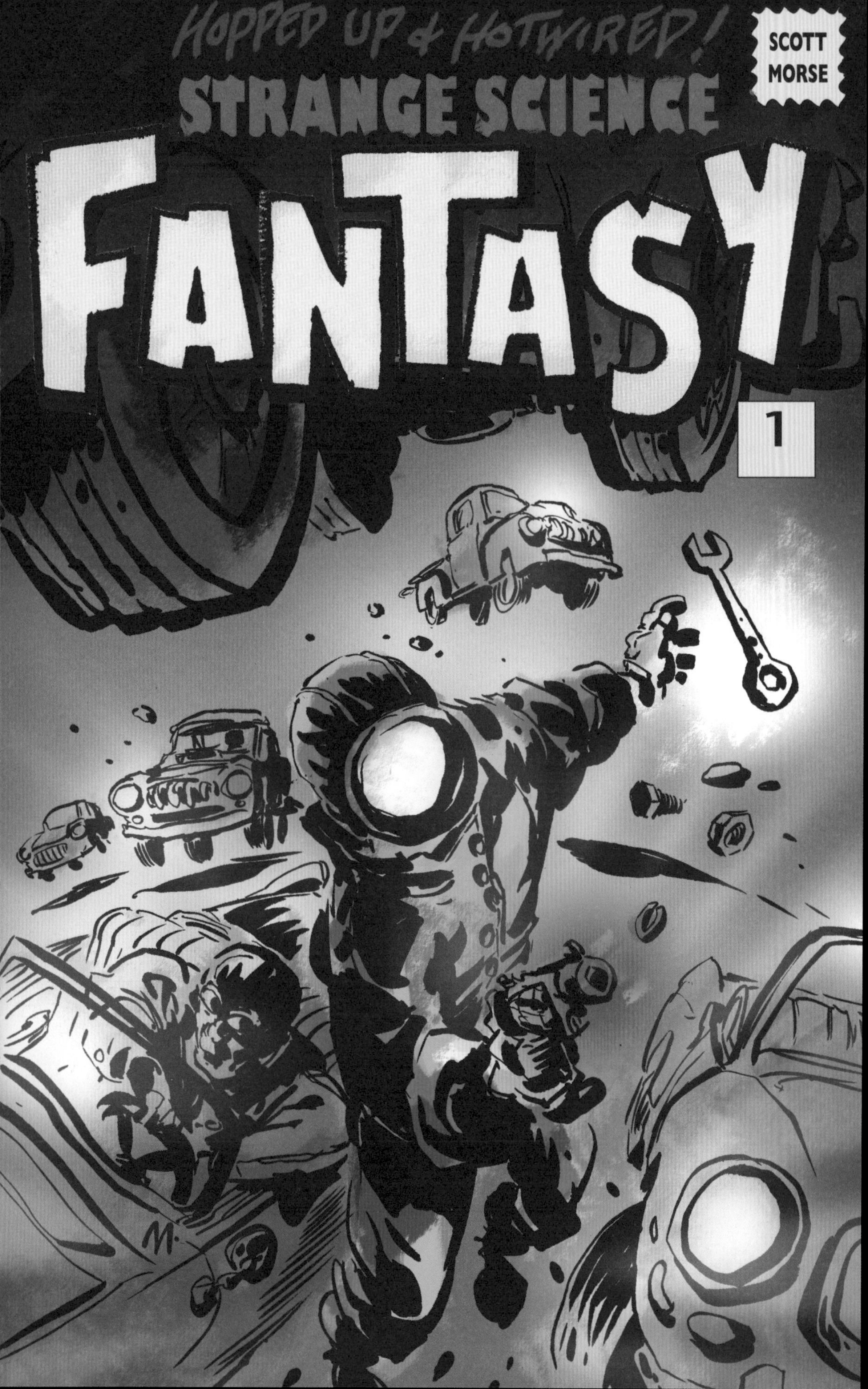
HOPPED UP & HOTWIRED!
STRANGE SCIENCE
FANTASY
SCOTT
MORSE
1

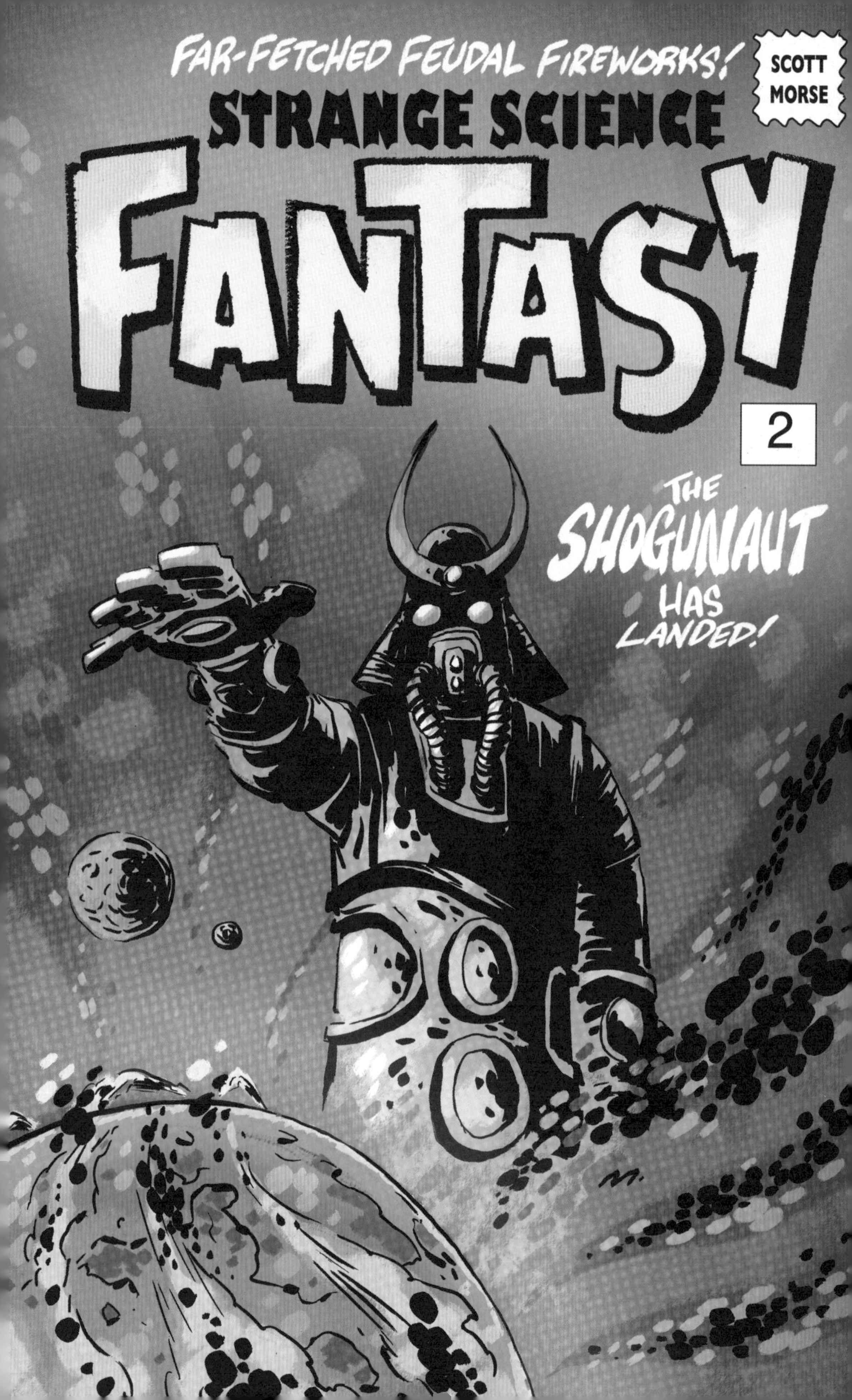
FAR-FETCHED FEUDAL FIREWORKS!
SCOTT MORSE
STRANGE SCIENCE
FANTASY
2
THE SHOGUNAUT HAS LANDED!

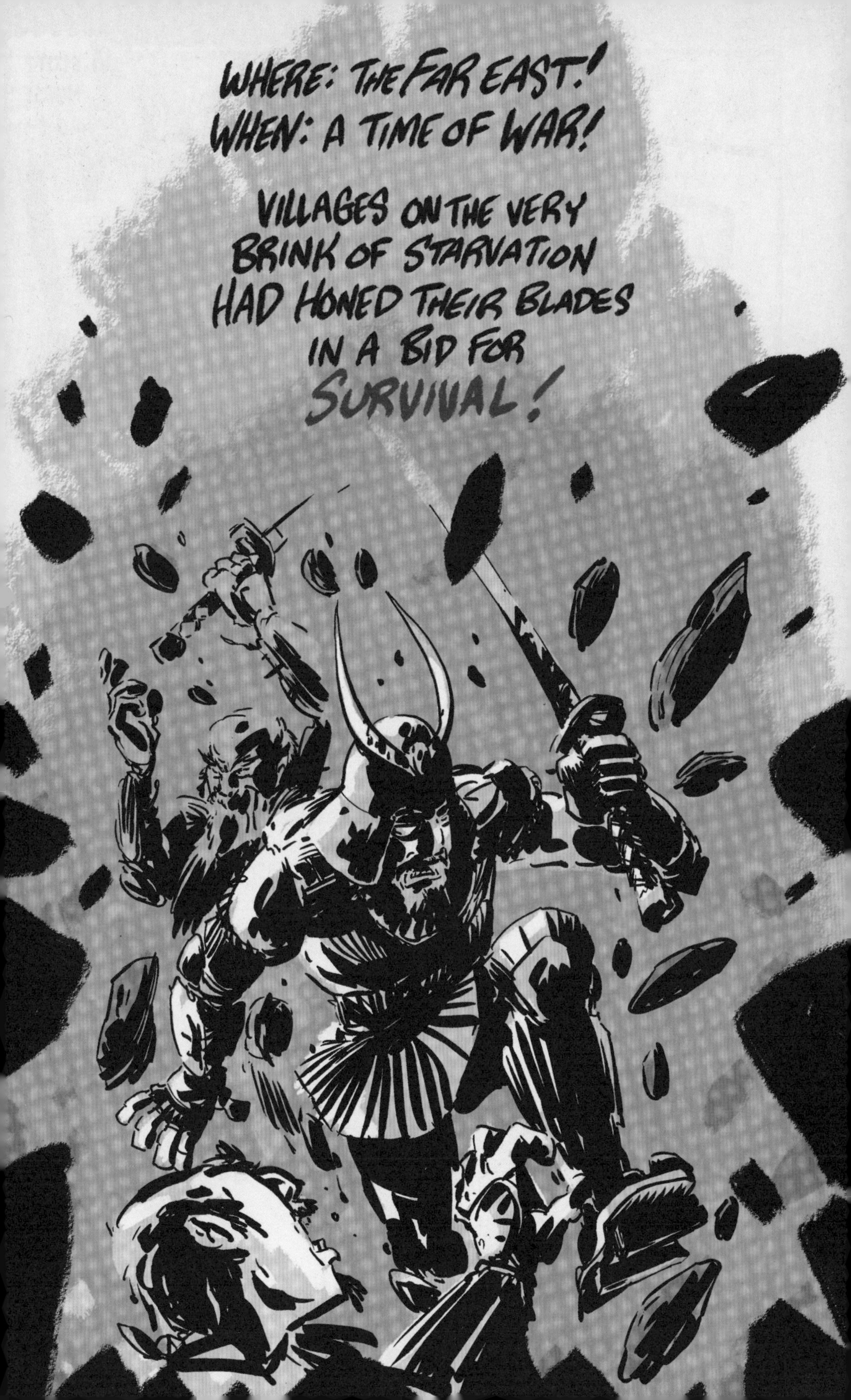
WHERE: THE FAR EAST!
WHEN: A TIME OF WAR!
VILLAGES ON THE VERY BRINK OF STARVATION HAD HONED THEIR BLADES IN A BID FOR SURVIVAL!

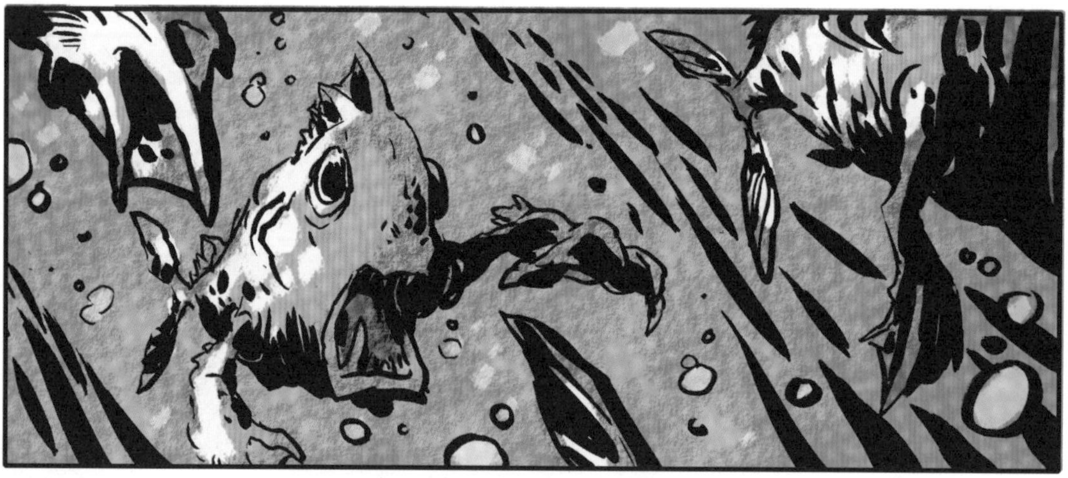

THE PROBLEM? FOOD!
SEA LIFE HAD EVOLVED INTO DEFENSIVE MACHINES!

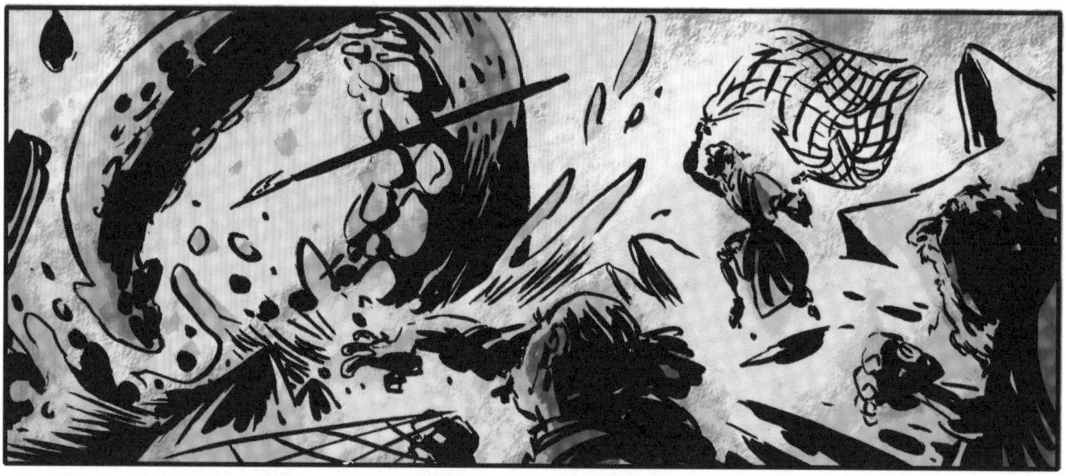

THE FIGHT FOR NOURISHMENT HAD TAKEN A DECISIVE TURN...

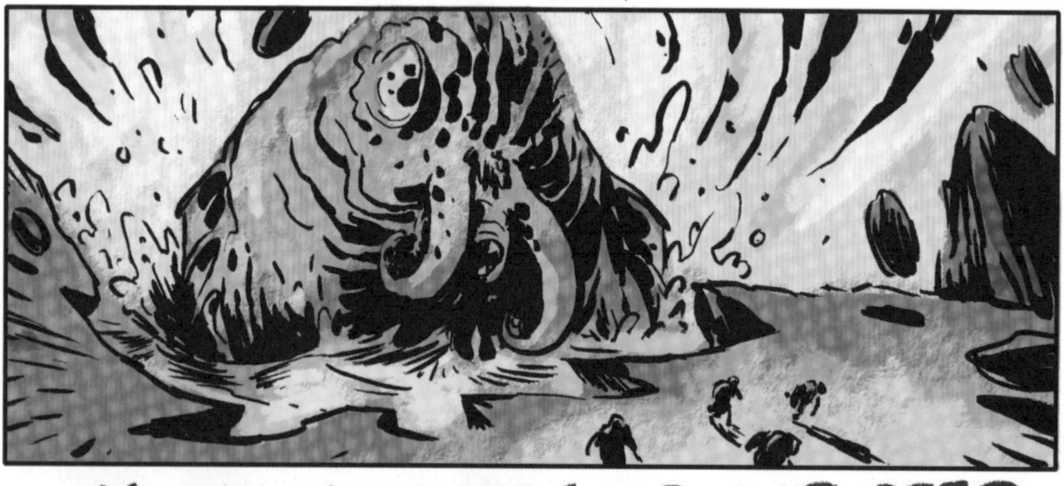

... AS THE MONSTERS OF THE DEEP BECAME THE HUNTERS OF MAN!

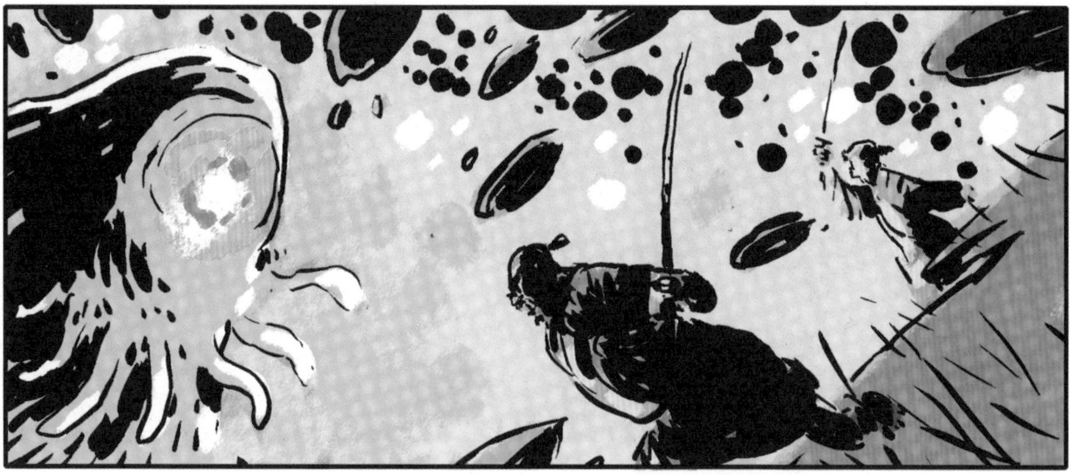

THE HUNT FOR FOOD WOULD
TAKE A BACK SEAT...

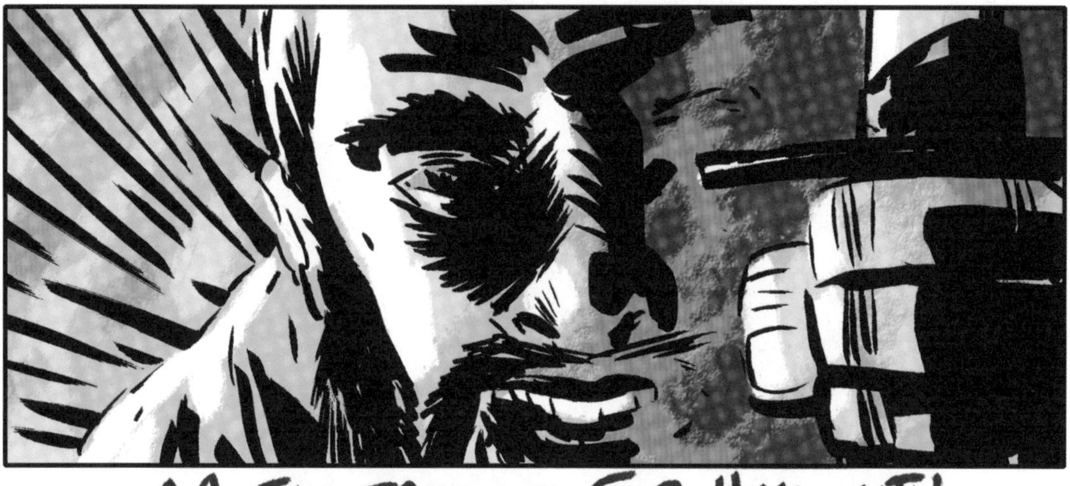

...AS THE BATTLE FOR HUMANITY
WAGED ONWARD.

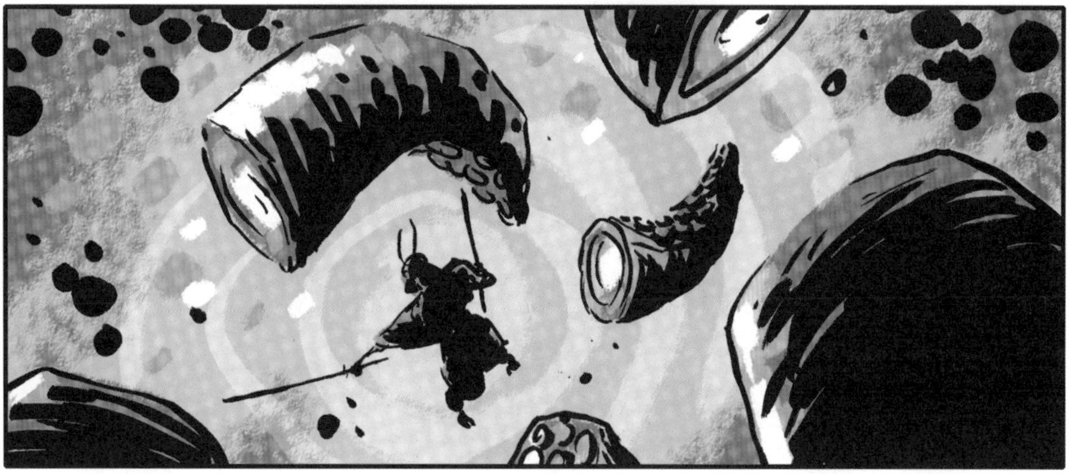

COLD STEEL DRAWING COLD BLOOD.

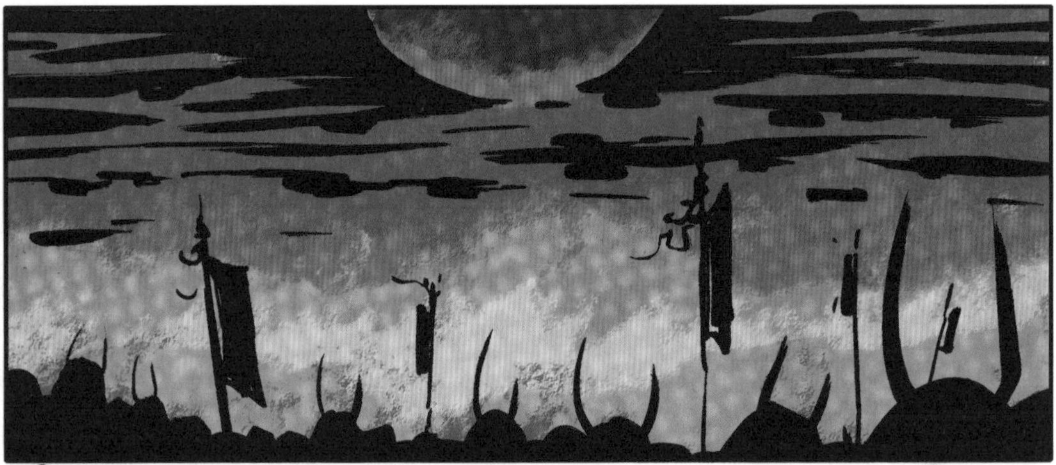

DISHEARTENED, THE SPIRIT OF MAN FOUND ITSELF SHREDDED TO PULP IN THE FACE OF THE MONSTROSITIES.

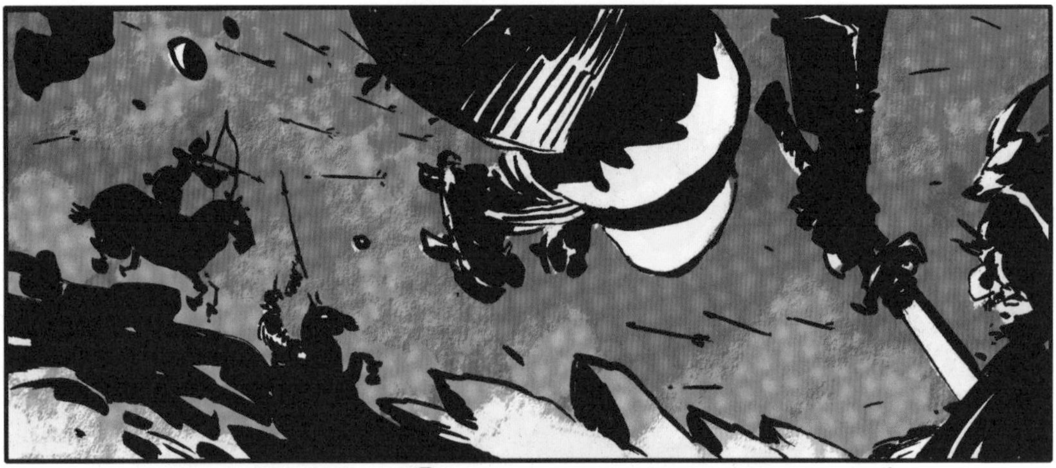

ANGER TURNED INWARD AS THE VILLAGES FLOUNDERED.

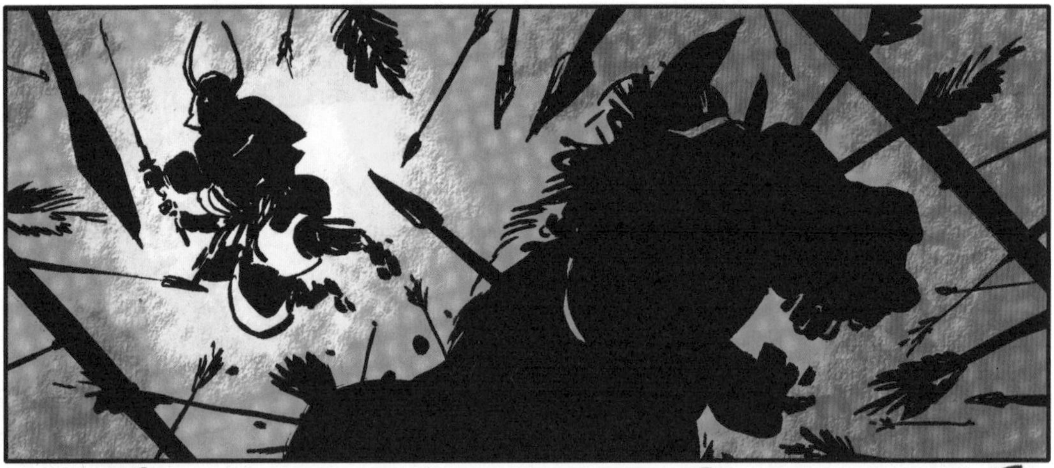

WITH FOOD STORES ANNIHILATED BY THE BEASTS OF THE DEEP AND UNITY BUT A BLUR OF THE PAST...

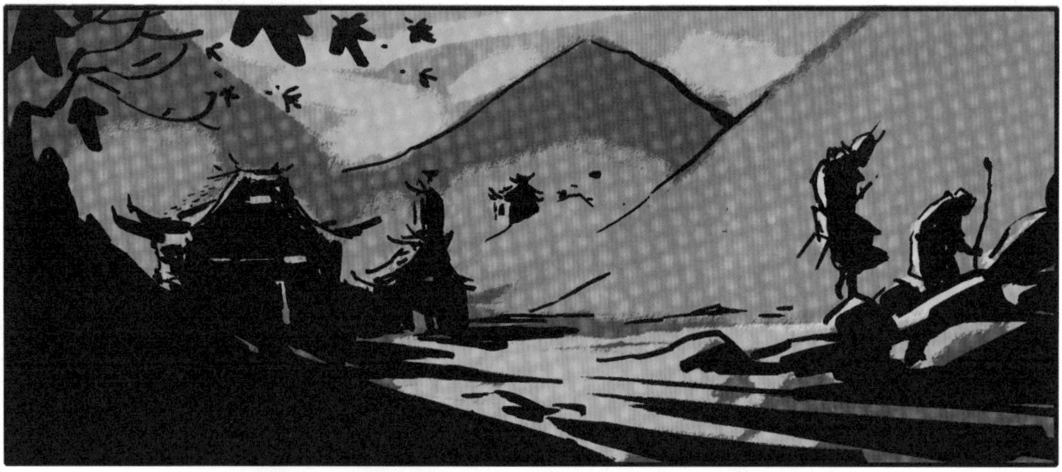

...THE SHOGUN THREW HOPE
TO THE FOUR WINDS.

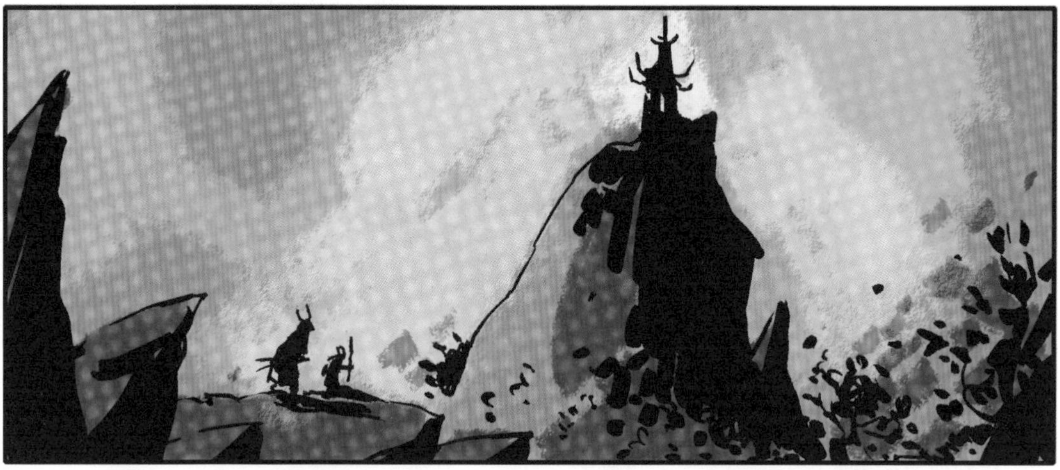

HE JOURNEYED TO THE HIGH PEAKS
OF SALVATION AND VIRTUE...

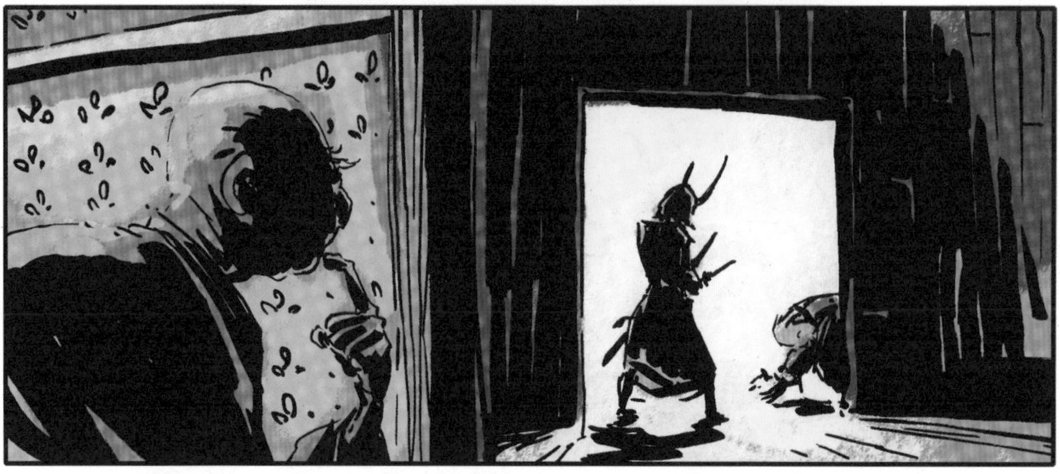

...TO A PLACE WHERE THE STORIED
WORKERS OF MAGIC RESIDE.

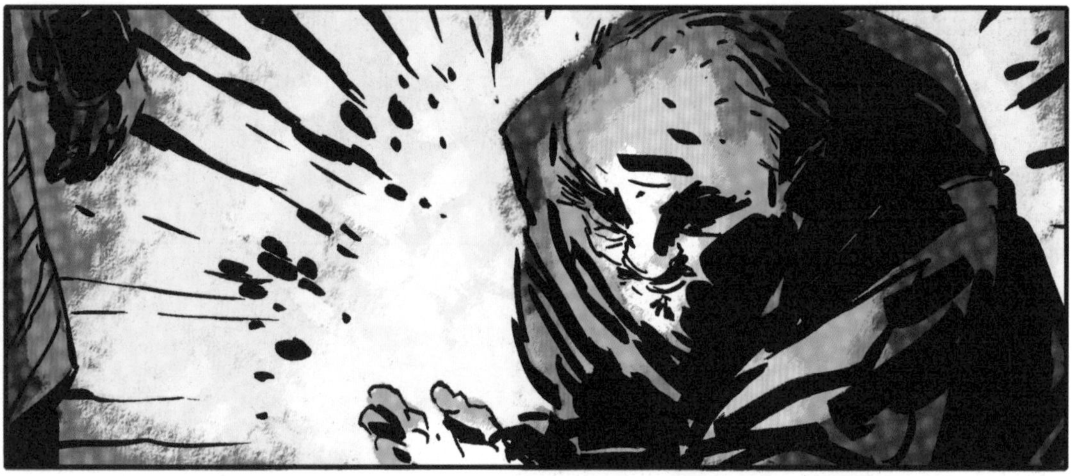

WOULD THE FUTURE HOLD STILL MORE MISFORTUNE?

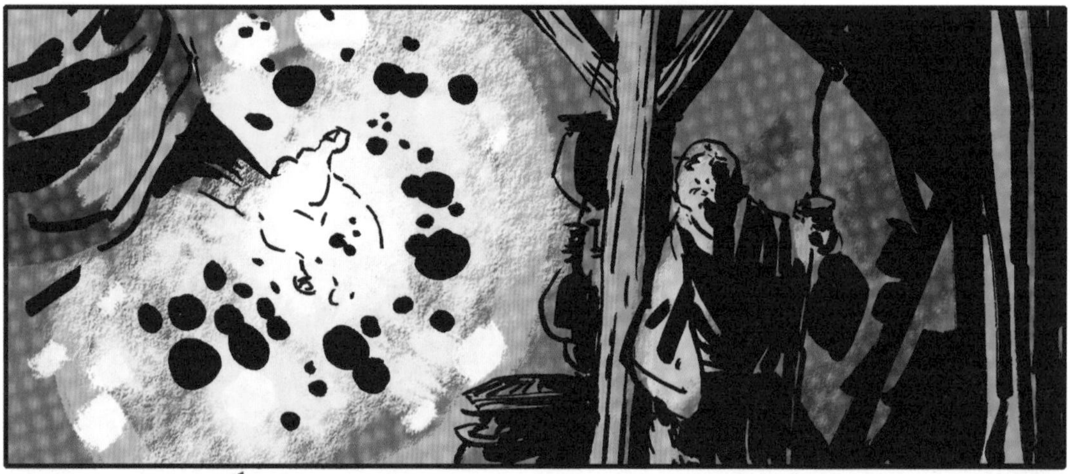

WOULD THERE BE A LAND OF PEACE AND HARMONY ON THE HORIZON?

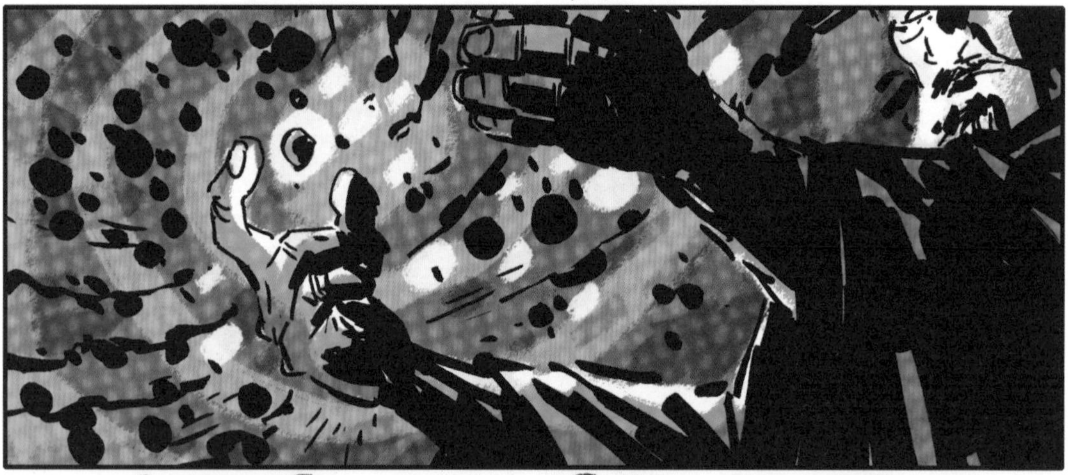

COULD THE WAYS OF THE ANCIENT MYSTICS HOLD A SOLUTION?

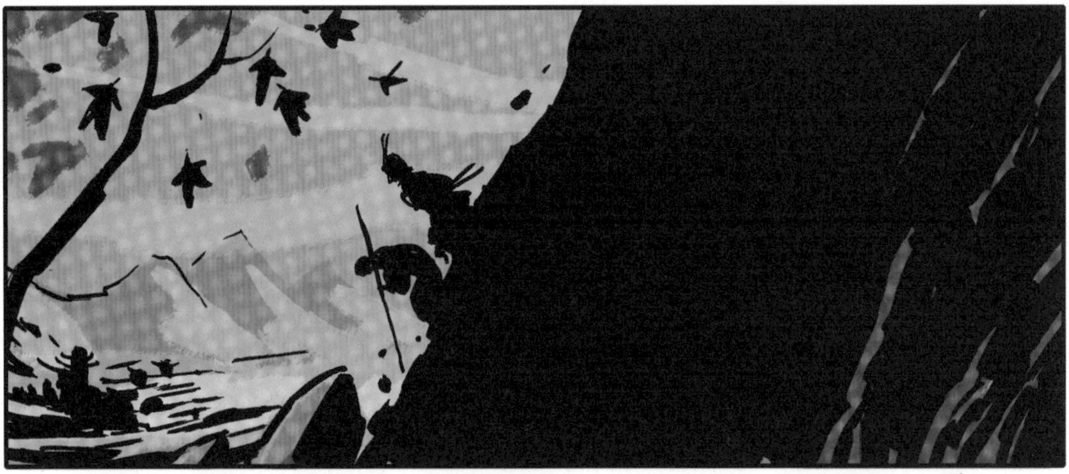

THE SHOGUN WOULD ALLOW TIME TO DECIPHER THESE ENIGMAS.

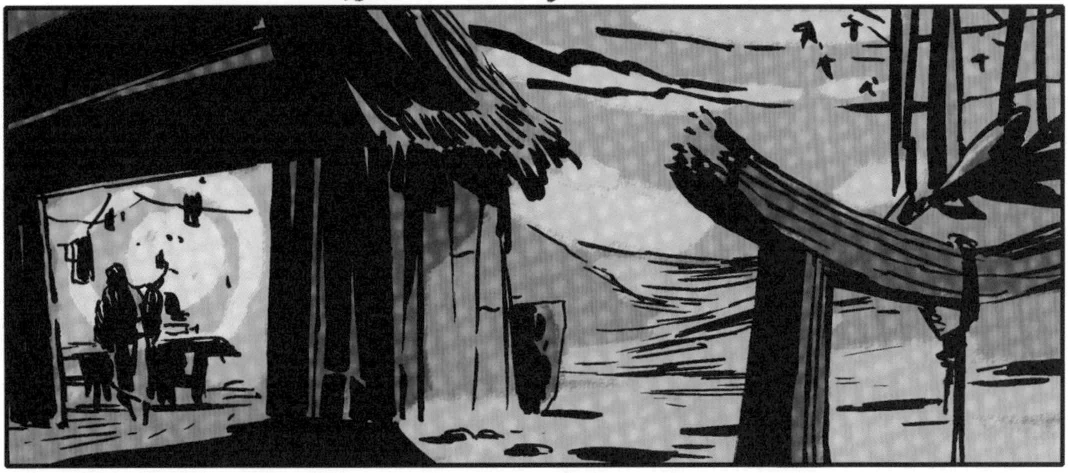

A GYPSY OF THE OUTER SPIRITS AND INNER INCANTATIONS WOULD FORGE THE ANSWER.

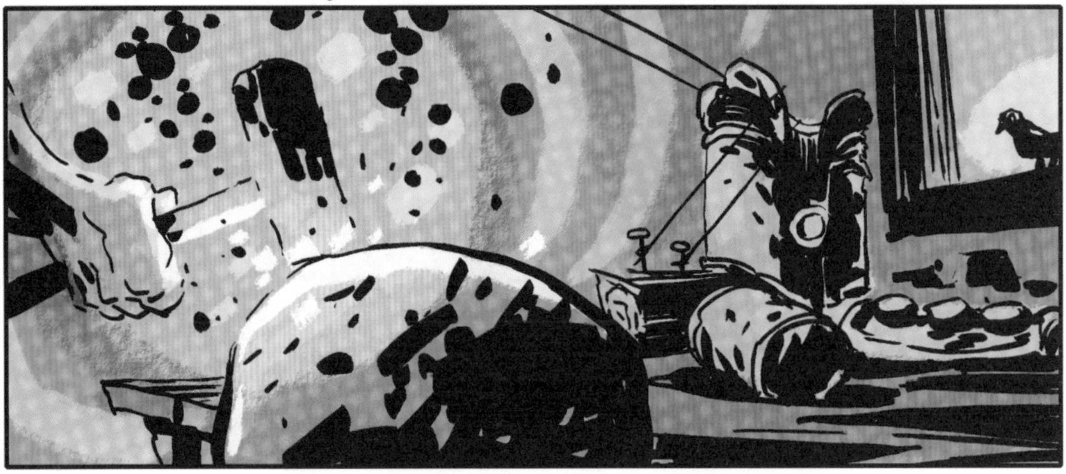

AN ALLOY OF METALS AND METTLE...

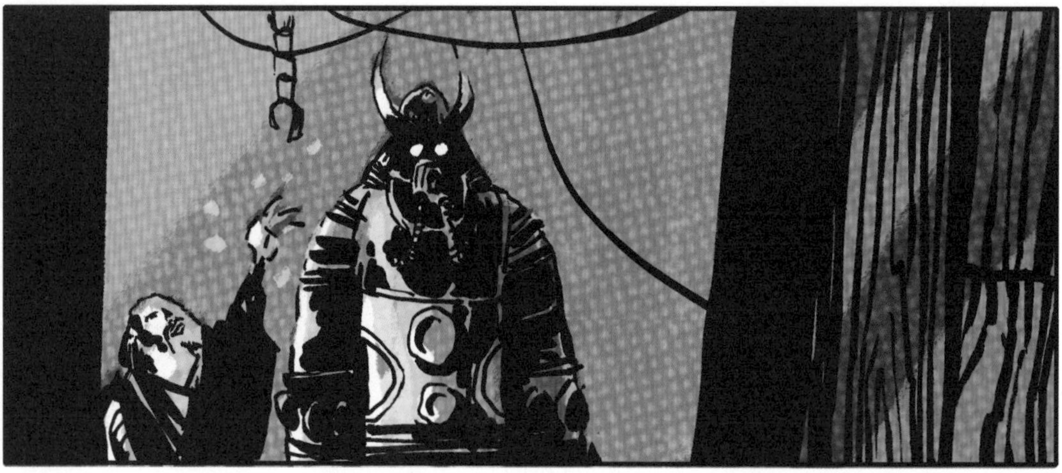

...A SOLUTION OF SORCERY AND SHEER STRENGTH.
SHOGUN... AND SHOGUNAUT!

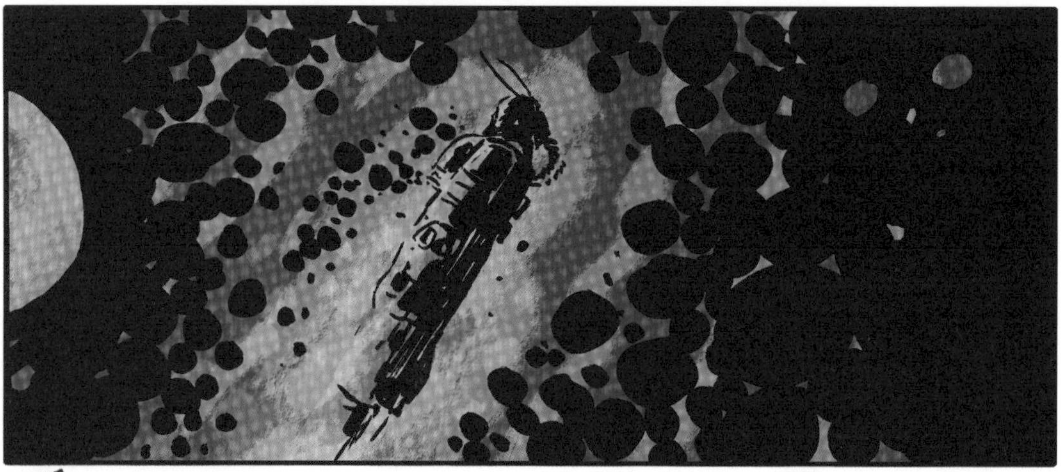

THE MYSTICS FELT ASSURED THAT THE
ANSWERS WOULD BE FOUND IN THE COSMOS...

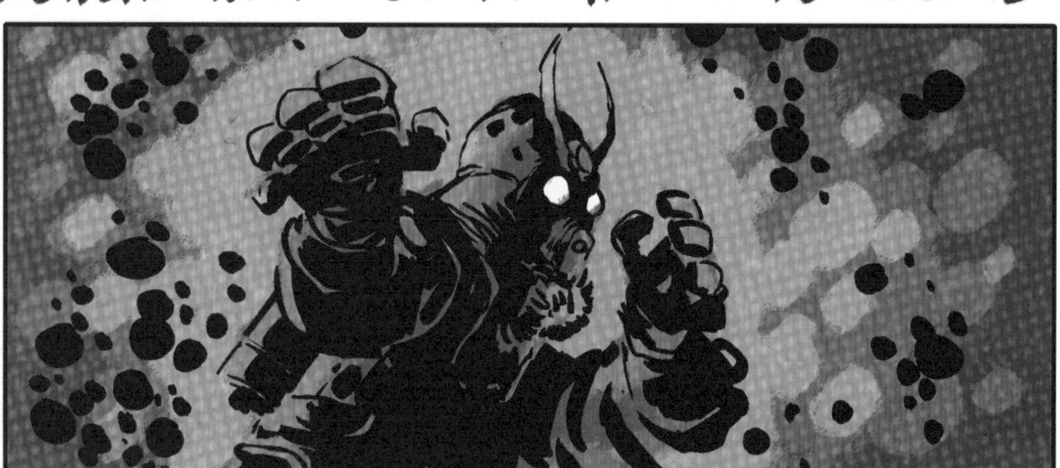

...AND THE COSMOS SPOKE!

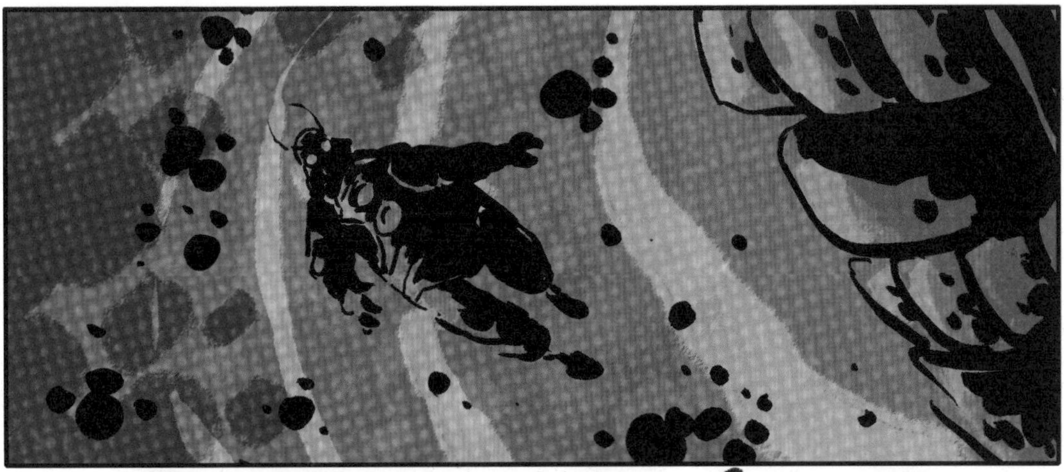

THE SHOGUNAUT FELL STILL AS NEW REALITIES TOOK TO ORBIT.

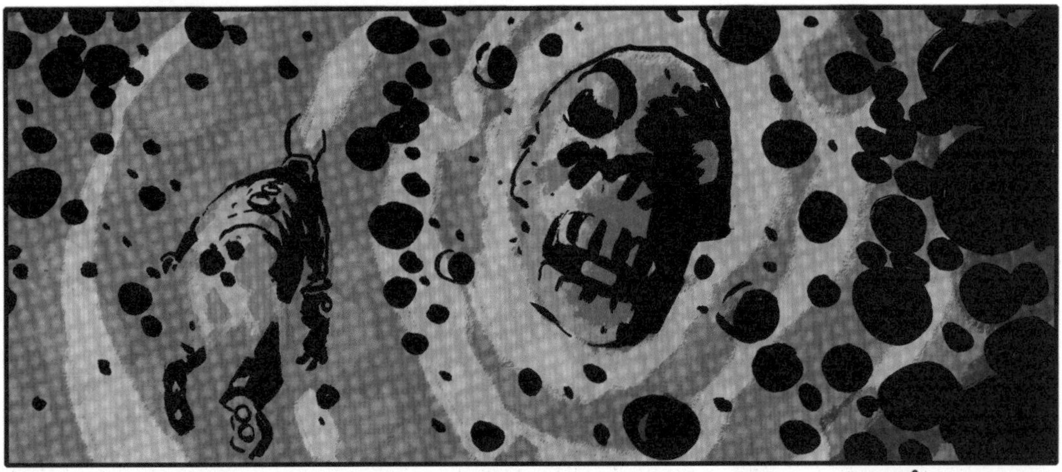

THE *COSMIC MIND* REVEALED THE ANSWERS THAT MIGHT AID THE EMBATTLED.

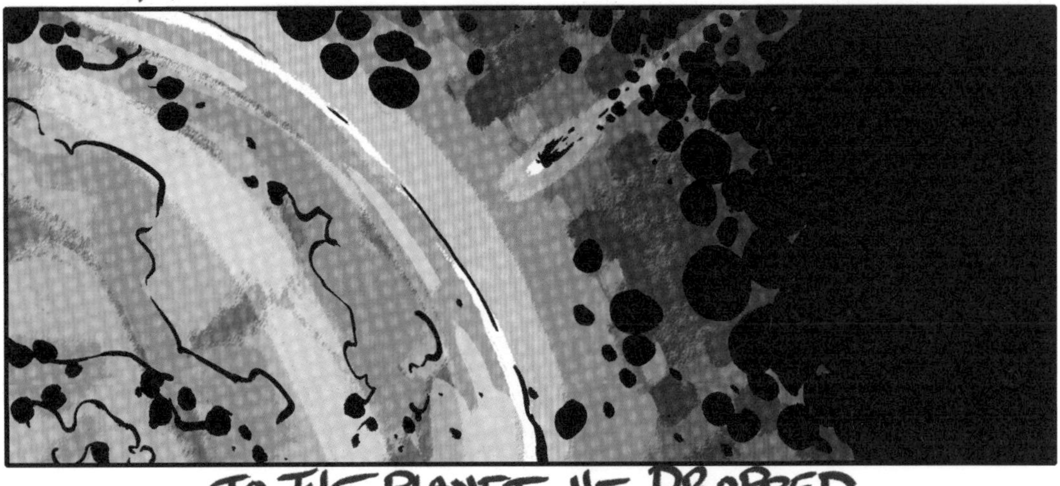

TO THE PLANET HE DROPPED,
A CHARGE OF APPREHENSION AFOOT
IN THE WILD ATMOSPHERE BELOW...

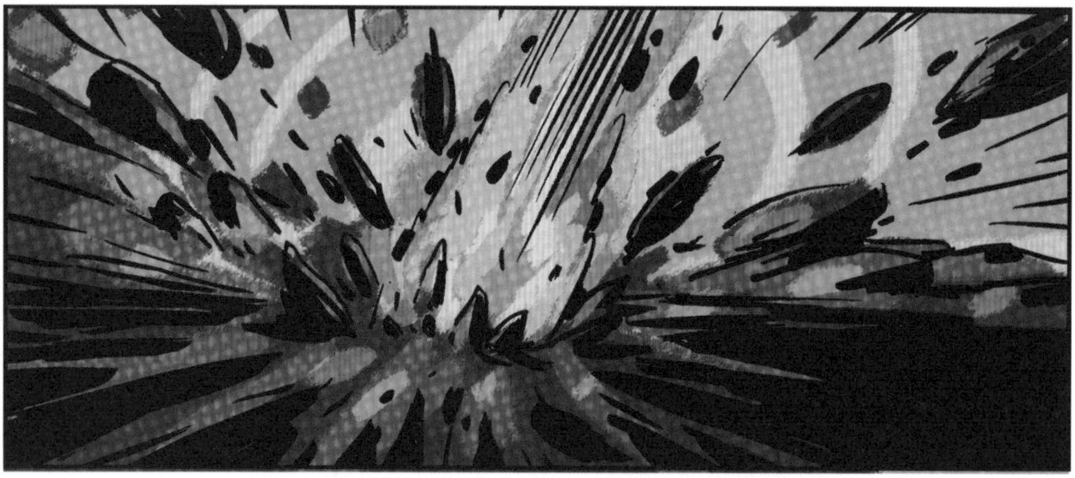

...THE GRAVITY OF THE SITUATION
PULLING AT HIS SOUL.

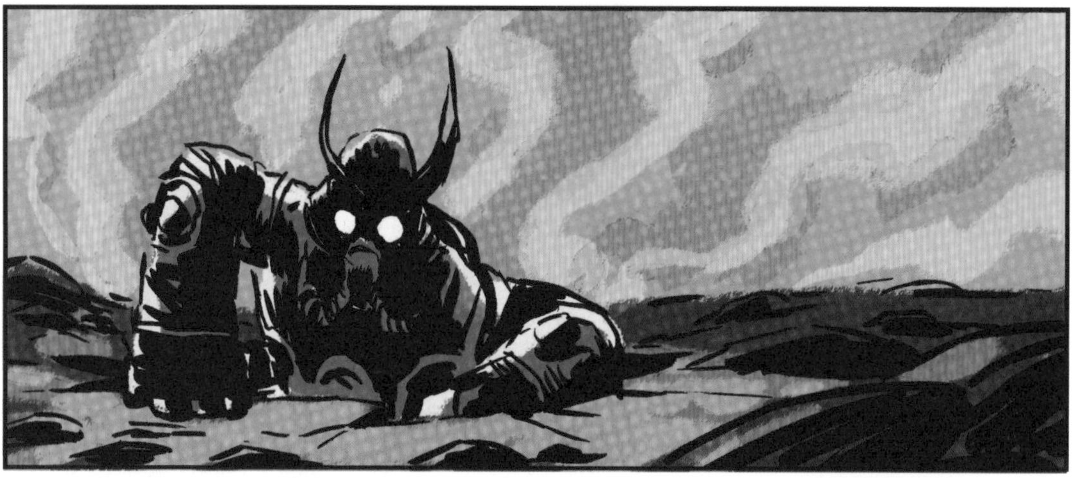

LIKE THE FOLDED METAL OF A FORGED
BLADE, HE ROSE WITH SOLID PURPOSE...

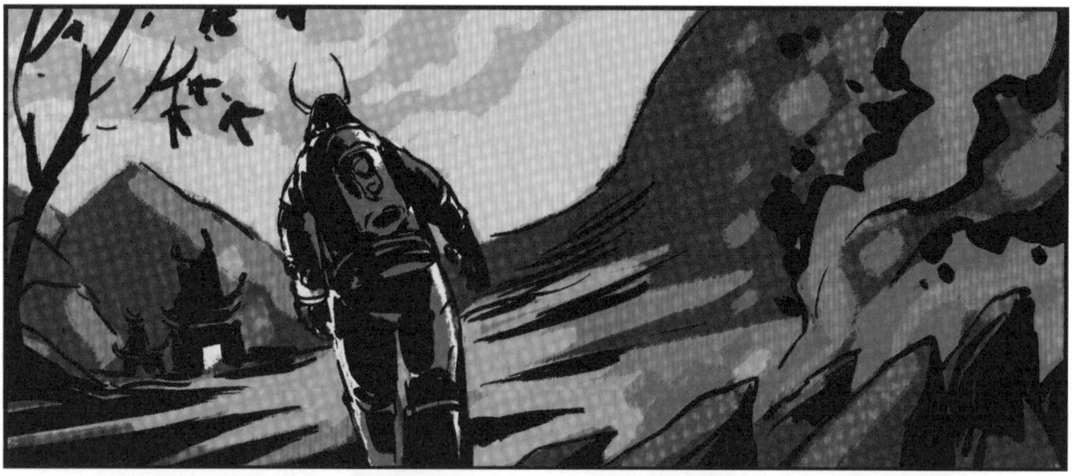

...HIS PATH STREWN WITH THE INFINITE
POSSIBLE OUTCOMES OF WHAT LAY AHEAD.

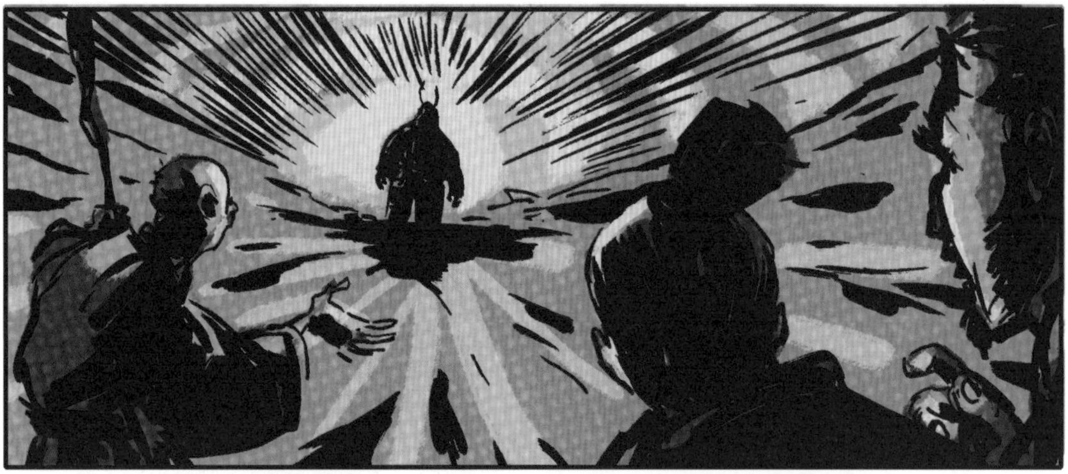

FACES MET HIM--FACES
DRESSED WITH ANTICIPATION.

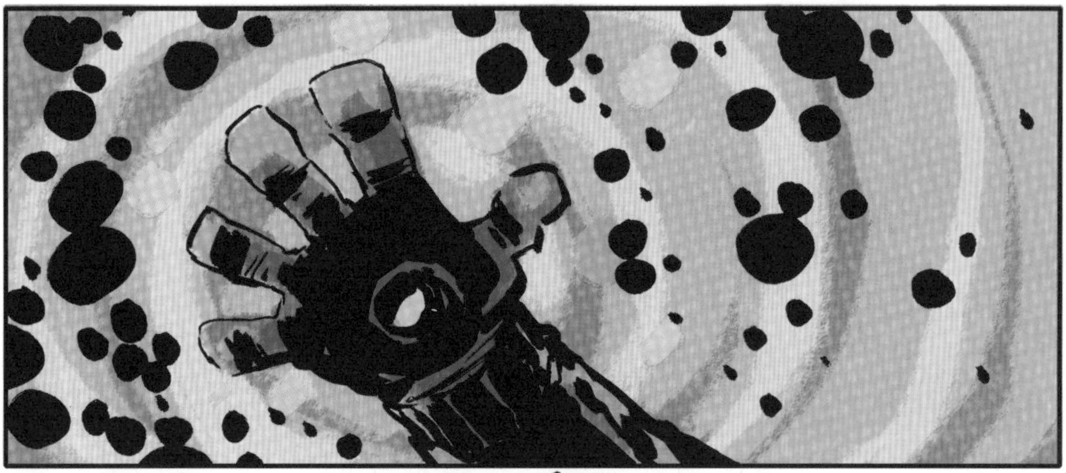

THE COSMIC MIND HAD SPOKEN, HE TOLD THEM...
SPOKEN A PLAN-- A TASK!

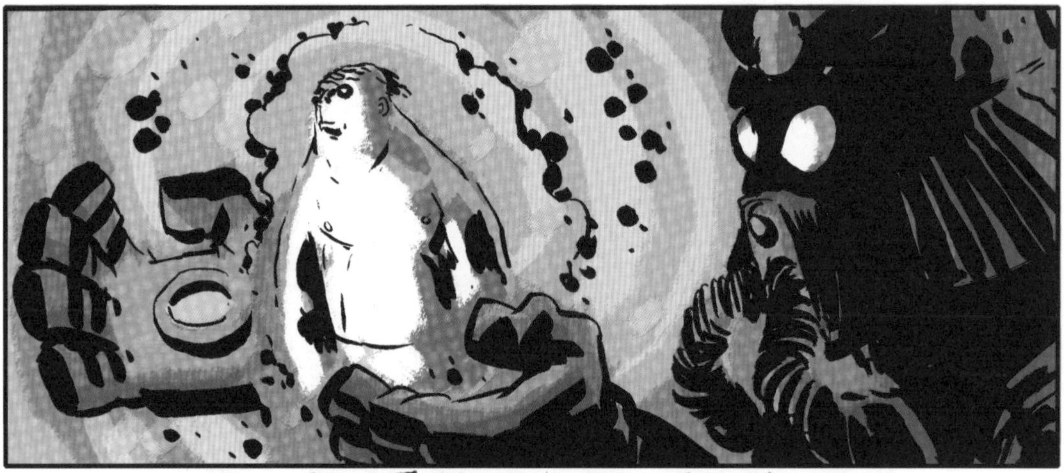

TO SAVE MANKIND FROM THE
FRAGILITY OF FAMINE AND FEAR...

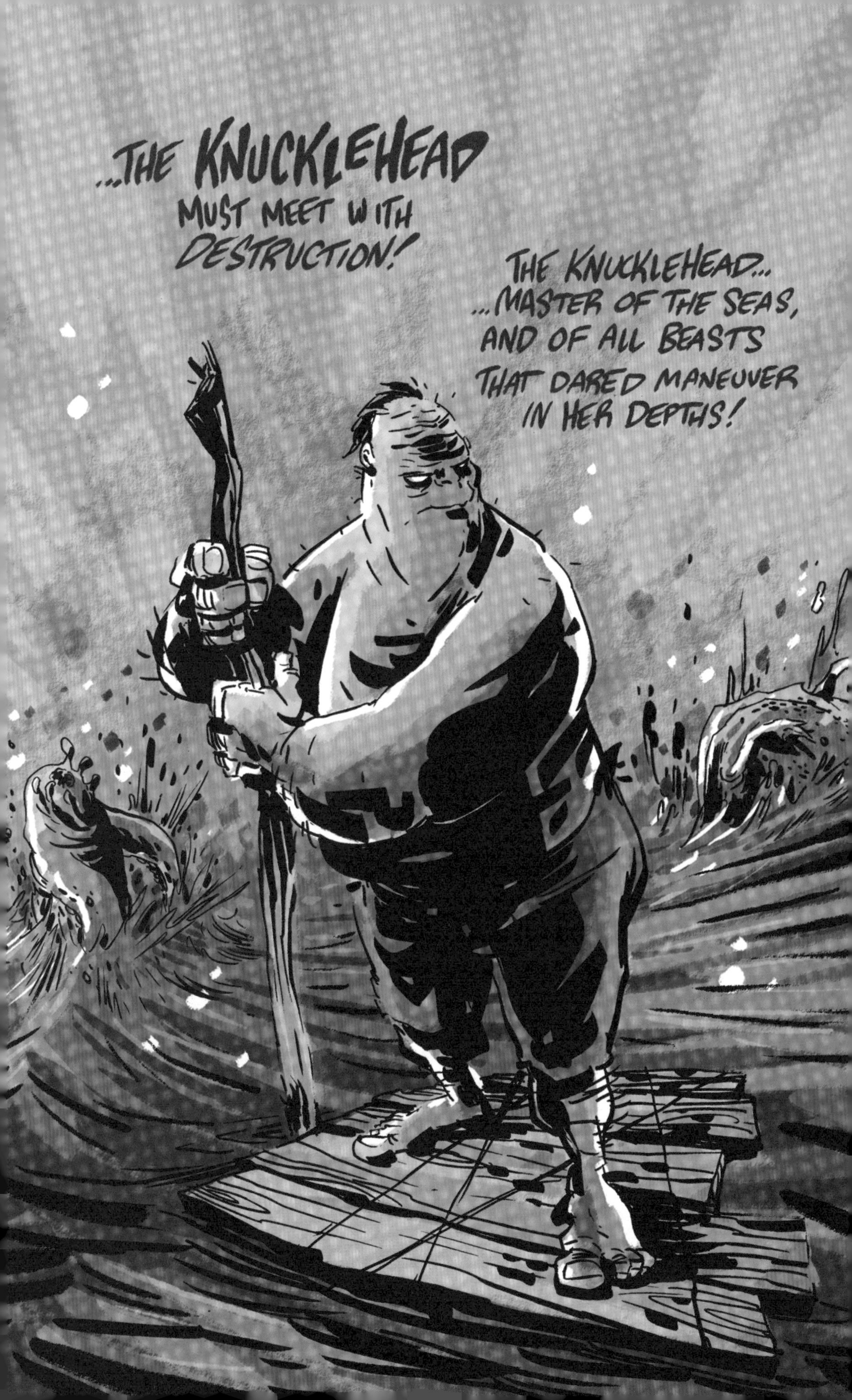
...THE KNUCKLEHEAD MUST MEET WITH DESTRUCTION!
THE KNUCKLEHEAD... ...MASTER OF THE SEAS, AND OF ALL BEASTS THAT DARED MANEUVER IN HER DEPTHS!

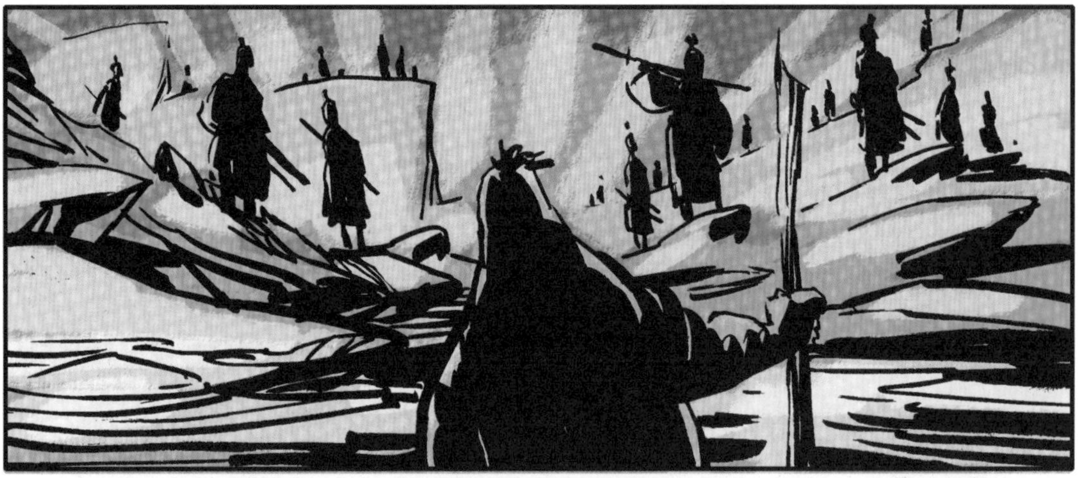

AT SEA SINCE THE DAWN OF MAN, THIS BRUTE WOULD NOW LAND ON THE SHORES OF *DESTINY*.

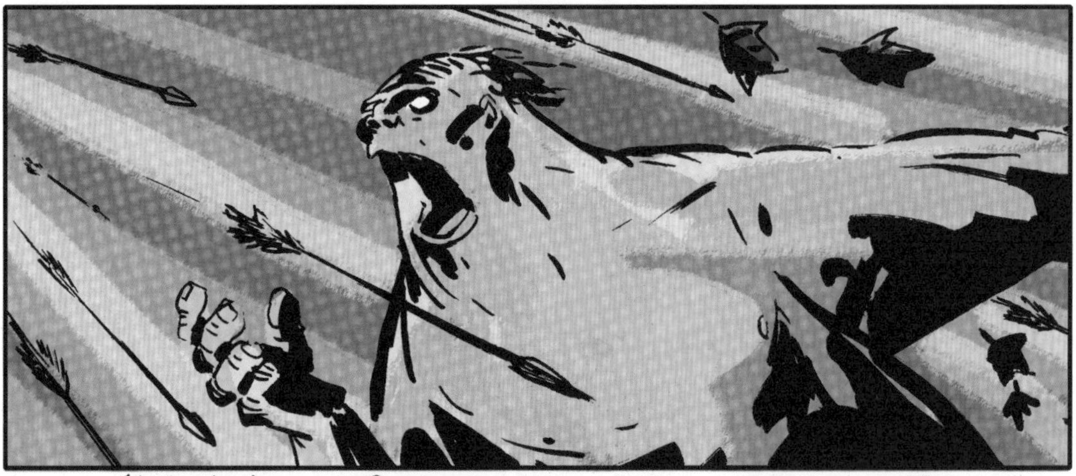

HIS HOSTILE RECEPTION WOULD ONE DAY BE REMEMBERED WITH SHAME AND EMBARRASSMENT.

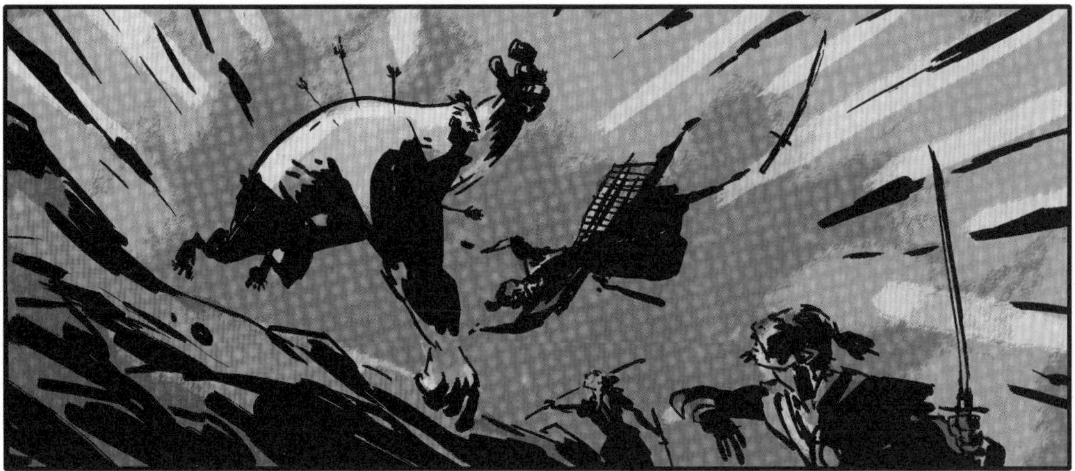

WHO AMONG THEM COULD HAVE KNOWN THE TRICKERY OF THE COSMIC MIND'S PROPHECY?

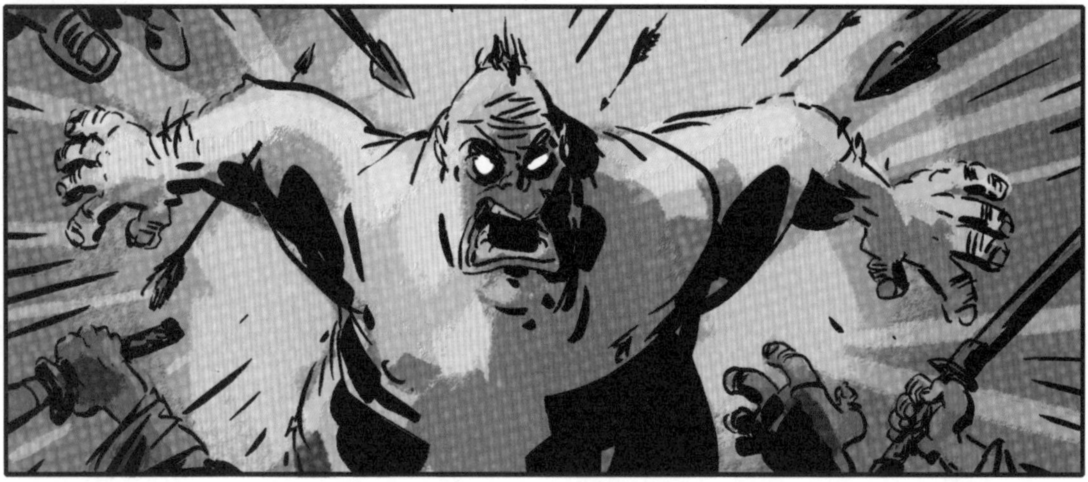

THEY HAD SIMPLY BEEN TOLD TO DESTROY THE KNUCKLEHEAD.

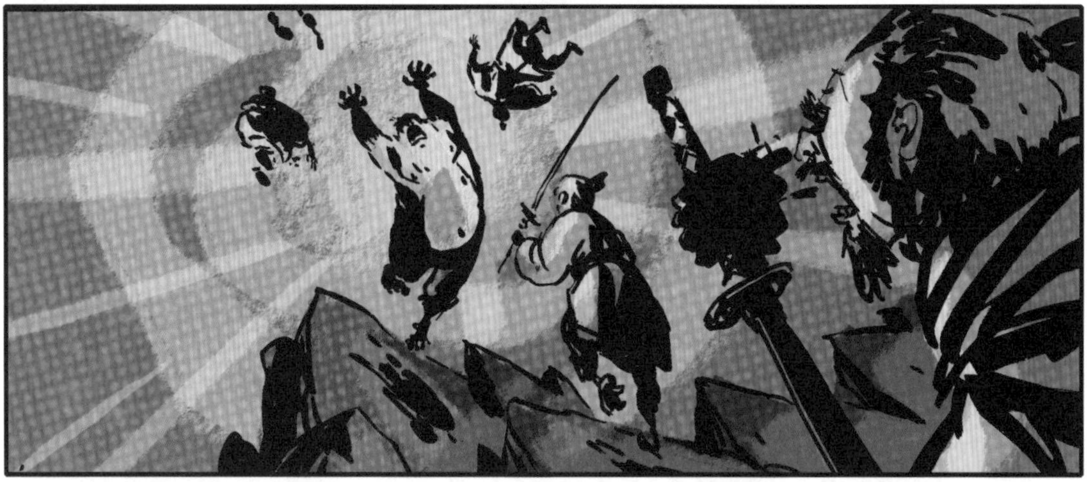

WHEN THE MARROW OF DIGNITY IS SUCKED FROM THE BONES OF HUMANITY...

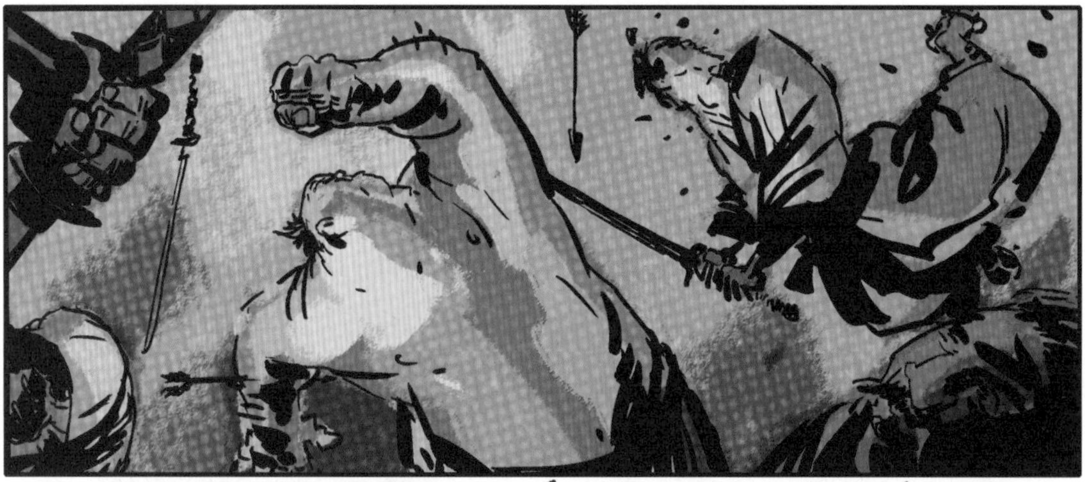

...HATRED PREVAILS IN THE BODY OF SOCIETY.

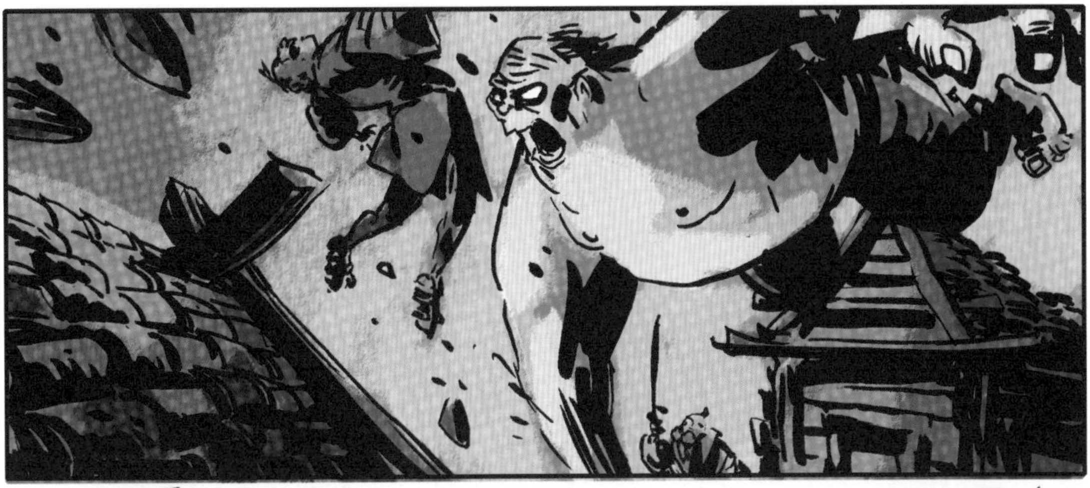

CONFRONTATION YIELDS ADRENAL ACCELERATION.
HOT BLOOD CAREENS THROUGH CONSTRICTED VEINS...

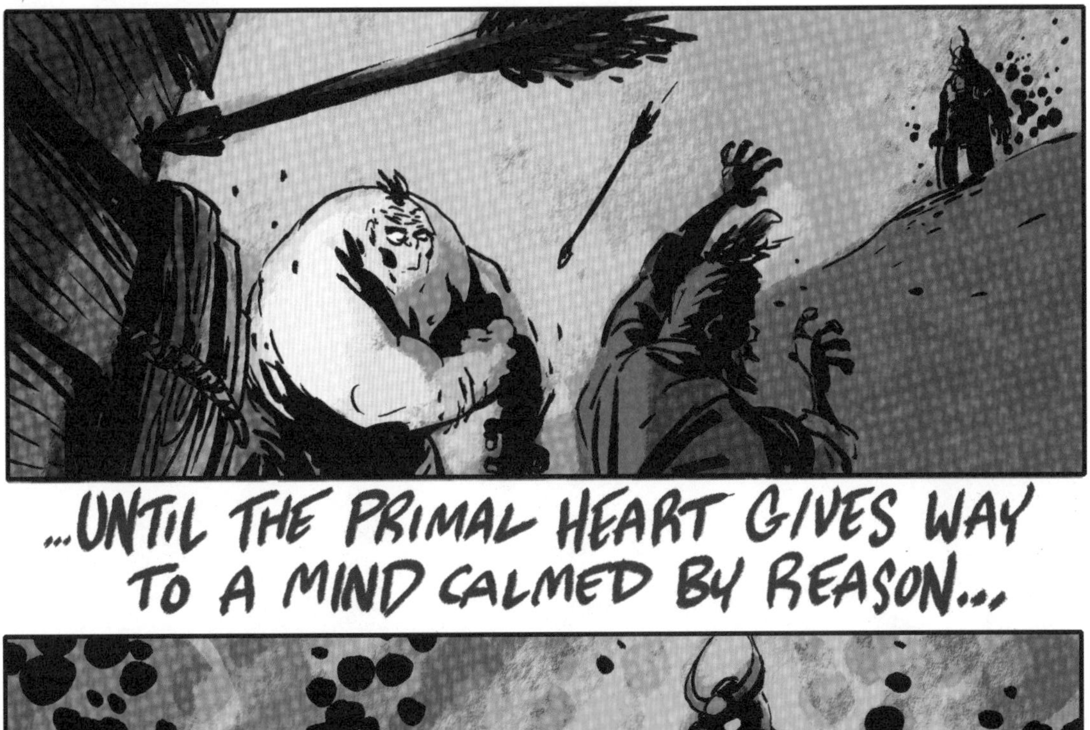

...UNTIL THE PRIMAL HEART GIVES WAY
TO A MIND CALMED BY REASON...

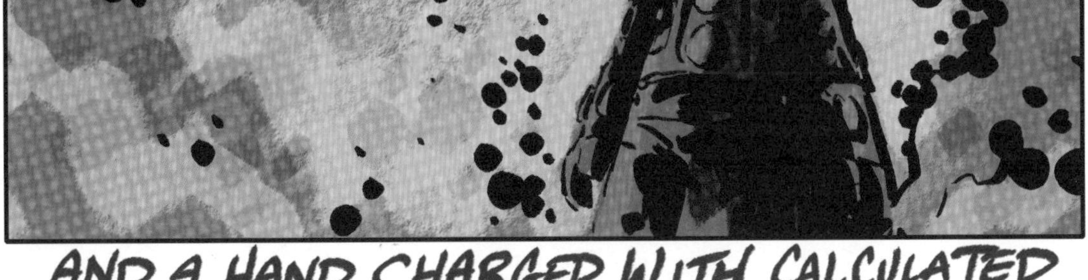

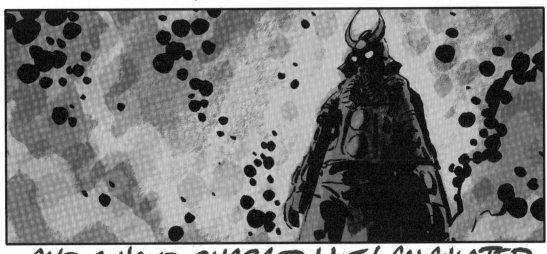

...AND A HAND CHARGED WITH CALCULATED
JUDGMENT.

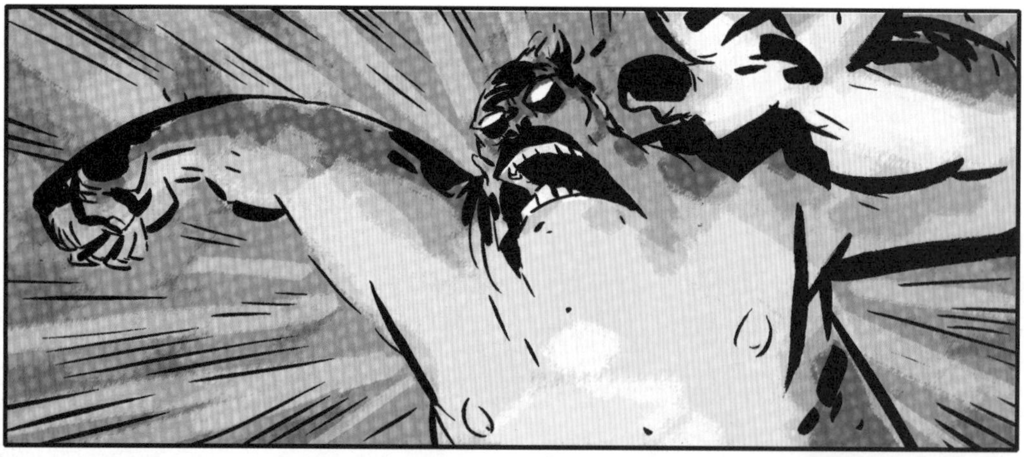

BUT WHEN TO PLAY THAT HAND IS THE QUESTION!

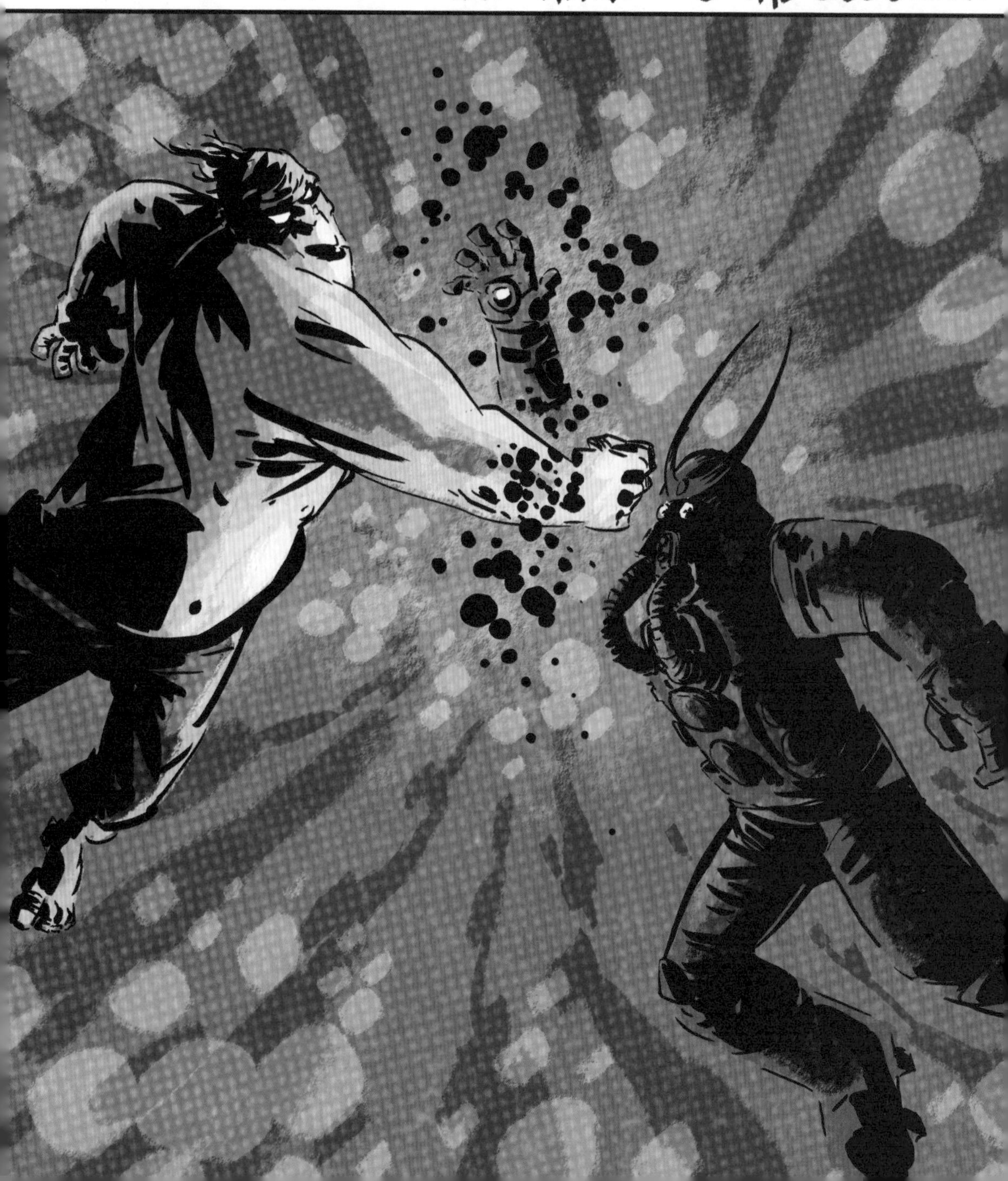

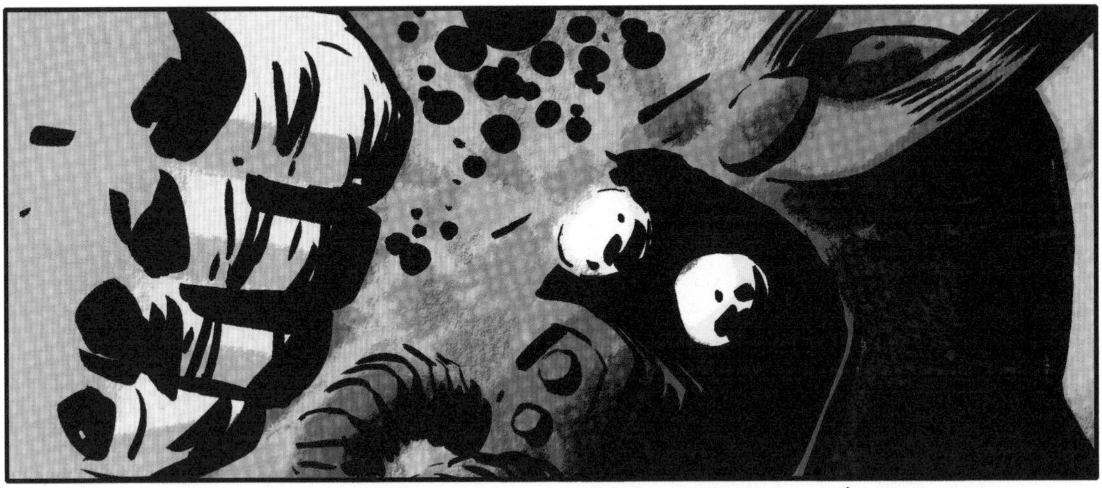

THE KNUCKLEHEAD KNEW WHEN TO PLAY SUCH A *HAND*.

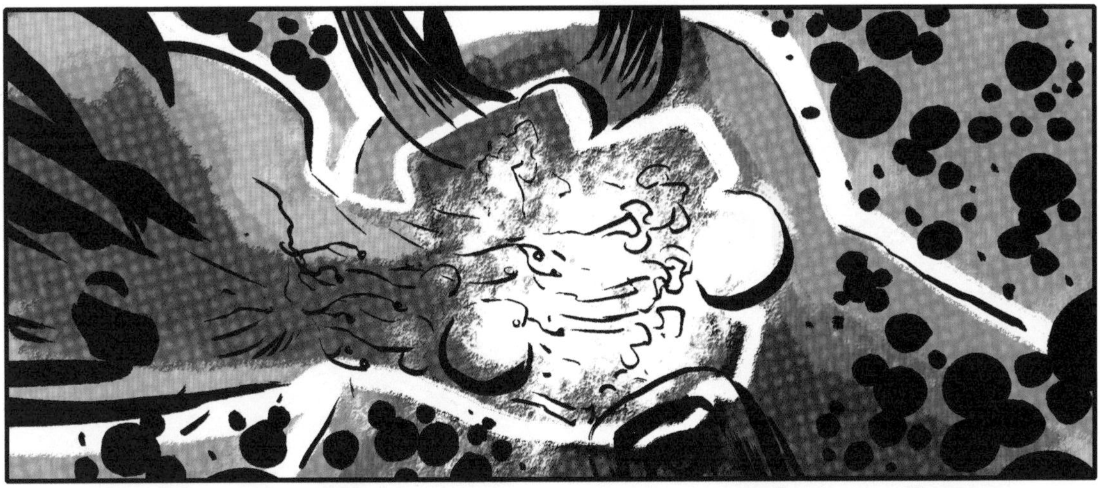

TO PLUG INTO THE MIND, THAT FIST WOULD LEAVE AN IMPRINT.

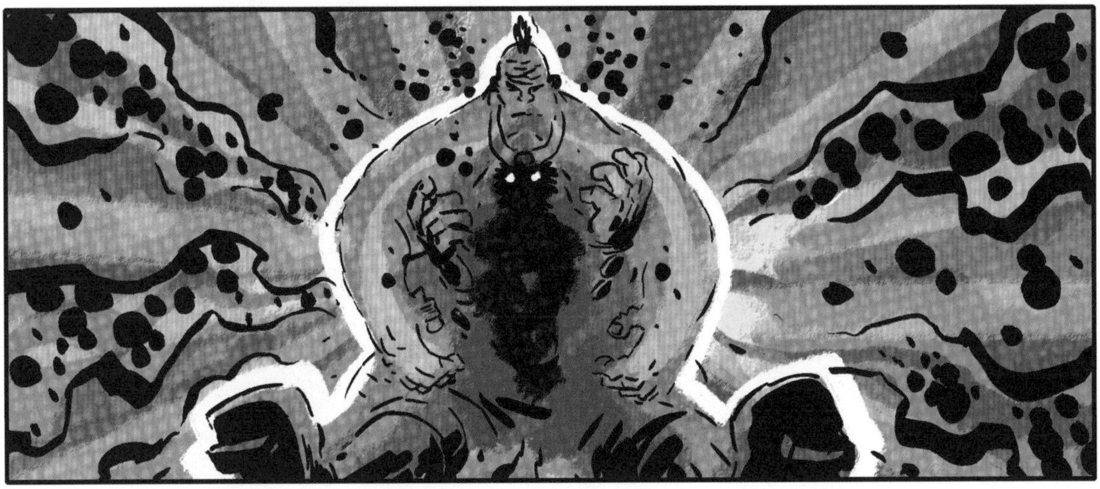

AN IMPRINT OF HIS PAST... ...HIS SOUL!

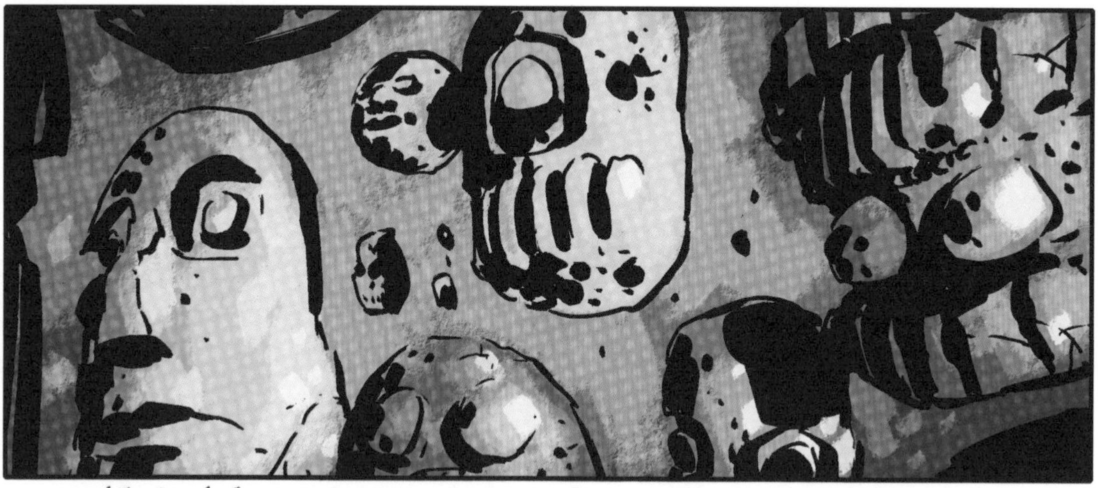

WELCOME TO THAT PAST... THE *AGE* OF *STONE!*
A TIME WHEN THE GODS ROAMED THE HEAVENS LIKE ASTEROIDS!

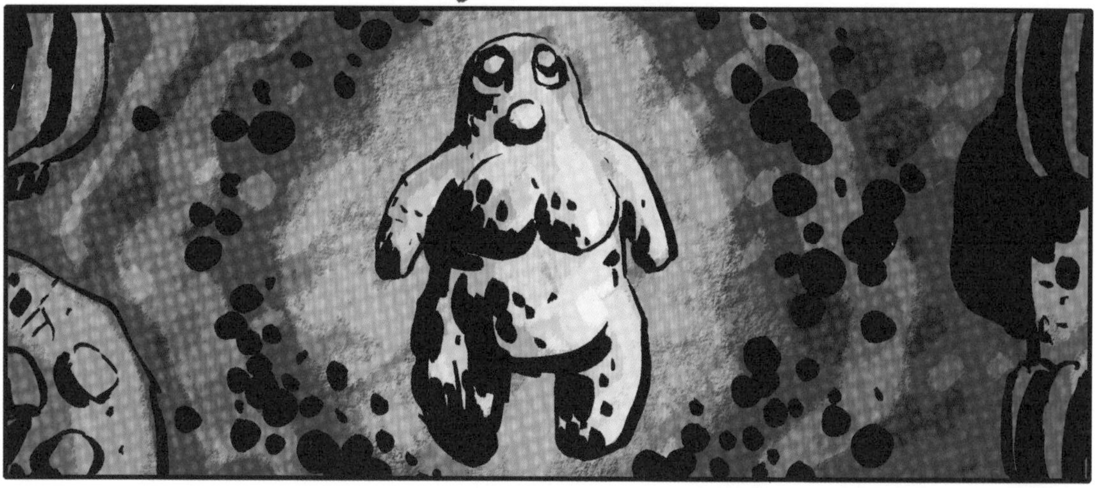

FROM THIS RIP IN *SPACE-TIME* SHE CAME...

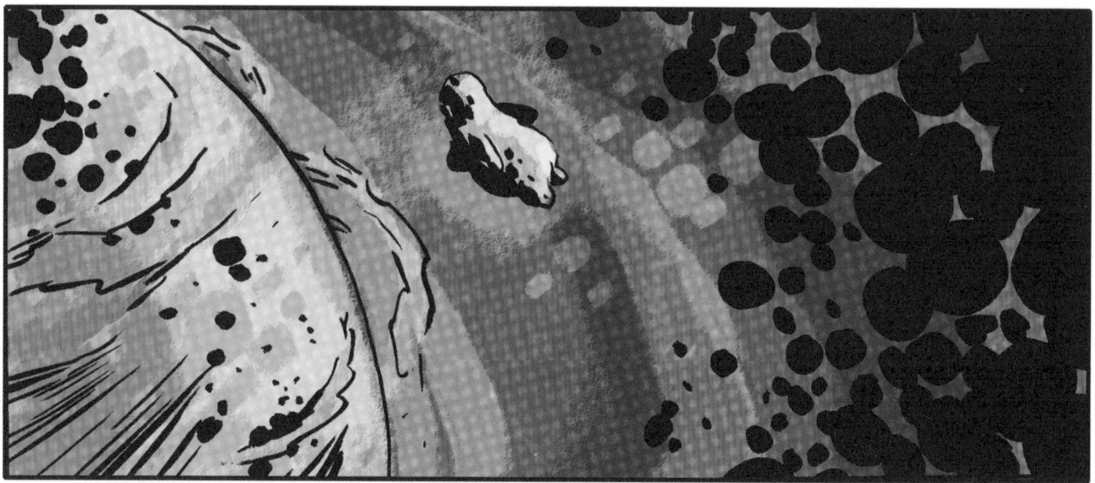

...LEAVING HER FAMILY IN SEARCH OF *MORE!*

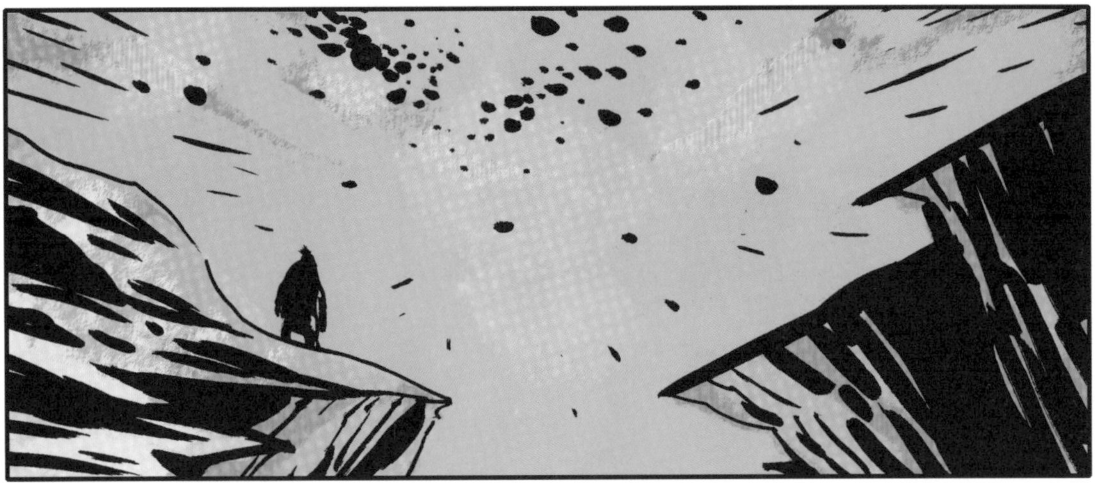

SHE FOUND HIM WAITING, ALONE.

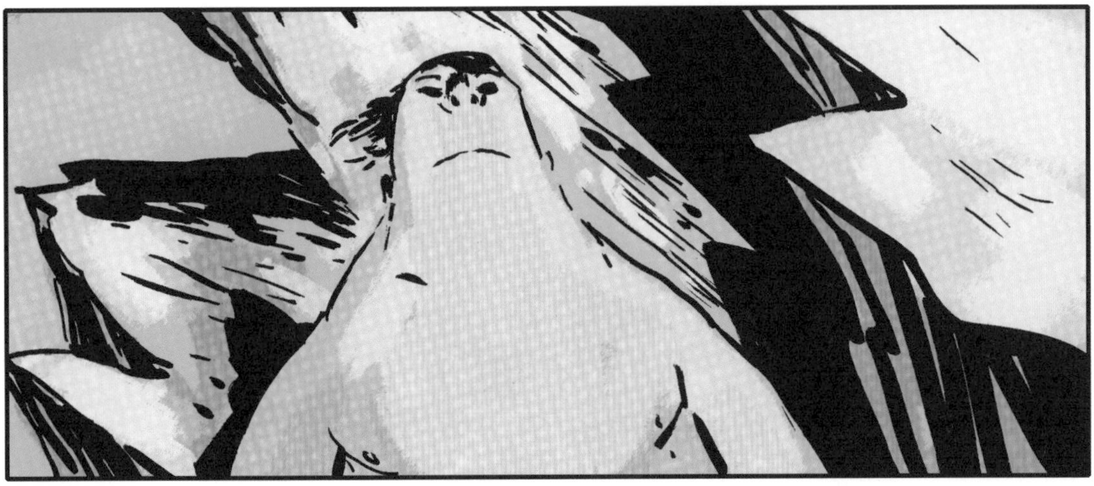

HE HAD LEFT HIS BELOVED SEA THAT DAY...

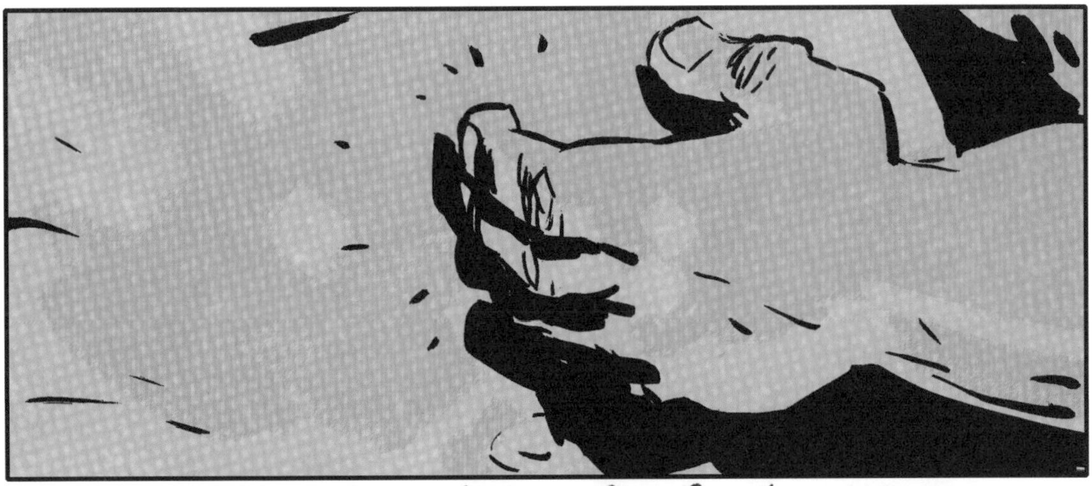

...DRAWN TO A SIREN SONG HE HEARD DEEP IN HIS HEART.

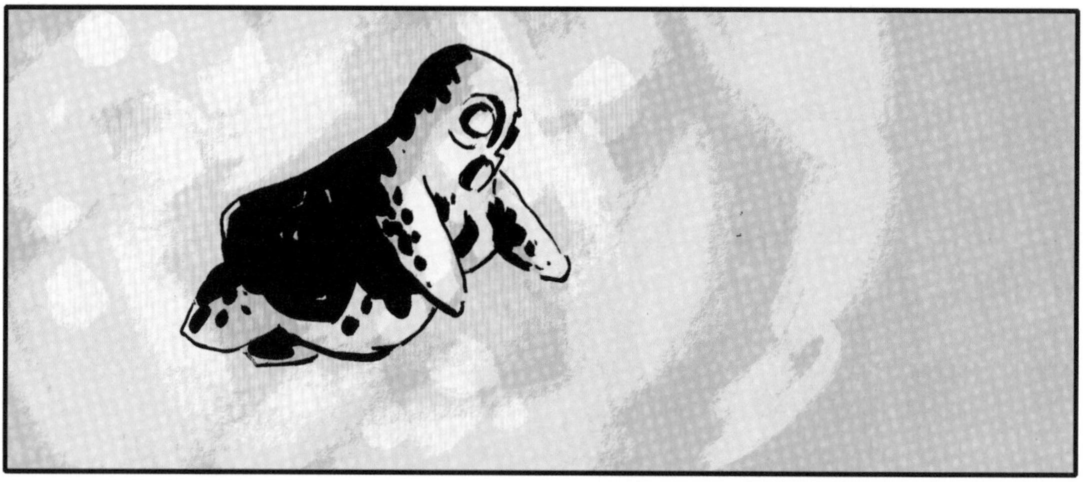

COULD THESE UNLIKELY WORLDS COLLIDE?

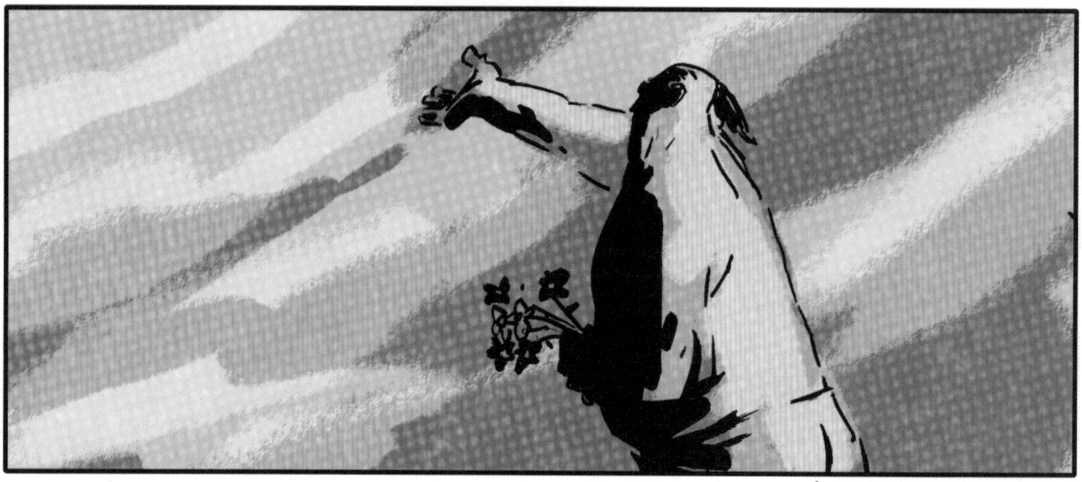

COULD THE FATES DESIGN A HAPPINESS BETWEEN SUCH ELEMENTAL FORCES?

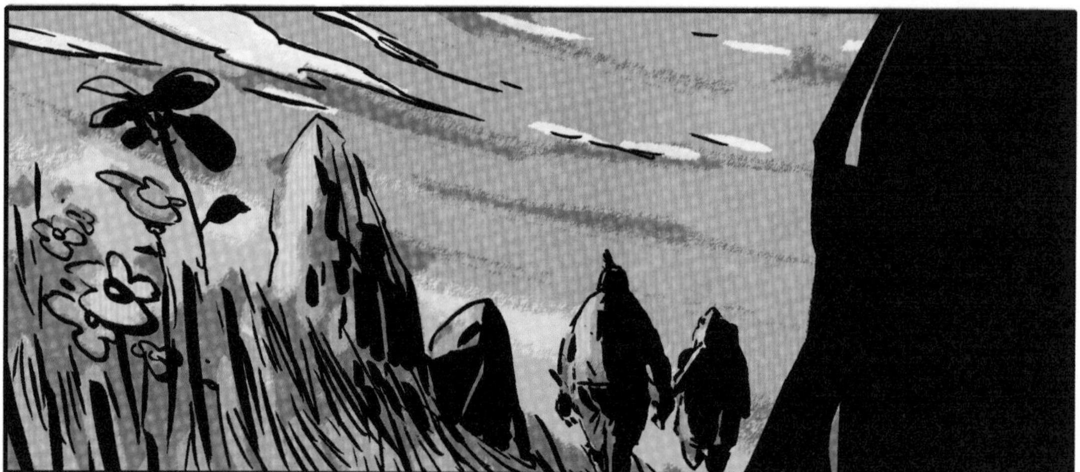

SUCH UNIONS, IT HAS BEEN ARGUED, ARE A RARE WORK OF ART.

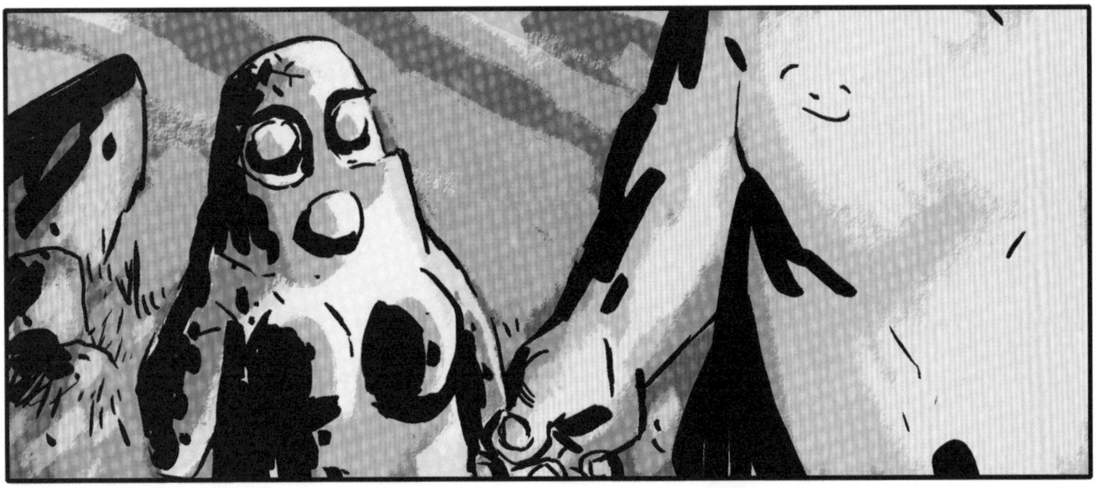

BEAUTY HAS ALWAYS LIVED IN THE EYE OF THE BEHOLDER, BUT WITH A BEAUTY SUCH AS THIS...

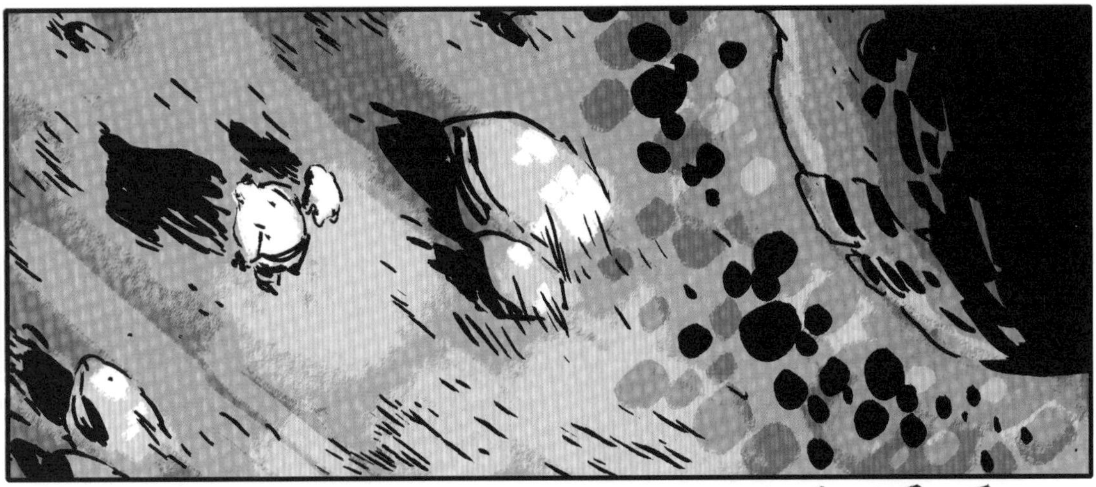

...THE PASSIONATE EYE OF A CRITIC IS ALWAYS AT HAND.

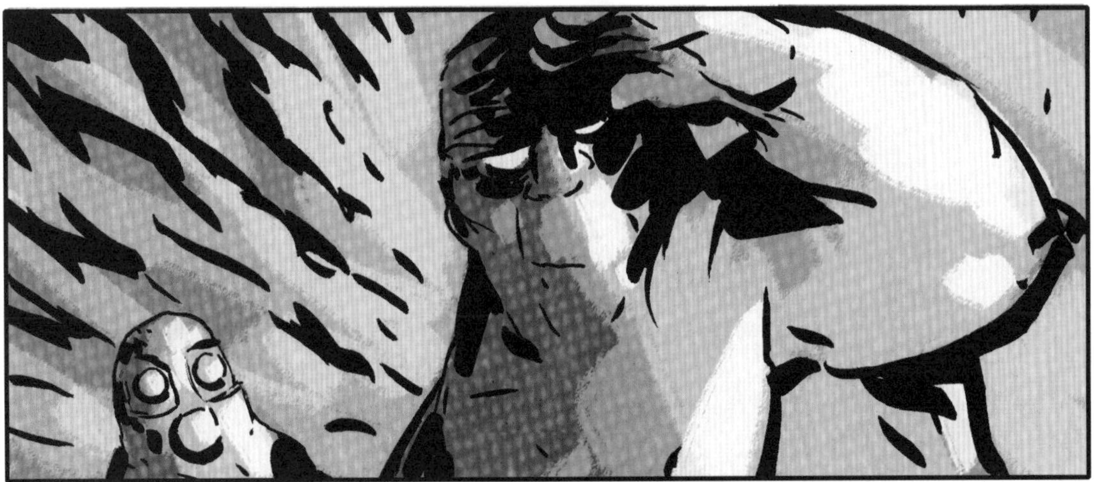

AND WHO HAS EVER PROVEN MORE CRITICAL...

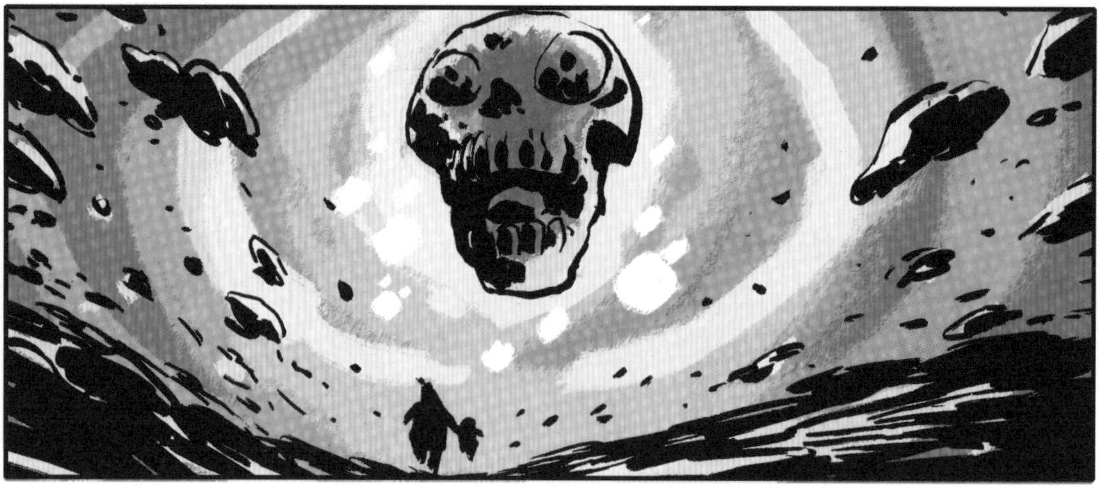

...THAN A *FATHER?*
"IT SHALL NOT *BE!*" HE THUNDERED.

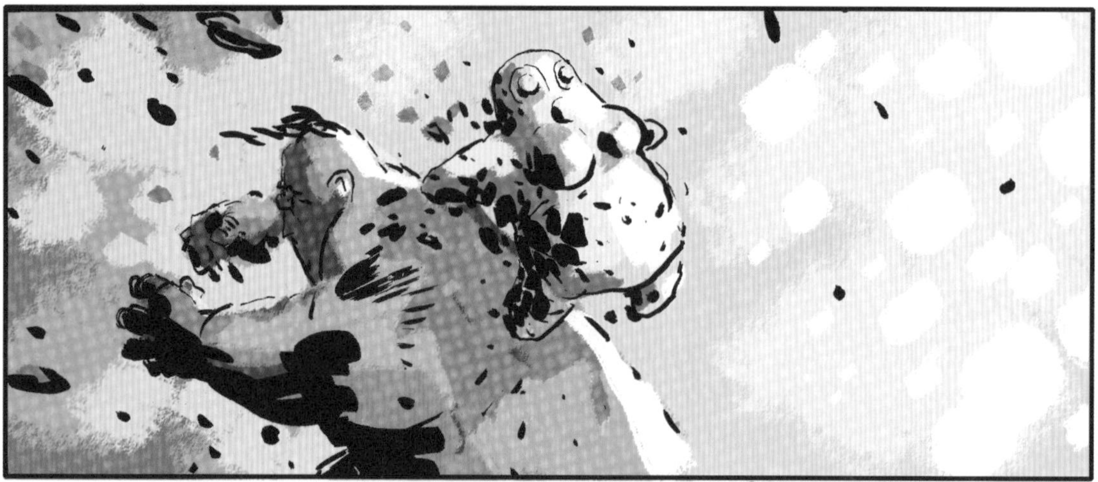

BUT THE CHILD WOULD NOT SEE HER
LOVE DESTROYED. SHE DOVE... NOW A STONE SHIELD...

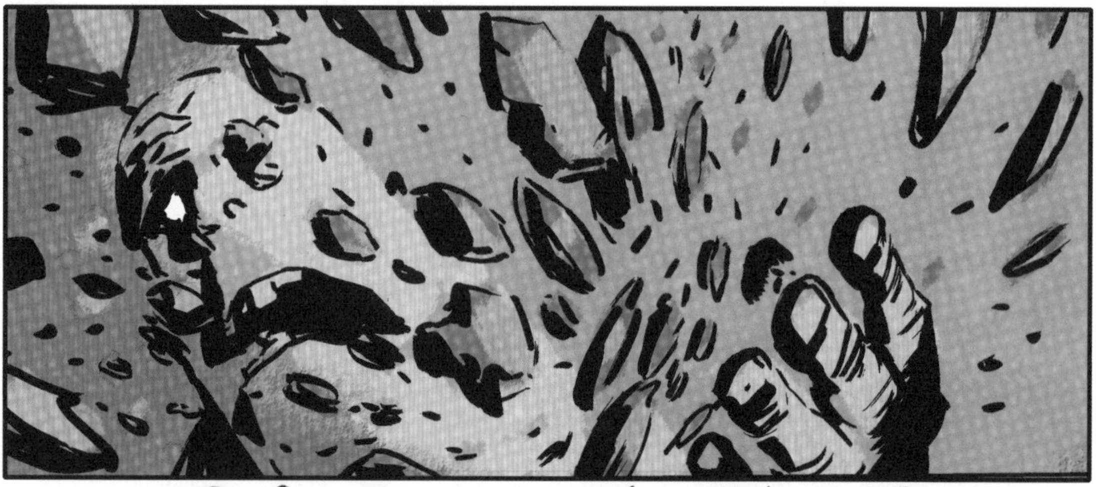

...AND SAVED THAT KNUCKLEHEAD
FROM THE IGNORANT COSMIC MIND!

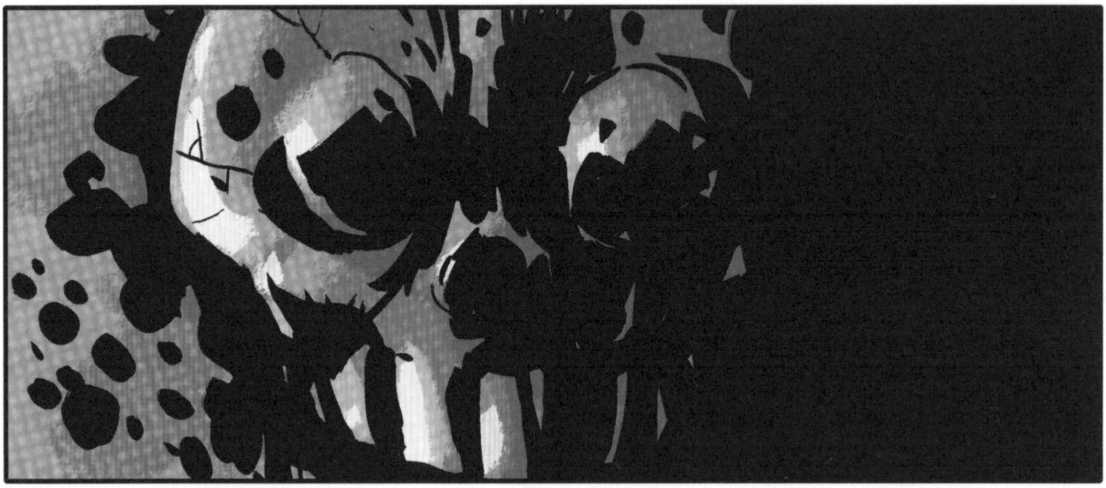

BUT THERE WOULD BE NO CHALLENGING
THE WILL OF THE GODS.

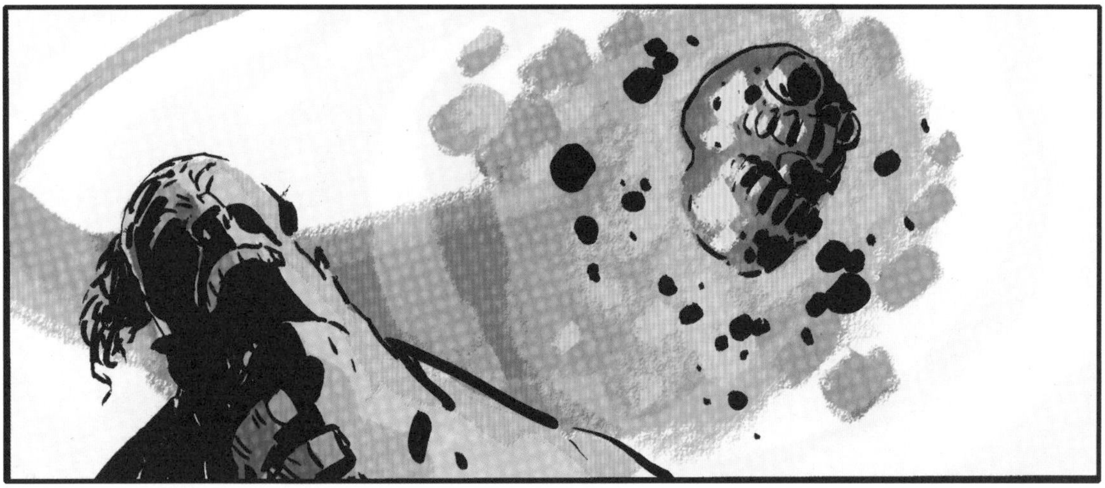

AND FROM THAT DAY FORWARD...

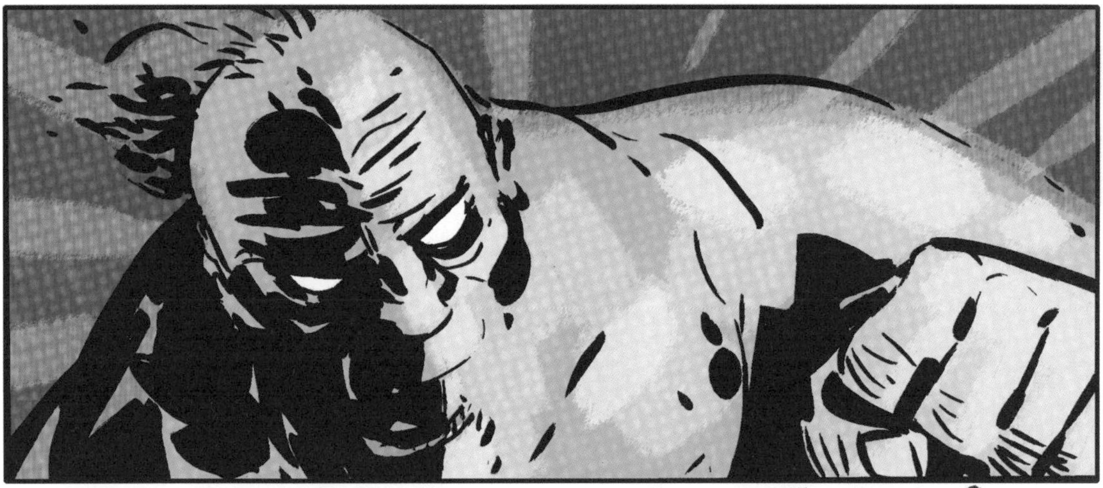

...THE KNUCKLEHEAD, LORD OF THE SEAS,
LET HIS LONELY HEART SEETHE...

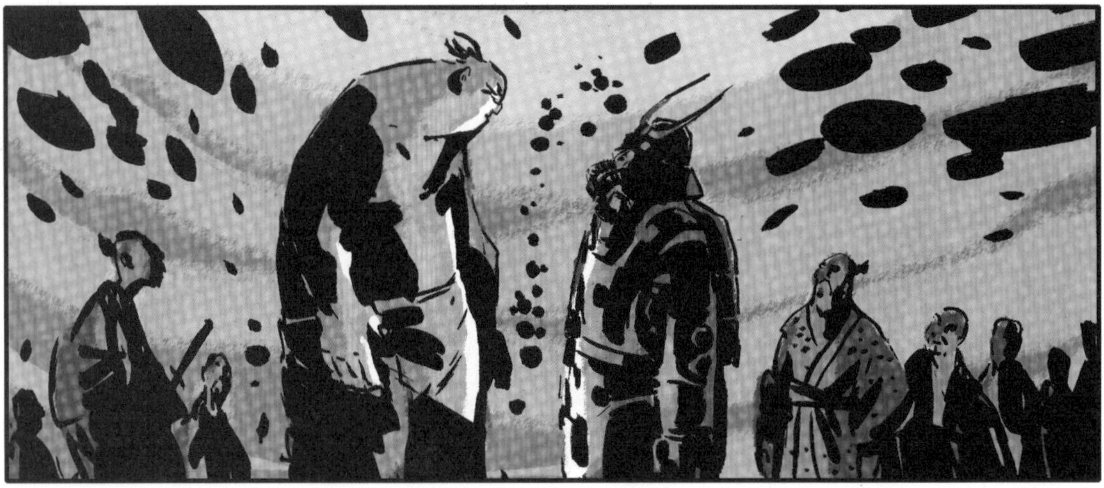

...HIS ANGUISH FEEDING THE CREATURES OF THE DEEP, TURNING THEM INTO MONSTERS.

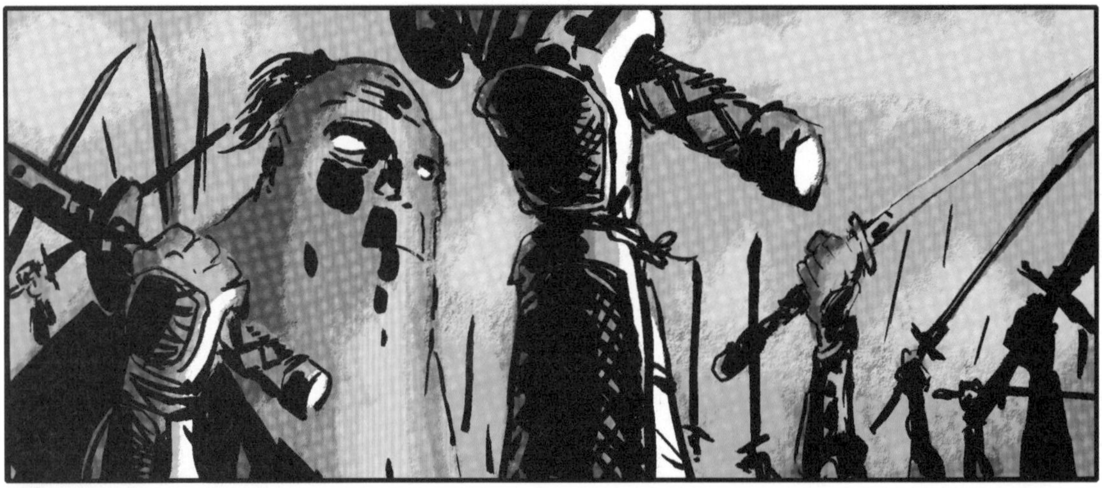

THE TALE RANG TRUE IN THE HEARTS OF THE VILLAGERS... THE COSMIC MIND WAS IN THE WRONG!

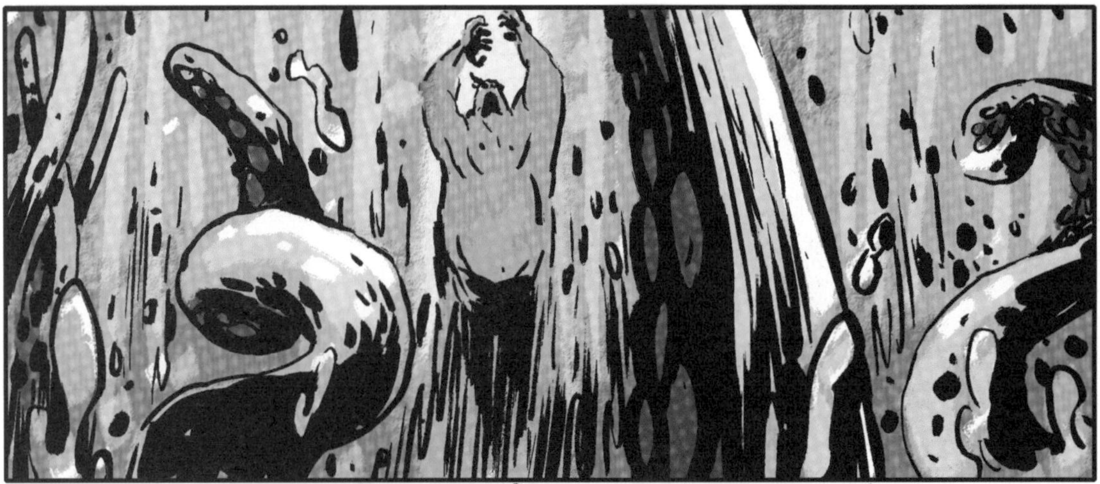

AN ALLIANCE WAS BORN! AN ARMY RAISED!

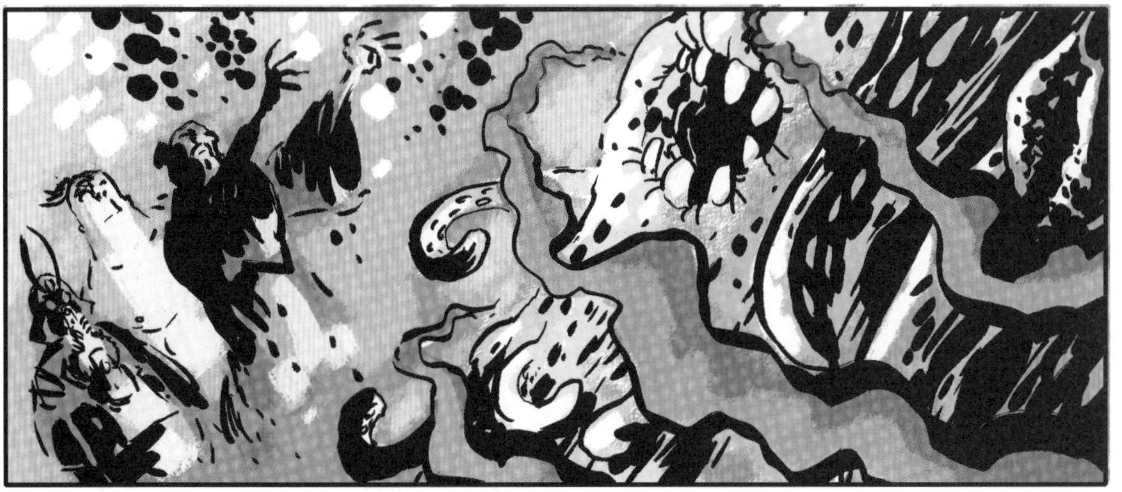

THE MAGIC OF THE MYSTICS PREPARED THEM...

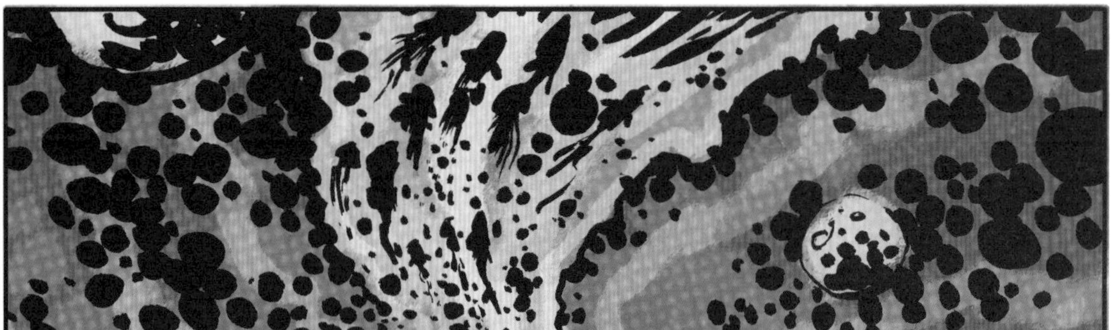

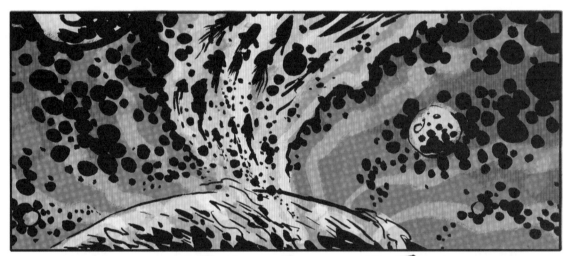

...AND THE CREATURES OF THE DEEP
SANK INTO THE DEPTHS OF SPACE!

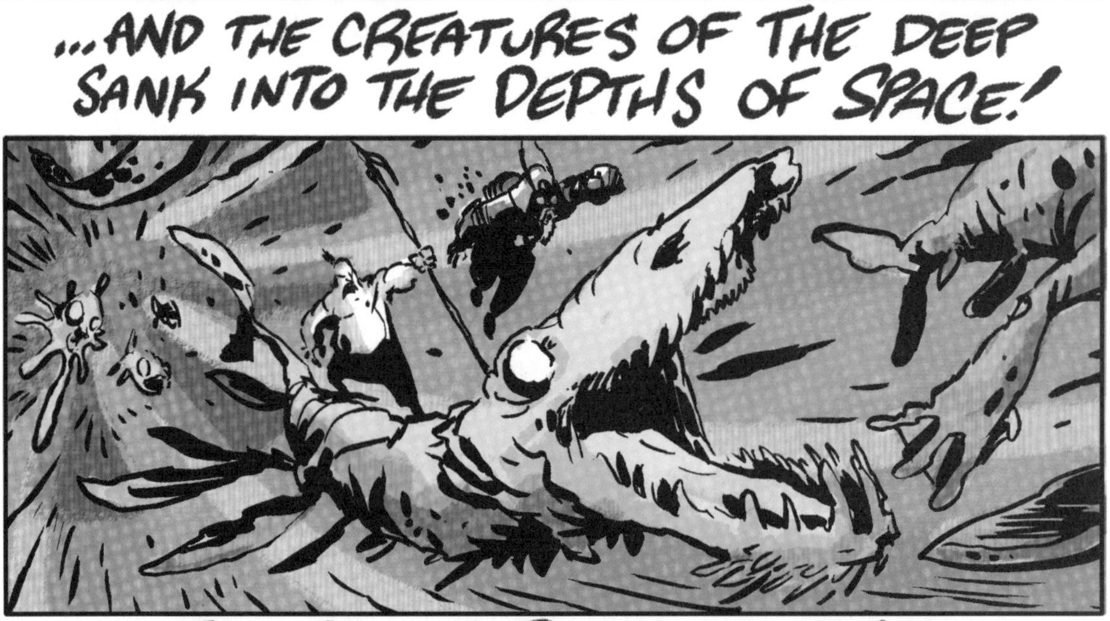

TWO FORCES, POWERING FORTH...
...THE SHOGUNAUT... THE KNUCKLEHEAD...

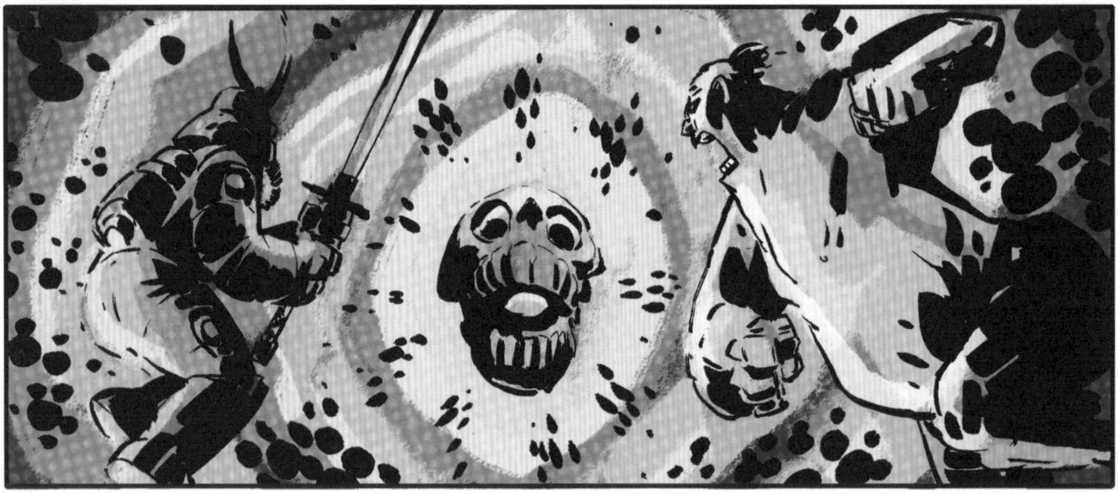

AND THE COSMIC MIND CRIED... FURY!

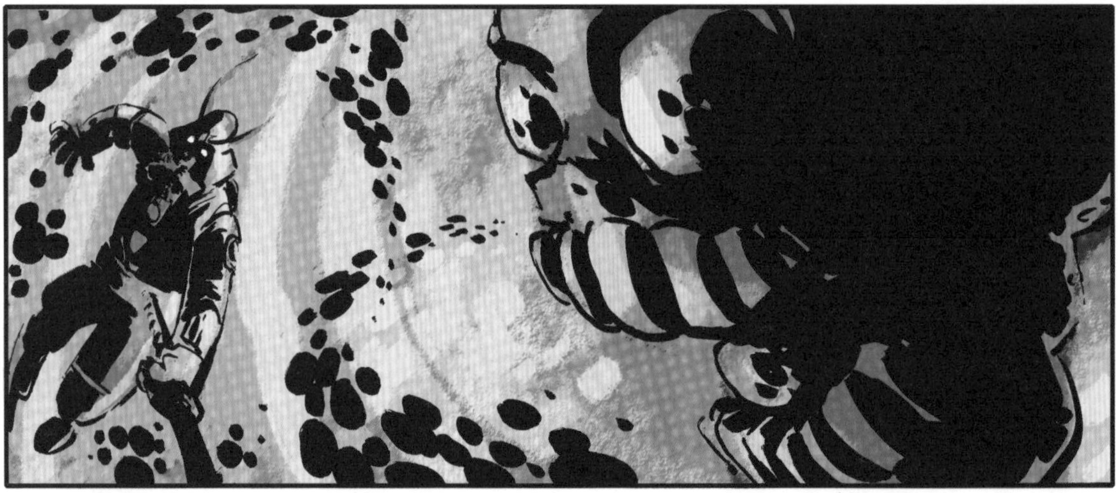

THE STONE GOD WOULD STAND STRONG! NO MORTAL COULD RIGHTFULLY CHALLENGE THE LOGIC OF THE COSMIC MIND!

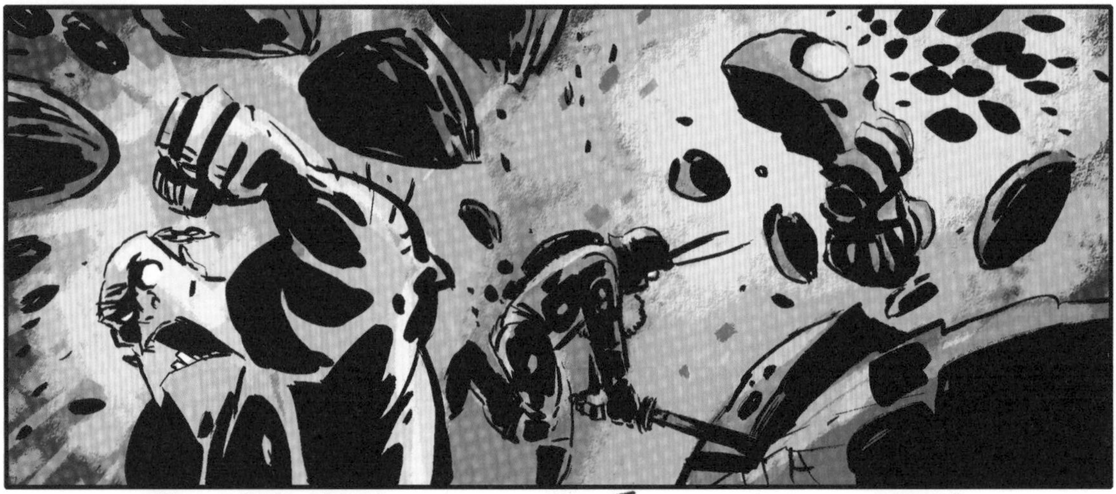

THE SHOGUNAUT CUT FIRMLY AS THE KNUCKLEHEAD DEALT A LONG-AWAITED BLOW...

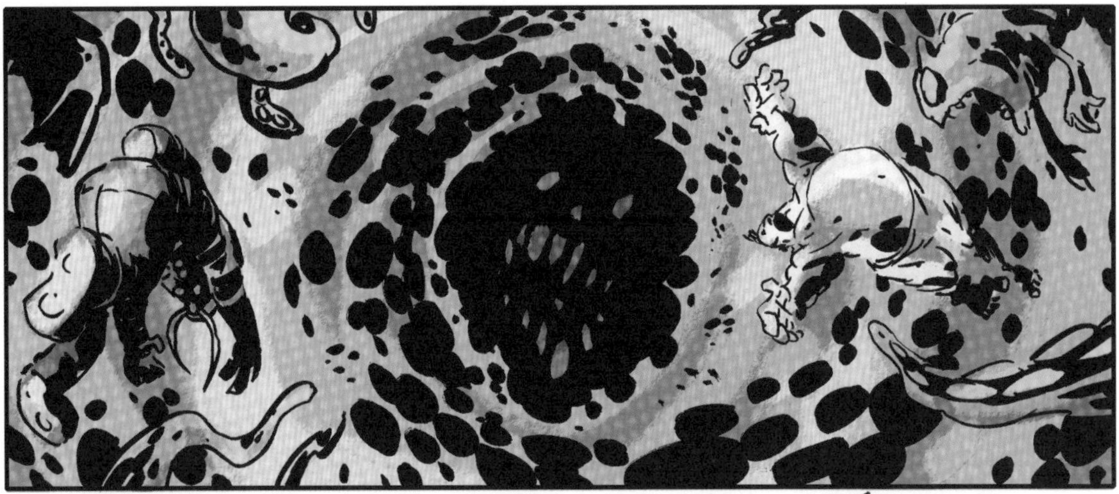

BUT THE COSMIC MIND HAD ONE LAST IDEA...
...TO FOLD... AND DRAW THEM FOREVER IN!

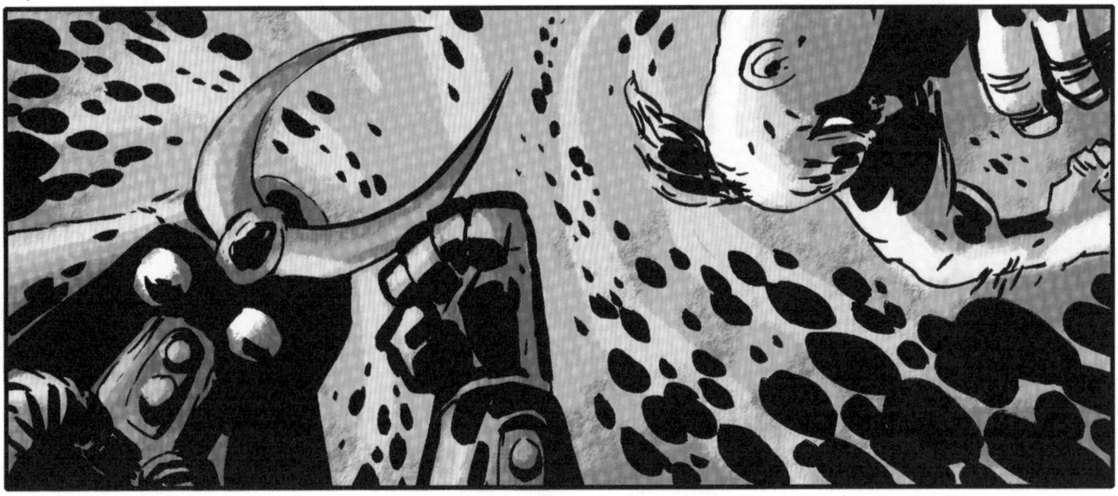

A BLACK HOLE...

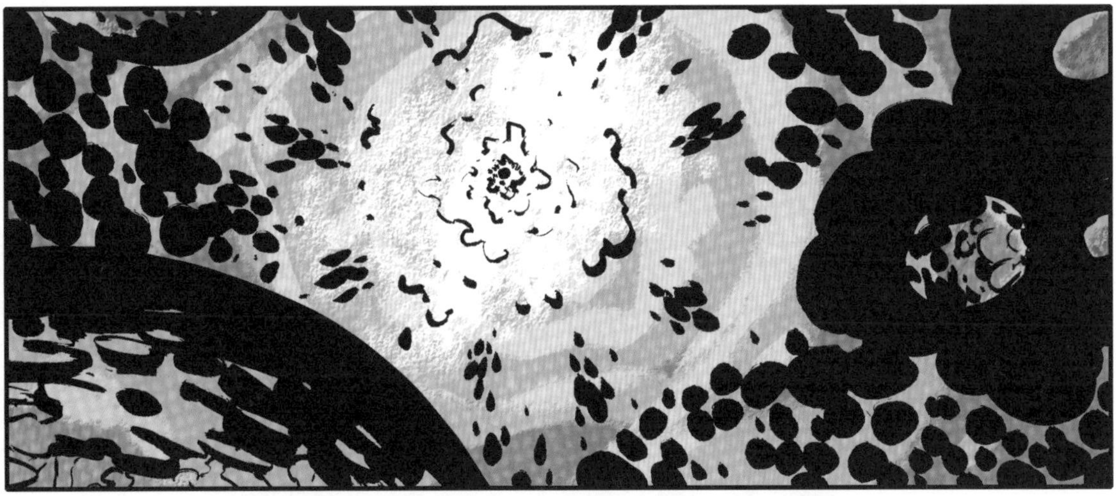

...AND NONE WOULD PASS.

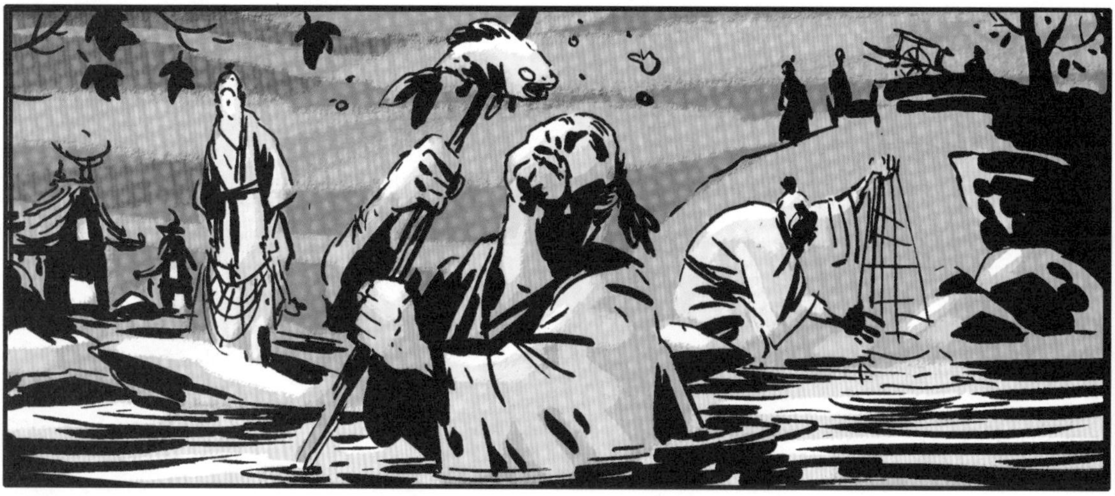

A PEACE, THEN, HAD BEEN FOUND... BUT AT WHAT PRICE?

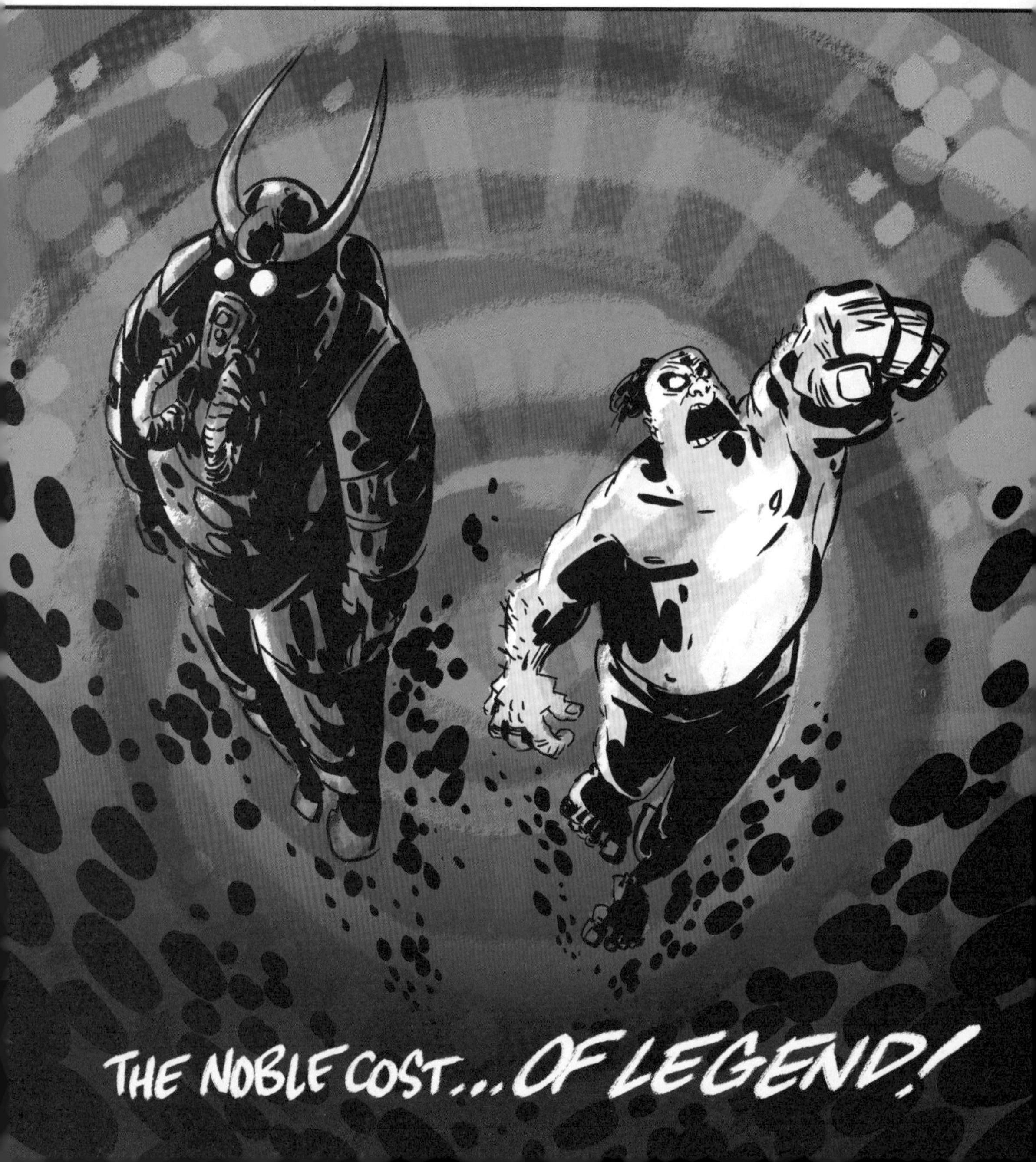
THE NOBLE COST... OF LEGEND!

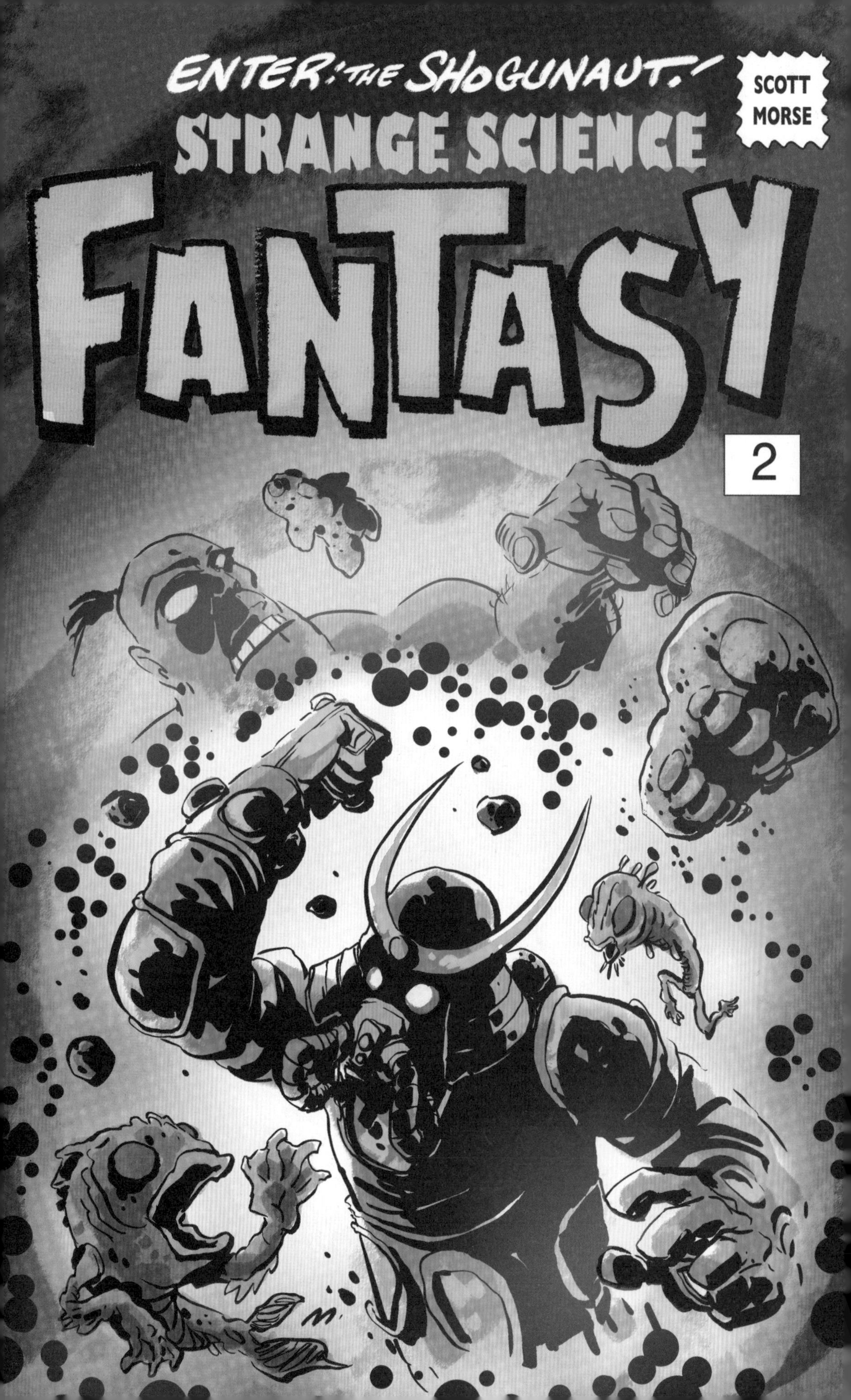
ENTER: THE SHOGUNAUT!
SCOTT MORSE
STRANGE SCIENCE
FANTASY
2

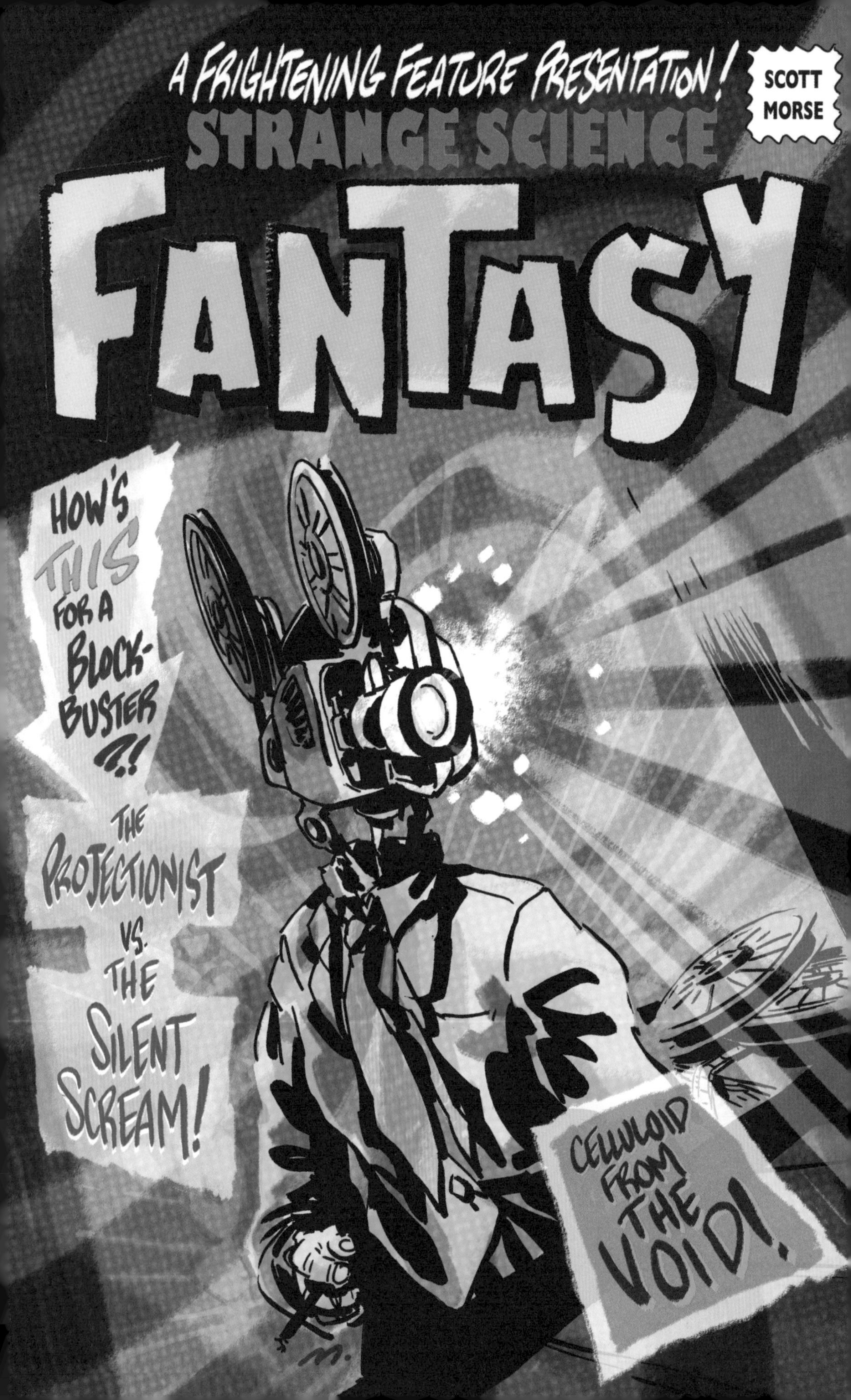
A FRIGHTENING FEATURE PRESENTATION!
SCOTT MORSE
STRANGE SCIENCE
FANTASY
HOW'S THIS FOR A BLOCK-BUSTER ?!
THE PROJECTIONIST VS. THE SILENT SCREAM!
CELLULOID FROM THE VOID!

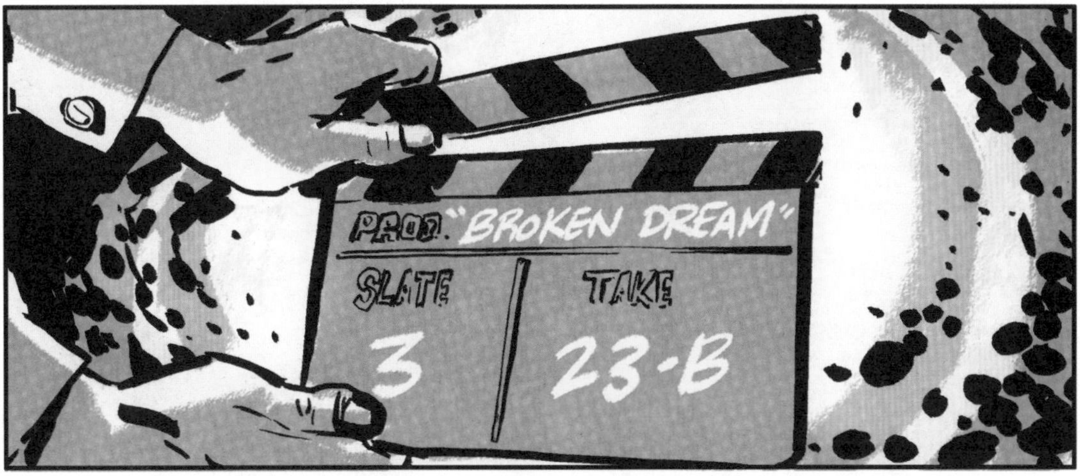
PROD. "BROKEN DREAM"
SLATE
TAKE
3
23-B

SURE, SURE! THE GOLDEN AGE IS WHAT THEY CALLED IT.

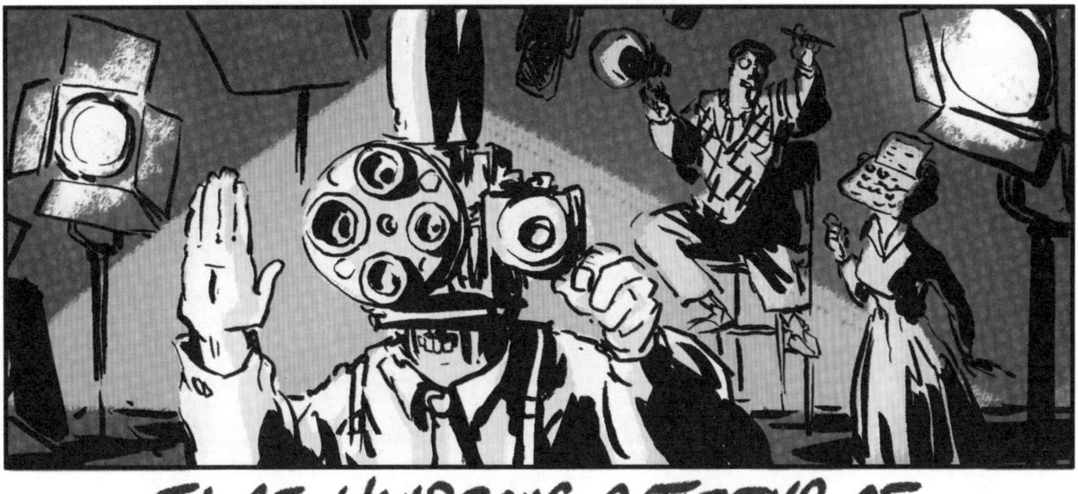

THOSE WONDROUS CITIZENS OF MOVIELAND WOULD WORK THEIR MAGIC...

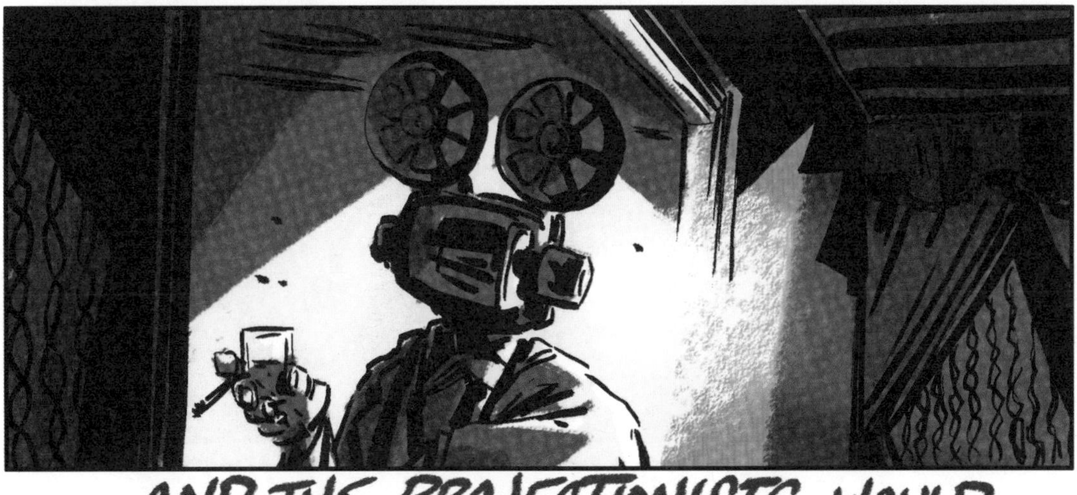

...AND THE PROJECTIONISTS WOULD SHOW IT TO THE WORLD!

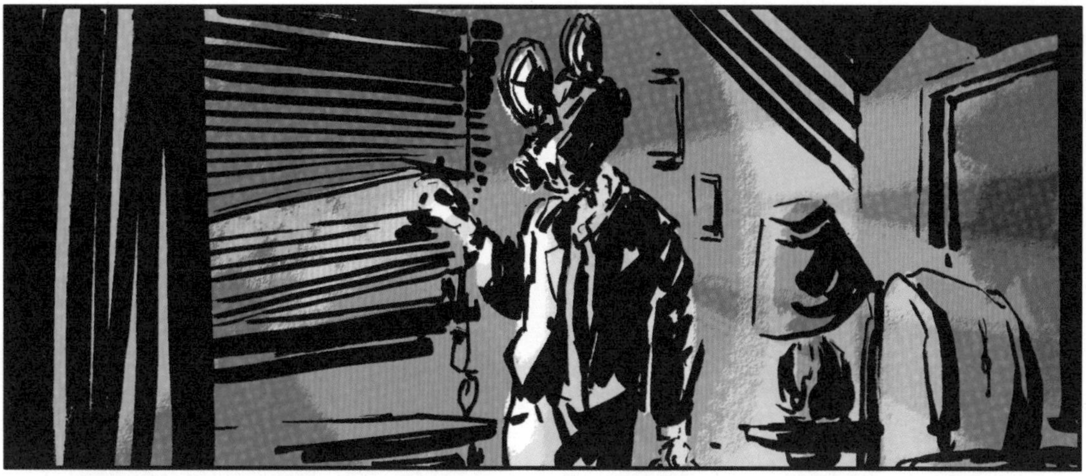

BUT SOMEONE WANTED THAT WORLD OF GLITTER AND TINSEL TO TAKE A *DIVE.*

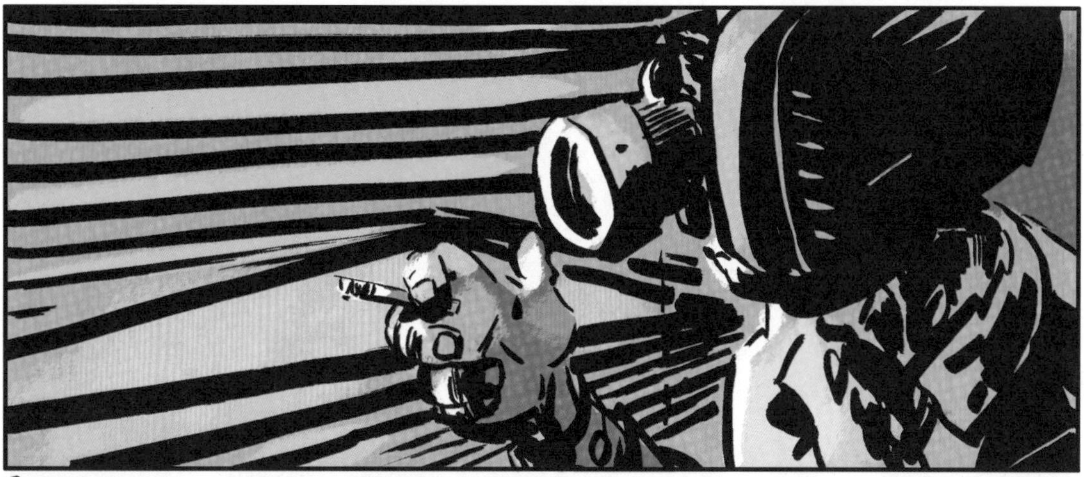

SOMEONE HAD BEEN KNOCKING OFF THE VERY GUYS THAT PAINTED THE BIG SCREENS WITH LIFE.

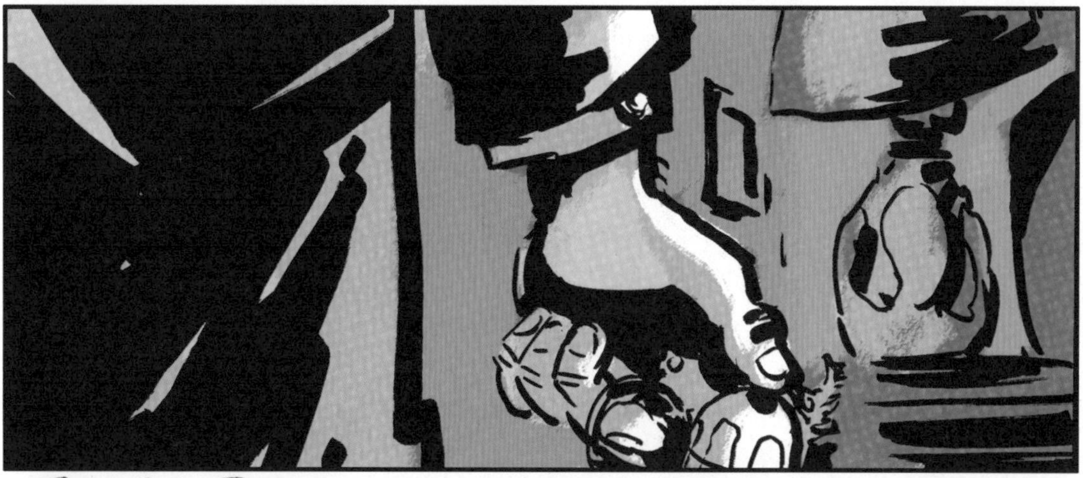

EVERY PROJECTIONIST IN TOWN HAD BEEN PUT TO BED FOR THE LONG SLEEP. EVERY PROJECTIONIST BUT ONE.

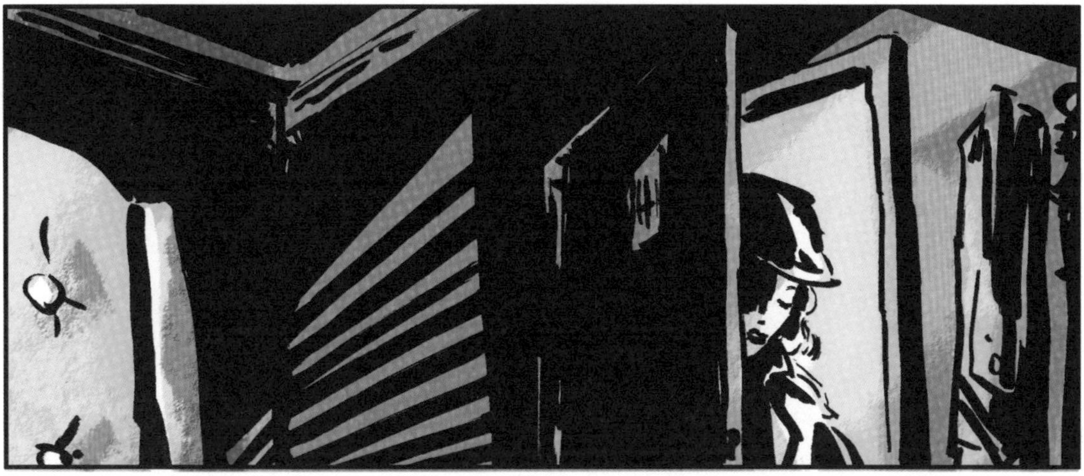

ENTER: THE SILENT SCREAM.

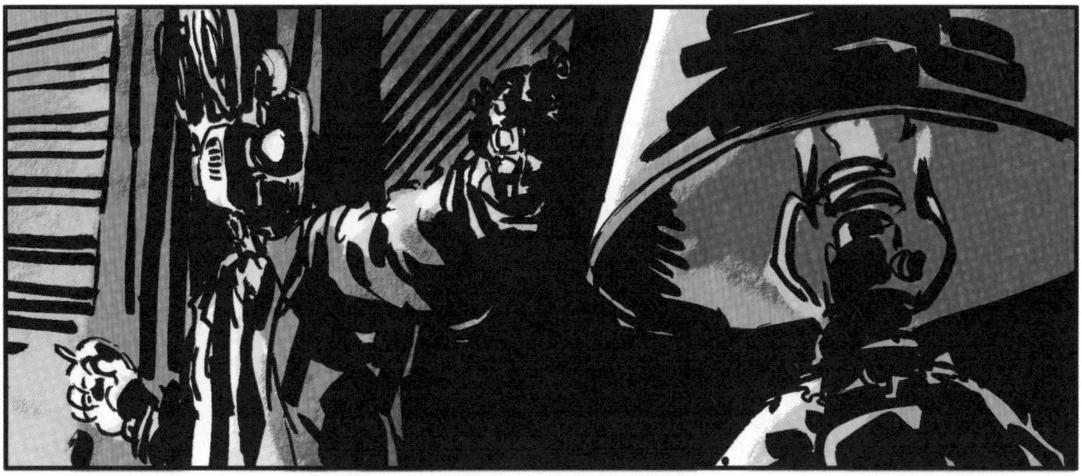

AN ACTRESS, DON'TCHA KNOW?

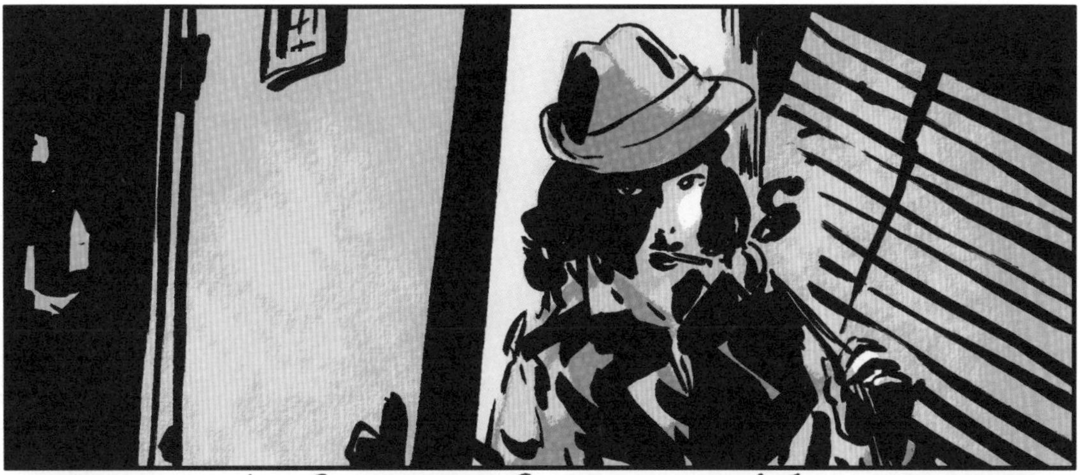

HER CHARACTERS ALWAYS WHINED VOLUMES WITHOUT SPEAKING A LINE.

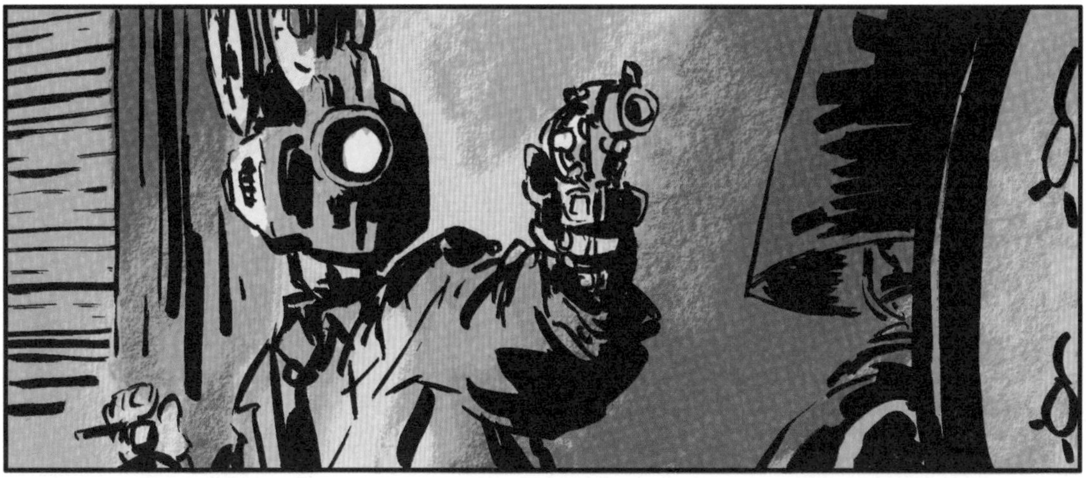

WHY WOULD A FACE LIKE THAT COME TO SEE A TWO-REELER LIKE THE PROJECTIONIST?

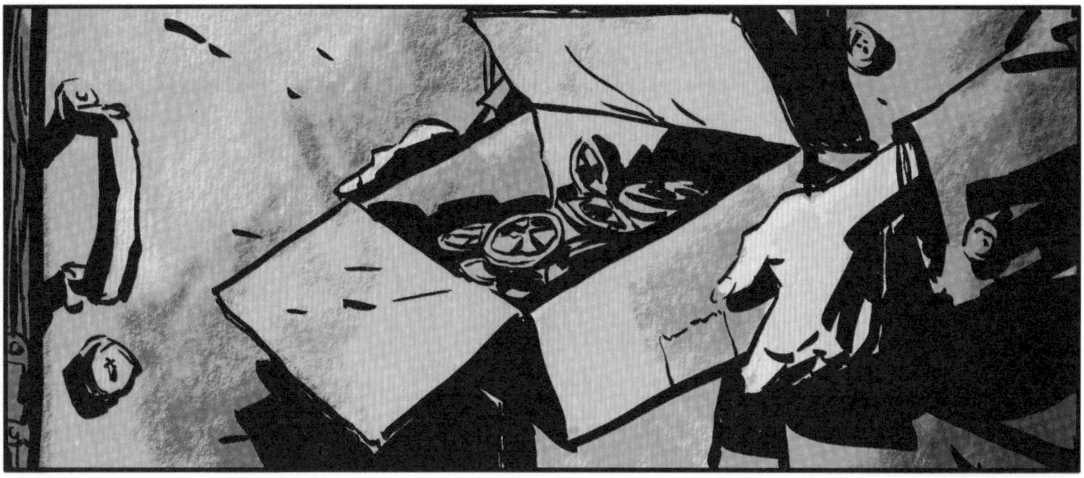

SHE SAID THAT SOMEONE HAD SENT A MESSAGE TO HER SET: "FILM IS DEAD."

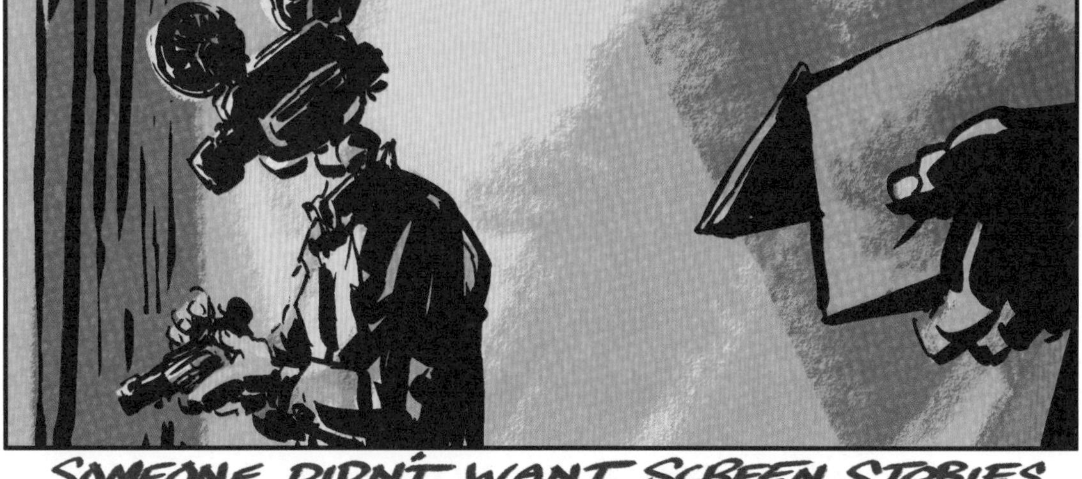

SOMEONE DIDN'T WANT SCREEN STORIES TOLD AND THEY WANTED EVERYONE TO KNOW IT.

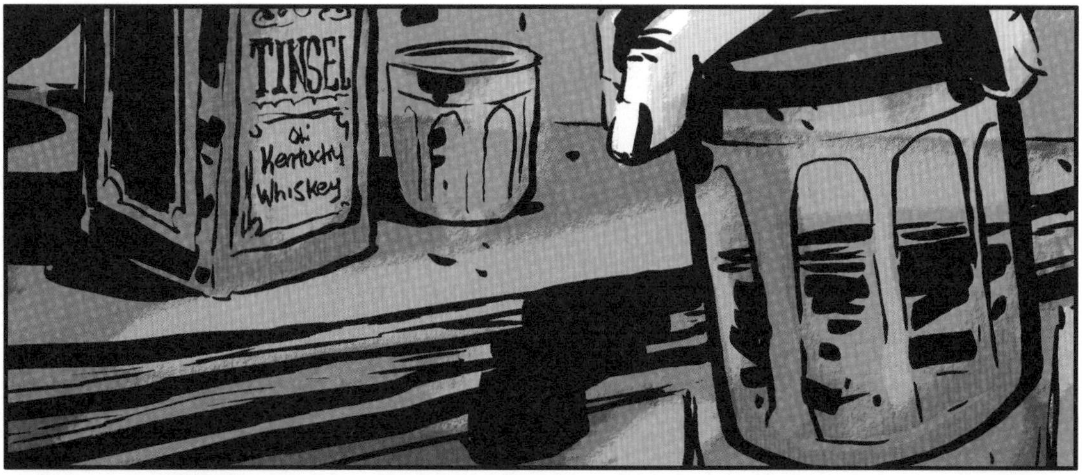
TINSEL
Ol' Kentucky Whiskey

BUT WHY KILL OFF THE PROJECTIONISTS?
THEY DIDN'T EVEN MAKE THE FLICKS.

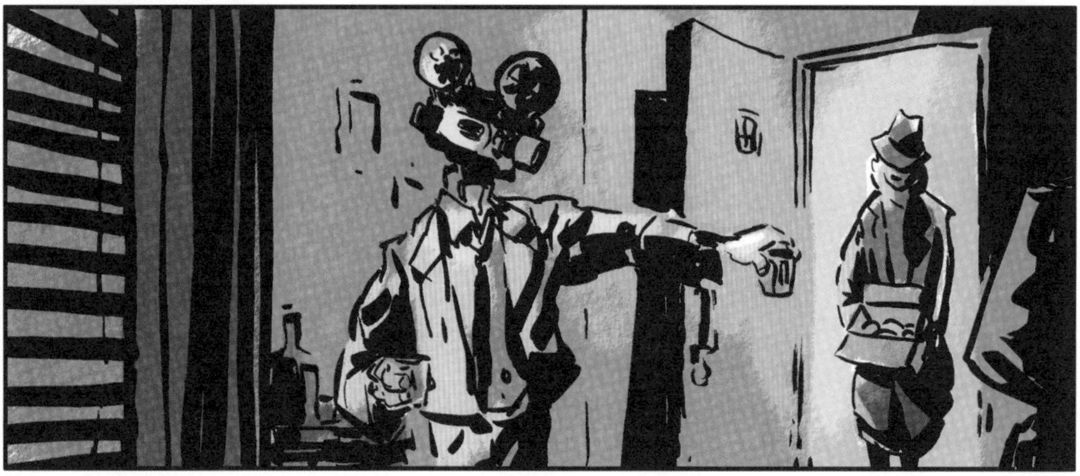

YOU WANT TO KILL A MOVIE, YOU GO TO THE TOP.
WRITER..., MAYBE DIRECTOR.

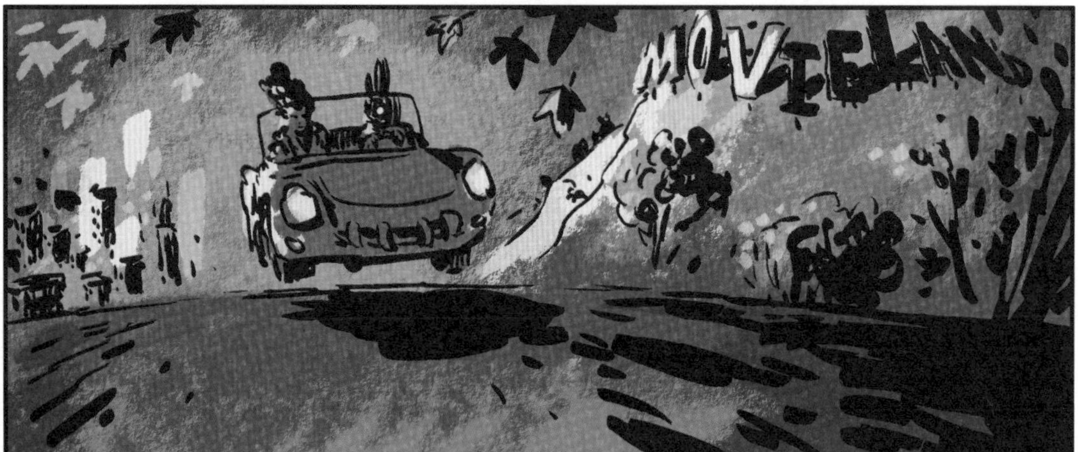

ONE THING WAS CERTAIN: STANDING IN THE DARK
WAS FOR USHERS.
ANSWERS WERE OUT ON THE TOWN.

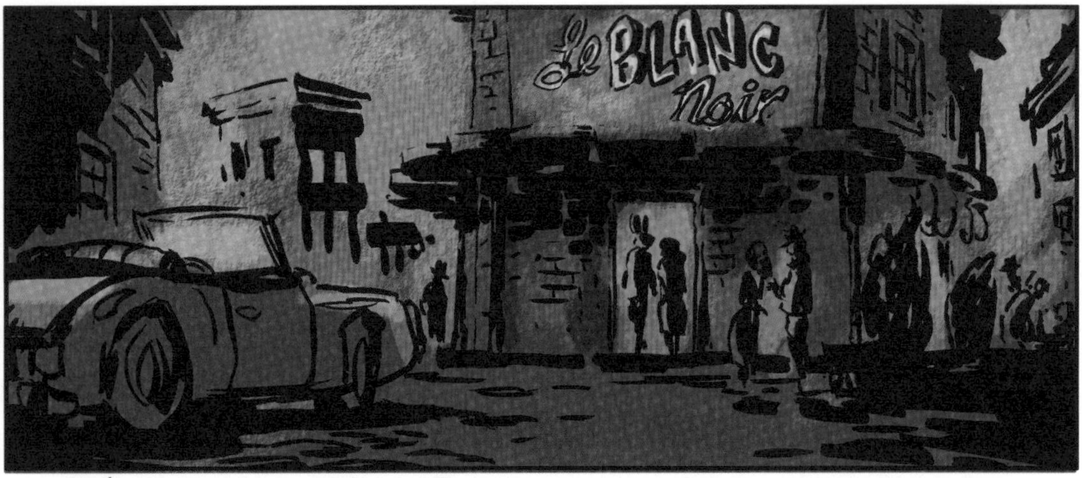
Le BLANC
Noir

WORD ON THE STREET WAS THAT THE SCREENWRITER HAD TAKEN A POWDER.

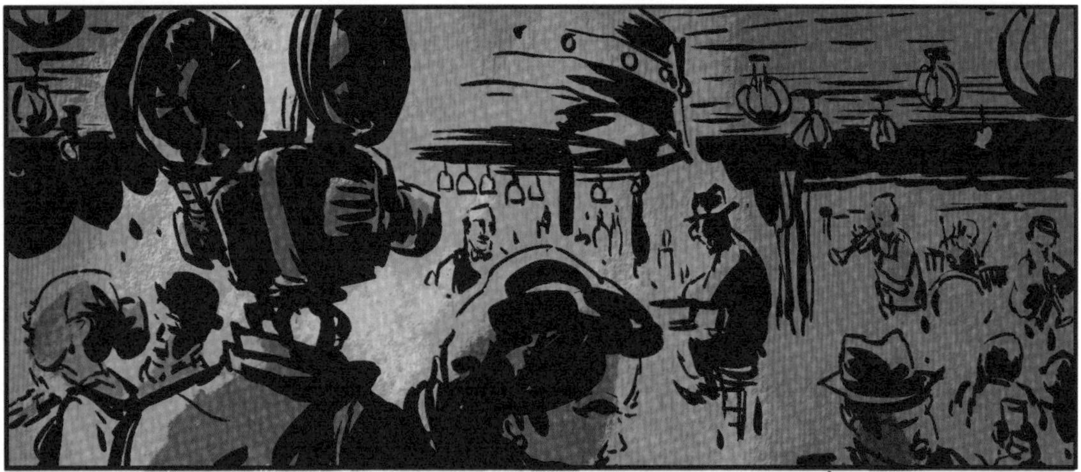

THE DIRECTOR, THOUGH, HE COULDN'T BE TOO FAR AWAY. IT WAS HIS PARTY, AFTER ALL.

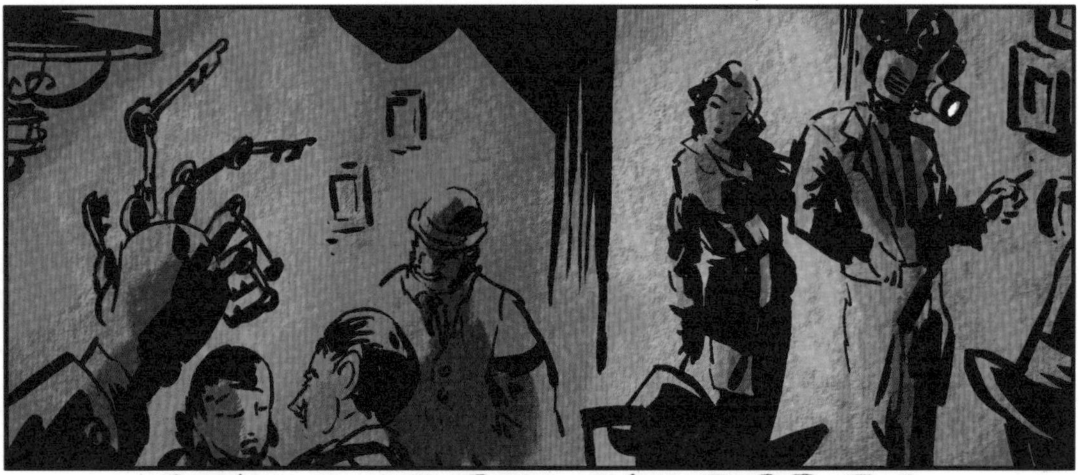

IF THEY COULD FIND THE DIRECTOR, THEY'D GET THE BIG PICTURE. THE KEY GRIP COULD SET IT ALL UP.

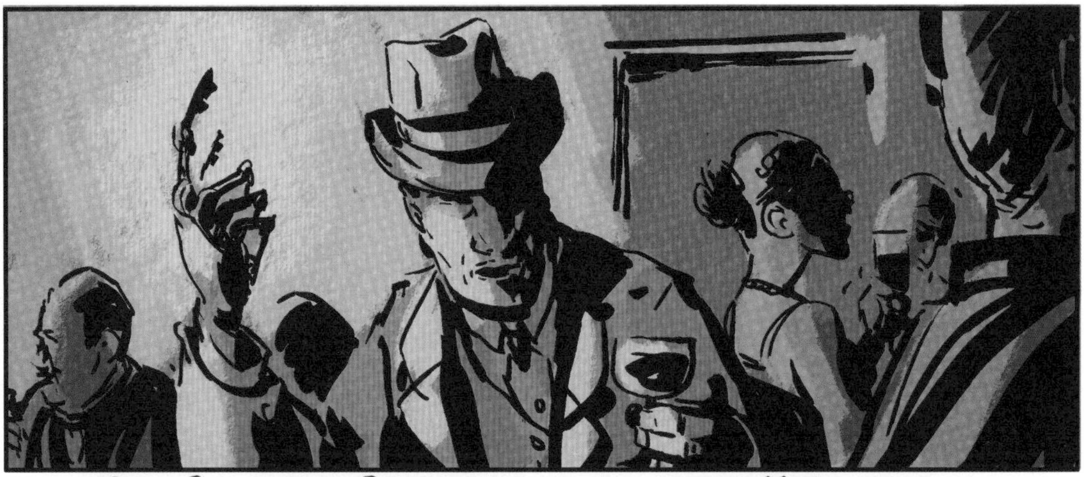

THE SILENT SCREAM HAD THE KEY GRIP WRAPPED AROUND HER FINGER. ACTRESSES... I TELL YA...

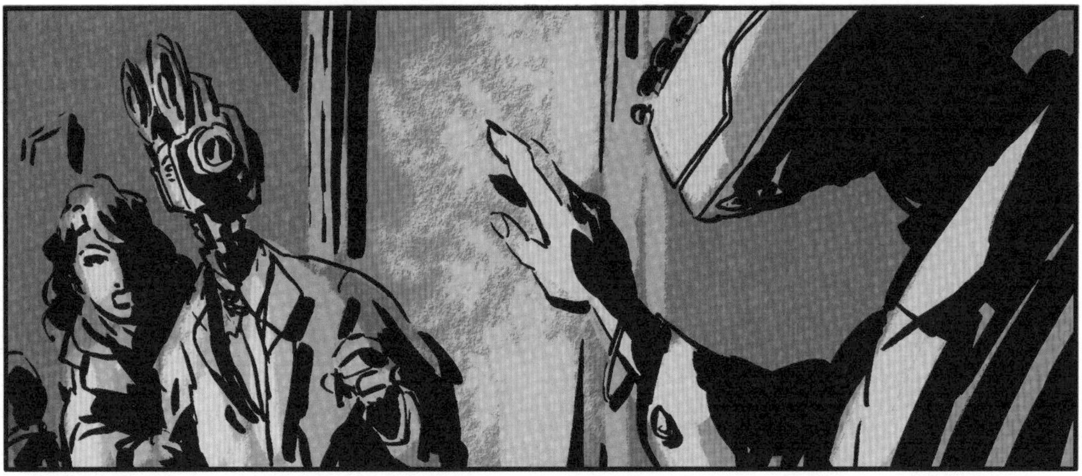

TURNS OUT SHE WAS PLAYING A *DIAL ROLE*. GOOD THING THE *SCRIPT GIRL* HAD READ AHEAD!

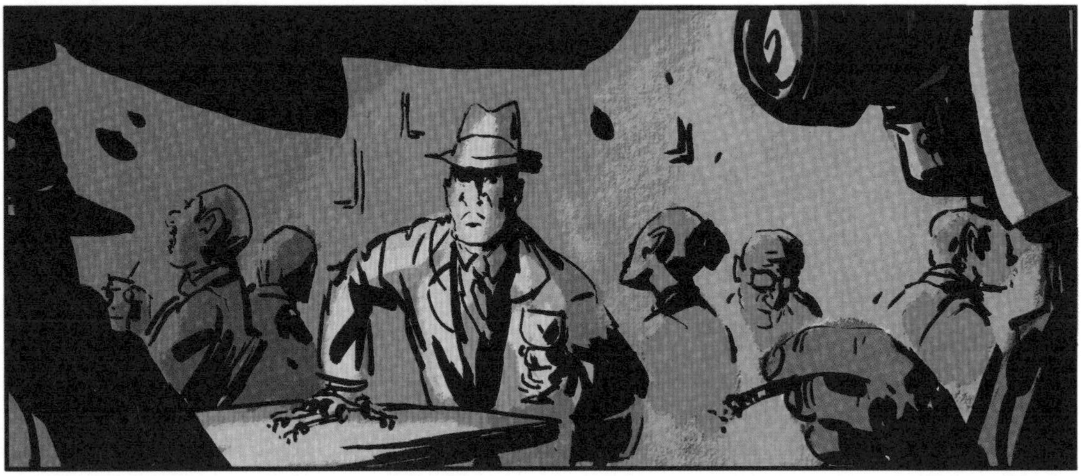

THAT WAS WHEN EVERYTHING WENT QUIET ON THE SET.

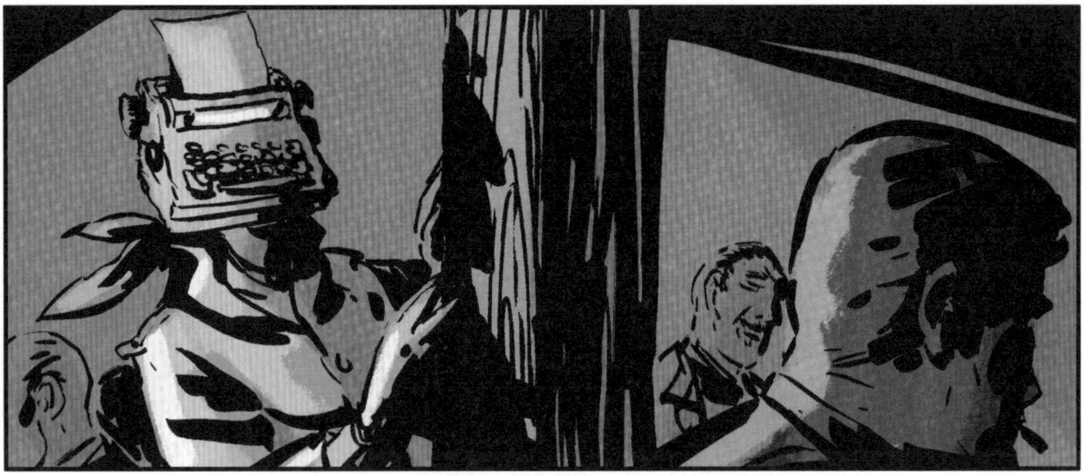

NOW, THE SCRIPT GIRL?
YOU COULD TRUST HER EVERY WORD.

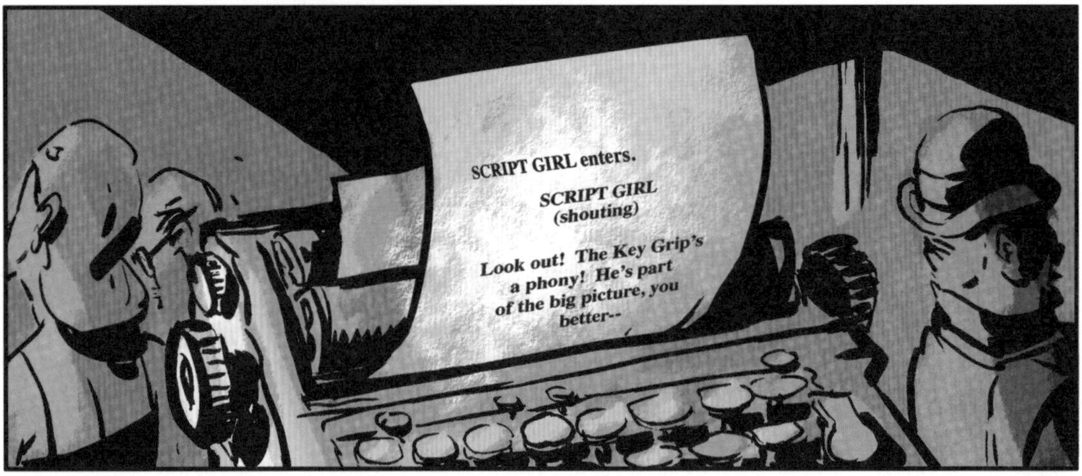
SCRIPT GIRL enters.
SCRIPT GIRL
(shouting)
Look out! The Key Grip's a phony! He's part of the big picture, you better--

SHE'D HEARD A RUMOR THAT SOMEONE HAD PLANS TO
STRIKE THE PROJECTIONIST'S SET AHEAD OF SCHEDULE.

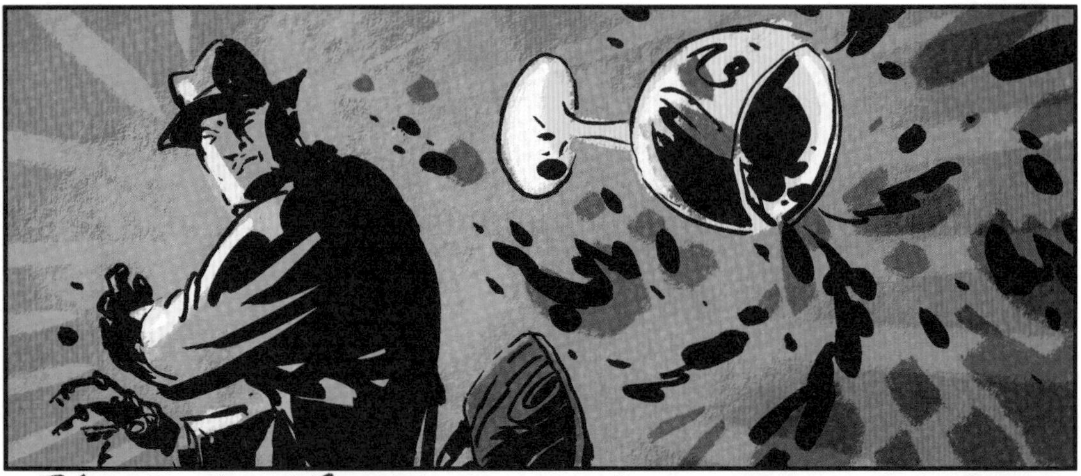

THAT KEY GRIP, HE WAS NO DAY PLAYER.
HE WAS RIGHT ON CUE, READY TO ROLL...

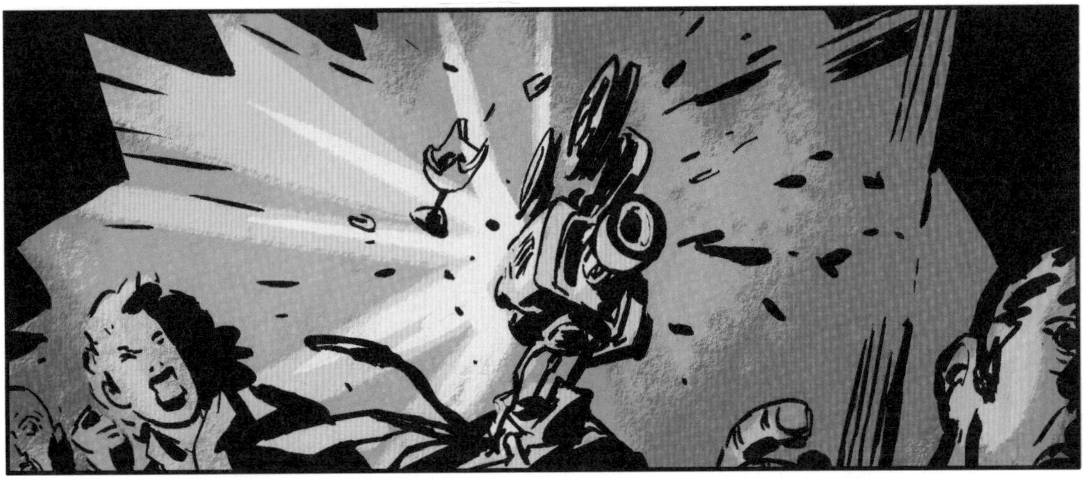

...READY TO THROW THE LIGHTS.

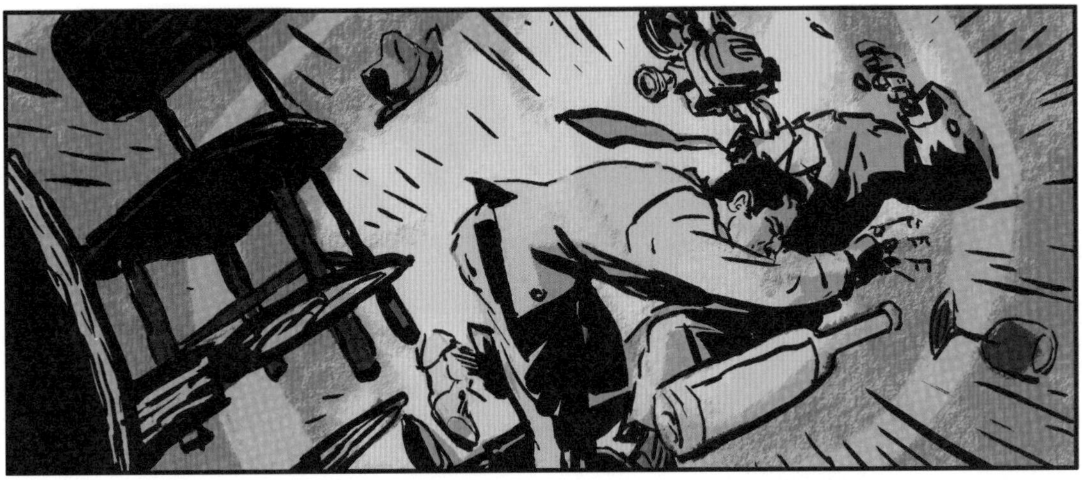

AND HE DIDN'T *DARE* USE A BOUNCE CARD
ON A SCENE LIKE *THIS*.

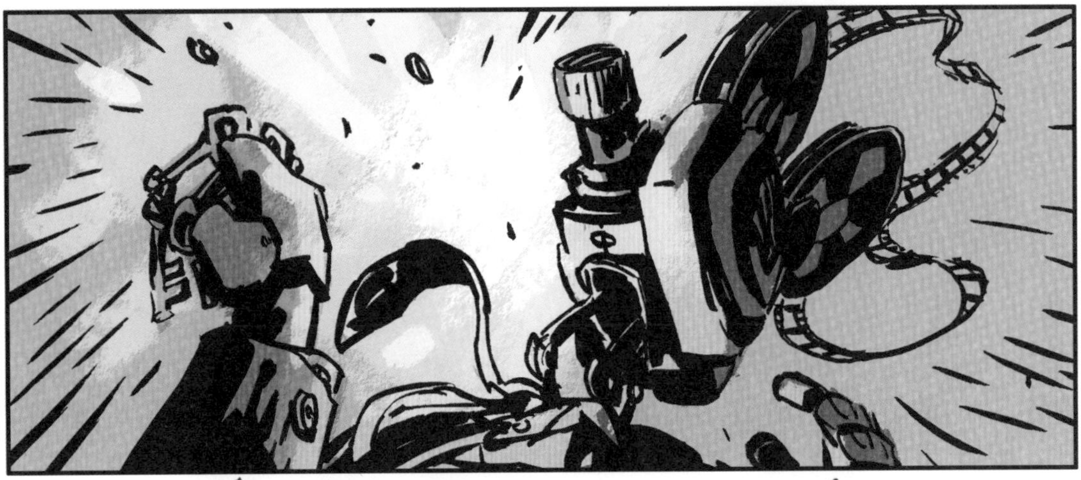

NO WAY, BROTHER. IT WAS
1000-WATT FLOODS, SO EVERYONE COULD SEE.

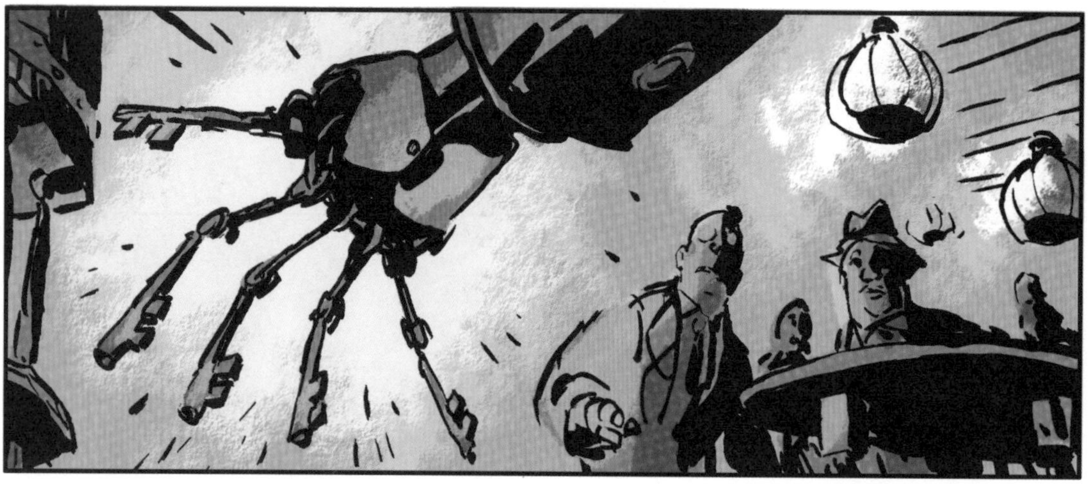

THE KEY GRIP HAD JUST THE RIGHT COMBINATION TO LOCK ANY MOMENT...

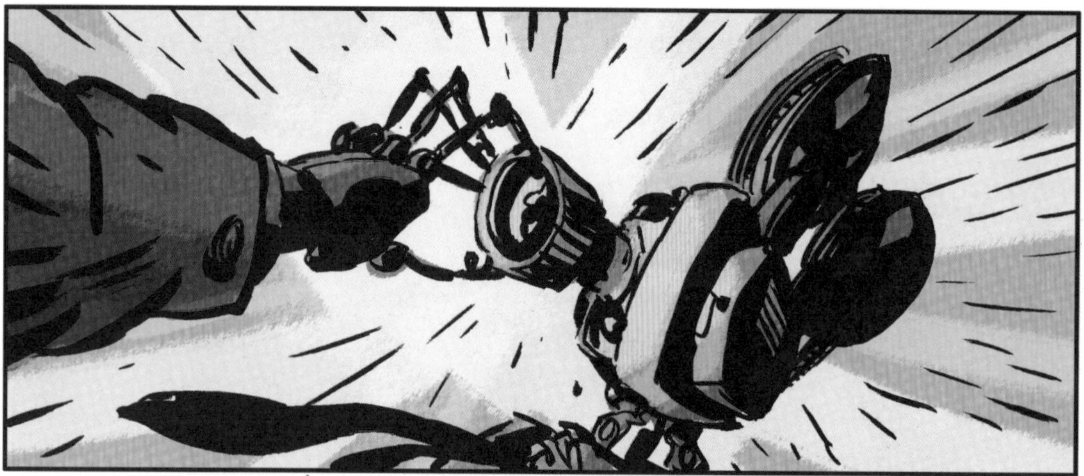

...KNEW JUST HOW TO TURN THE EMOTIONS OF A CAPTIVE AUDIENCE...

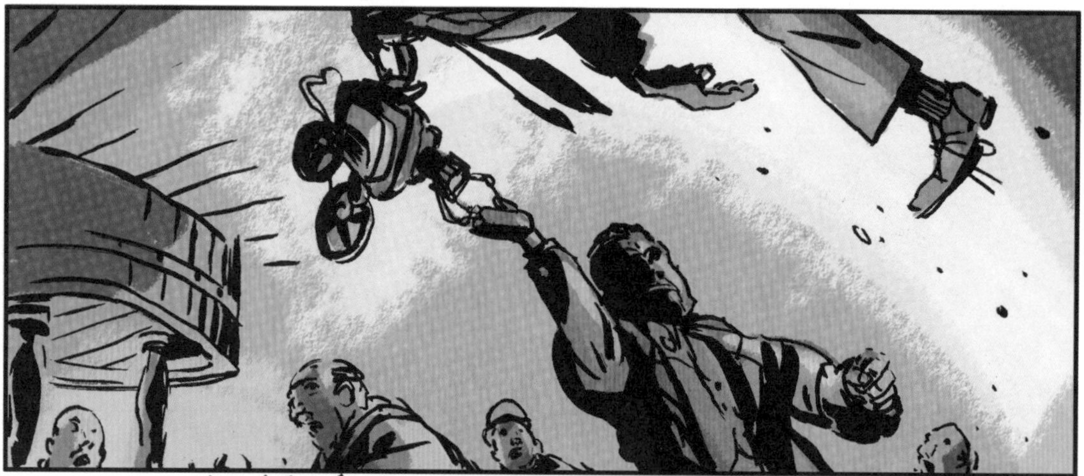

...KNEW JUST HOW TO MAKE THEM JUMP OUTTA THEIR SEATS.

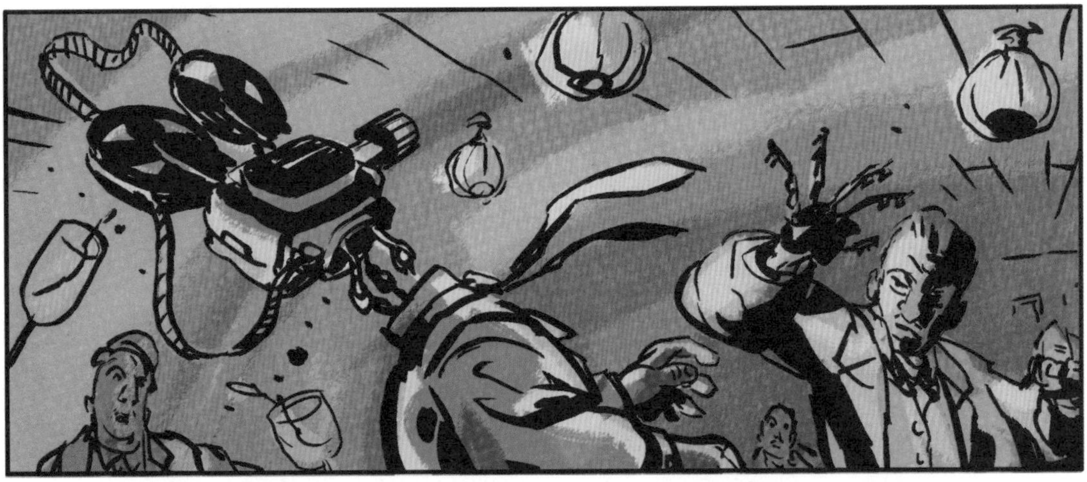

THE PROJECTIONIST KNEW HE'D BETTER SWITCH REELS FAST.

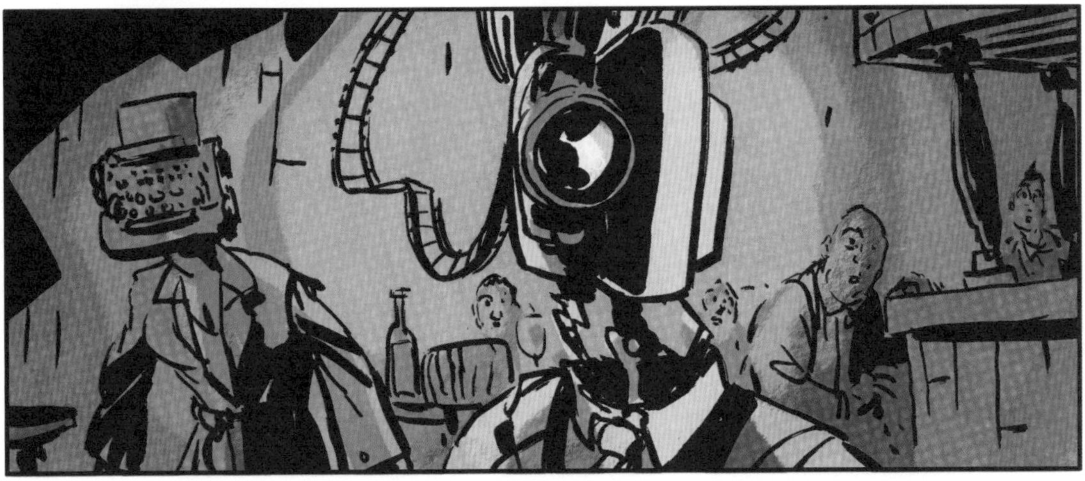

HE WAS LOSING *LIGHT*.

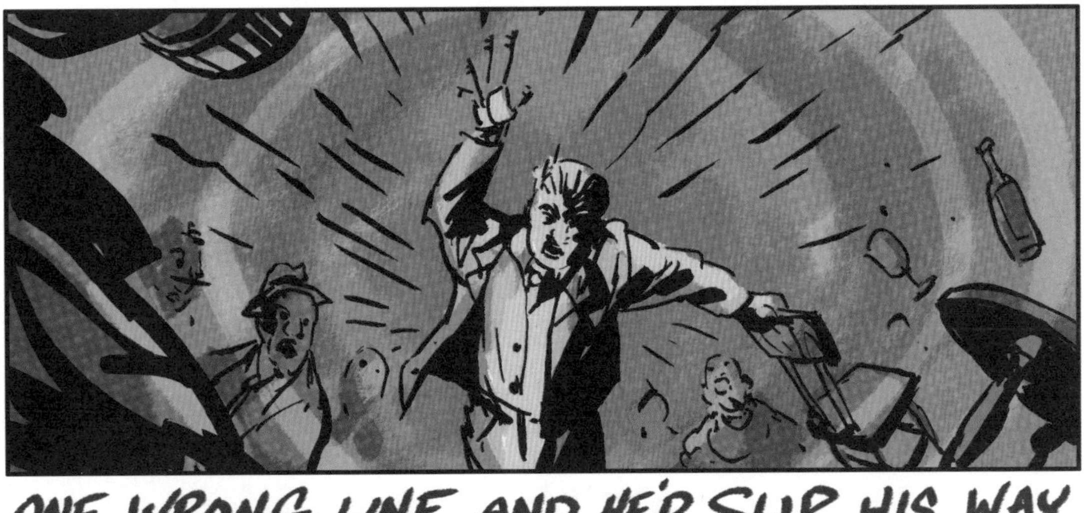

ONE WRONG LINE AND HE'D SLIP HIS WAY ONTO THE CUTTING-ROOM FLOOR.

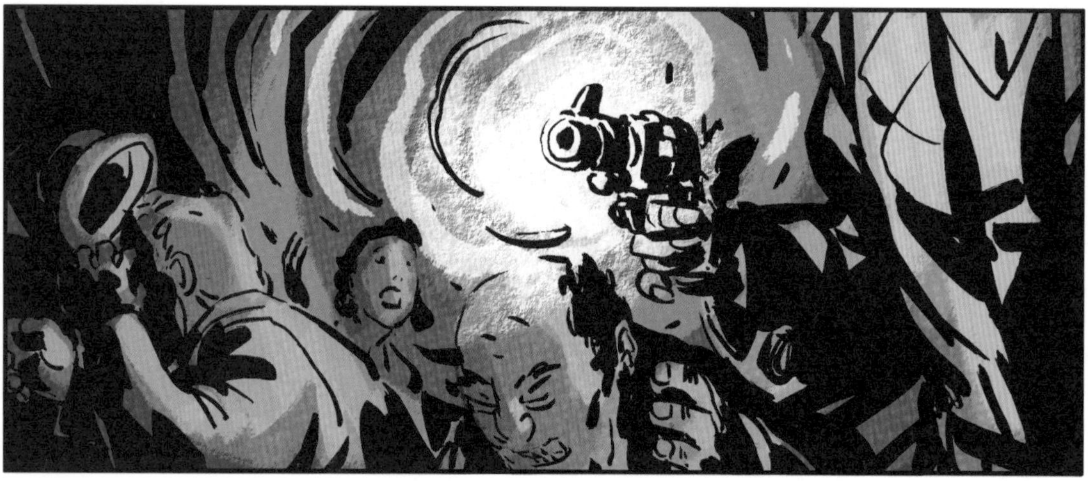

THEN--*BANG!!*

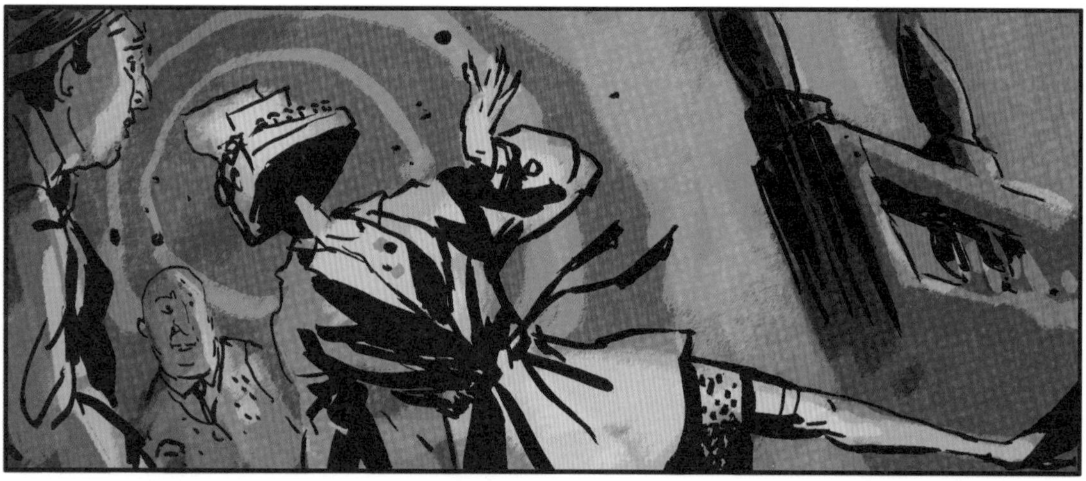

SOMEONE HAD CALLED A *REWRITE.*

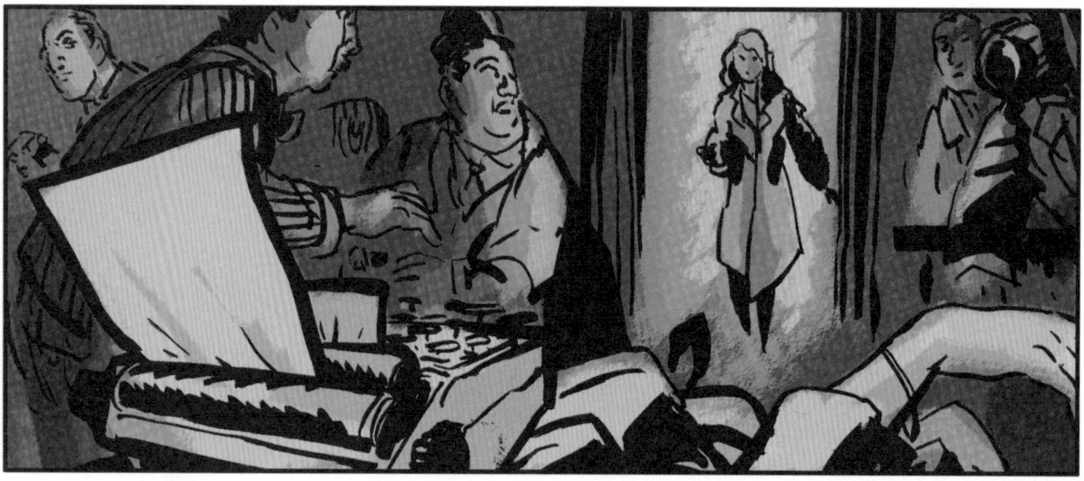

WITH *LEAD,* APPARENTLY.

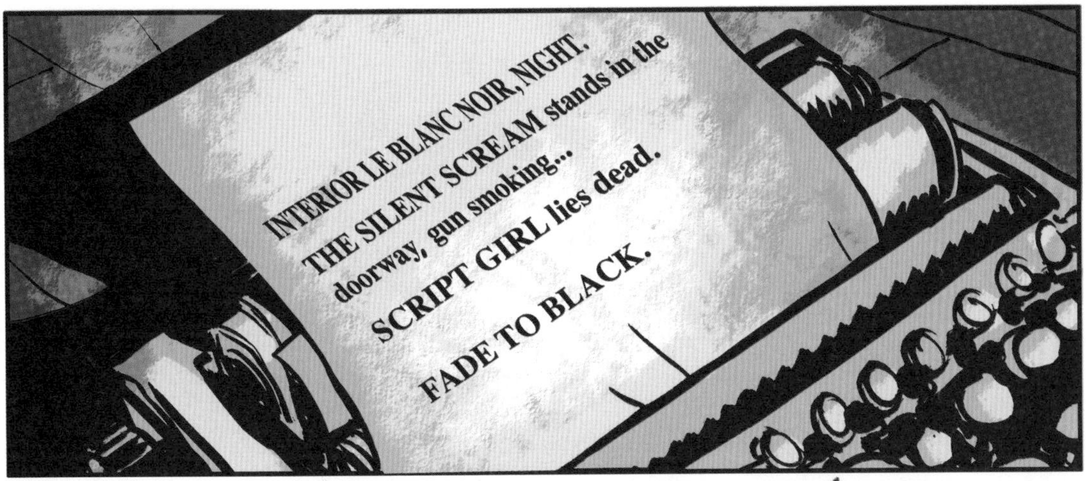
INTERIOR LE BLANC NOIR, NIGHT.
THE SILENT SCREAM stands in the doorway, gun smoking...
SCRIPT GIRL lies dead.
FADE TO BLACK.

NO ONE COULD HAVE GUESSED THAT THEY'D KILL OFF THE *SCRIPT GIRL*.

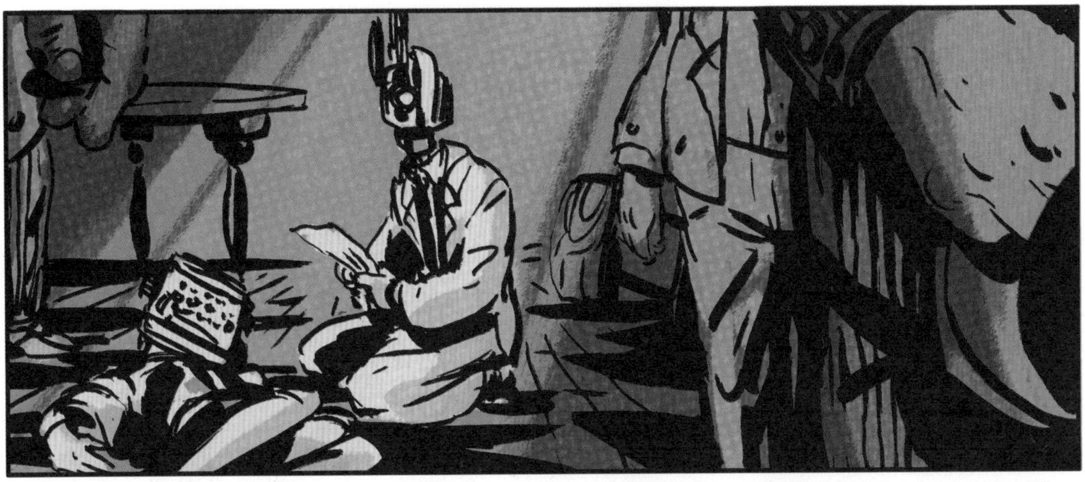

THE KEY GRIP HAD EXITED STAGE LEFT. THE SILENT SCREAM, TOO.

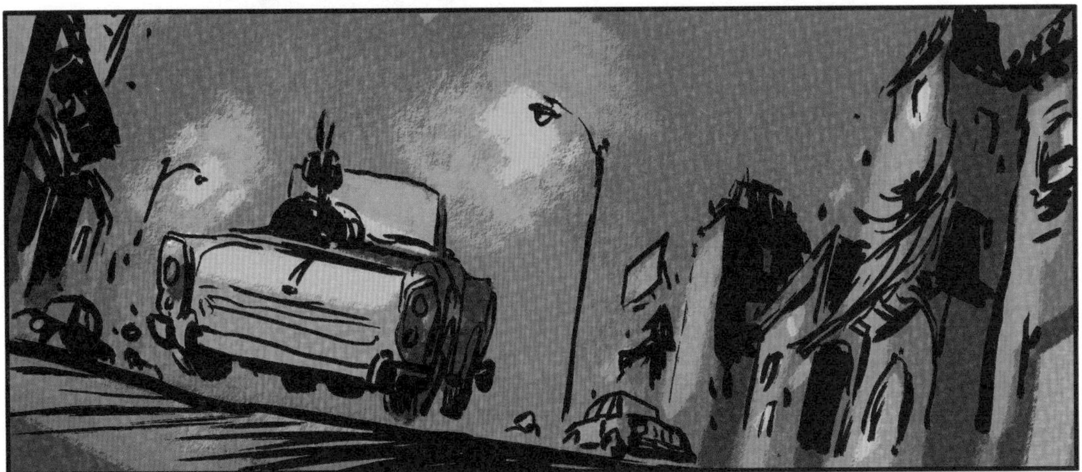

THAT MEANT SHE WAS *IN* ON THIS PLOT TWIST... ...*BUT WHY?*

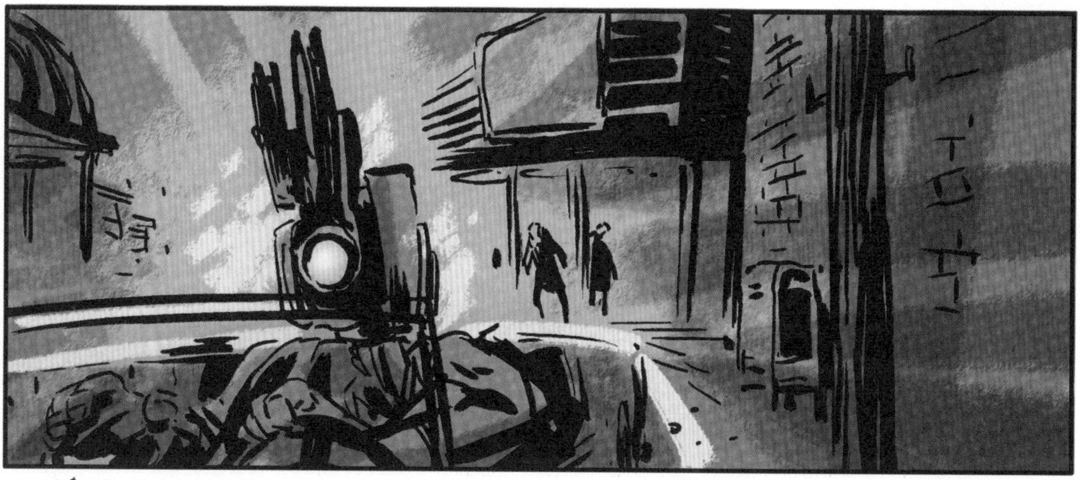

HE TURNED A CORNER AND REALIZED THEY INTENDED TO SHOOT THIS THING WITH NO PERMITS.

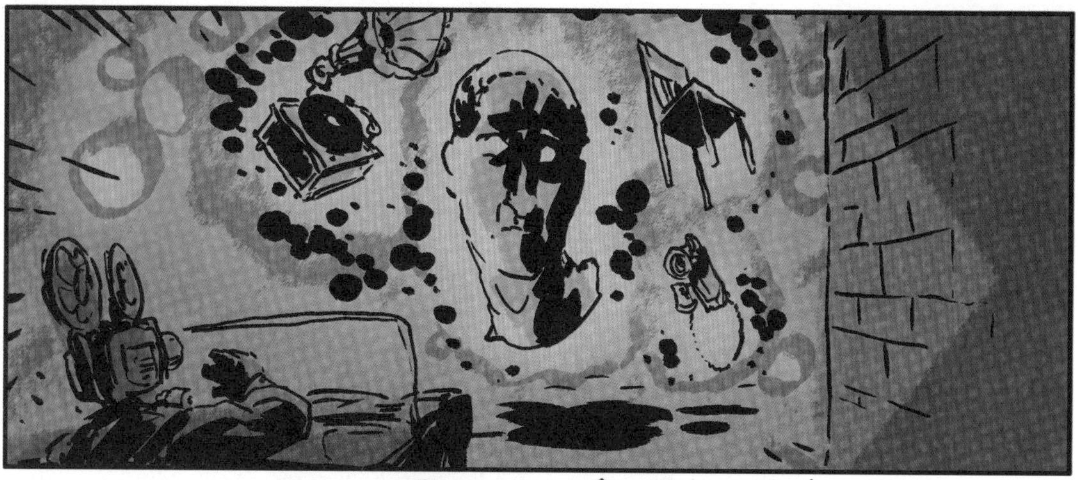

THE *PROP MASTER!* SOMEONE WAS REALLY BLOWIN' THE BUDGET.

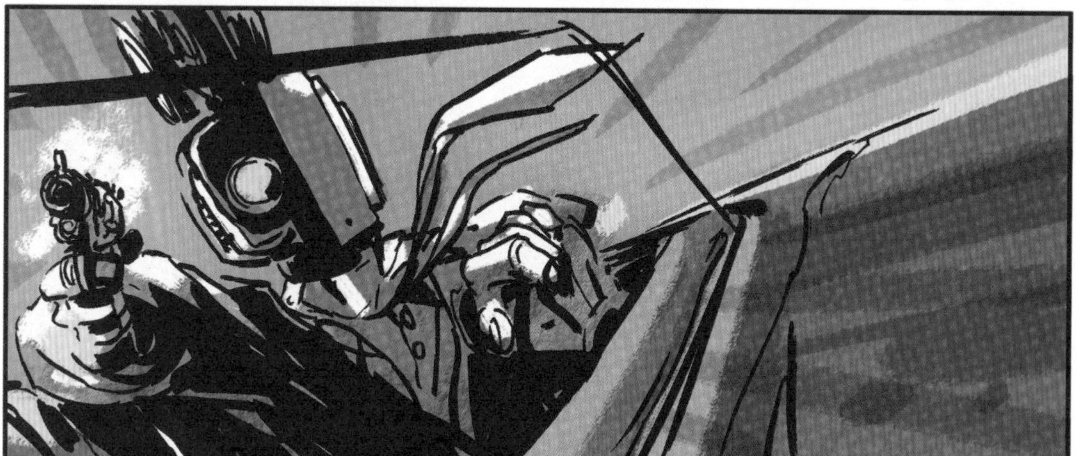

THEY WERE THROWING EVERYTHING BUT THE KITCHEN SINK AT HIM!

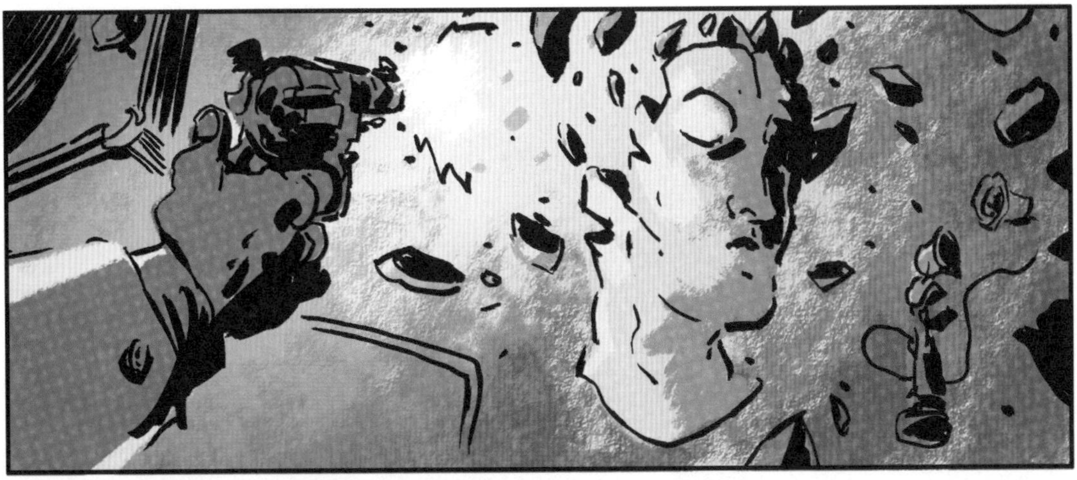

GOOD THING THE PROP MASTER WAS JUST A PILE OF CHICKEN WIRE AND PLASTER WHEN YOU GOT DOWN TO IT.

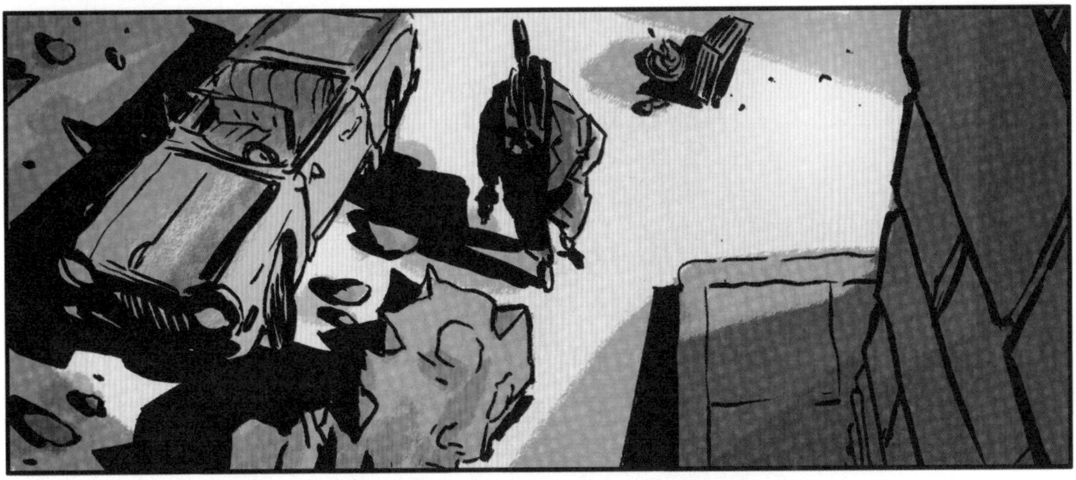

AND PLASTER AN' BULLETS...
...THEY DON'T MIX.

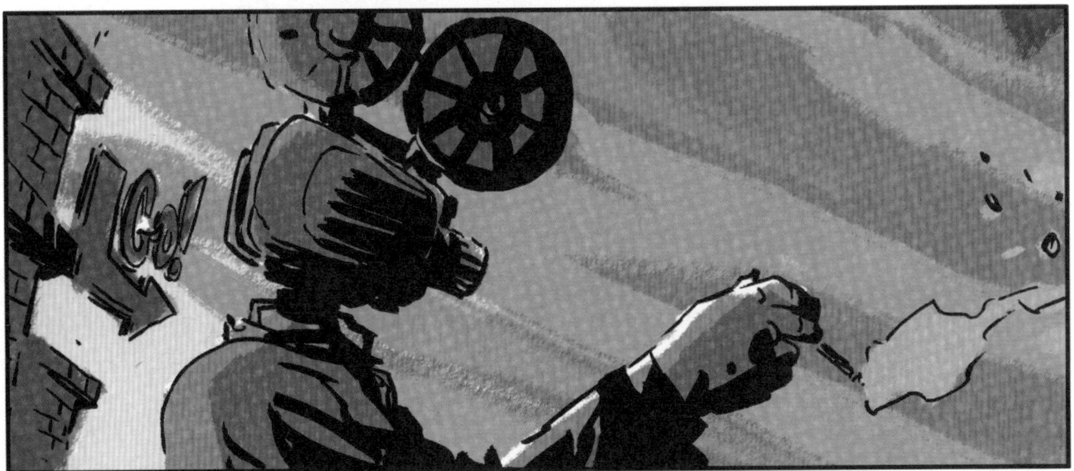
GO!

NOW, COULD THE NEXT REEL POSSIBLY HOLD THE WHEREABOUTS OF THE DIRECTOR...?

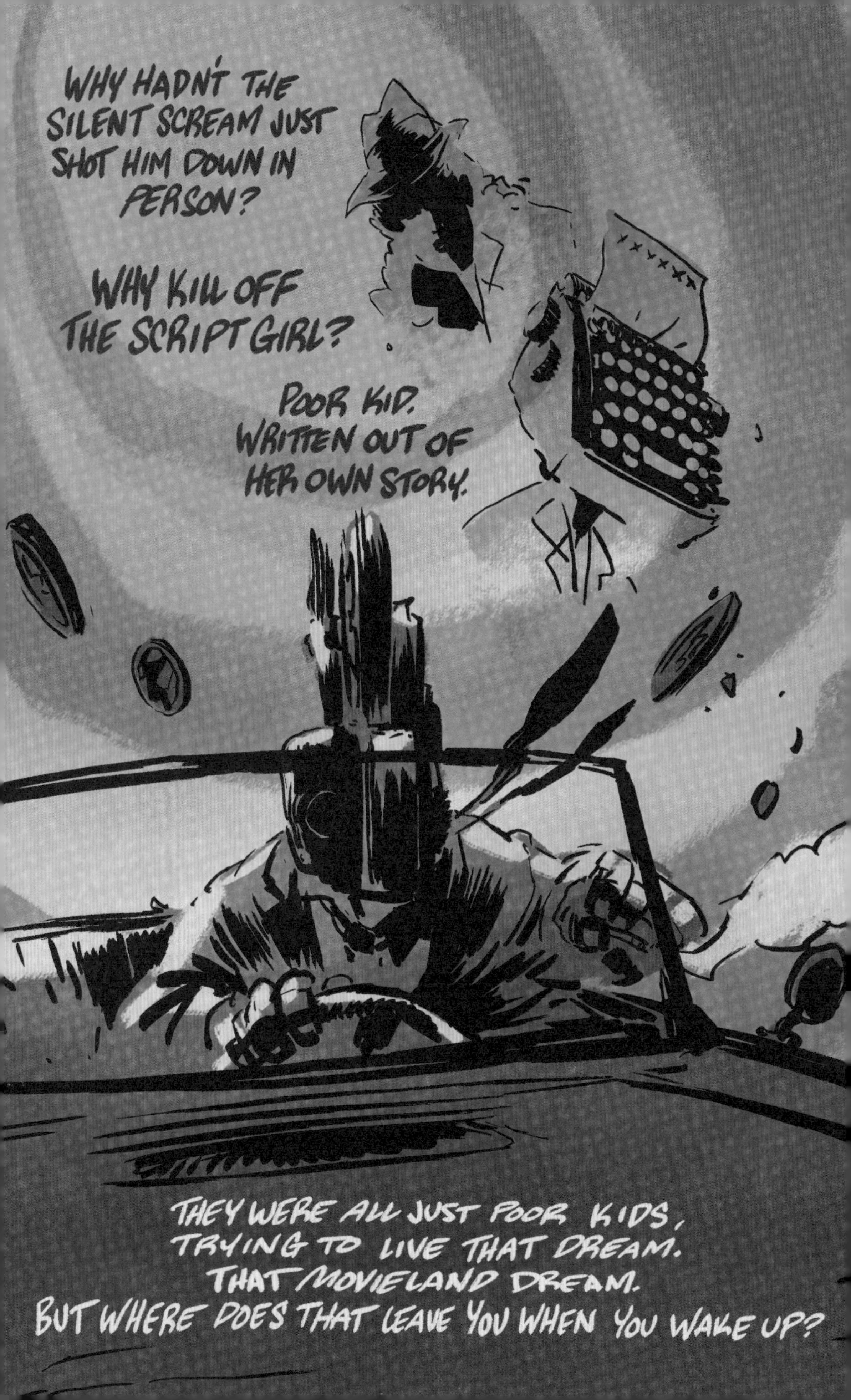
WHY HADN'T THE SILENT SCREAM JUST SHOT HIM DOWN IN PERSON?
WHY KILL OFF THE SCRIPT GIRL?
POOR KID. WRITTEN OUT OF HER OWN STORY.
THEY WERE ALL JUST POOR KIDS, TRYING TO LIVE THAT DREAM. THAT MOVIELAND DREAM. BUT WHERE DOES THAT LEAVE YOU WHEN YOU WAKE UP?

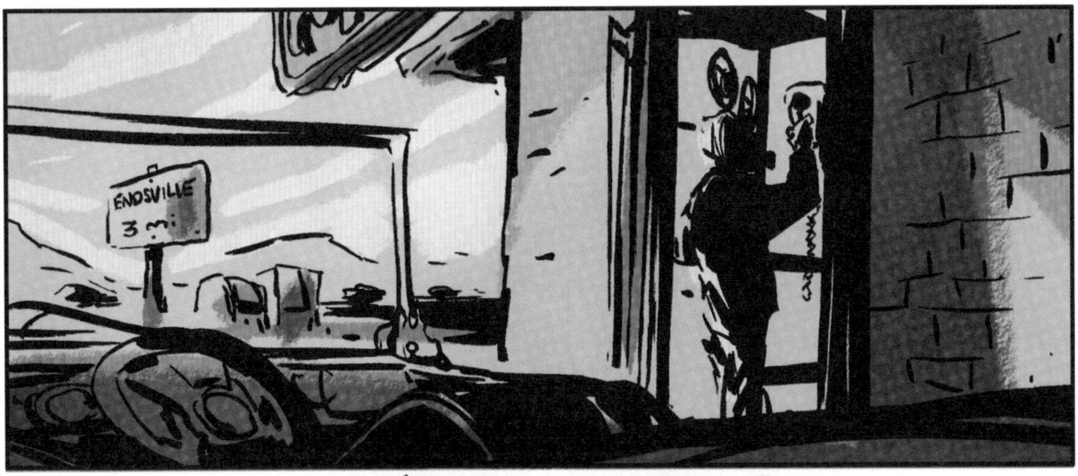
ENDSVILLE
3 mi

WHERE INDEED?
JUST A THIN DIME AWAY...

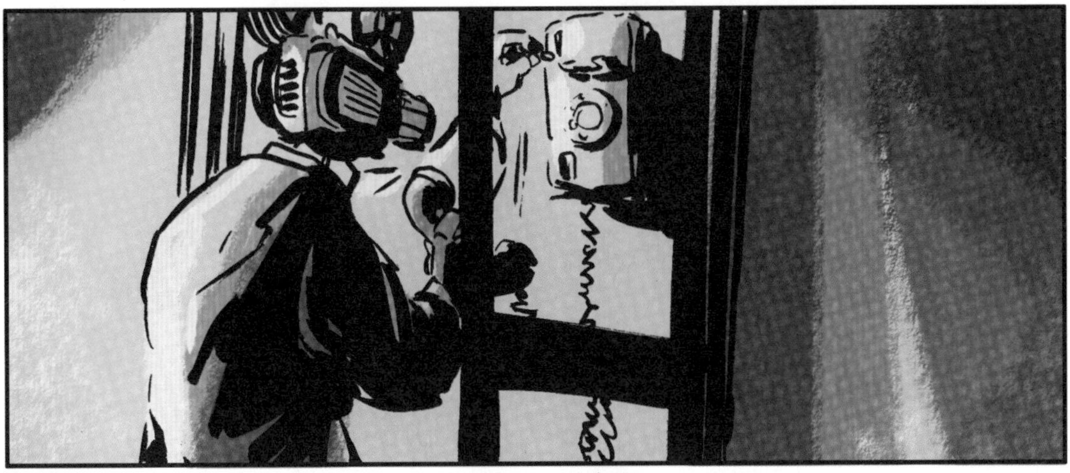

...TO THE
LOCATION SCOUT!

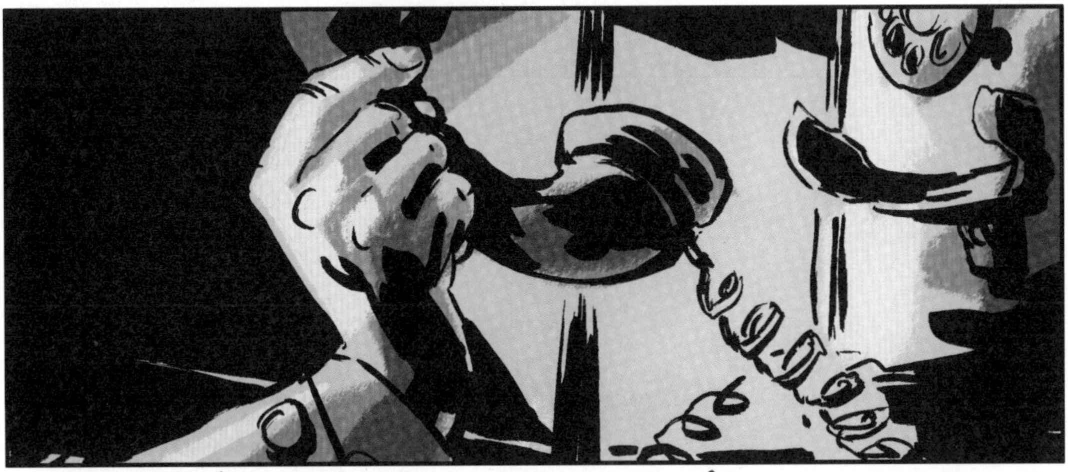

HE MIGHT NOT KNOW *WHO* WAS YELLING "ACTION,"
BUT HE'D KNOW *WHERE* TO START LOOKING.

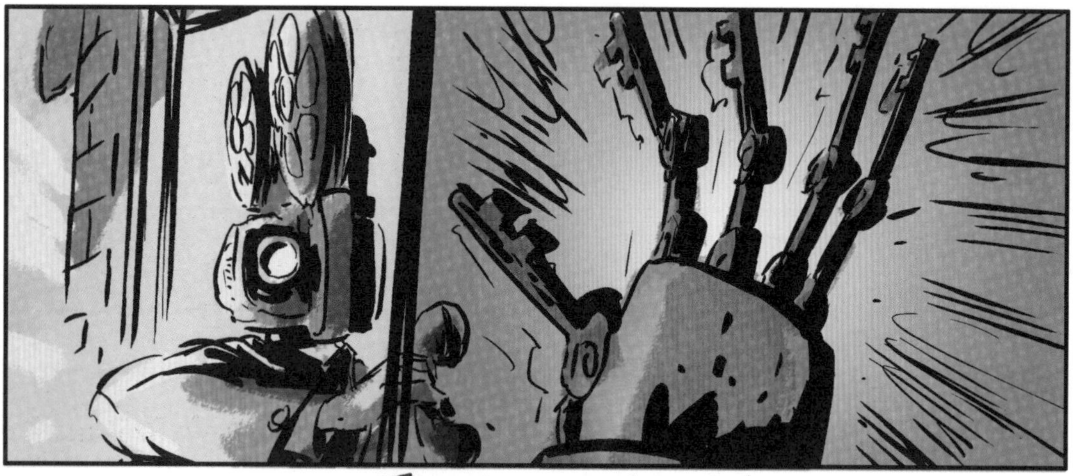

THEN-- WHAM!
THOSE KEYS CLATTERED OUT OF NOWHERE.

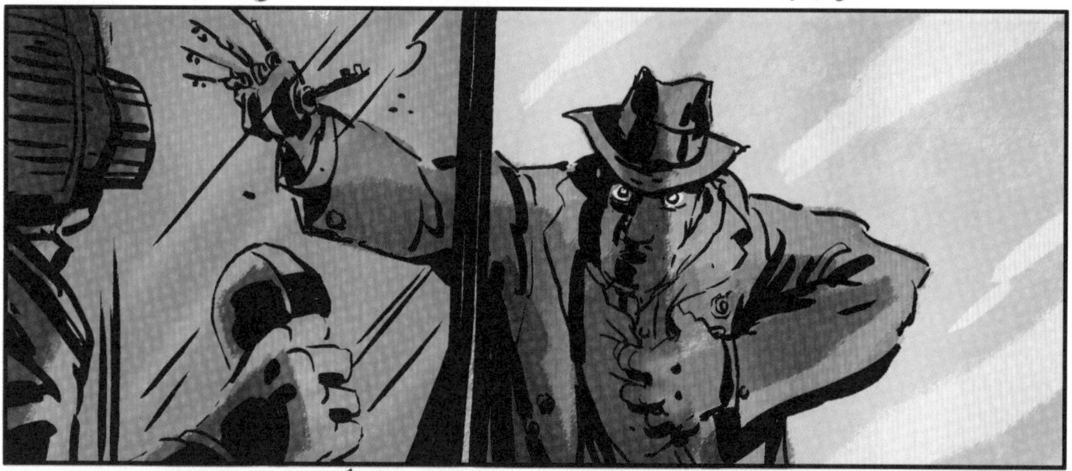

BUT THEY'D FINALLY LOST THEIR GRIP.
THE SILENT SCREAM WAS DOING FREELANCE AS AN EDITOR.
CUTTING HER TIES.

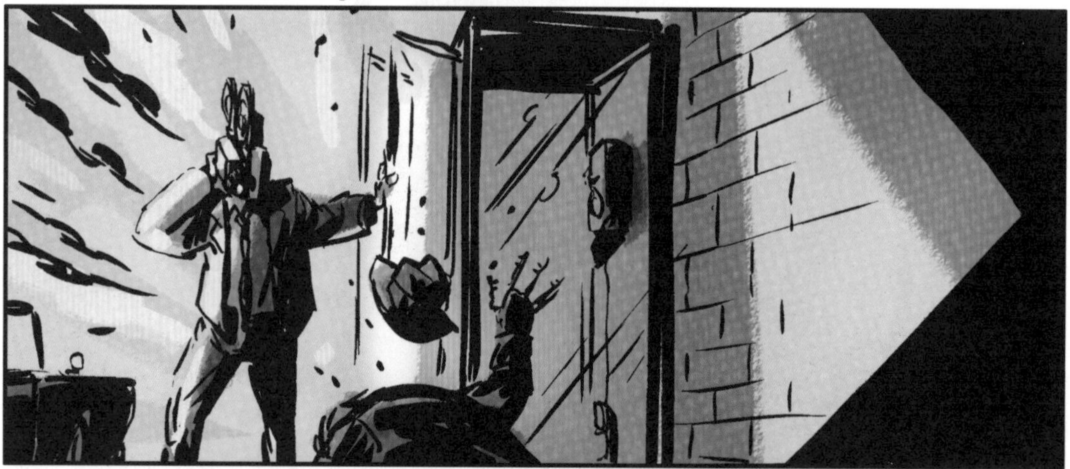

THE SET-UP GUY HAD BEEN SET UP HIMSELF.
THAT'S HOW IT WORKS FOR TWO-BIT
DAY PLAYERS AND EXTRAS.

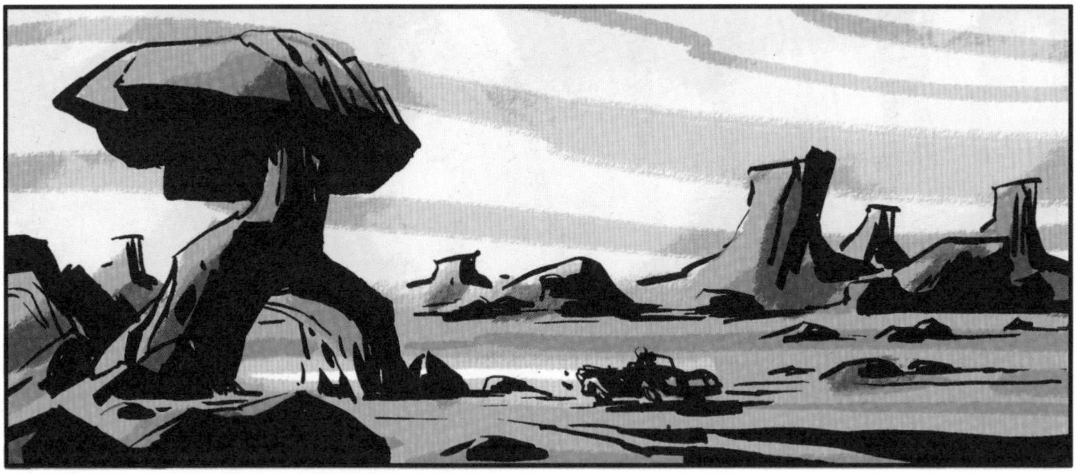

THE KEY GRIP ENDED UP DOING HIS OWN STUNTS
AND JUMPED THE SHARK--

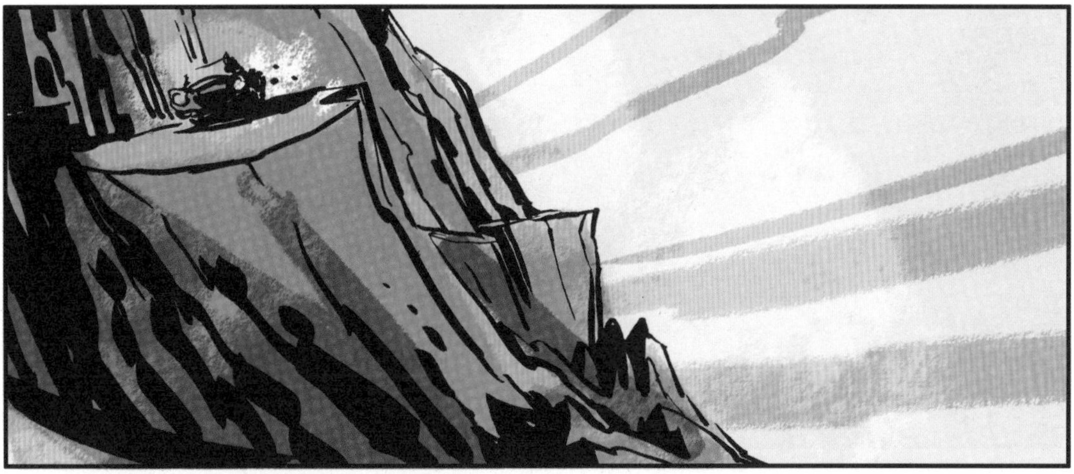

--BUT NOT BEFORE THE LOCATION SCOUT
AGREED TO A RENDEZVOUS.

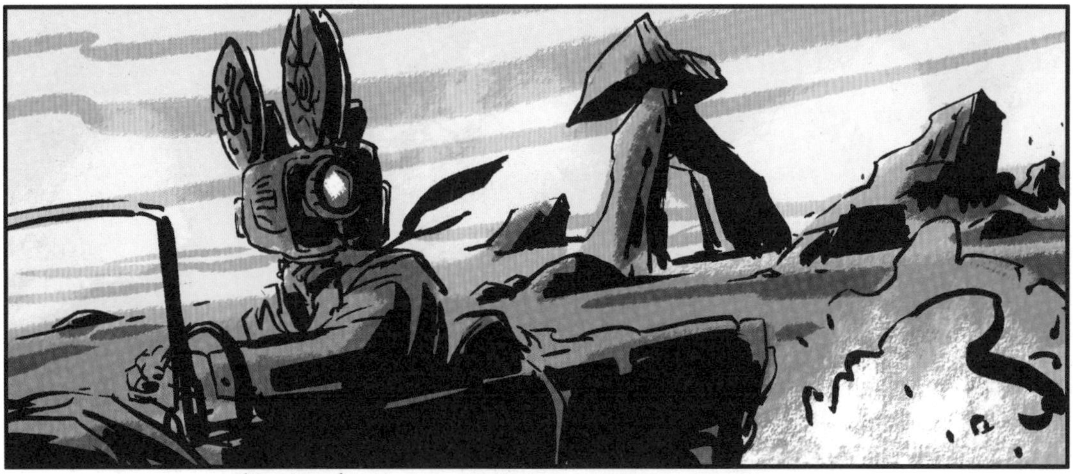

HE WAS A *REAL* CHARACTER--
--AND ALWAYS *IN* CHARACTER.
HE WANTED TO MEET SOMEWHERE "*SCENIC*."

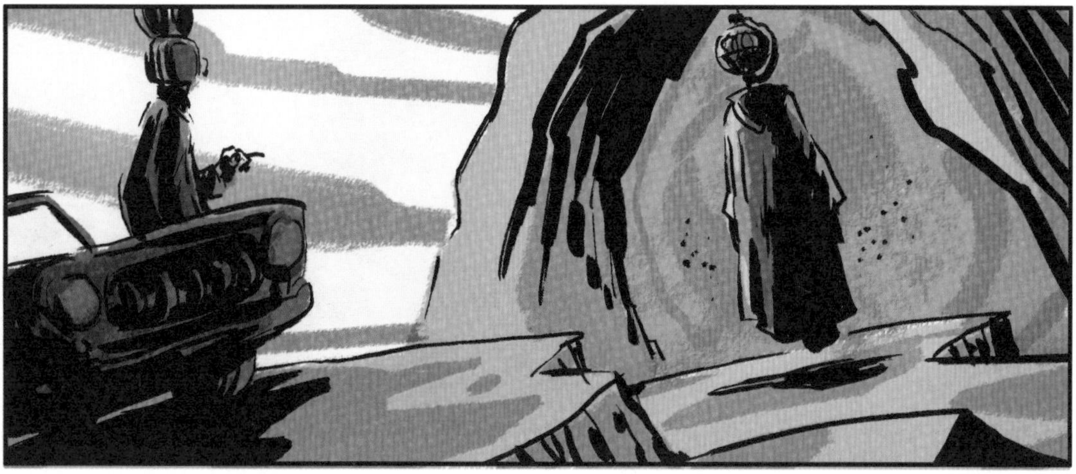

IT FIGURES THE LOCATION SCOUT WOULD BE "OUT THERE," YOU KNOW?

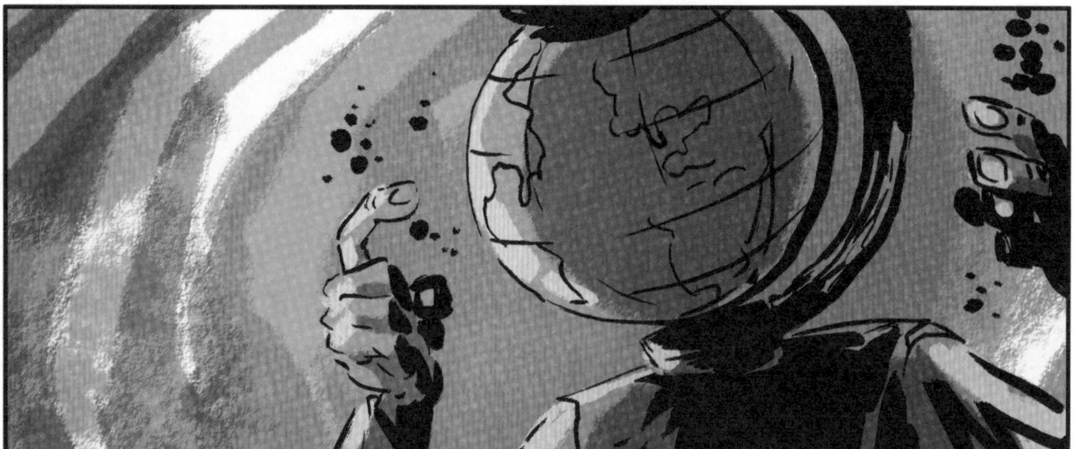

THIS GUY HAD GONE PLACES. CIRCLED THE PLANET. HE COULD FIND ANYONE, ANYWHERE.

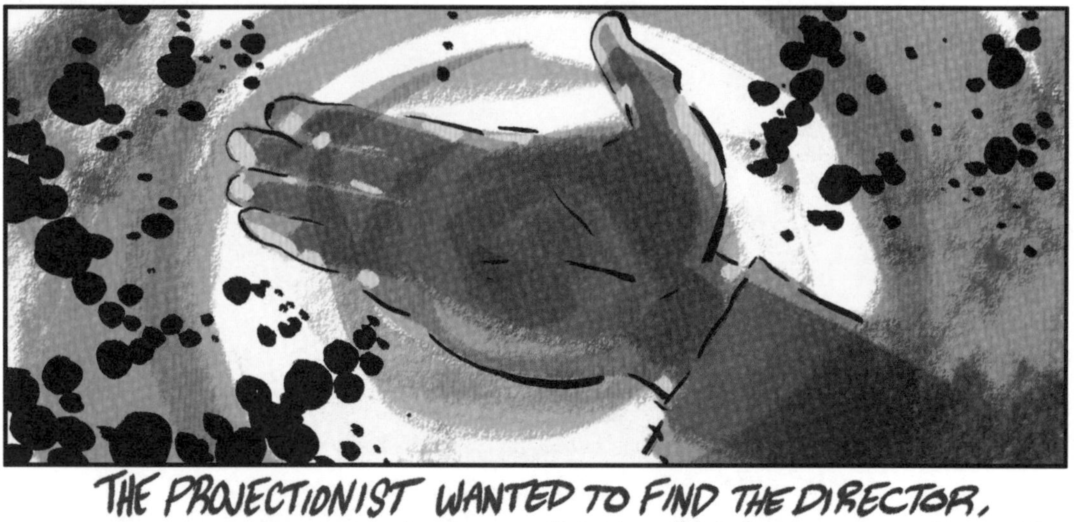

THE PROJECTIONIST WANTED TO FIND THE DIRECTOR. SIMPLE ENOUGH, FOR SOMEONE LIKE THE LOCATION SCOUT.

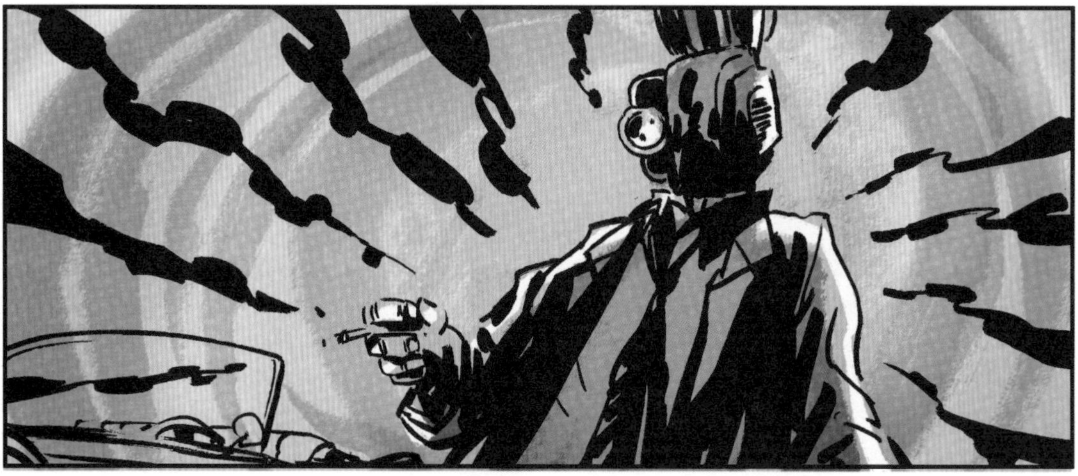

STILL, THE PROJECTIONIST WAS CUT OF A DIFFERENT CLOTH!
IN "THE BUSINESS," SURELY--

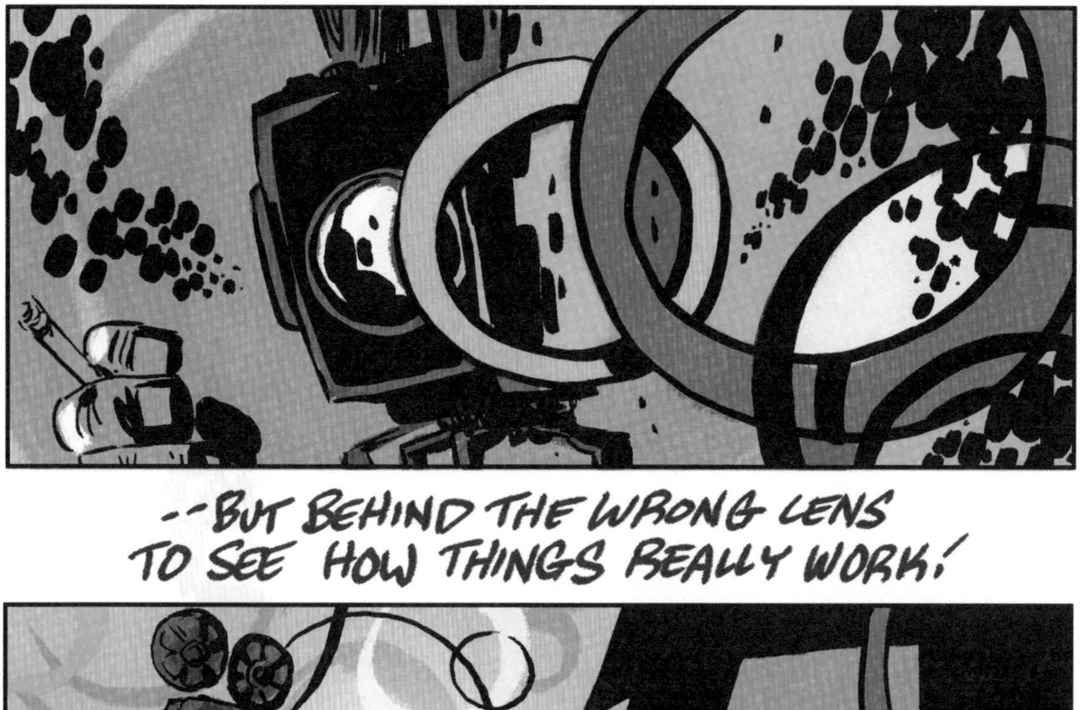

--BUT BEHIND THE WRONG LENS
TO SEE HOW THINGS REALLY WORK!

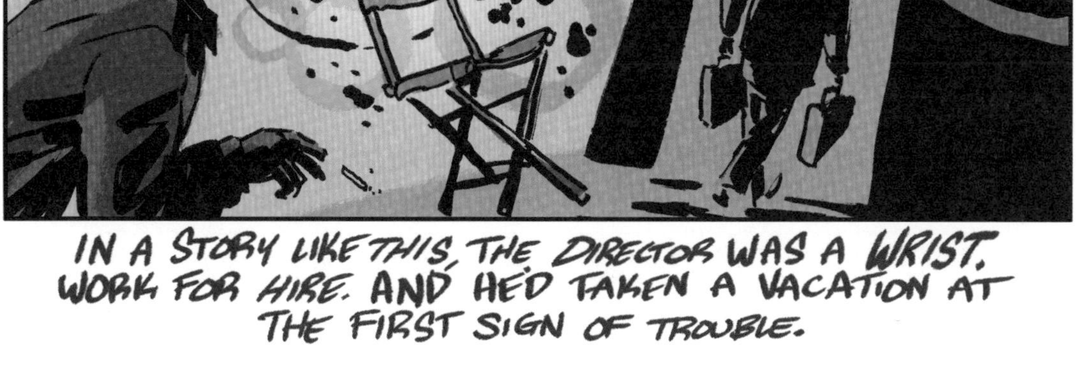

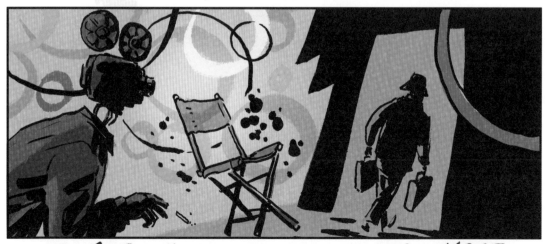

IN A STORY LIKE THIS, THE DIRECTOR WAS A *WRIST.*
WORK FOR HIRE. AND HE'D TAKEN A VACATION AT
THE FIRST SIGN OF TROUBLE.

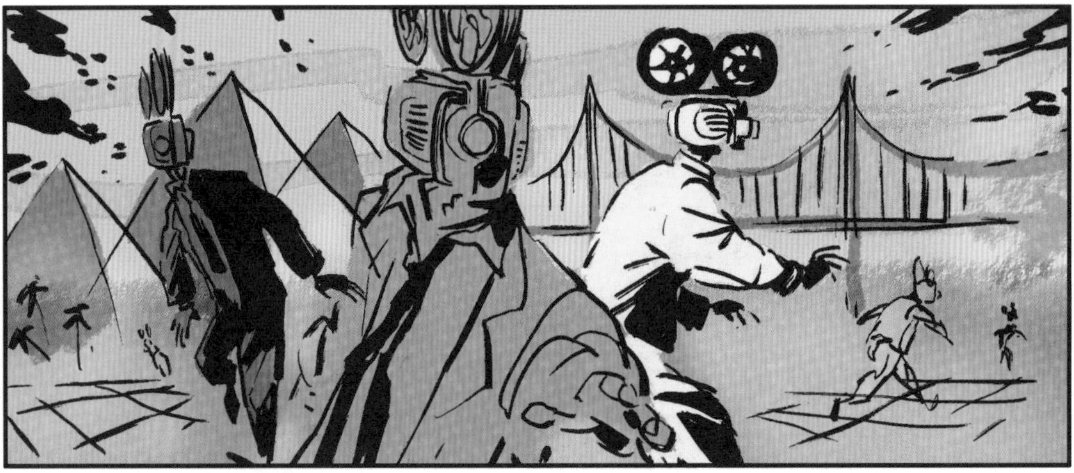

BUT IT WASN'T THE DIRECTOR HE NEEDED.
IT WAS BIGGER THAN THAT, HE SOON REALIZED.

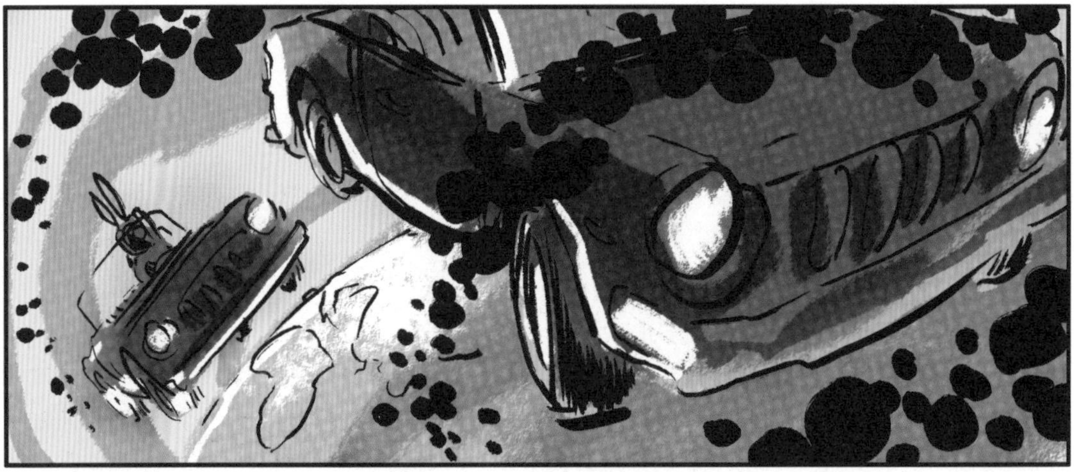

THE PRODUCER WOULD BE HOLDING THE RECEIPTS
AT THE END OF THE DAY.

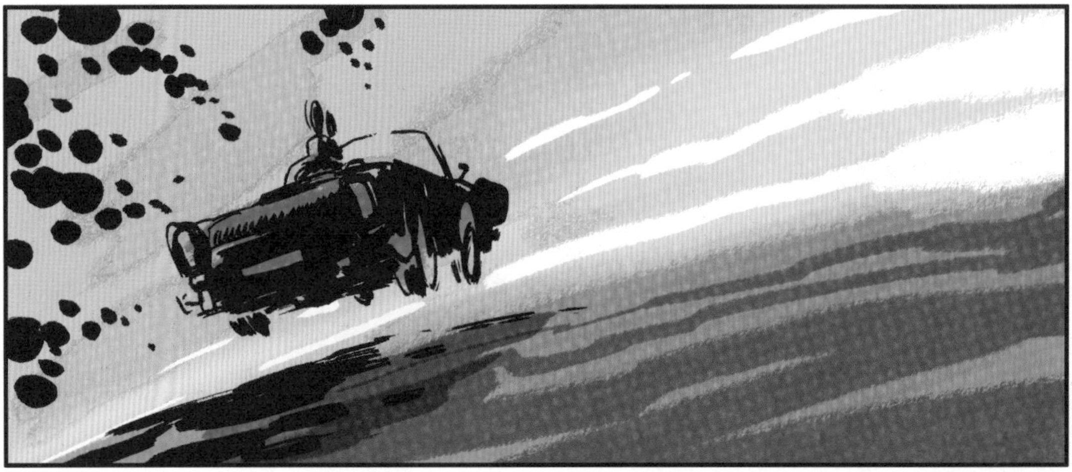

IT WAS THE PRODUCER HE NEEDED TO FIND!

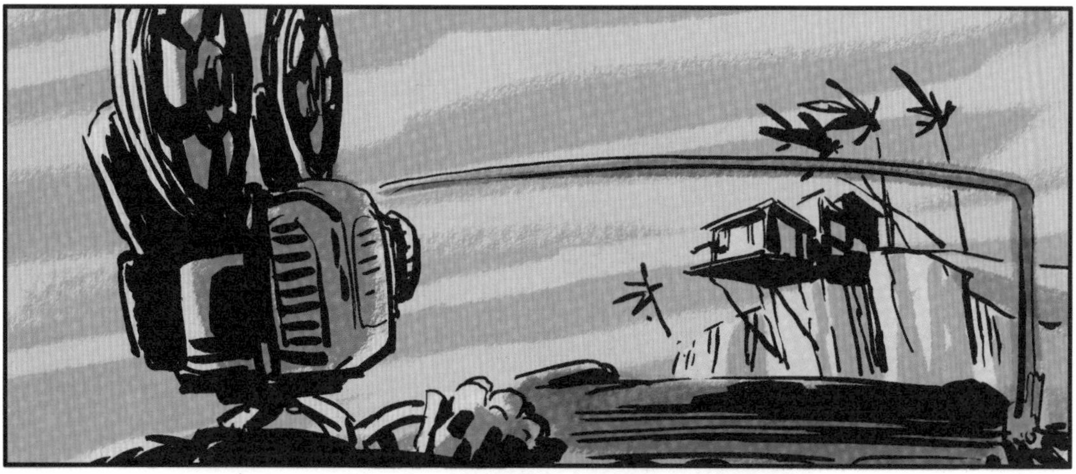

THE PRODUCER. OF COURSE!

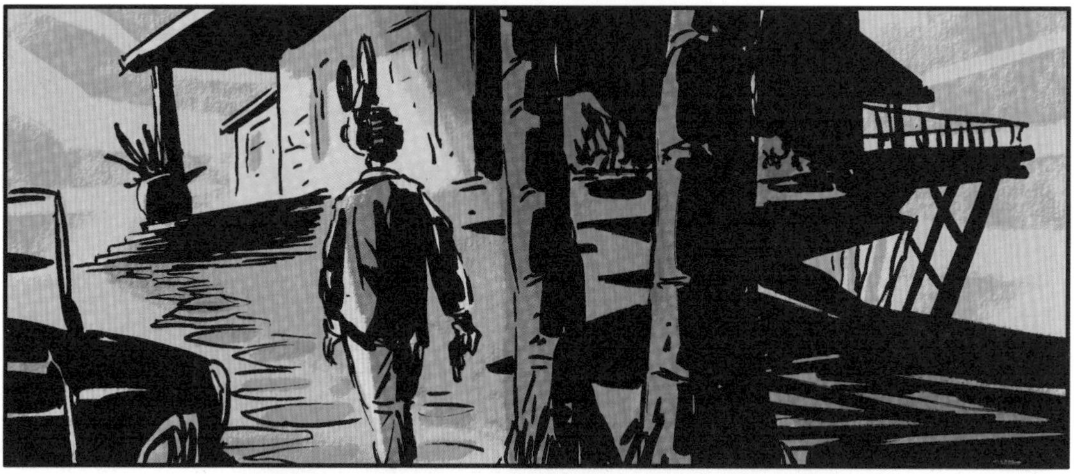

THE GUY THAT ALWAYS LIVED LARGE.

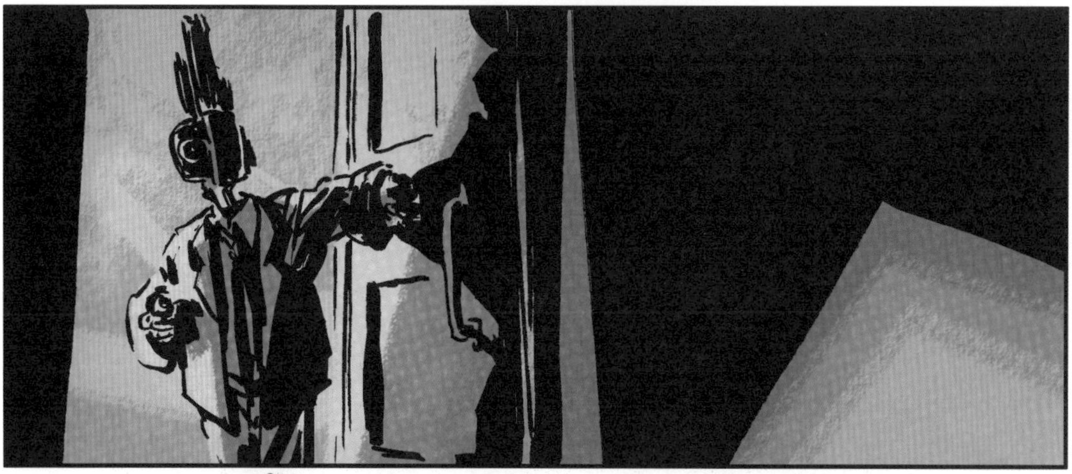

THE ONE WHO COULD REALLY AFFORD TO MAKE THINGS HAPPEN.

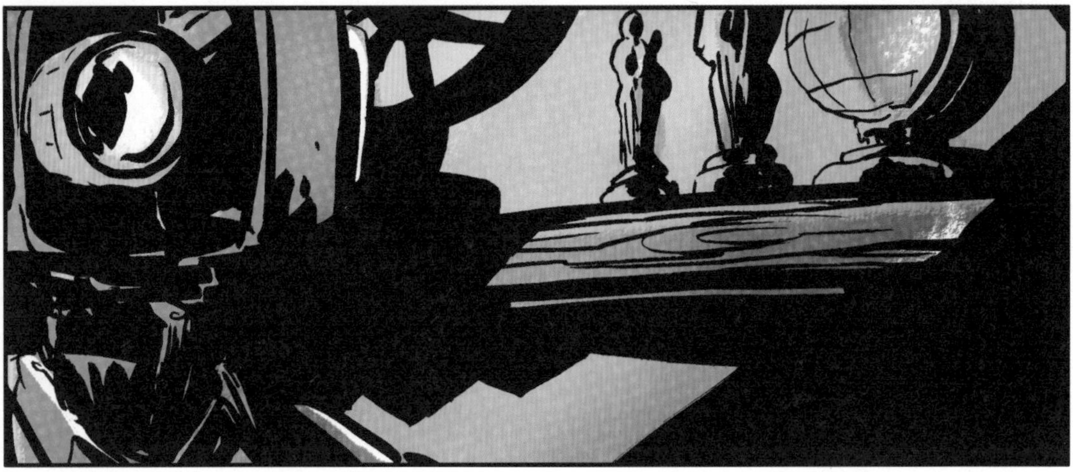

HE'S THE KID WHO ALWAYS MANAGES TO STAY IN THE PICTURE.
AND COME AWARDS SEASON, IT WAS ALWAYS "HIS IDEA," RIGHT?

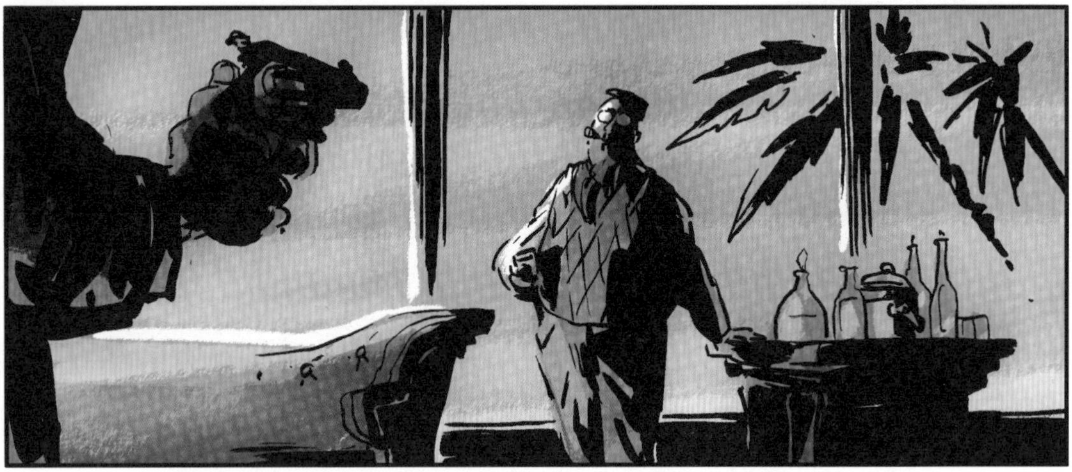

SO THE PROJECTIONIST FINALLY SPLICED
THE PRINT TOGETHER AND PULLED FOCUS. *BRAVO!*

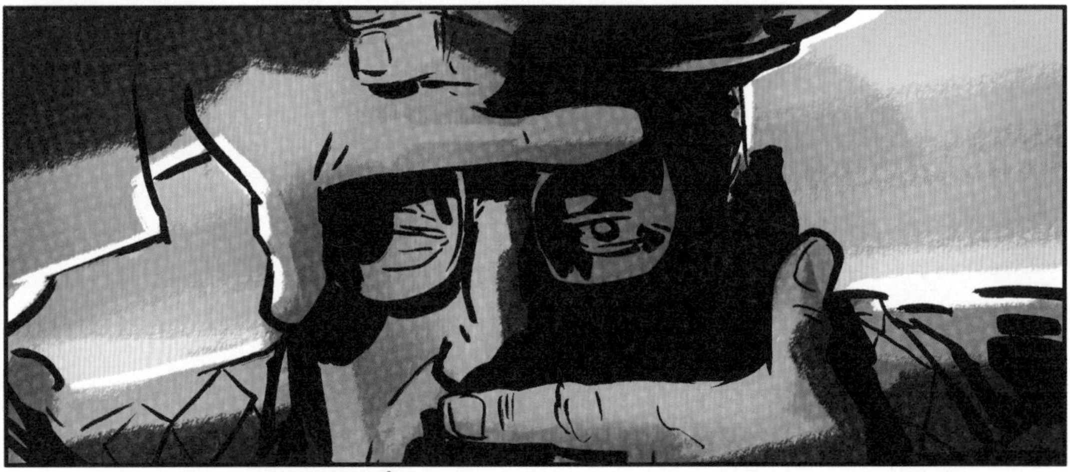

STILL, THERE'S ALWAYS A LITTLE MAGIC
JUST OFF-SCREEN!

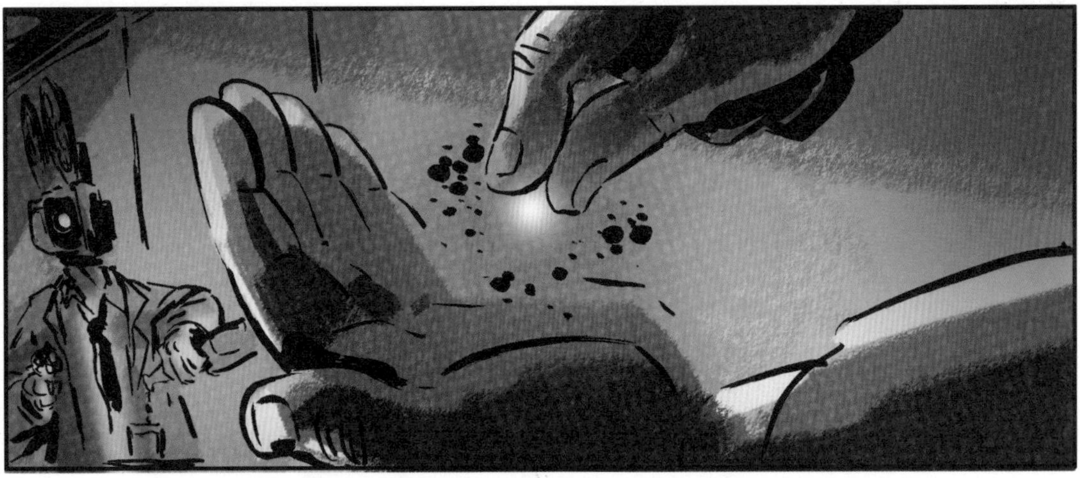

YOU'VE ALWAYS GOT TO STAY FOR
THE CREDITS TO "ROLL."

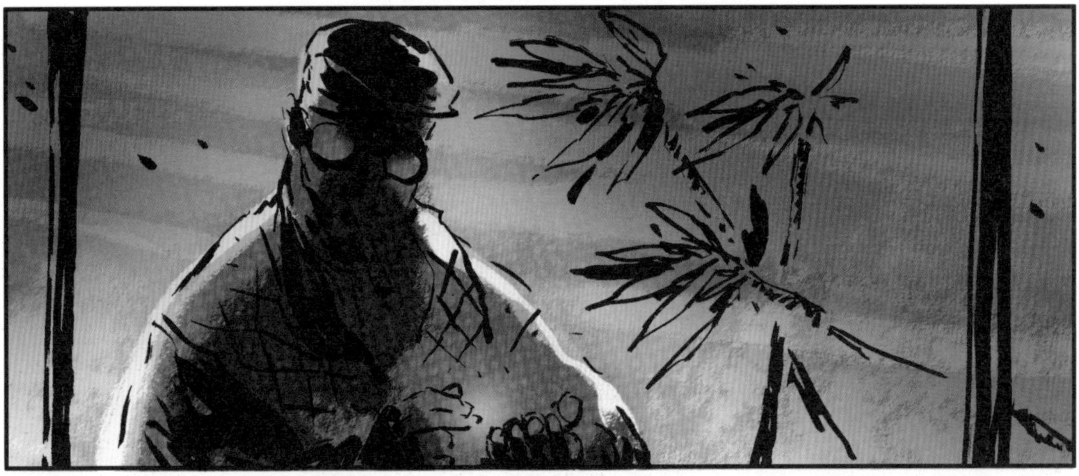

SEE, EVEN THE PRODUCER COULD END UP BEING RECAST.
LET'S TURN THE SPOTLIGHT ON THE REAL STAR.

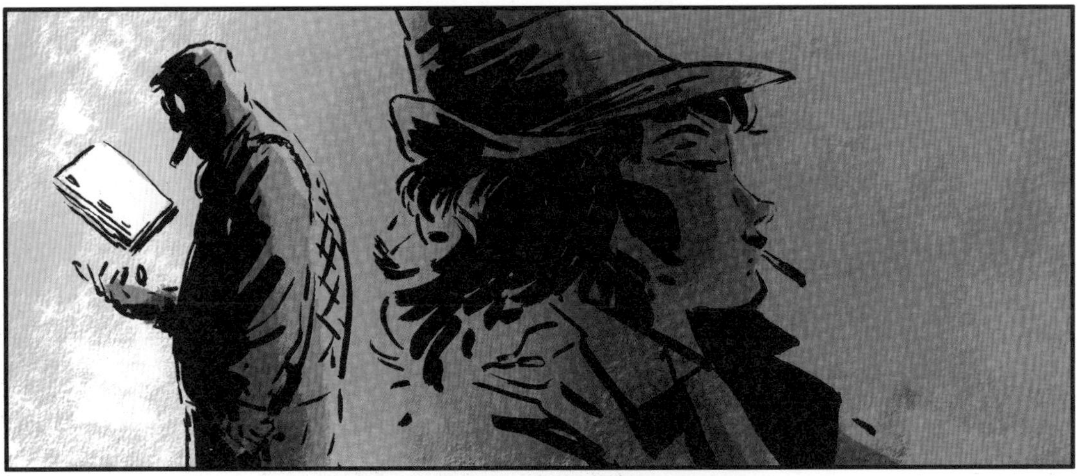

THE SILENT SCREAM.
WORKING HER OWN QUIET ANGLE
FROM THE FIRST FRAME ON.

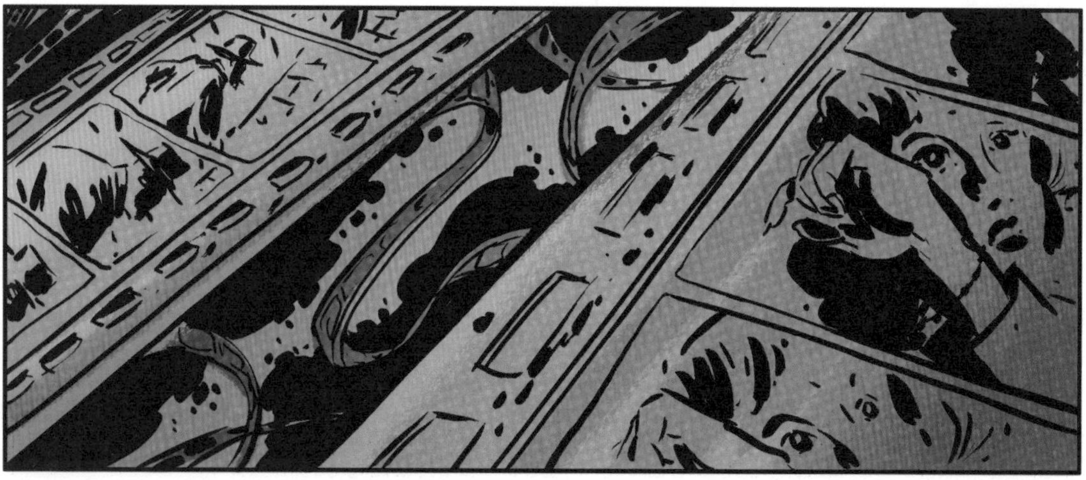

FILM, SHE THOUGHT, WASN'T AN ACTOR'S TRUE MEDIUM.
A PERFORMANCE COULD BE CAPTURED ON FILM. *TRAPPED.*

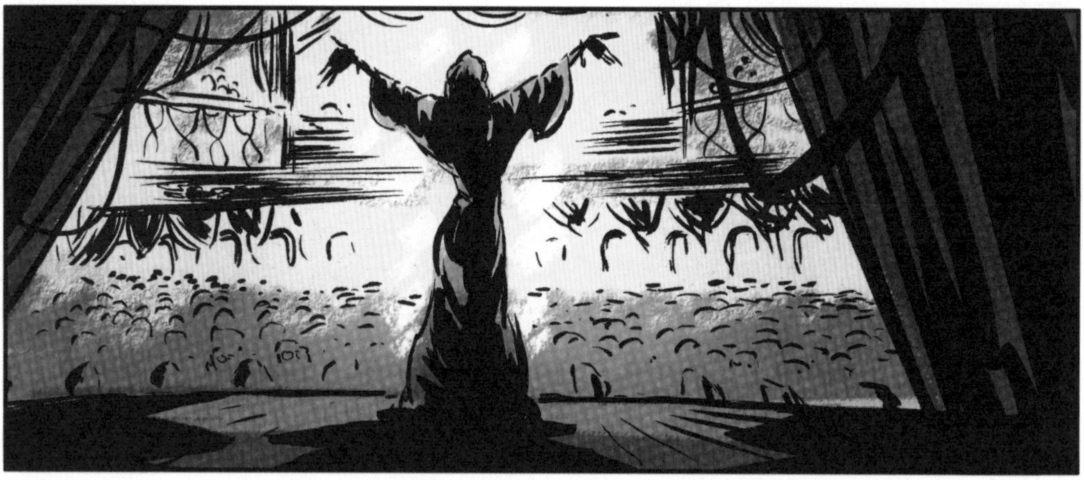

TO *HER*, A PERFORMANCE SHOULD *LIVE*. ON *STAGE*.
ALIVE, AND BEAUTIFULLY *FLEETING*.

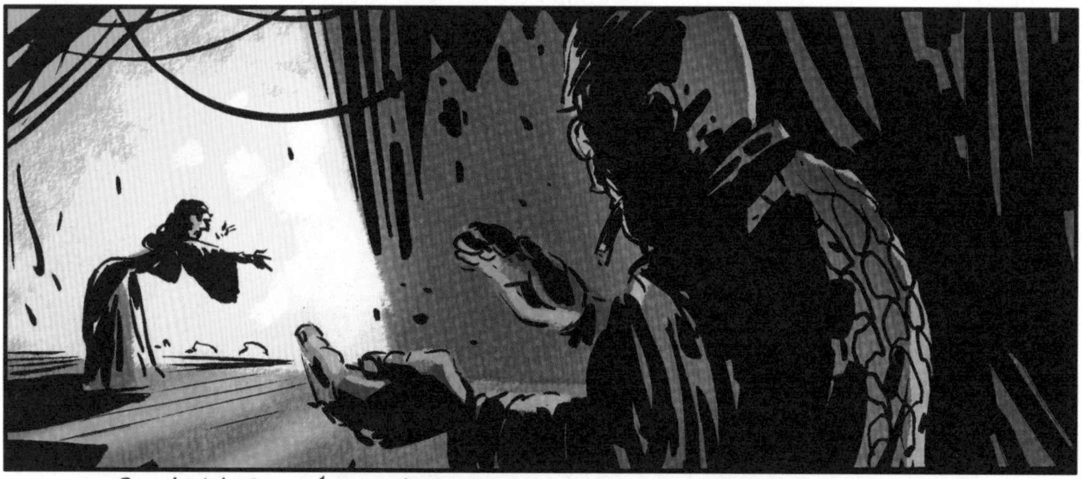

A ROMANTIC NOTION TO BE SURE... AND SHE ROMANCED
IT RIGHT INTO THE HEART OF THE PRODUCER.
FOR A MOMENT.

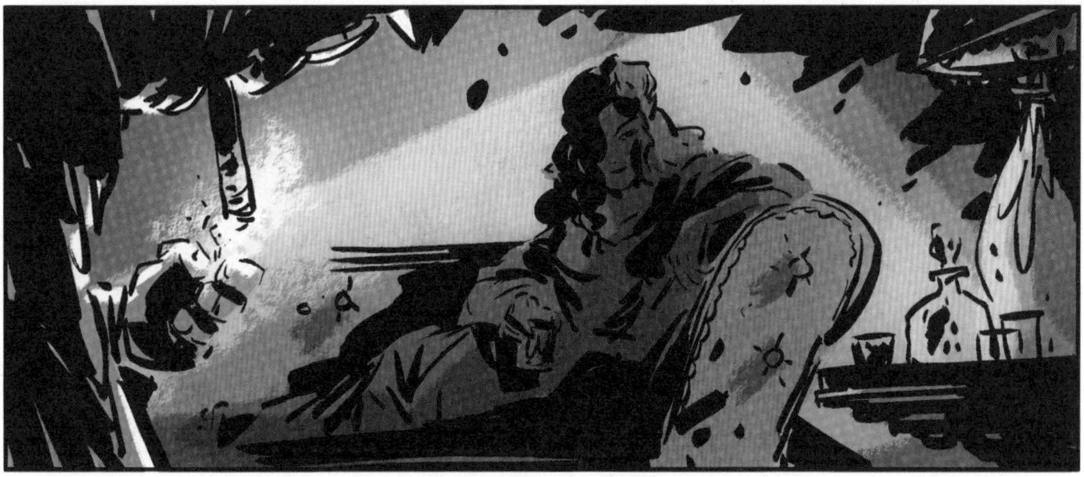

WITH HIS BUDGET... HIS CREW... SHE KNEW SHE COULD ZOOM-IN AND WIPE OUT CINEMA FROM THE CASTING COUCH...

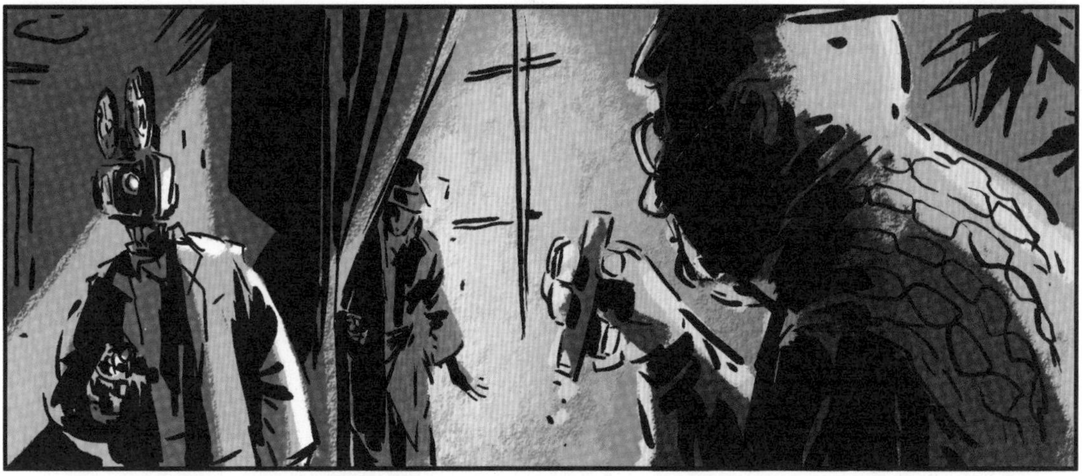

...LEAVING LIVE THEATER AS THE ONLY GAME IN TOWN, WITH HER CENTER-STAGE!

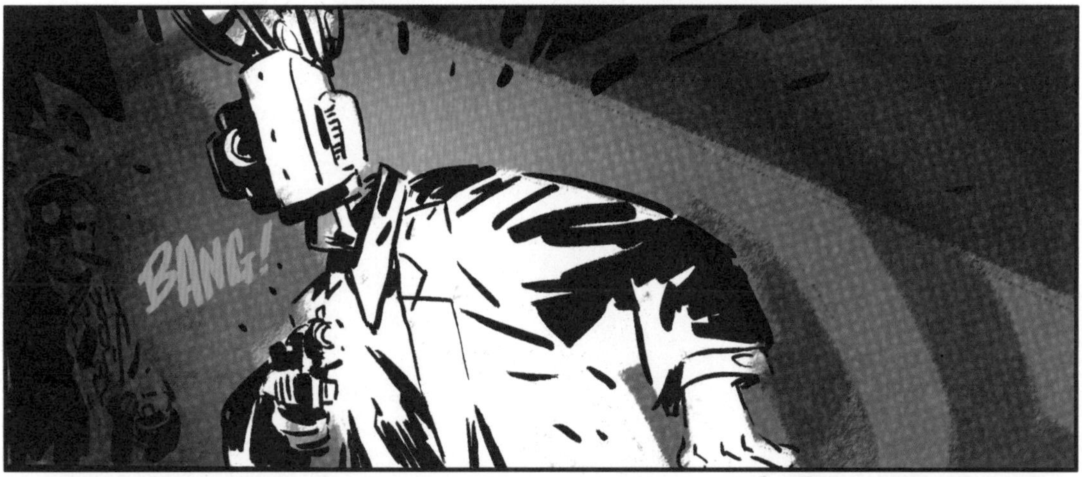
BANG!

AND THAT, MOVIE FANS, WOULD LEAVE ALL OF THEM SCHLEPS LIKE THE PROJECTIONIST OUT OF A JOB--OR WORSE!

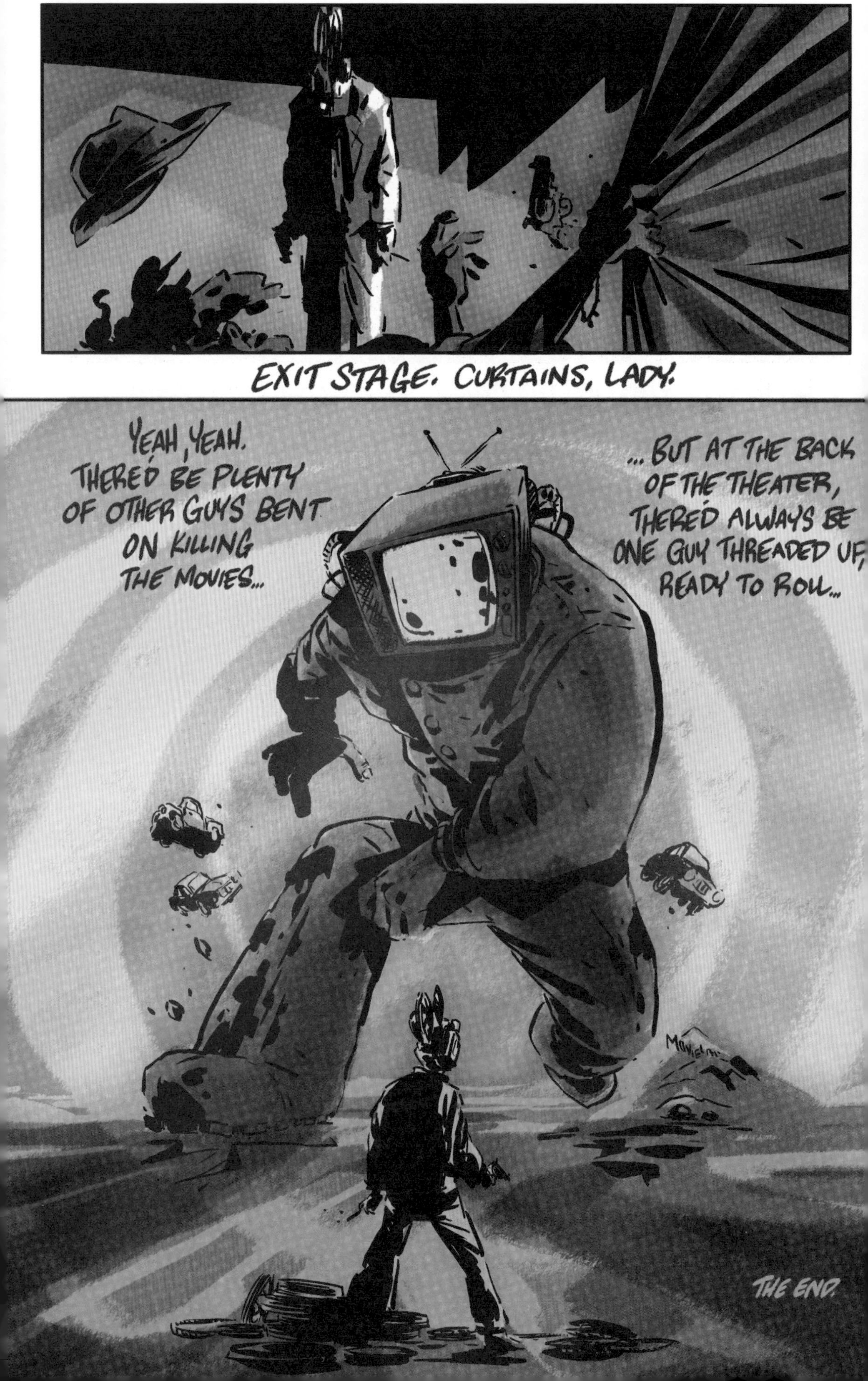
EXIT STAGE. CURTAINS, LADY.
YEAH, YEAH. THERE'D BE PLENTY OF OTHER GUYS BENT ON KILLING THE MOVIES...
... BUT AT THE BACK OF THE THEATER, THERE'D ALWAYS BE ONE GUY THREADED UP, READY TO ROLL...
THE END.

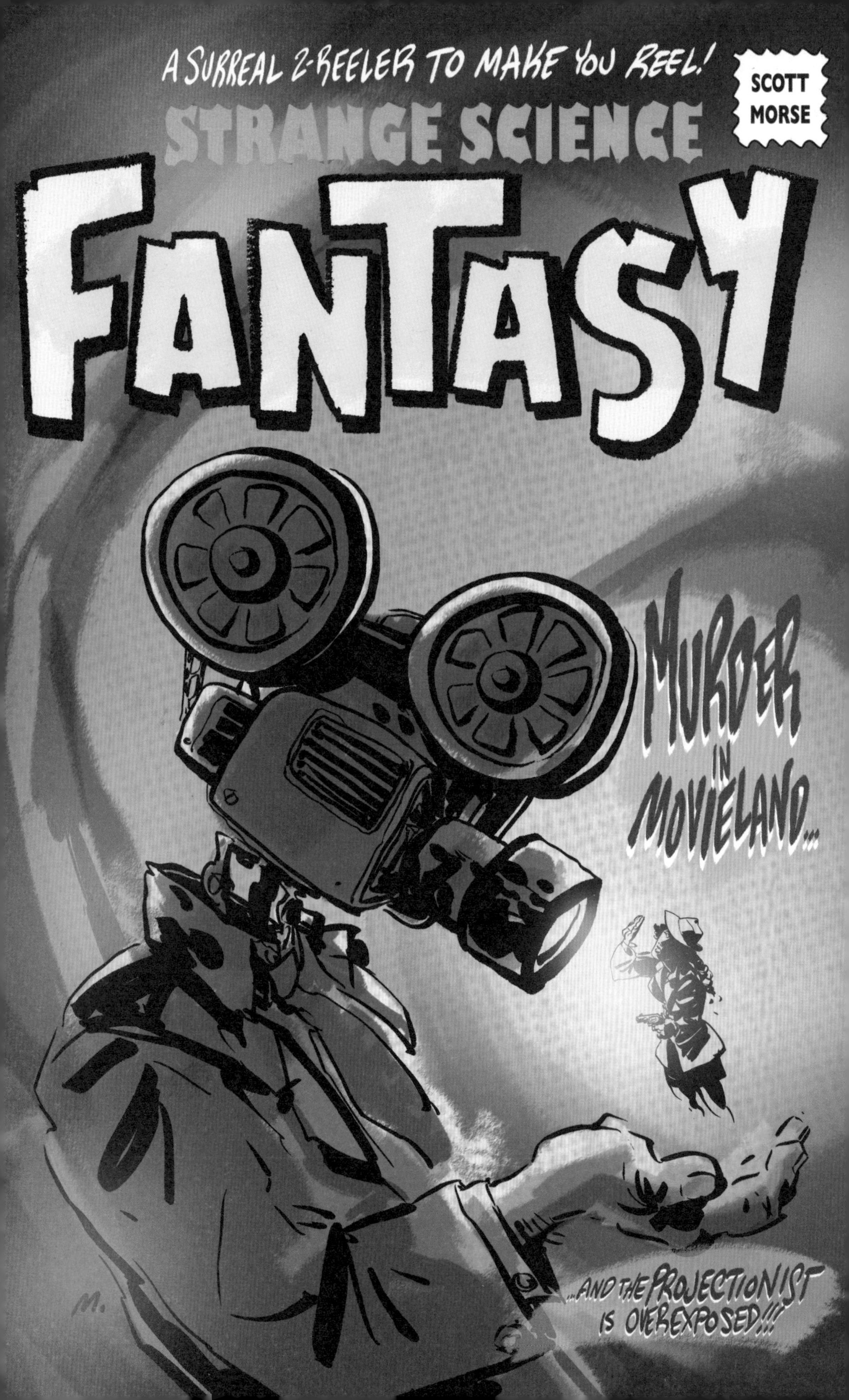
A SURREAL 2-REELER TO MAKE YOU REEL!
SCOTT MORSE
STRANGE SCIENCE
FANTASY
MURDER IN MOVIELAND...
...AND THE PROJECTIONIST IS OVEREXPOSED!!!
M.

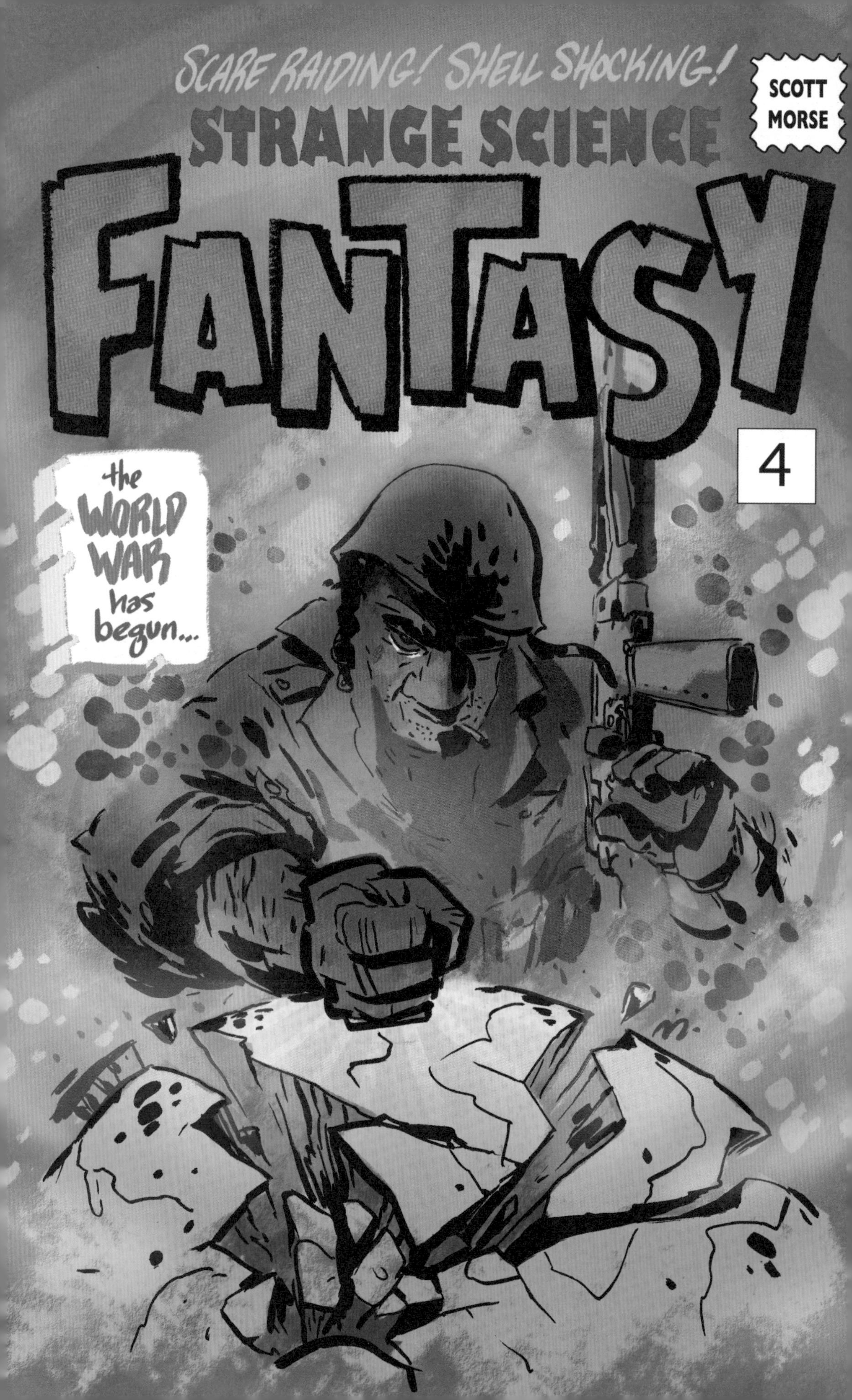
SCARE RAIDING! SHELL SHOCKING!
SCOTT MORSE
STRANGE SCIENCE
FANTASY
4
the WORLD WAR has begun...

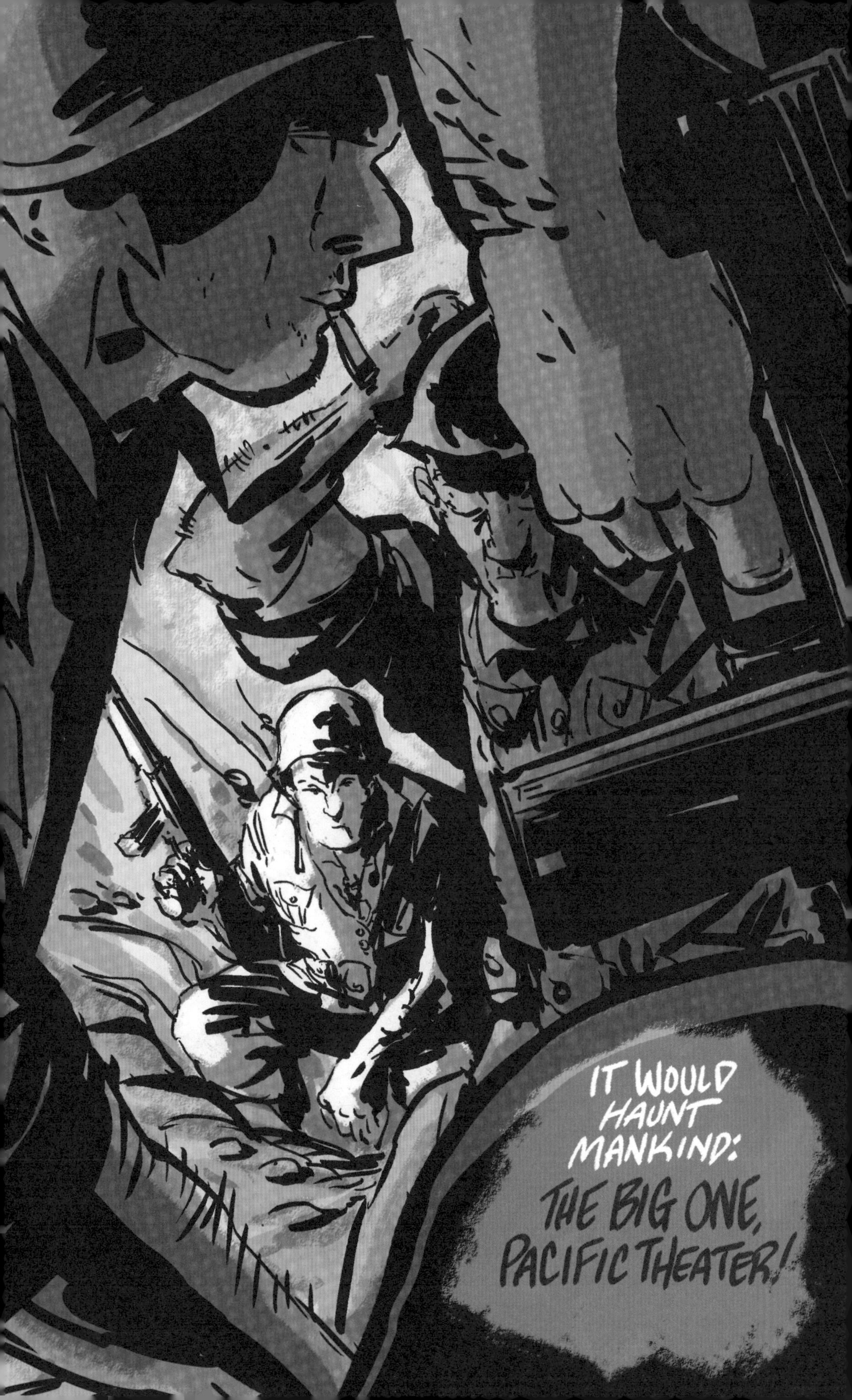
IT WOULD HAUNT MANKIND:
THE BIG ONE, PACIFIC THEATER!

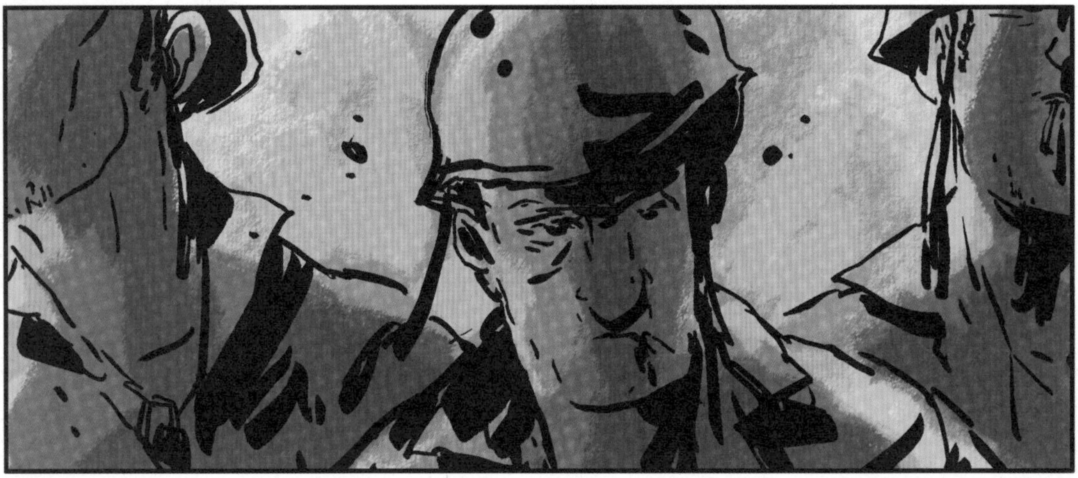

THAT SNEAK ATTACK ON PEARL MEANT THEY HAD TO SACK UP AND SHIP OUT.

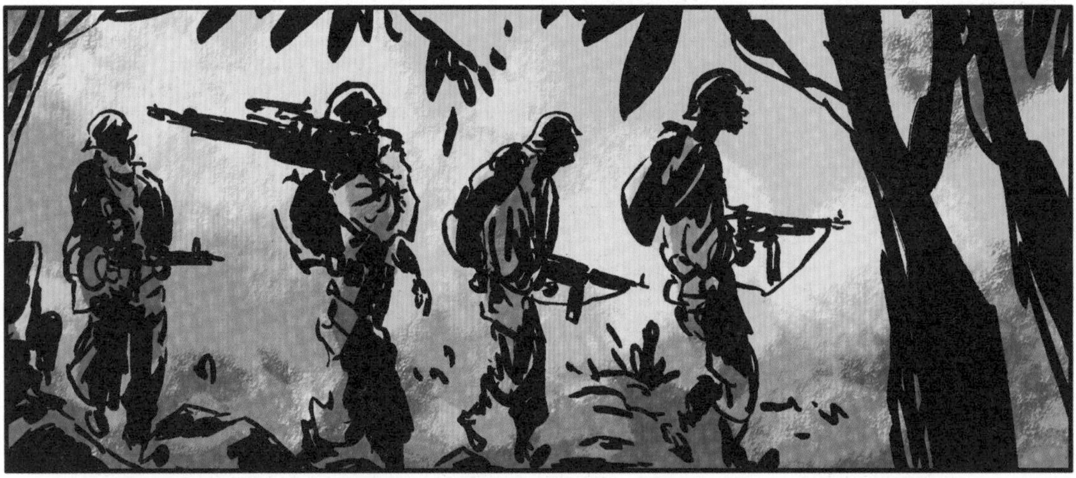

THOSE GYRENES HAD IT TOUGH IN THE ISLAND PITS OF MOISTURE AND MISERY!

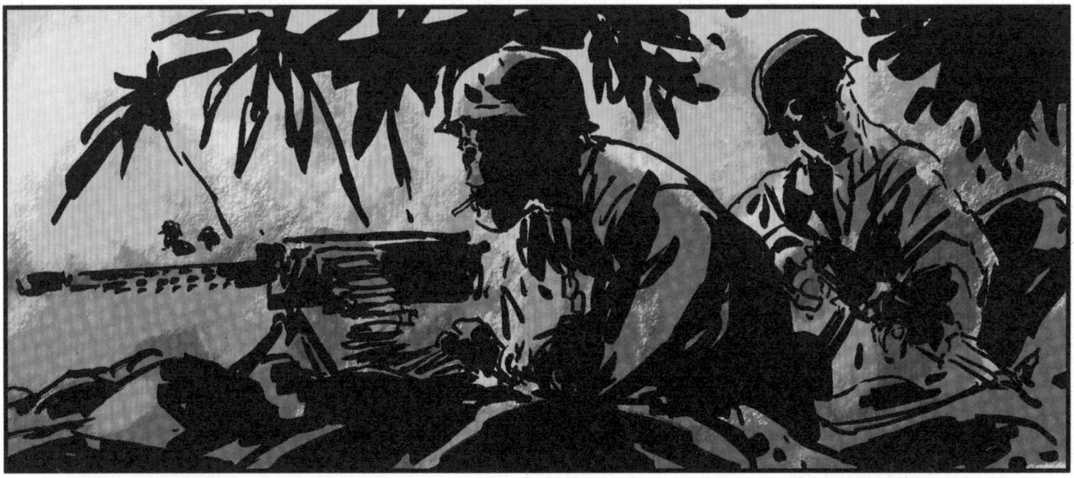

JUNGLE ROT. MALARIA. NO WATER.

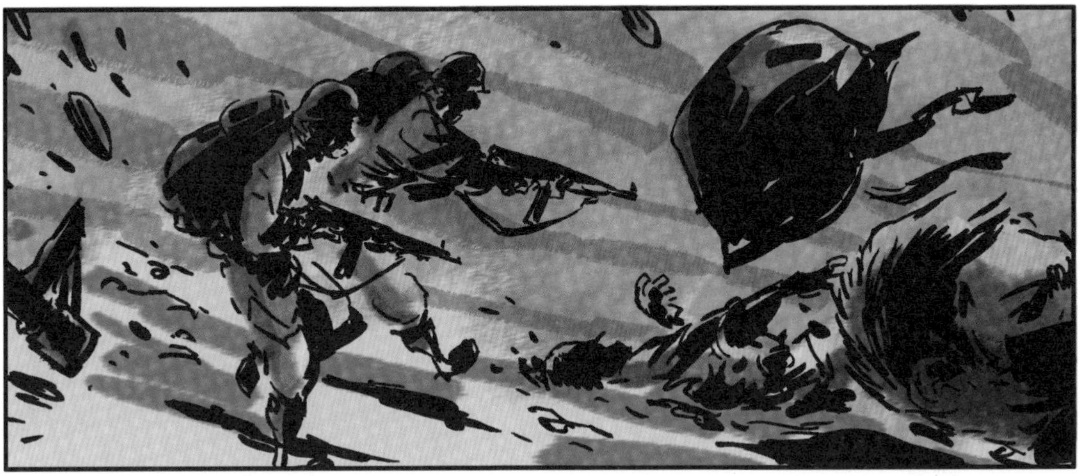

NO SUPPLIES. NO BOOZE, EVEN.

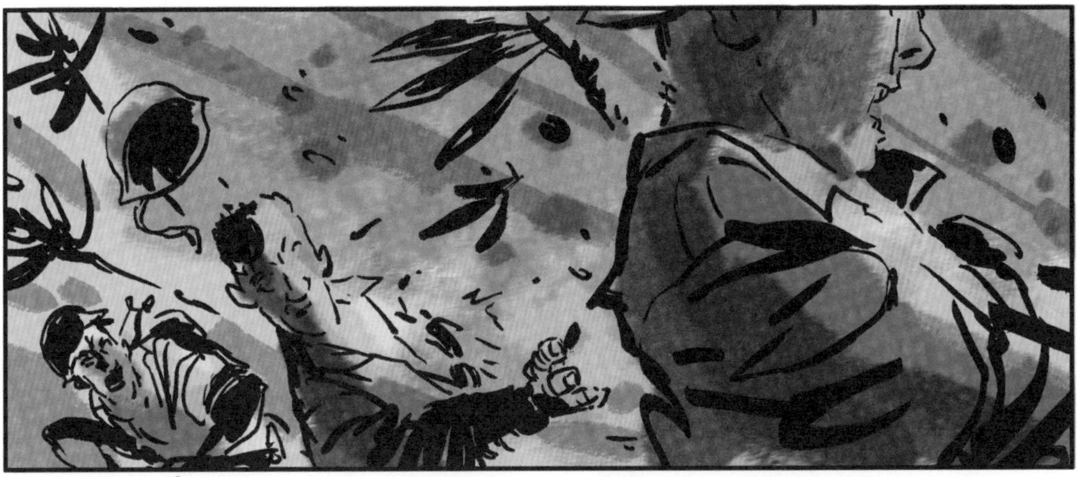

NO GIRLS. ALL RIGHT, A FEW NURSES, BUT
NEVER WHERE THEY COULD DO YOU ANY GOOD.

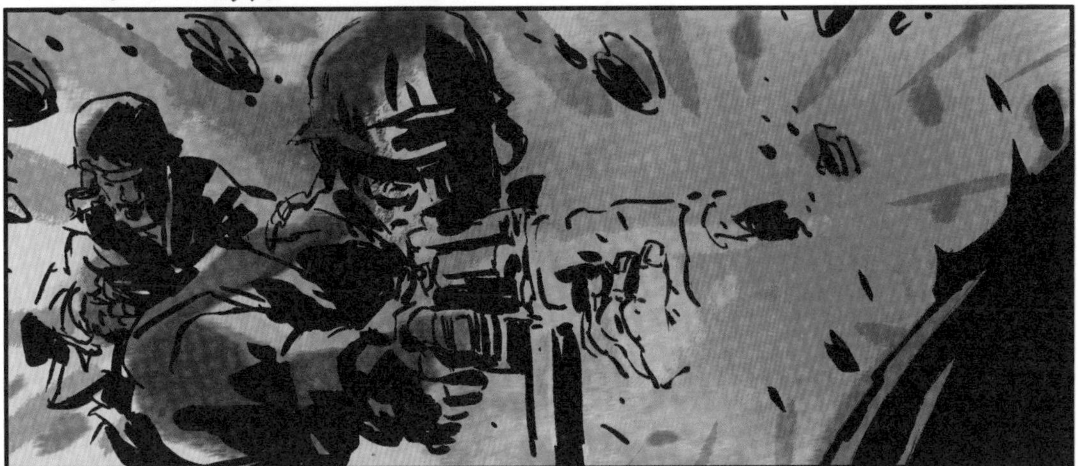

YOU HAD TO LOVE YOUR COUNTRY TO FIGHT IN THAT MUD.
YOU HAD TO LOVE YOUR FREE WORLD.

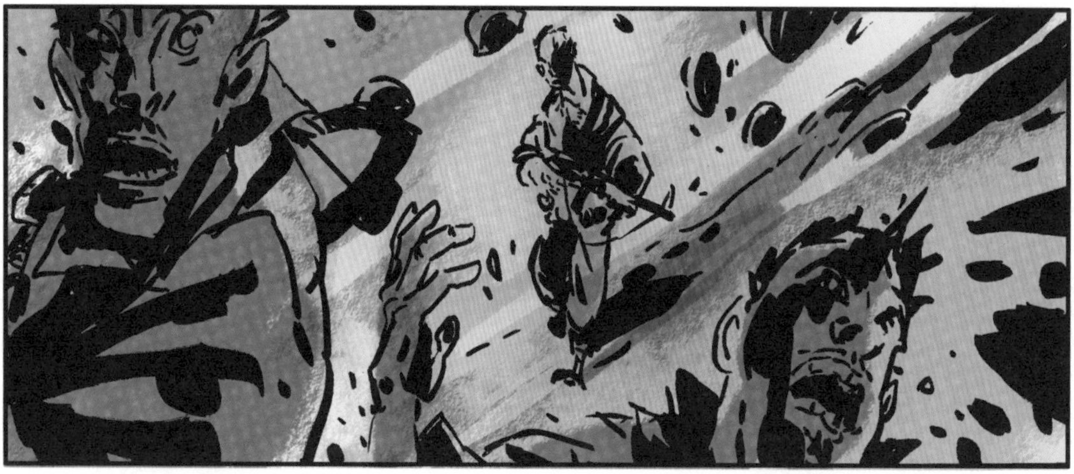

PRIVATE CHARLIE GANTIC WAS JUST POURING OVER WITH LOVE.

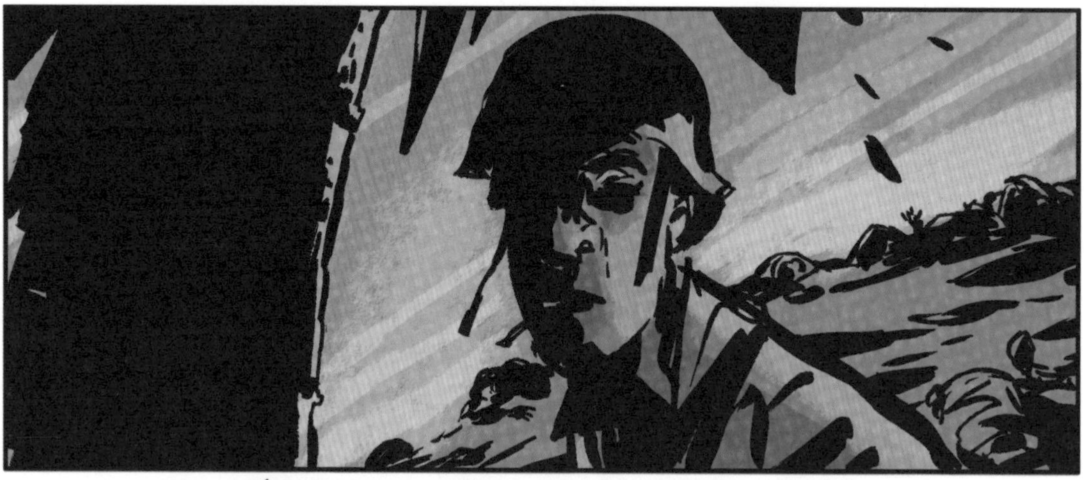

HE LOVED HIS WAY INTO THE ONLY SURVIVING SPOT IN HIS UNIT.

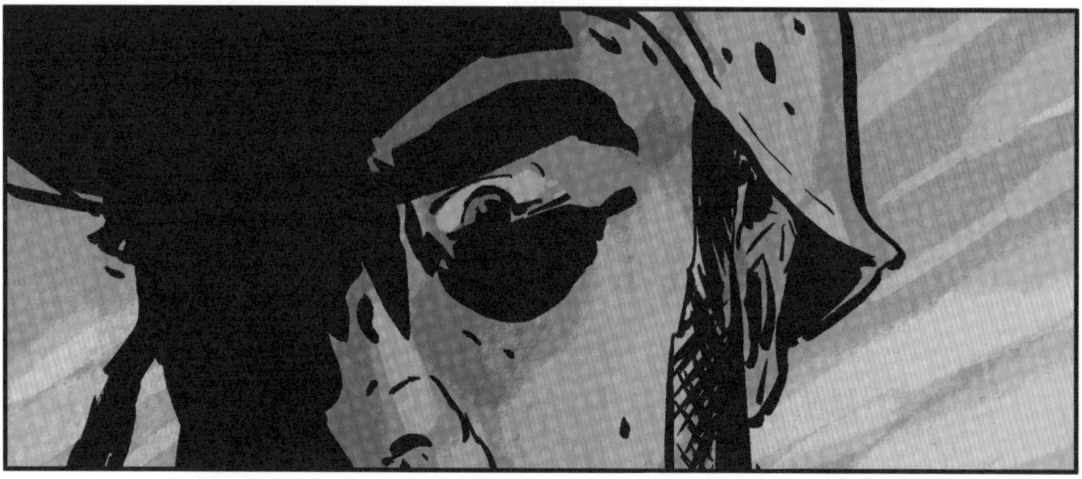

LAST MAN STANDING.

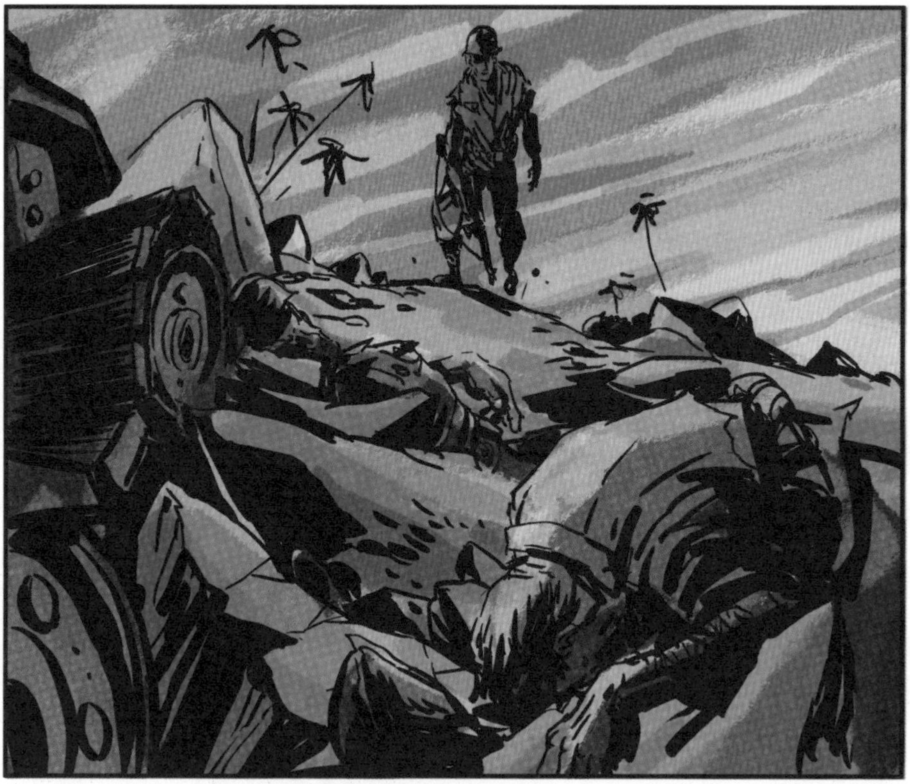

SOMEHOW UNTOUCHED.
UNTOUCHABLE.

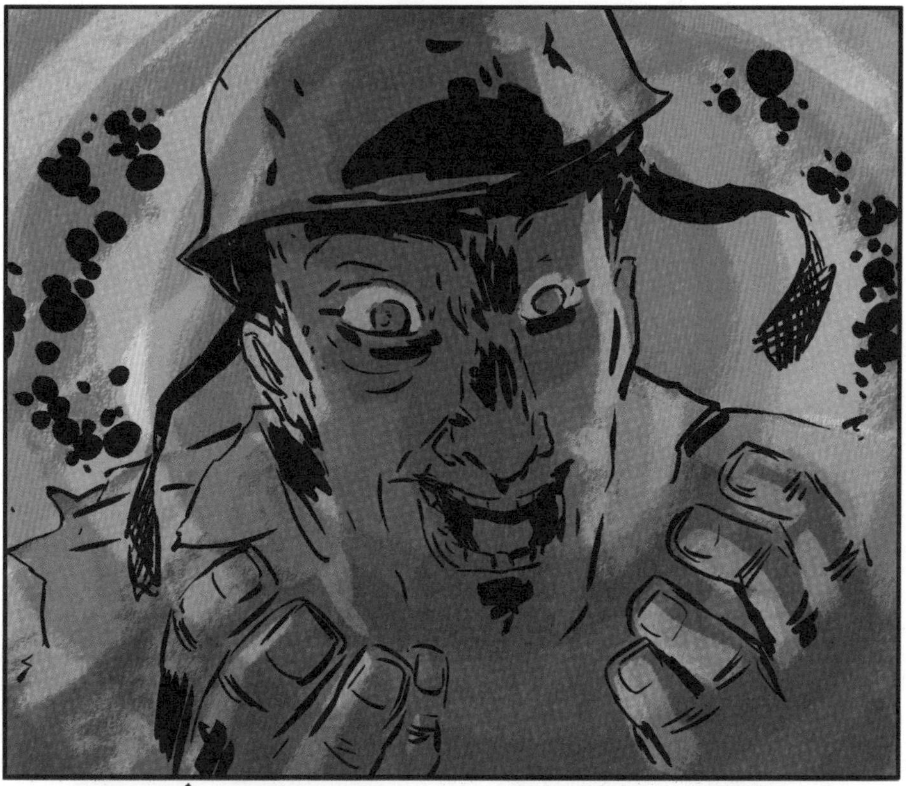

THAT'S ENOUGH TO GIVE A FELLA
DELUSIONS OF GRANDEUR.

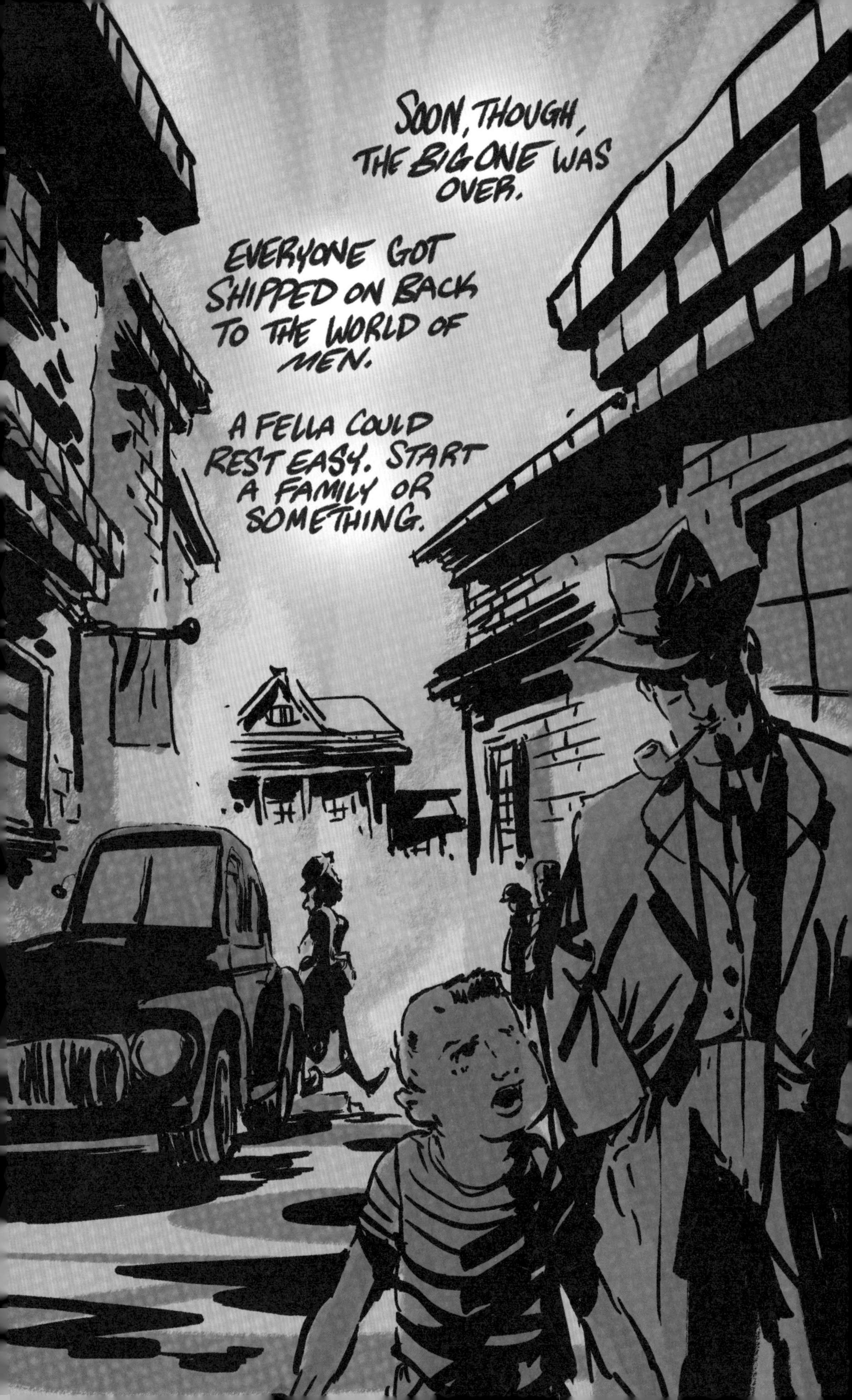
SOON, THOUGH, THE BIG ONE WAS OVER.
EVERYONE GOT SHIPPED ON BACK TO THE WORLD OF MEN.
A FELLA COULD REST EASY. START A FAMILY OR SOMETHING.

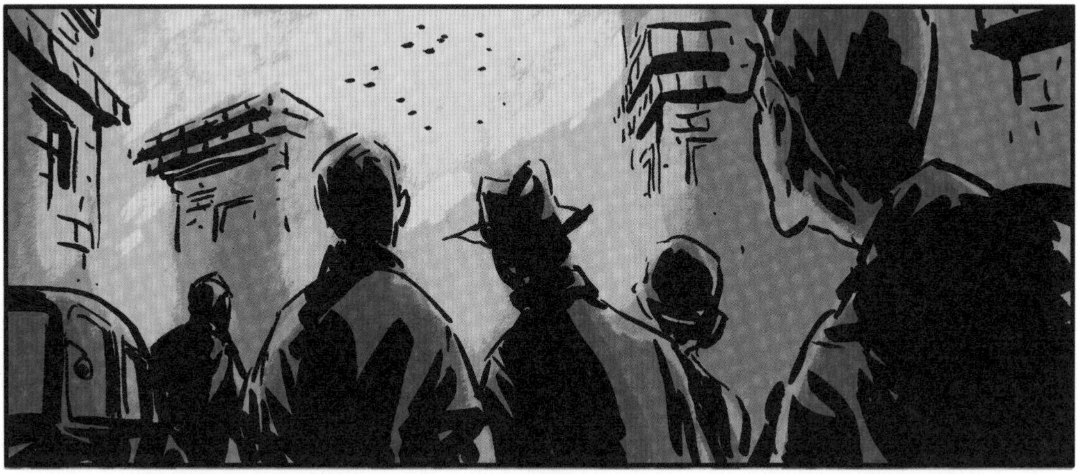

WOULDN'T YOU KNOW IT, THOUGH?
THERE'S NO REST FOR MAN. DON'T KID YERSELF.

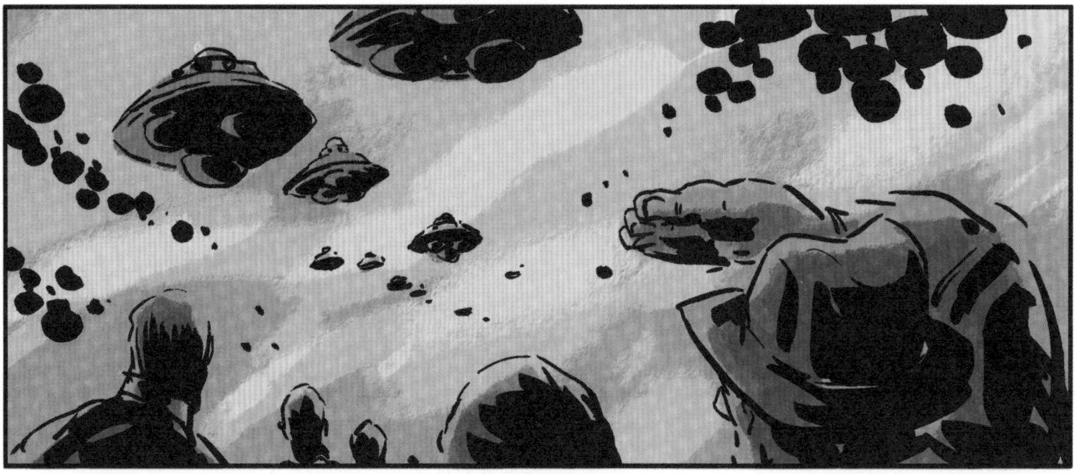

YOU CAN GO AN' SURVIVE A MAN'S WAR,
BUT THAT DOESN'T MEAN SOME OTHER GUY OUT THERE...

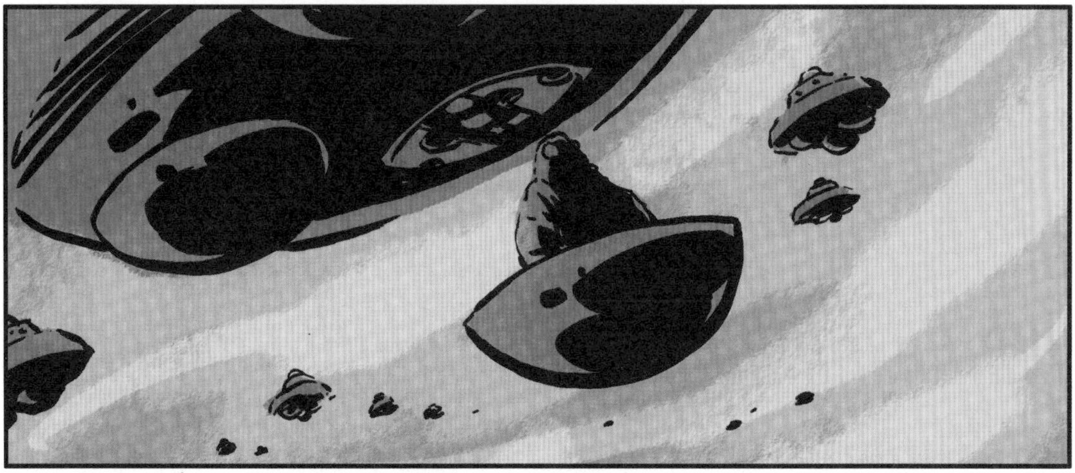

...AIN'T GONNA NOT COME ALONG AN' START
PLAYIN' GOD?

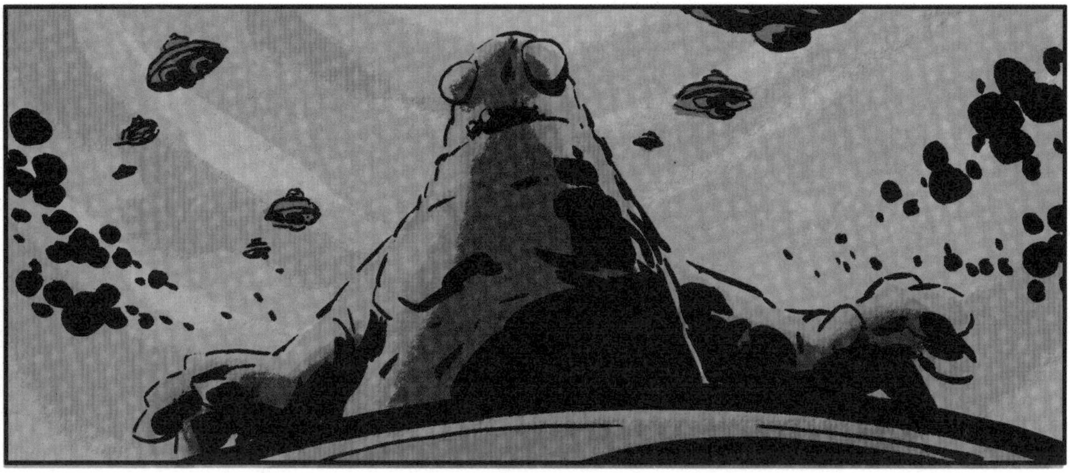

THEIR DISH-SHAPED SHIPS OF WONDER FILLED THE SKY LIKE THE CHURCHBELLS OF TOMORROW.

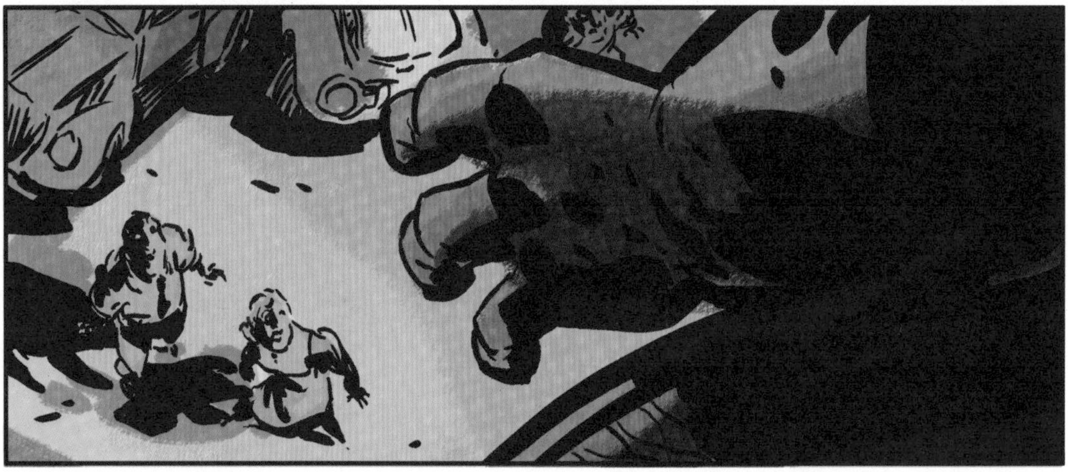

THE RINGING CLARION CALL OF *CHANGE* SOUNDED LOUDLY AS THEIR OTHERWORLDLY ENGINES WHINED.

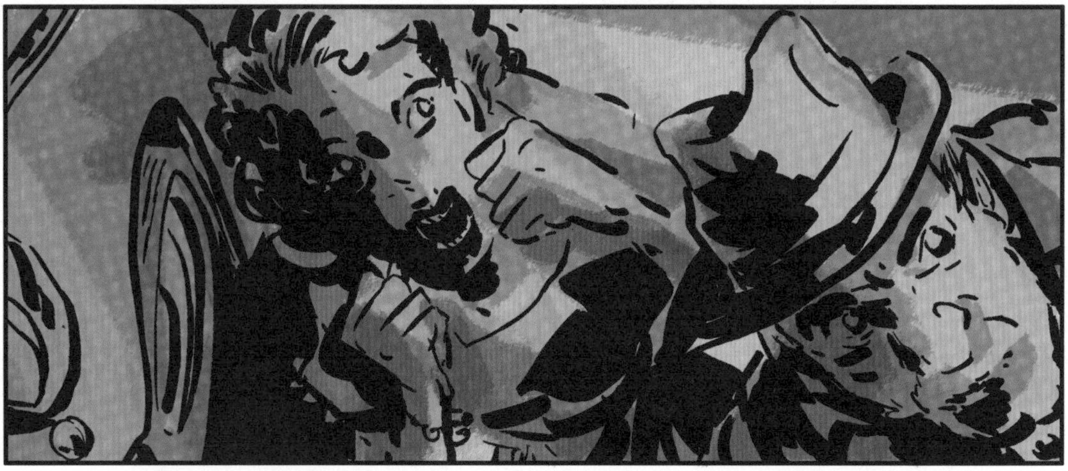

BUT THESE WERE CHERUBS OF DESTRUCTION. THERE WOULD BE NO CHORUS OF HALLELUJAH.

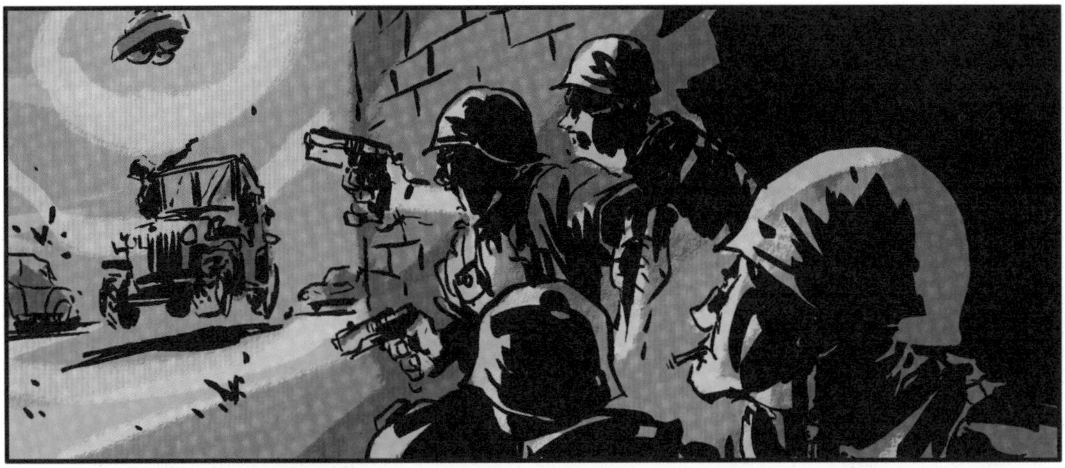

OUR FIGHTING FORCES OFFERED THEM AN HONEST AND FIRM RECEPTION OF DEFIANCE.

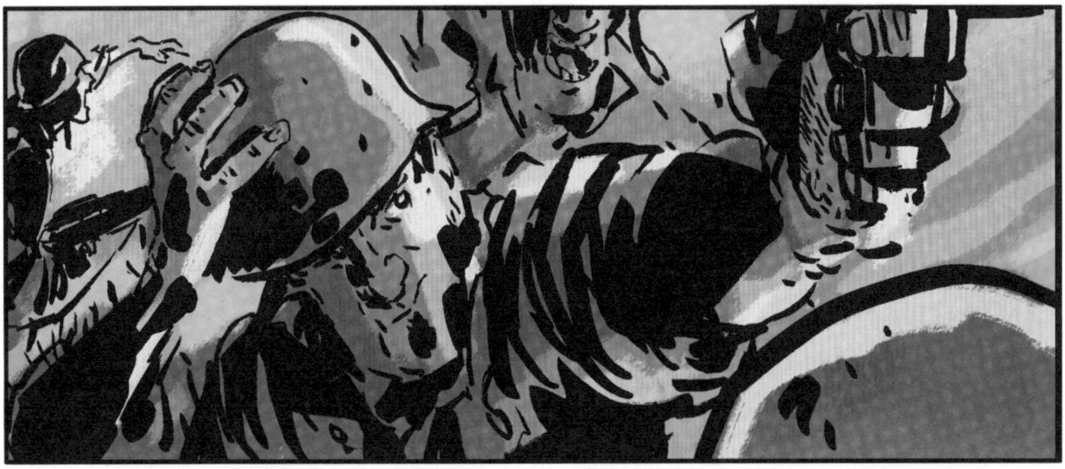

OUR BOYS KNEW JUST WHICH HAND TO EXTEND IN A SALUTATION OF SCORN.

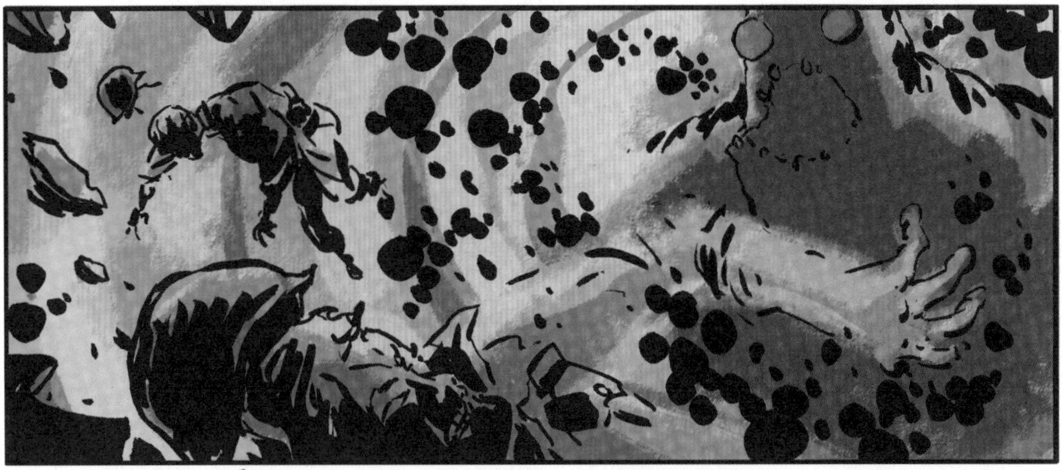

OUR GOOD MANNERS WERE MET FIERCELY BY THEIR EXHALATIONS OF ALIEN CARNAGE.

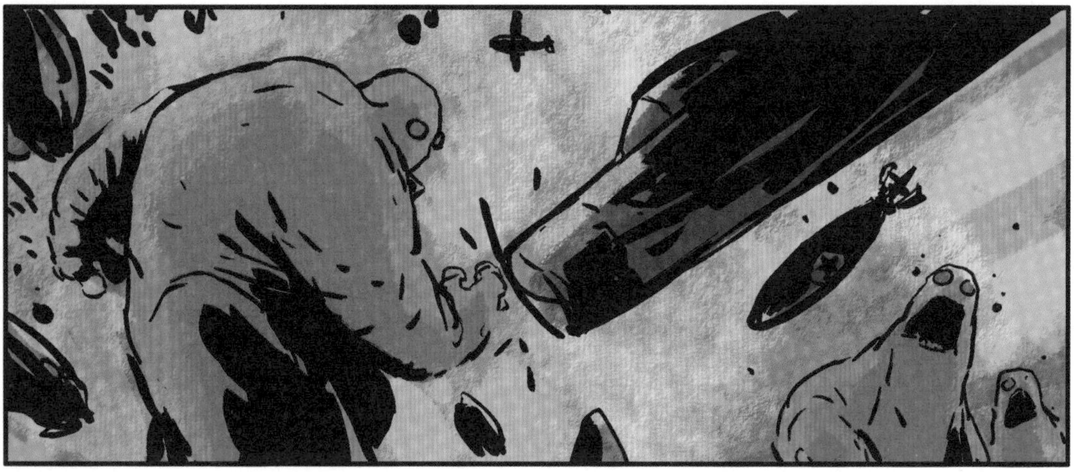

WE OFFERED THEM A STUNNING DISPLAY OF TERROR FROM ABOVE...

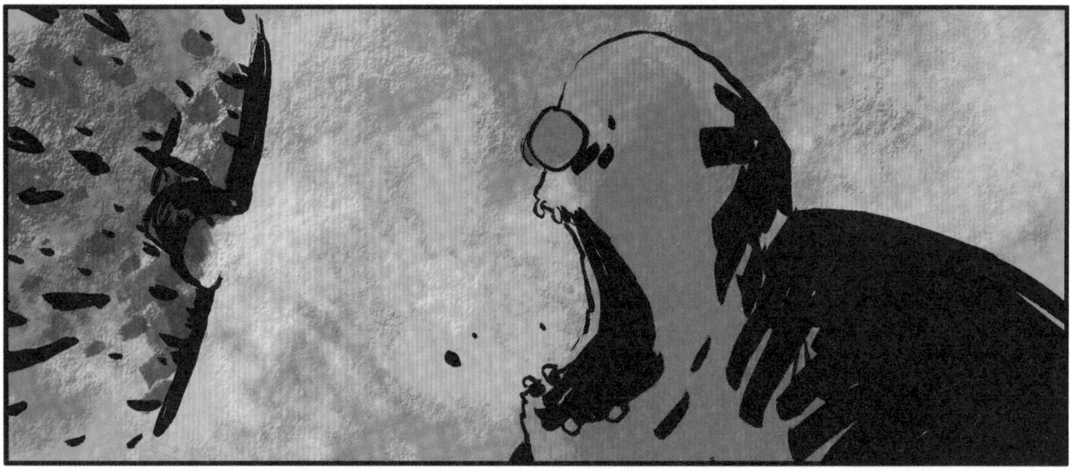

THE WIND FROM THEIR OTHERWORLDLY LUNGS CRUSHED US WITH A HARSH BREATH OF REALITY:

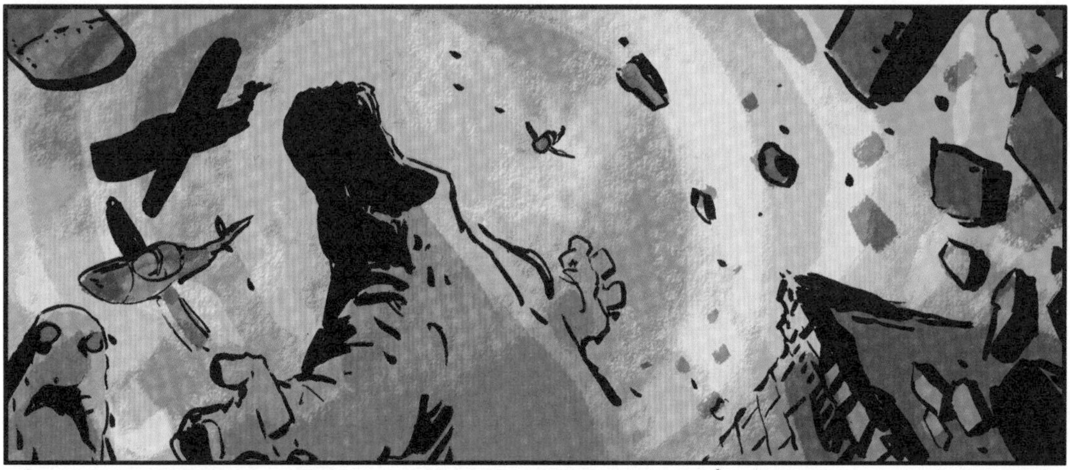

THESE CREATURES MEANT TO *BREAK* US. OUR TOWNS. OUR WORLD. OUR SPIRIT.

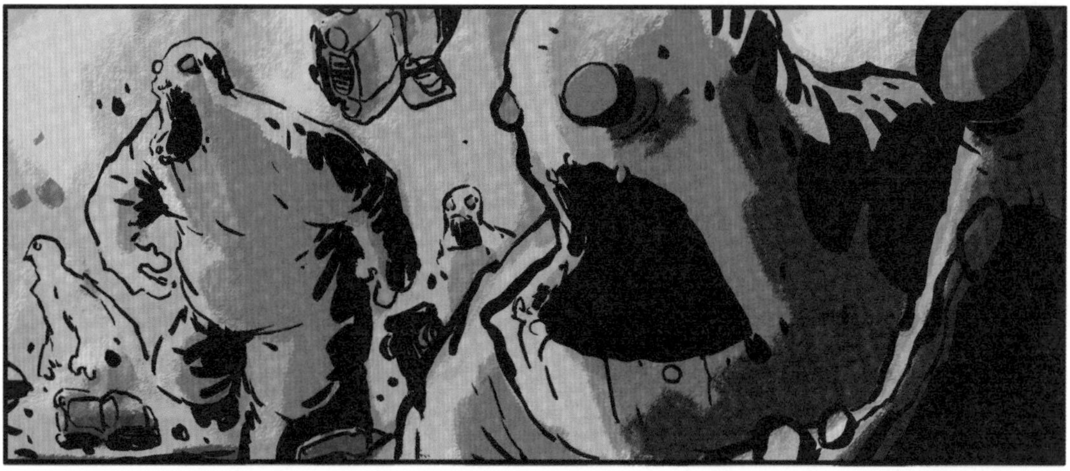

IT IS A HARSH FACT TO LEARN THAT THERE MIGHT TRULY BE A BIGGER HAND AT WORK IN THE UNIVERSE.

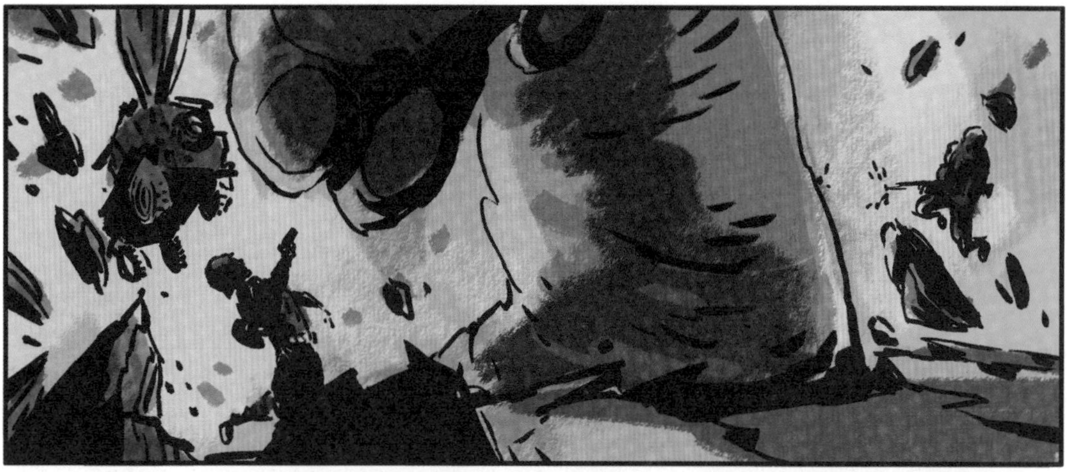

STILL MORE HARSH IS THE PAIN INFLICTED BY THAT HAND'S SWIFT WORK.

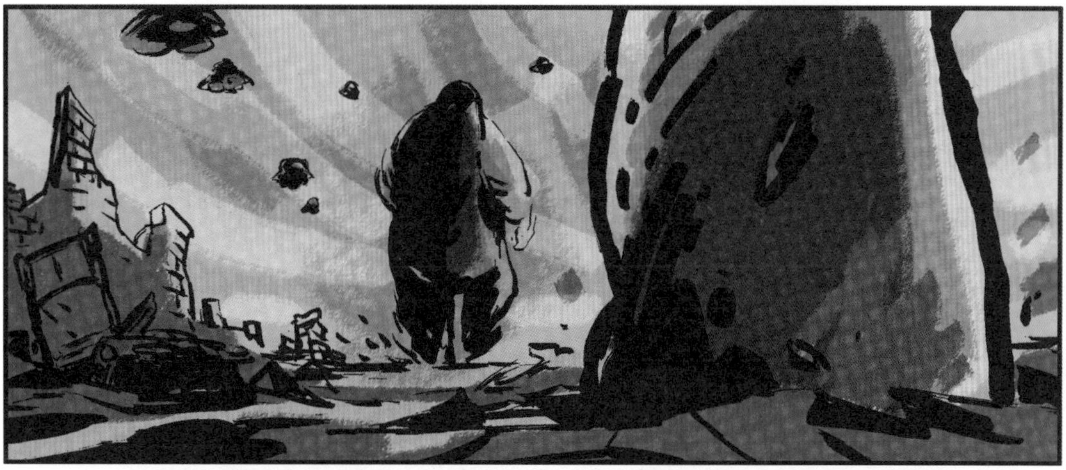

IF THIS BE THE SOUND OF HARMONY, THEN MAN MIGHT BE BETTER OFF WITH THE EARS OF THE DEAF.

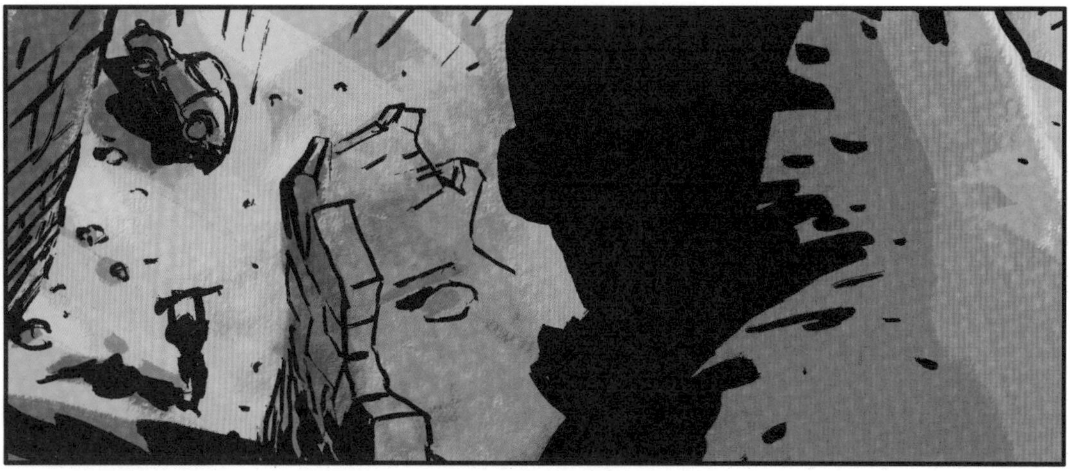

OUR BOYS HAD BEEN ON HOPELESS GROUND BEFORE.
THEY'D DONE THIS VERY THING, PLOWING DOWN THE FIELDS OF ENEMIES.

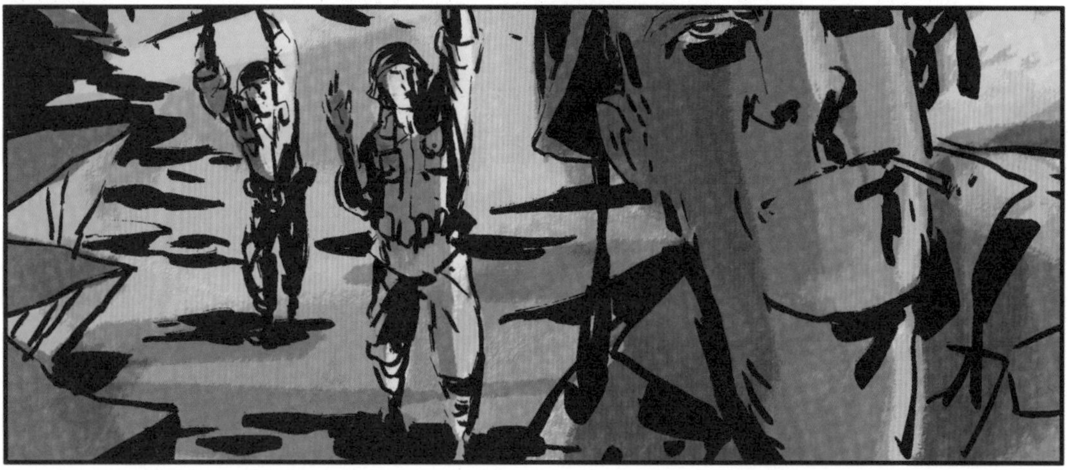

ALL IN THE NAME OF FREEDOM.

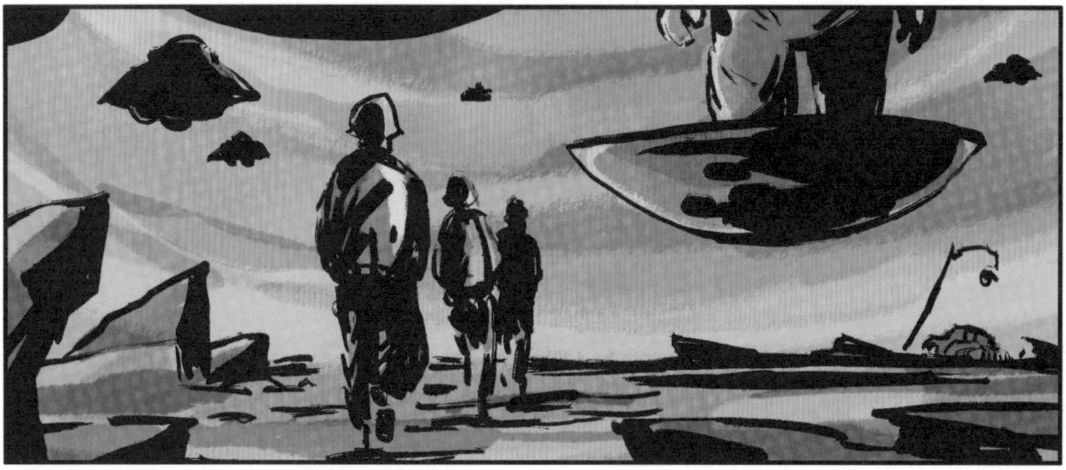

NOW, WOULD SURRENDER YIELD PEACE FOR MANKIND?

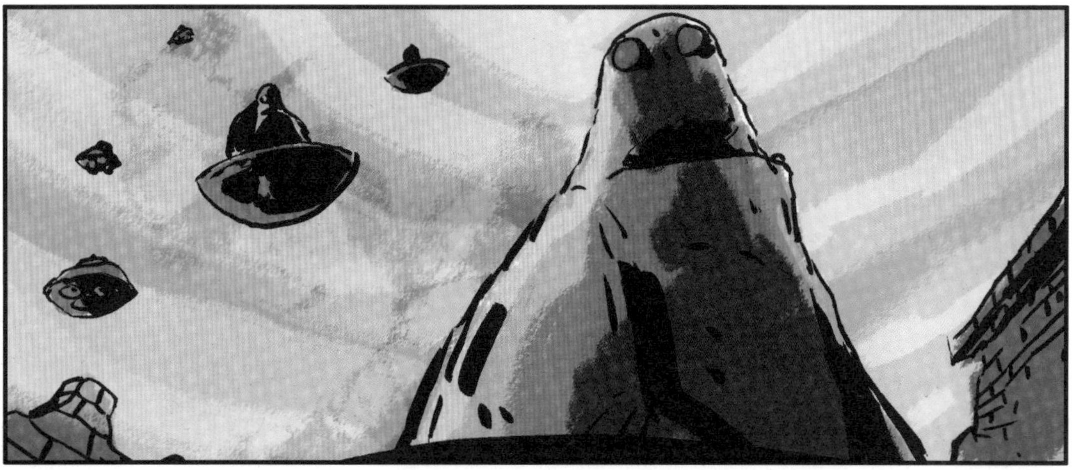

A GUTTURAL CHUCKLE RODE THE WIND.
THERE WOULD BE NO SURRENDER.

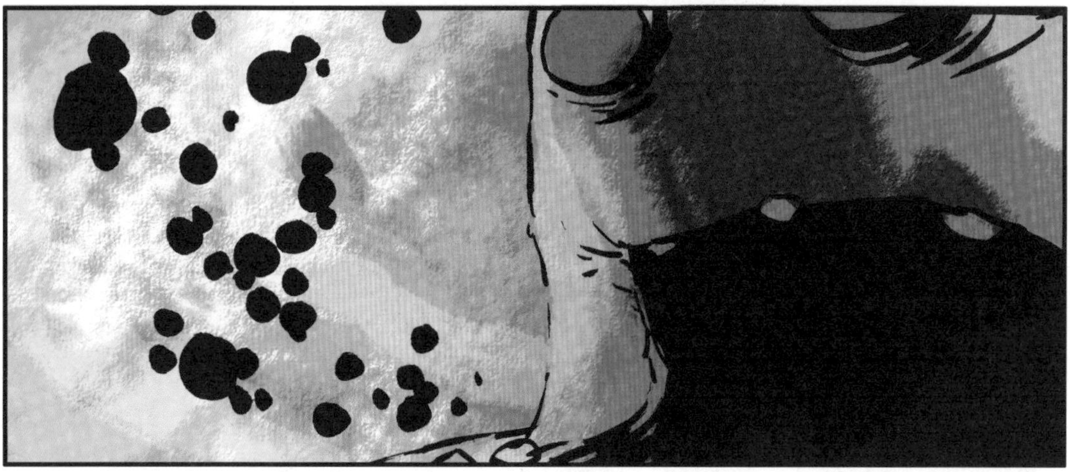

THEY HAD COME TO BLOW THE DUST OF MANKIND
FROM THE FACE OF HISTORY.

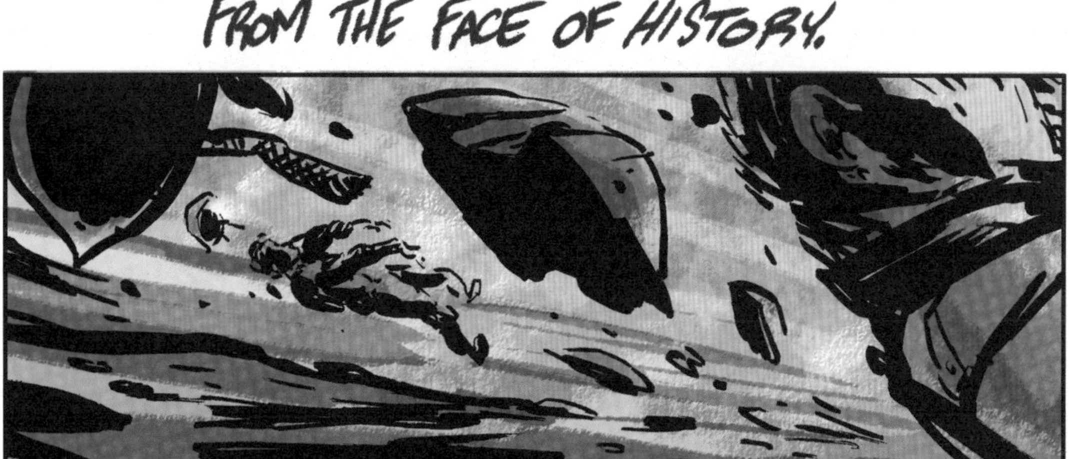

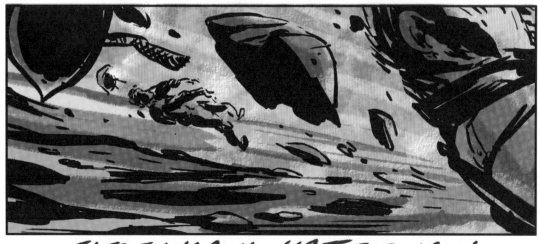

THERE WAS NO USE FOR MAN.

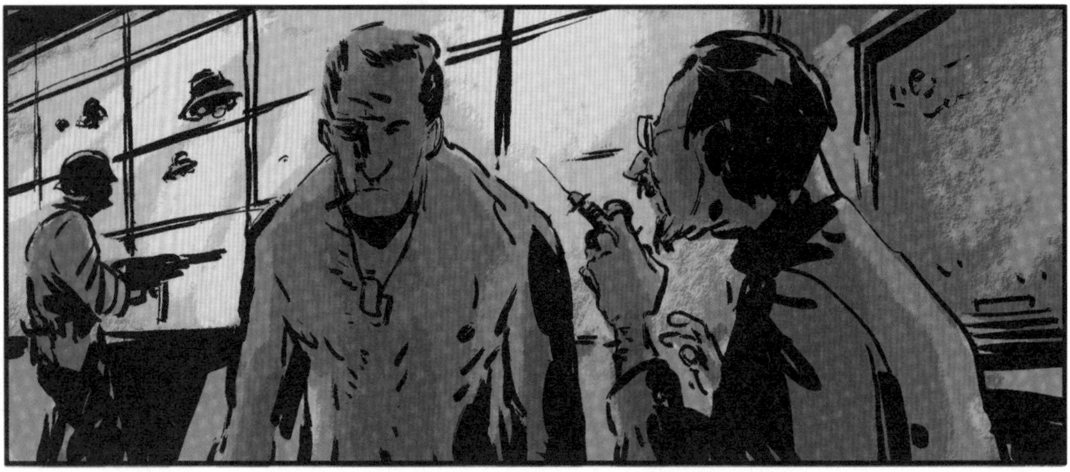

IT WAS FOR MORE THAN FREEDOM, THEN.
IT WAS FOR SURVIVAL.

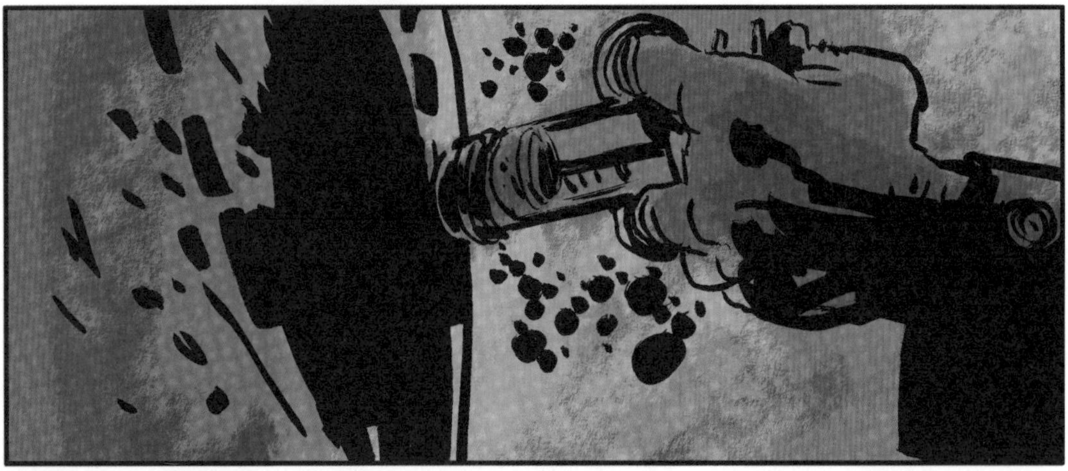

NOW THAT THE OBJECTIVE WAS CLEAR,
MAN COULD ADJUST HIS FIGHT WITH CLARITY.

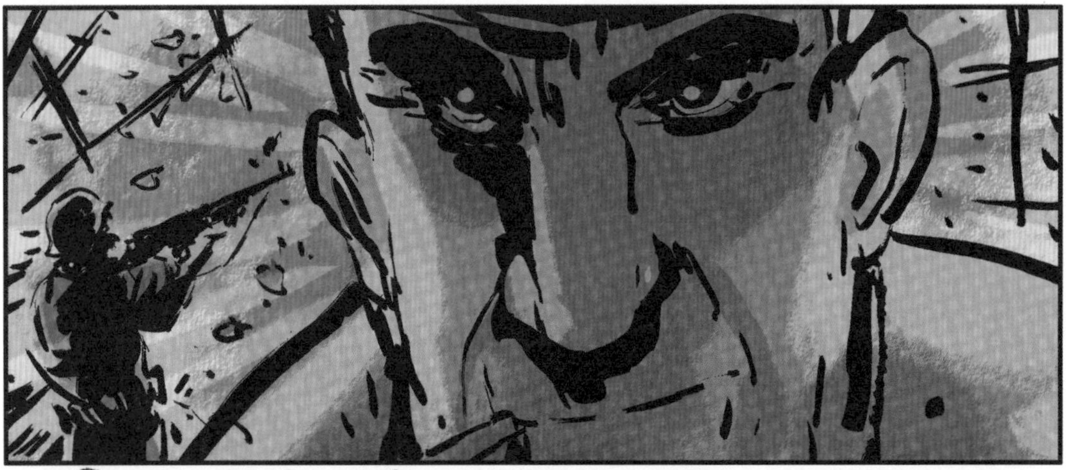

PRIVATE CHARLIE GANTIC KNEW ABOUT CLARITY.
HE'D CHEATED ALL THE GODS, REMEMBER?

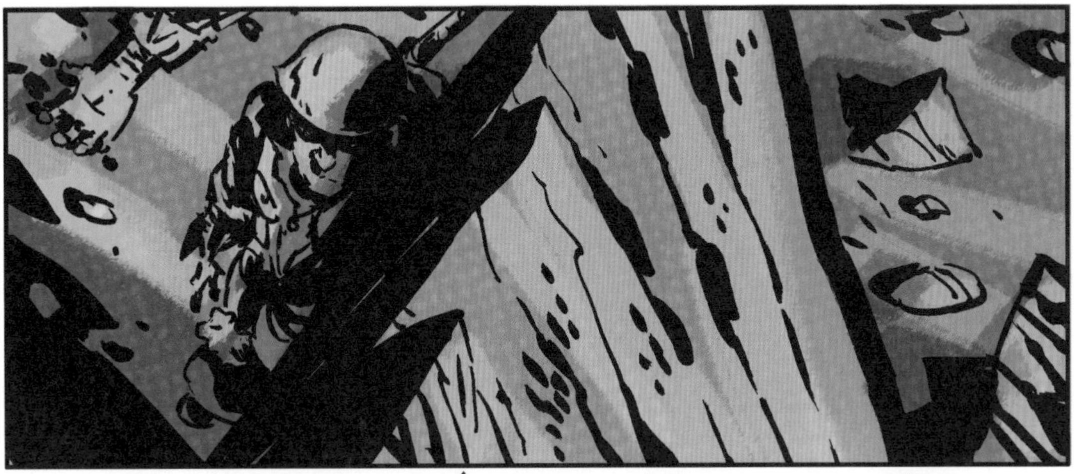

NO MATTER WHO SET FOOT IN THE EVER-LOVIN' PATH OF MAN...

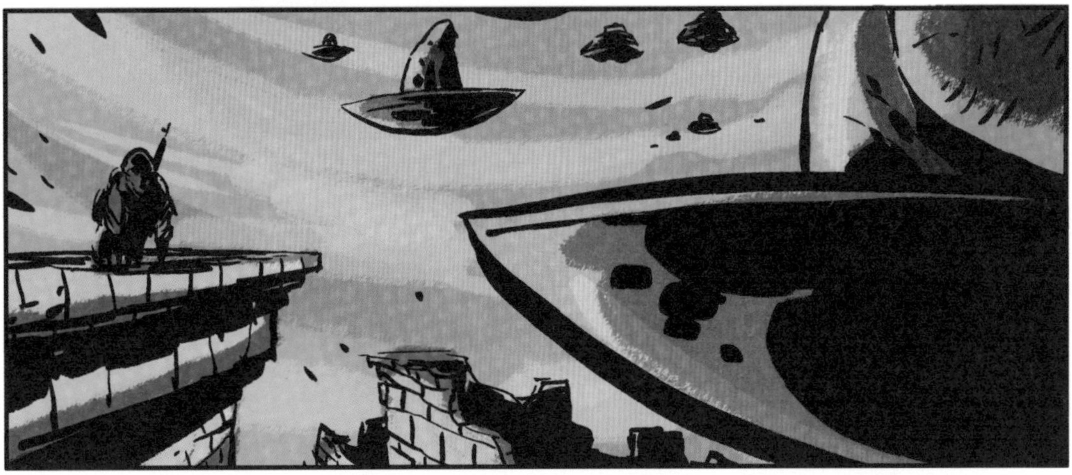

...PRIVATE CHARLIE GANTIC FIGURED HE MIGHT BE JUST THE GUY TO TRIP 'EM UP.

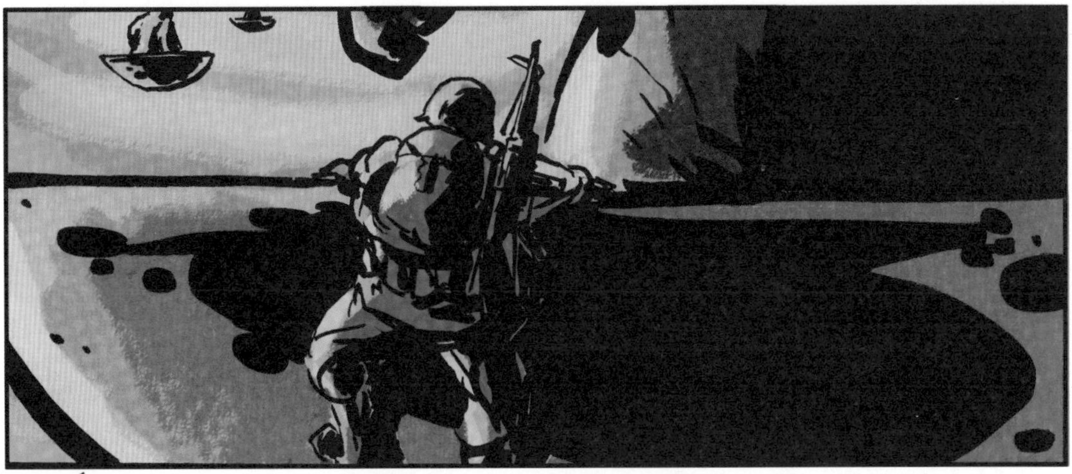

WHAT WAS ONE MORE SUICIDE MISSION TO THE GUY THAT CHEATED DEATH?

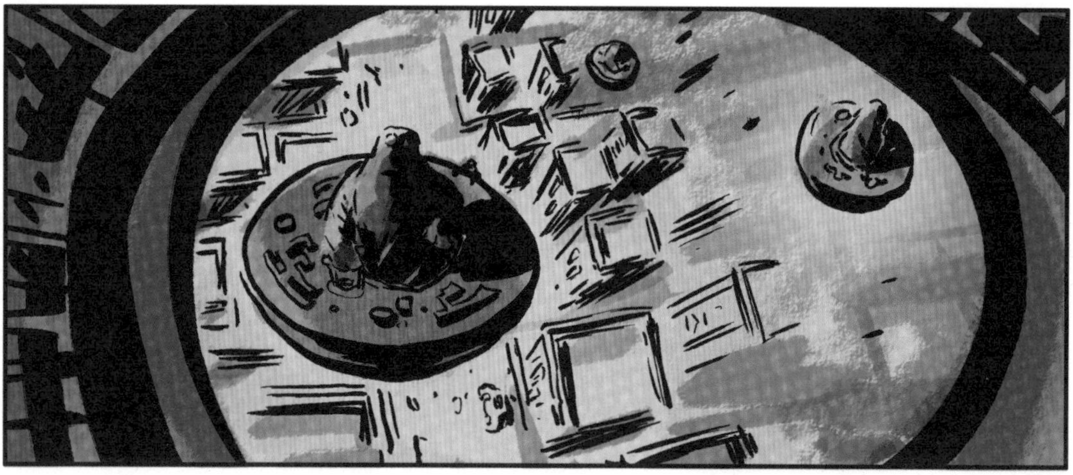

THE WAY CHARLIE FIGURED IT, EARTHMEN DIDN'T NEED TO STAY ON EARTH TO BE MEN.

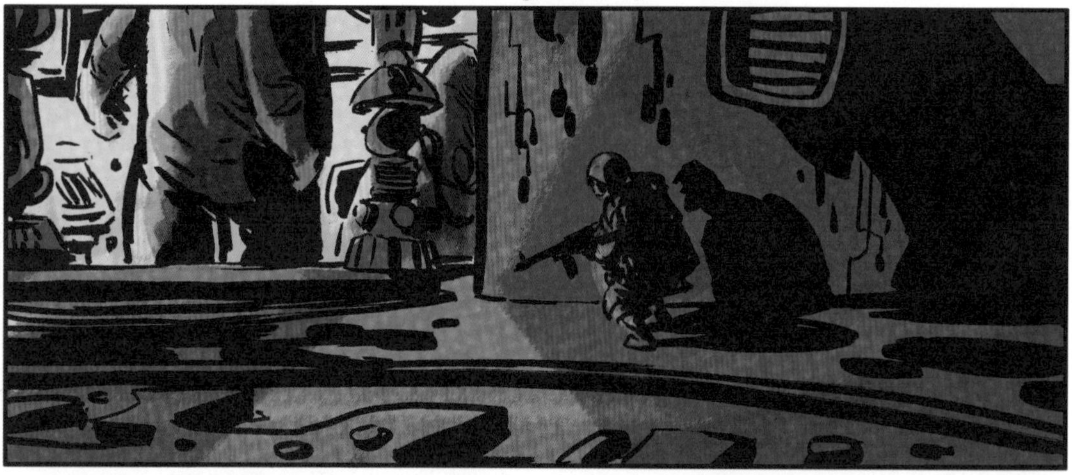

EVEN STRANGE VISITORS FROM ANOTHER PLANET NEEDED TO RE-SUPPLY.

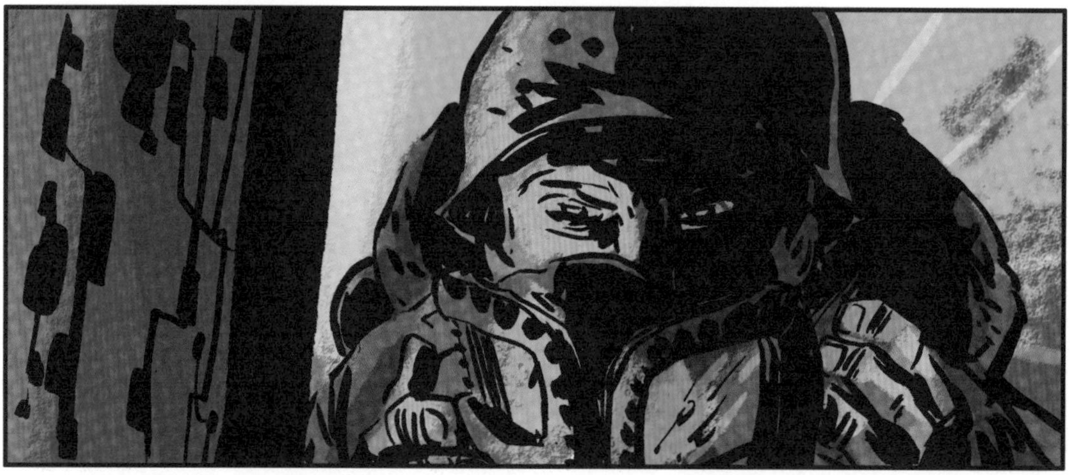

CHARLIE WOULD SHOW 'EM THAT COURAGE FLOWS STRONG THROUGH MAN'S VEINS.

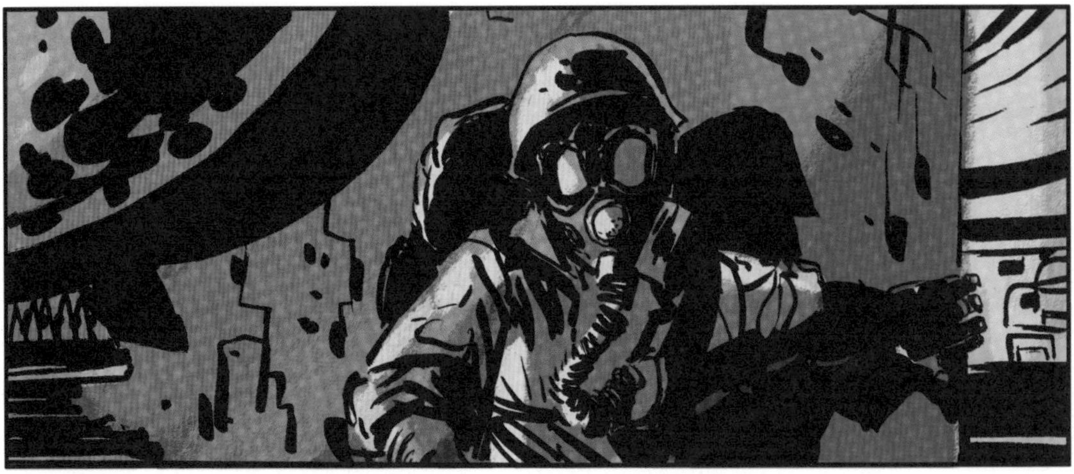

AND IN PRIVATE CHARLIE GANTIC'S VEINS, NOT JUST COURAGE.

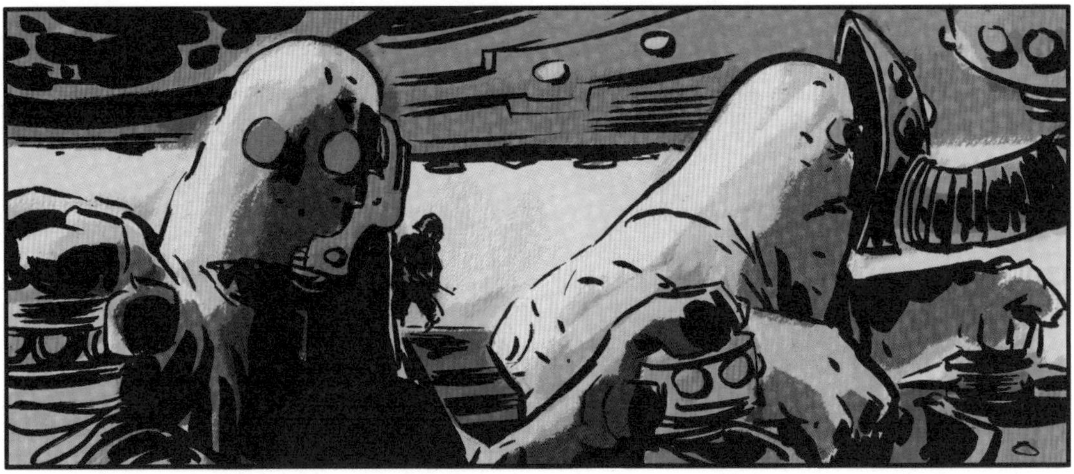

SEE, JUST LIKE CHARLIE WAS HITCHIN' A RIDE...

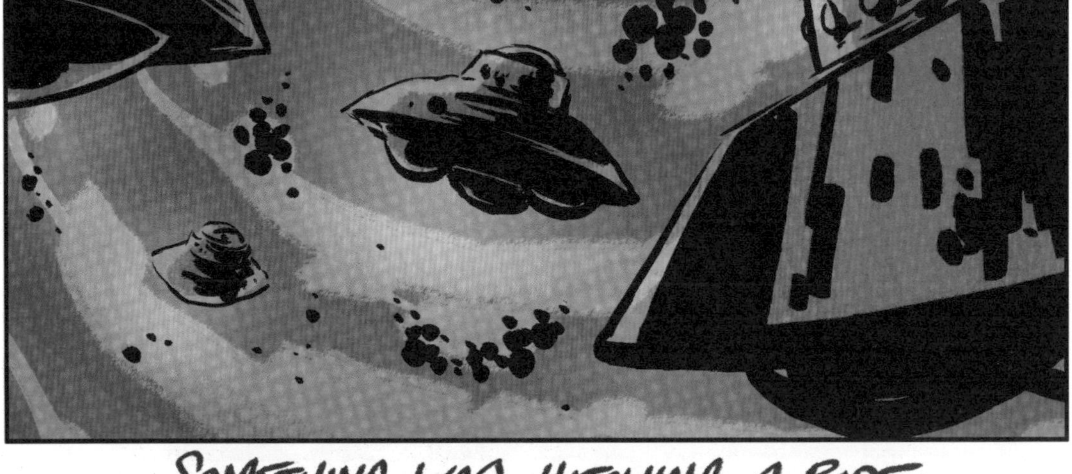

...SOMETHING WAS HITCHING A RIDE INSIDE PRIVATE CHARLIE GANTIC.

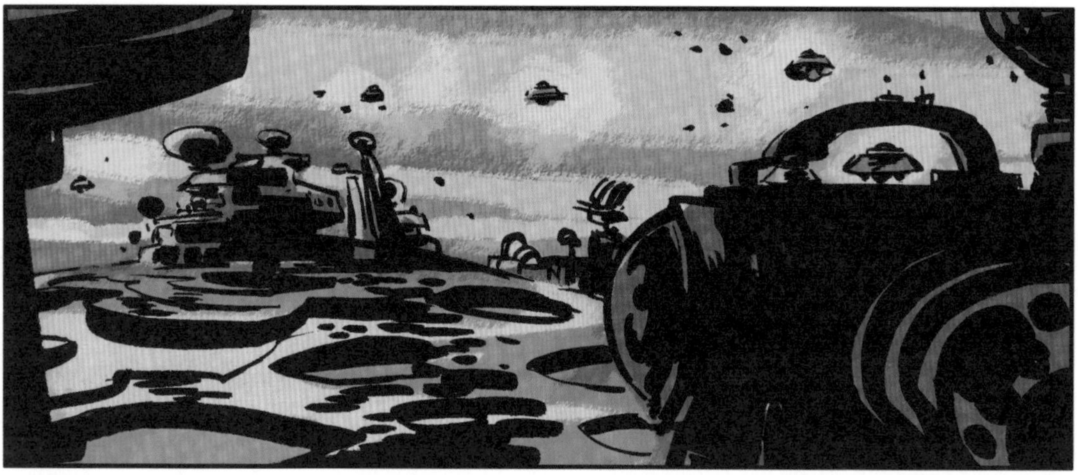

...ALL THE WAY BACK TO WHERE THE TERROR HAD BEEN BORN!

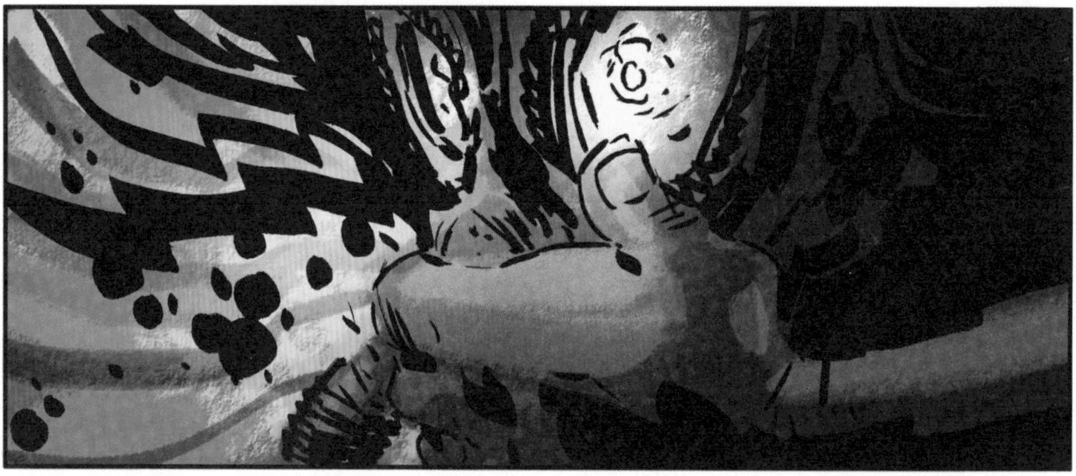

IT WAS A SURPRISE FROM THE BRIGHTEST SCIENTIFIC MINDS ON OUR PLANET.

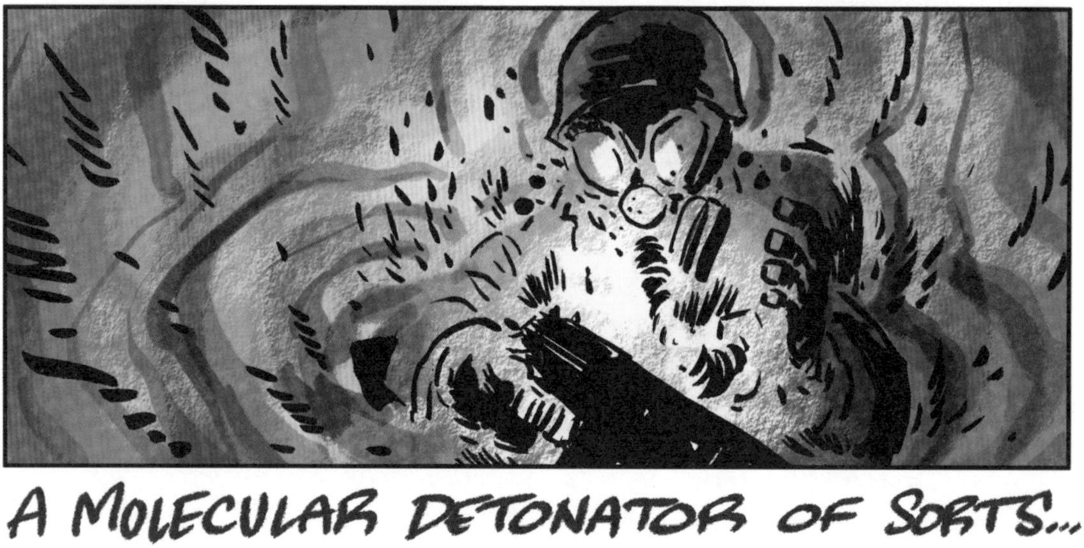

A MOLECULAR DETONATOR OF SORTS...

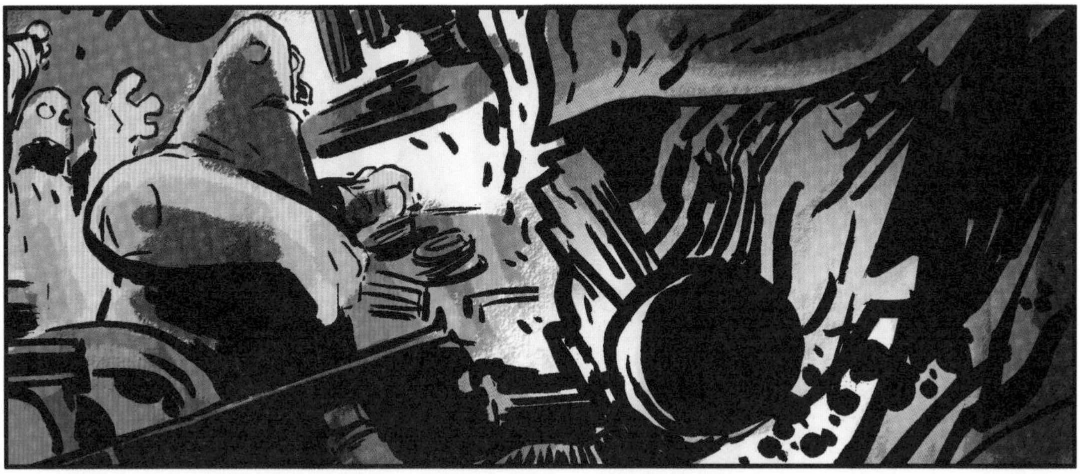

...SET TO BLOW WHEN CHARLIE SAW FIT.

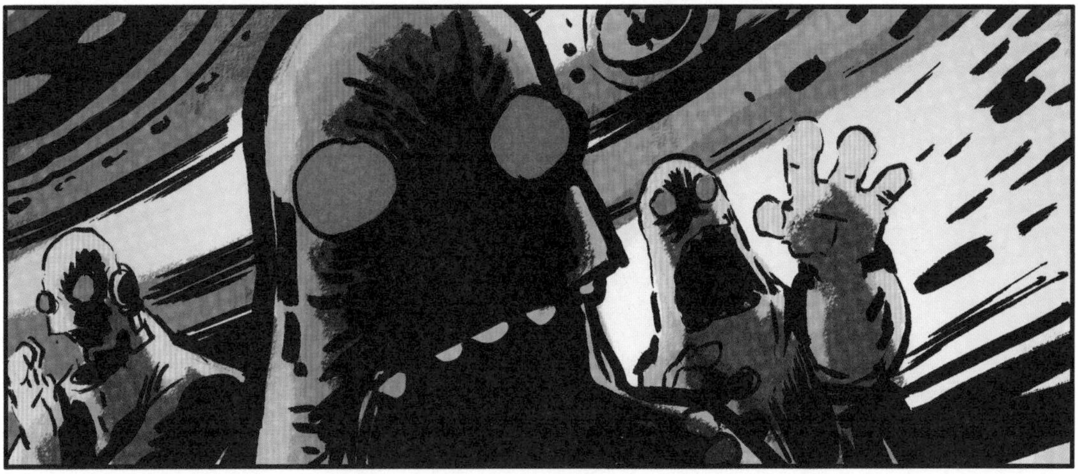

NOW, PRIVATE GANTIC HAD STORMED BEACHES BEFORE...

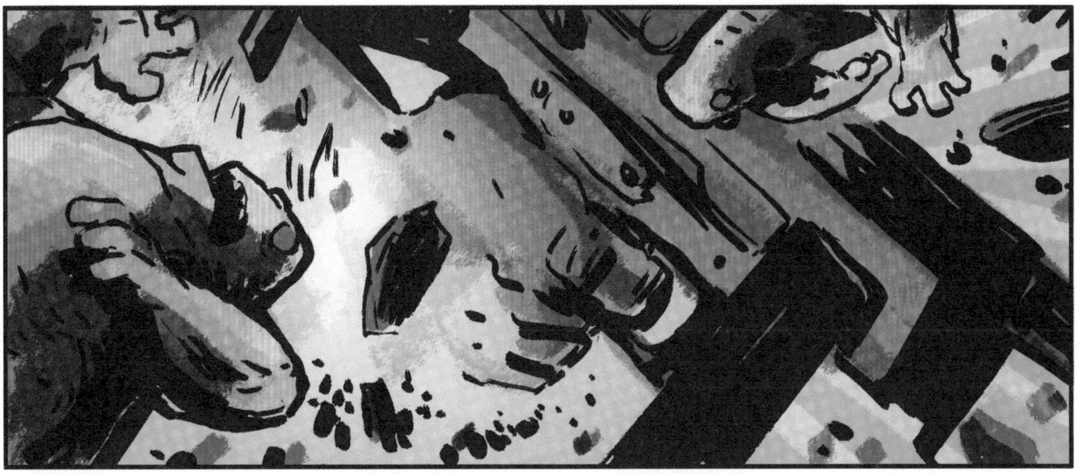

...BUT THIS WAS A NEW TYPE OF LANDFALL.

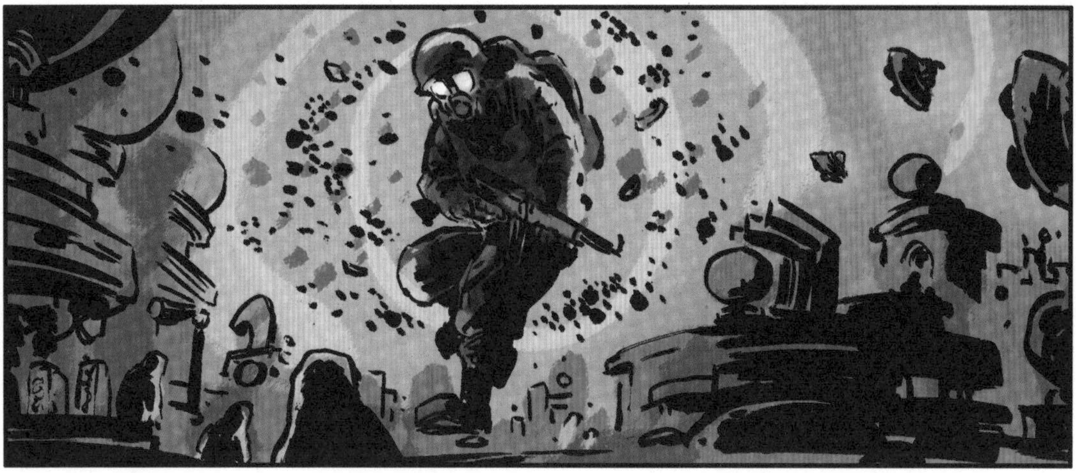

THIS WAS ONE FOR ALL MANKIND.

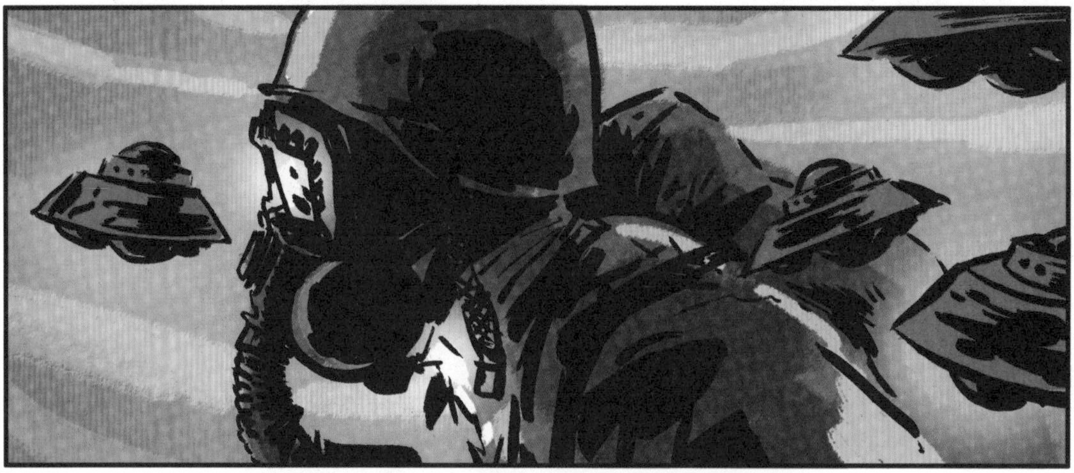

G.I.GANTIC.

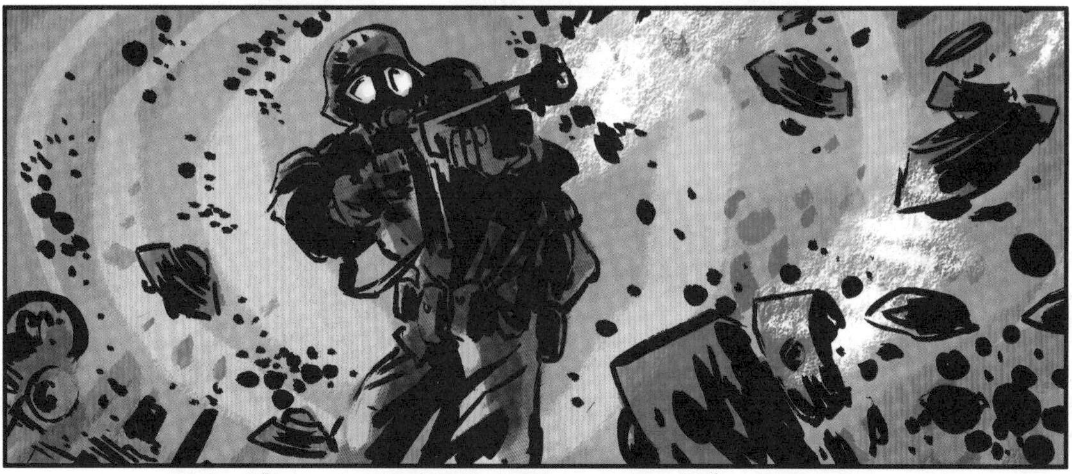

OH, HOW LOFTY THE VIEW FROM A TABLE TURNED?

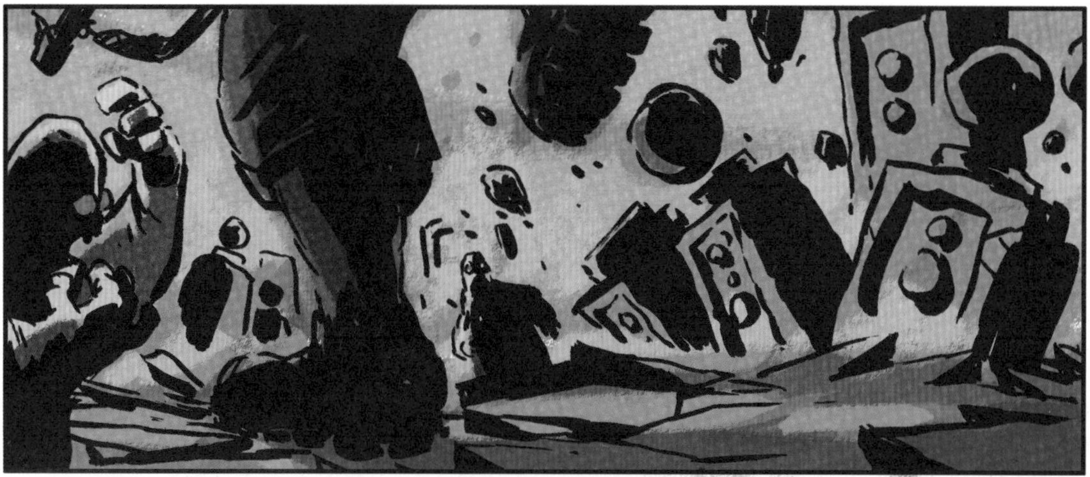

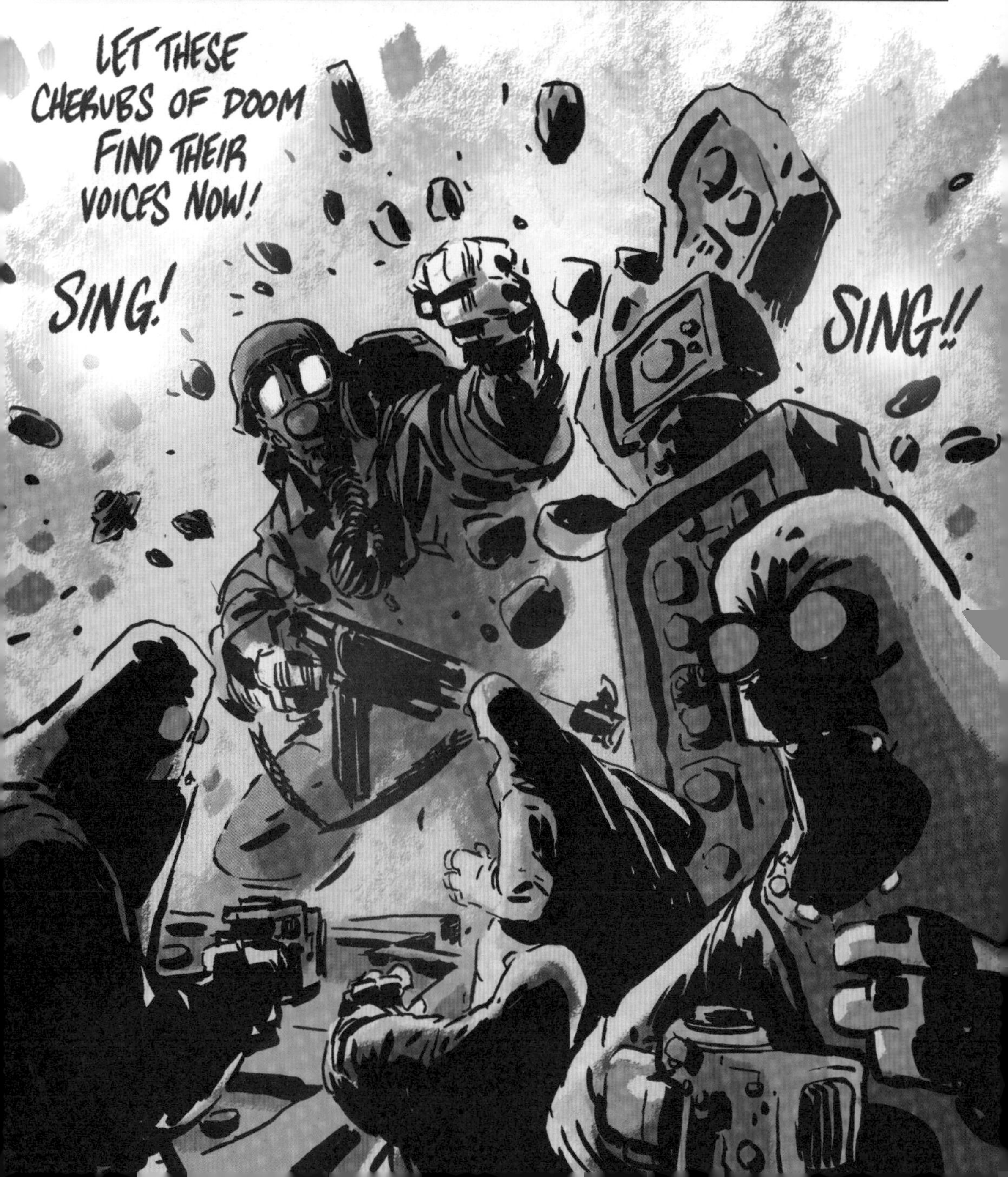
LET THESE CHERUBS OF DOOM FIND THEIR VOICES NOW!
SING!
SING!!

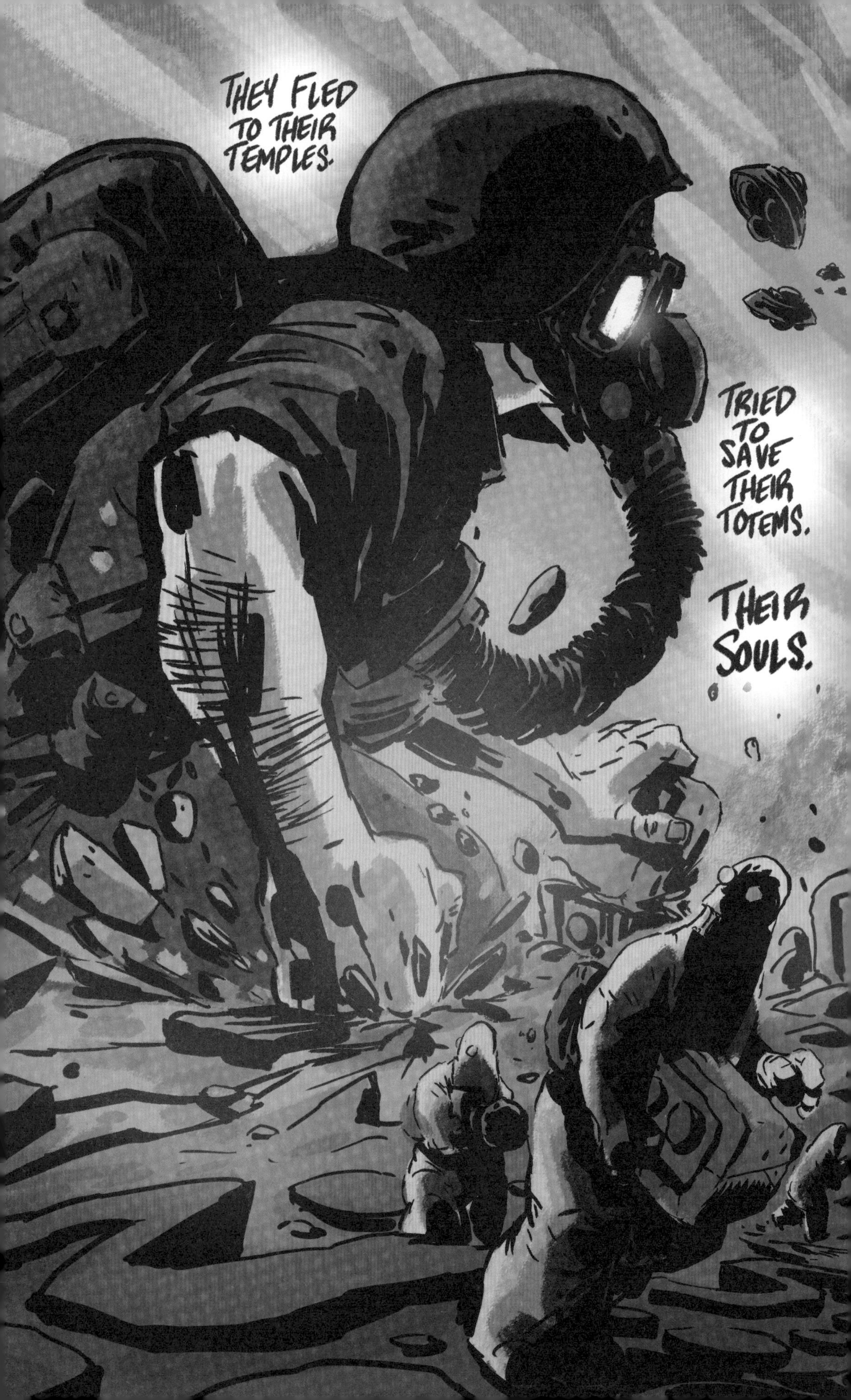
THEY FLED TO THEIR TEMPLES.
TRIED TO SAVE THEIR TOTEMS.
THEIR SOULS.

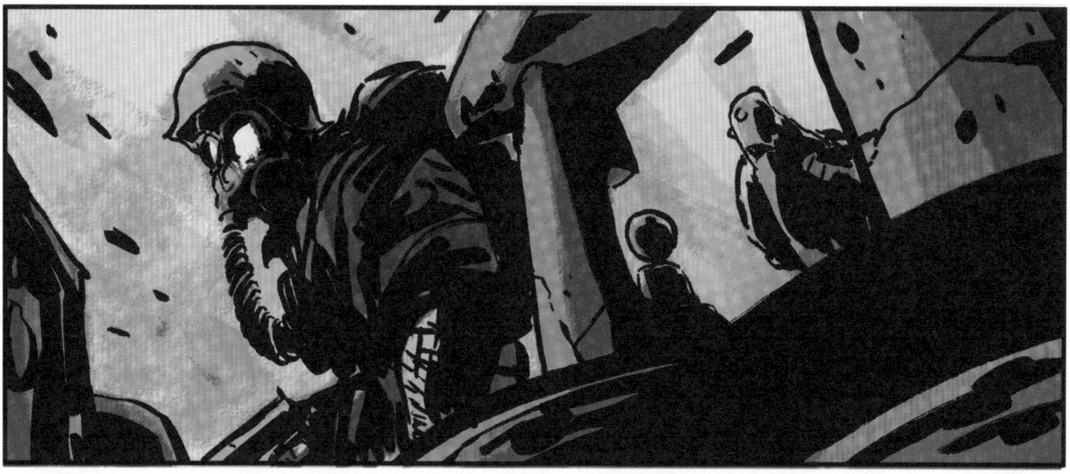

BUT NOTHING COULD HIDE FROM THE EYES OF G.I. GANTIC.

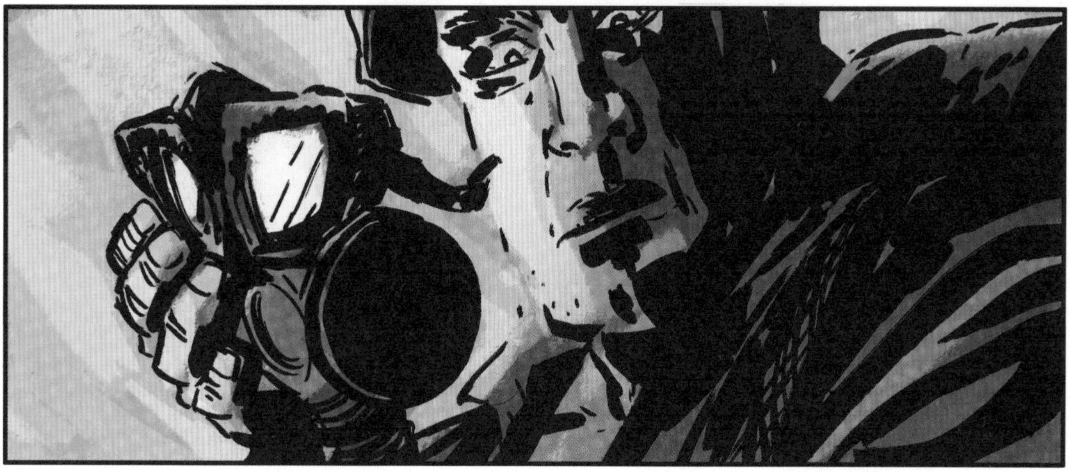

ESPECIALLY NOT THE TRUTH.

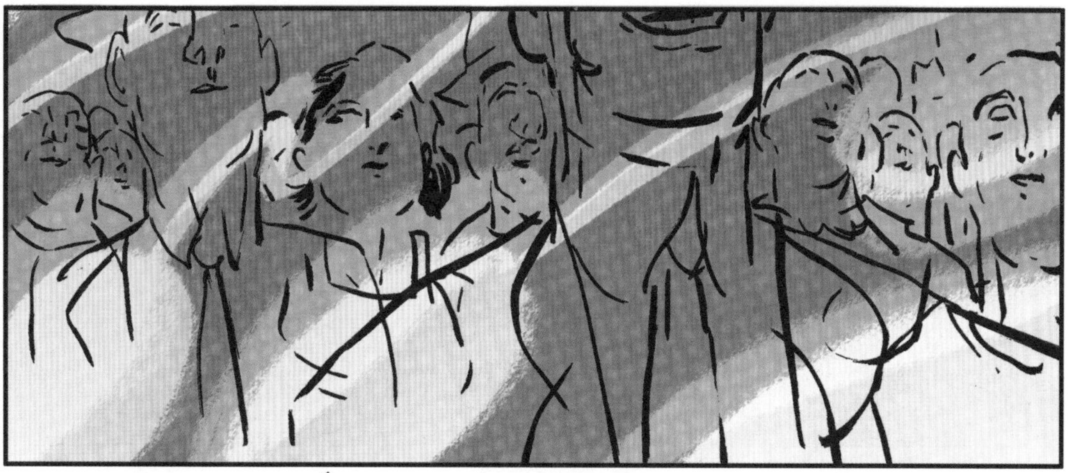

MANKIND'S GREATEST MYSTERY.

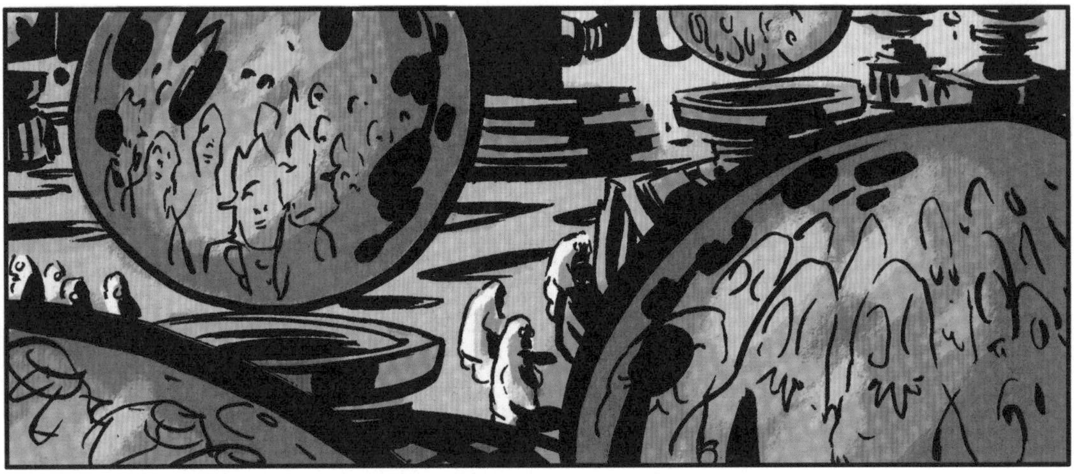

WHERE DO WE COME FROM?

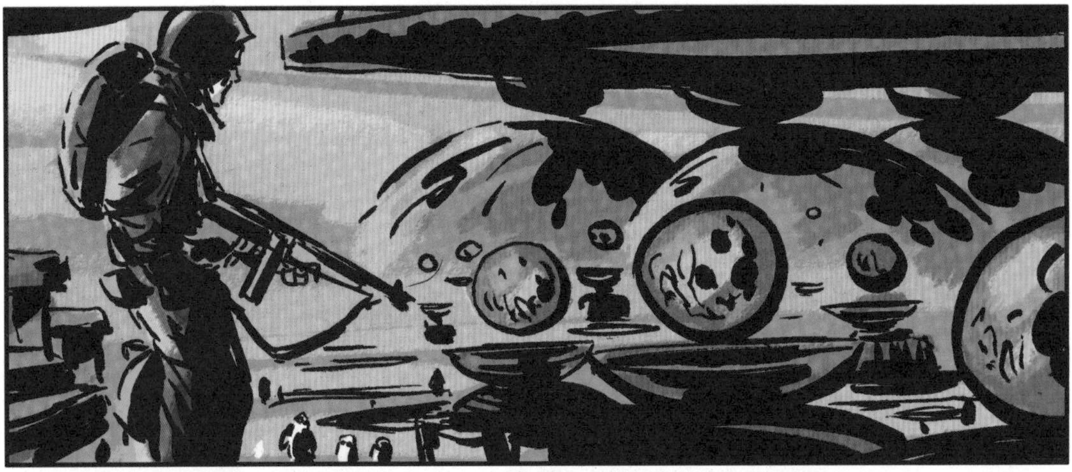

WAS THE SPIRIT OF MAN JUST A PRODUCT OF...
...THEM?

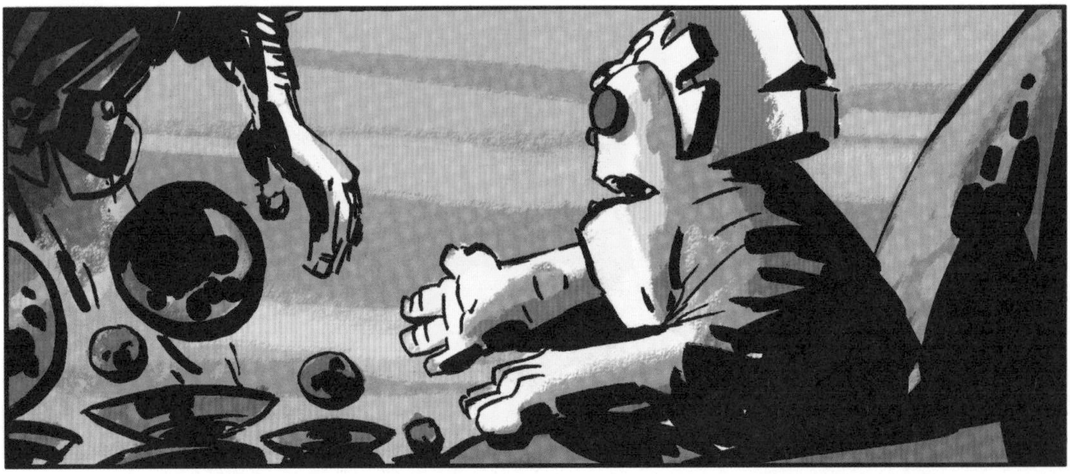

THEIR LEADER CLAIMED, "YES!"

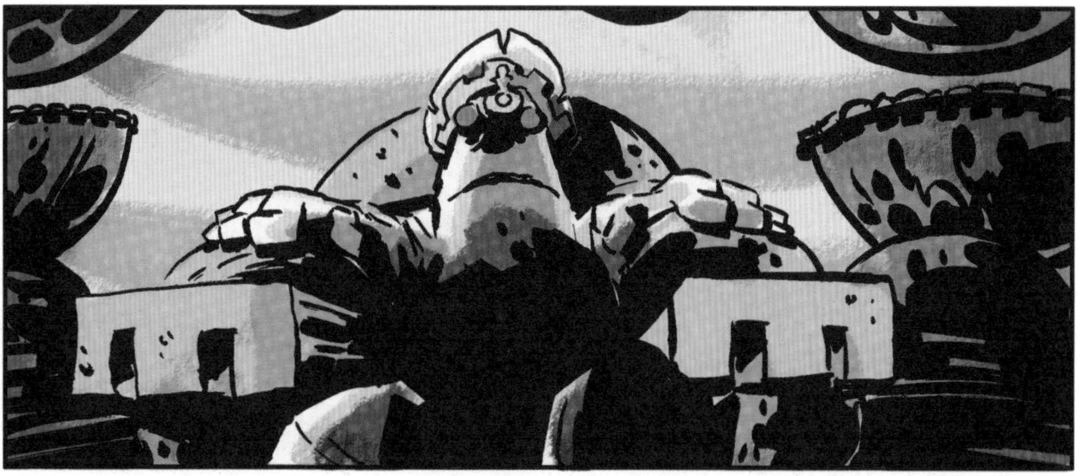

THE GRAND DESIGN, SPRUNG FORTH
FROM THE CANVAS OF THEIR WORLD ALONE!

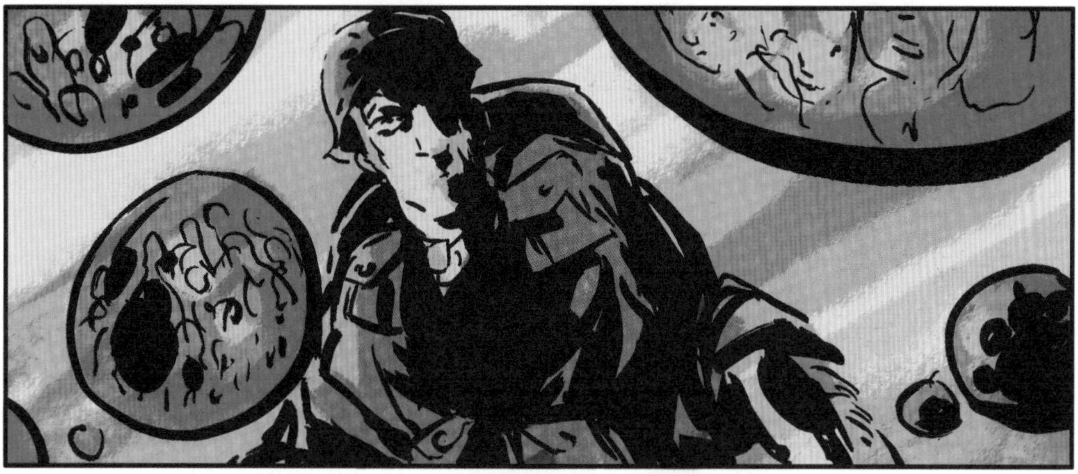

ALL WORLDS... EXPERIMENTS ON THE
ASTRAL SLIDE OF THE COSMOS.

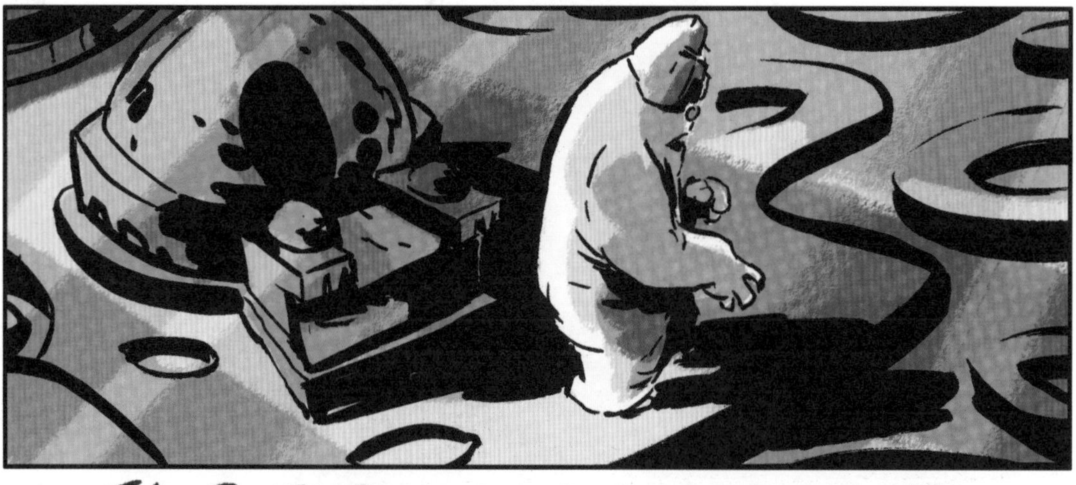

THEIR BURDEN OF CURIOSITY HAD
LEFT THEM BUT TINKERERS IN THE VOID.

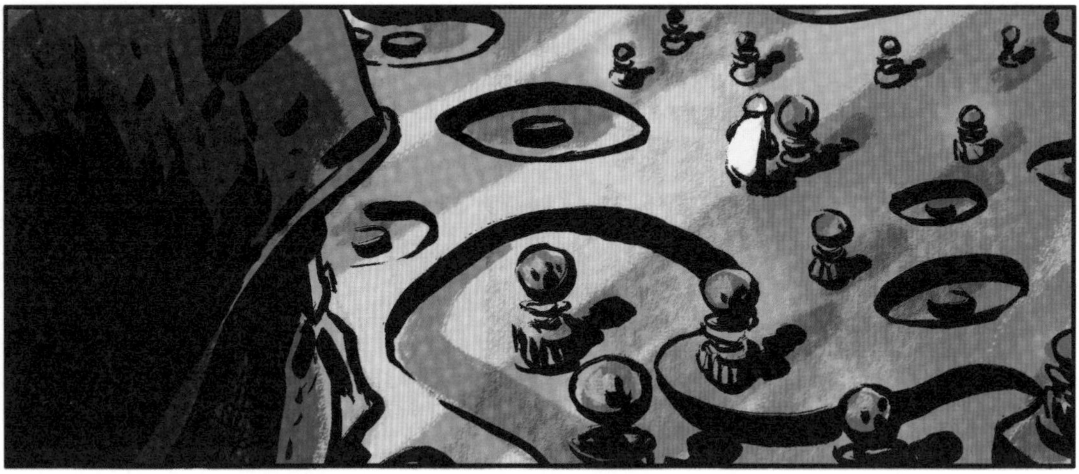

IMAGINE THEIR CHORE, EARTHMAN:
TO CREATE FROM SCRATCH THE PEOPLES OF THE GALAXY.

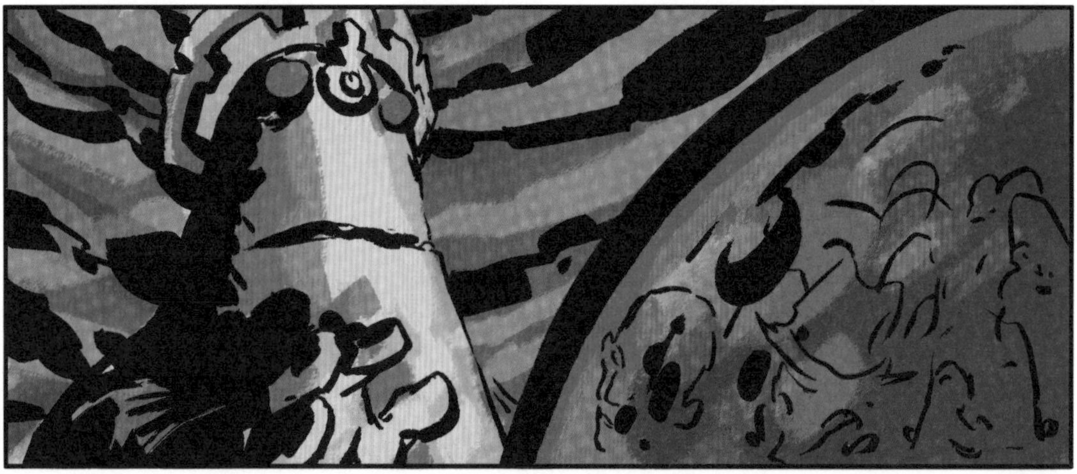

TO SET THEM FREE TO GROW... LEARN... LIVE.
TO SOMETIMES FAIL.

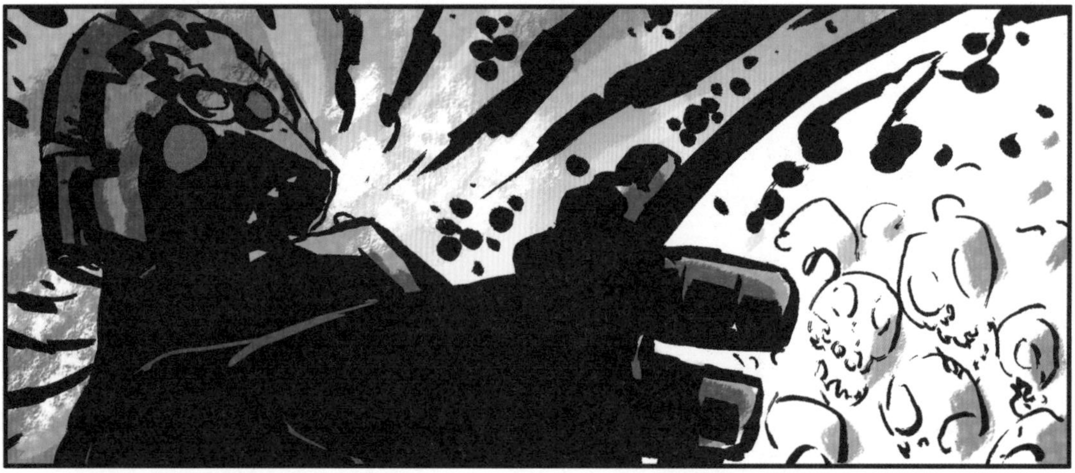

AS EARTH HAD. AS MAN HAD.

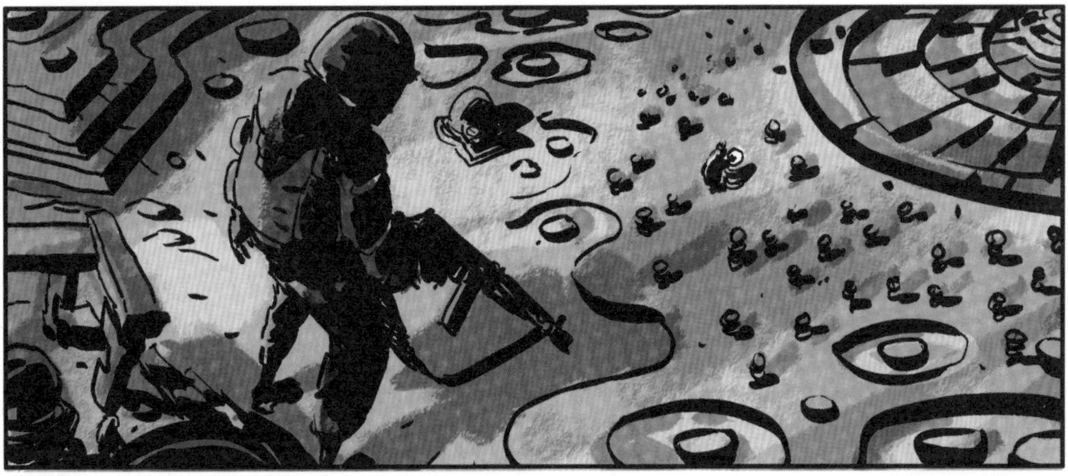

MANKIND WAS A SELF-DESTRUCTIVE, FAILED EXPERIMENT.
ONE OF MANY MESSES TO BE CLEANED UP.

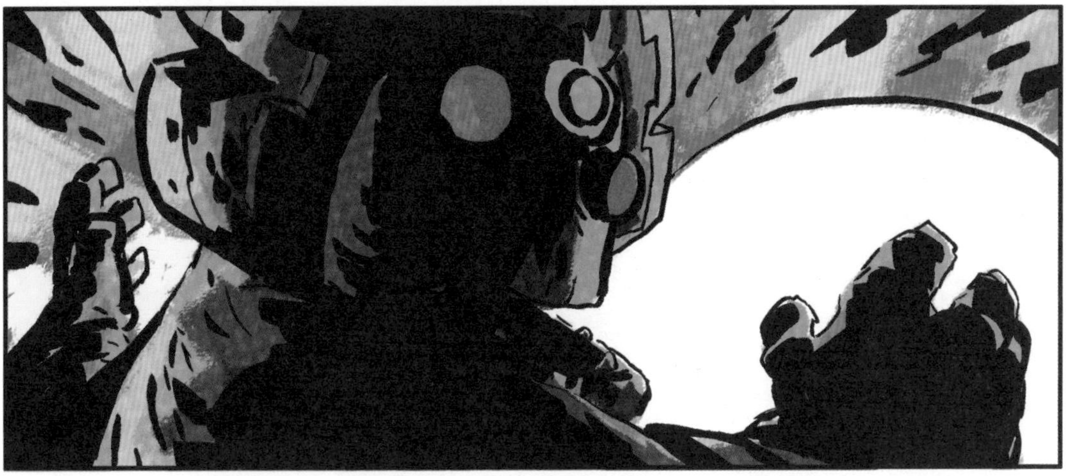

HOLD THEM NOT RESPONSIBLE!
MANKIND WAS THEIR PROBLEM TO SOLVE!

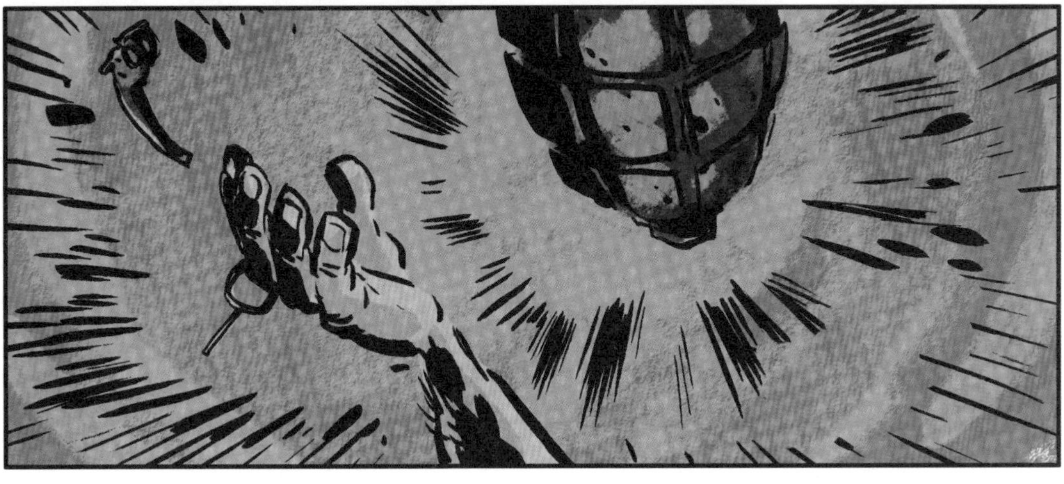

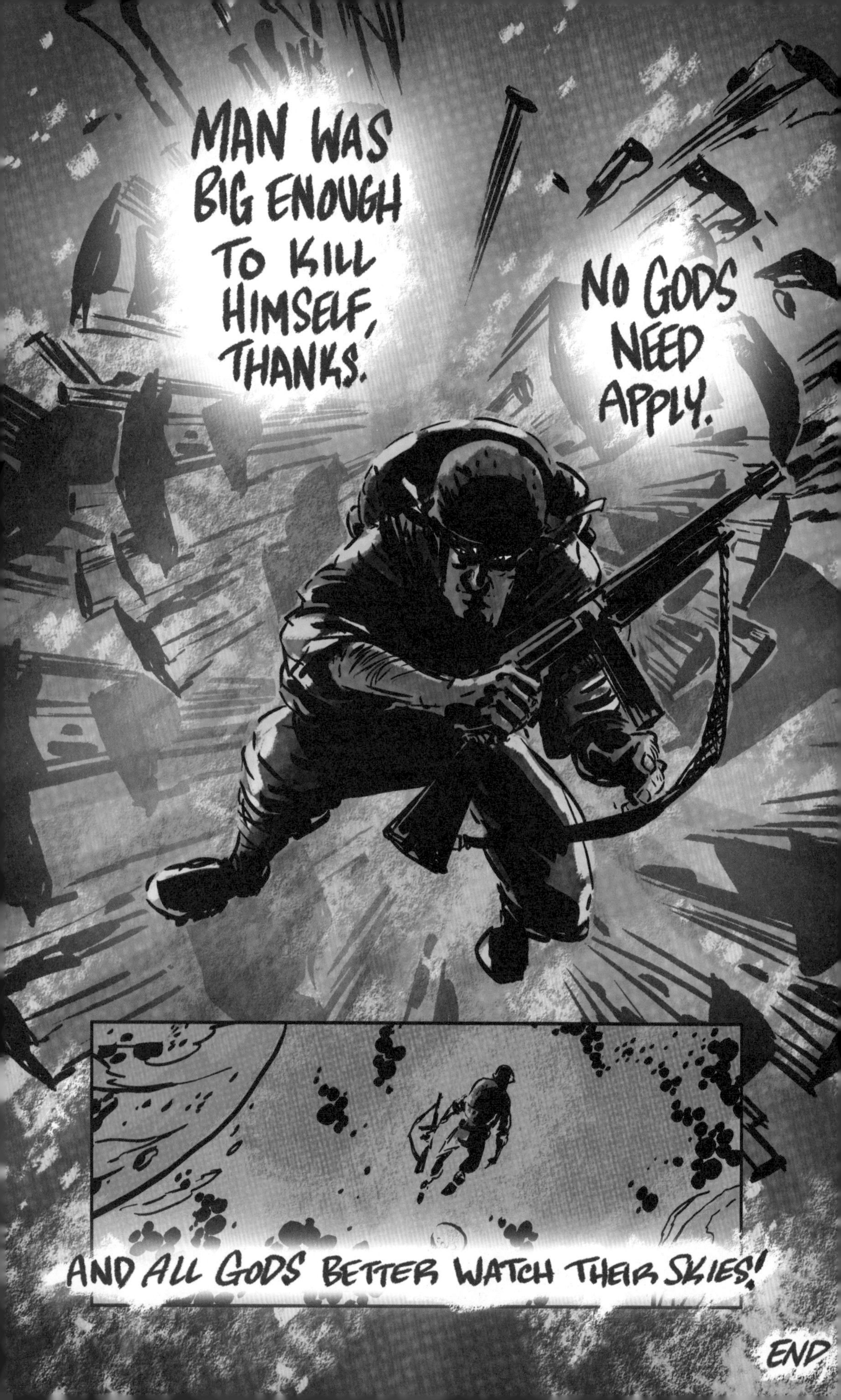

MAN WAS BIG ENOUGH TO KILL HIMSELF, THANKS.
NO GODS NEED APPLY.
AND ALL GODS BETTER WATCH THEIR SKIES!
END

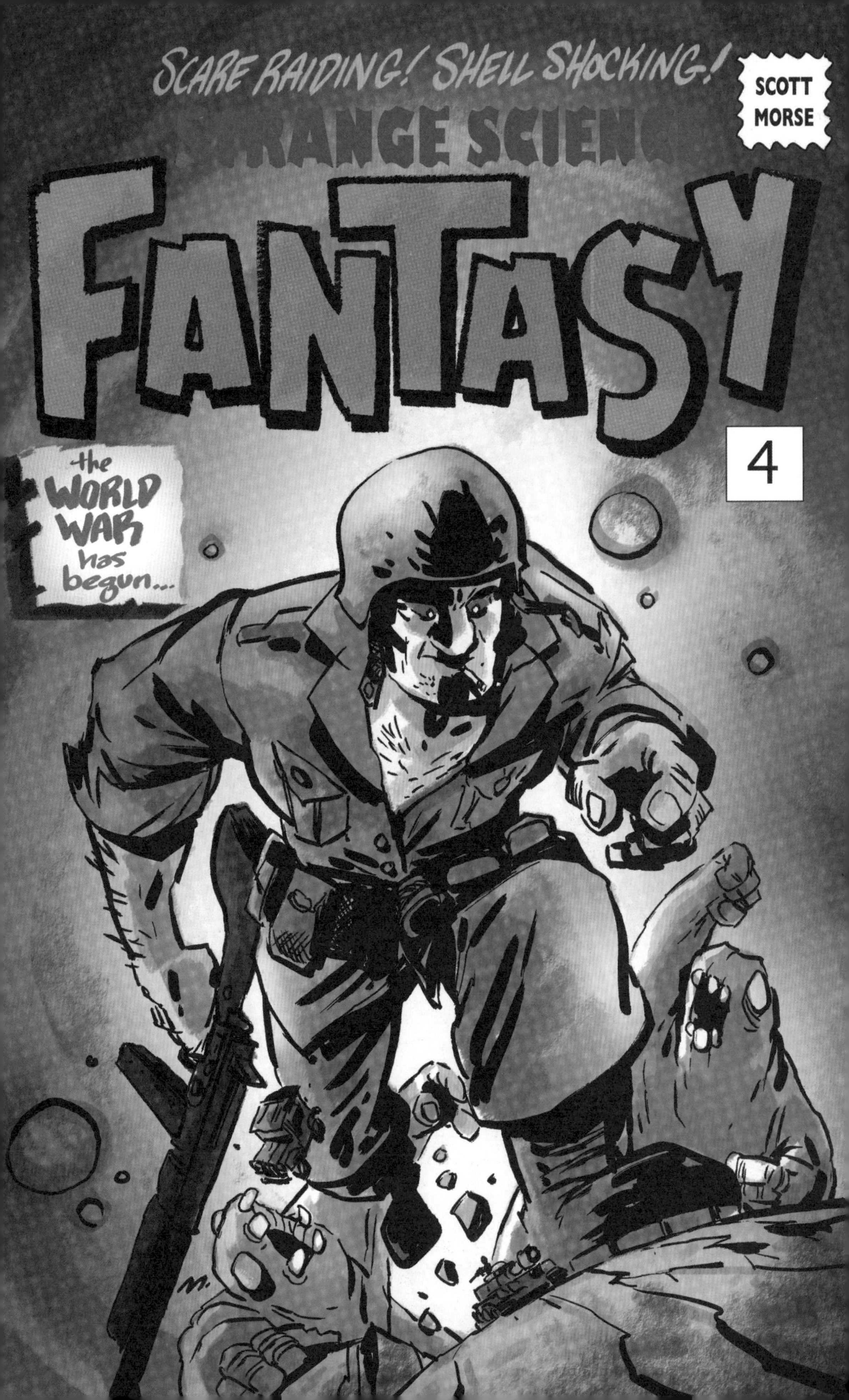
SCARE RAIDING! SHELL SHOCKING!
SCOTT MORSE
...RANGE SCIEN...
FANTASY
4
the WORLD WAR has begun...

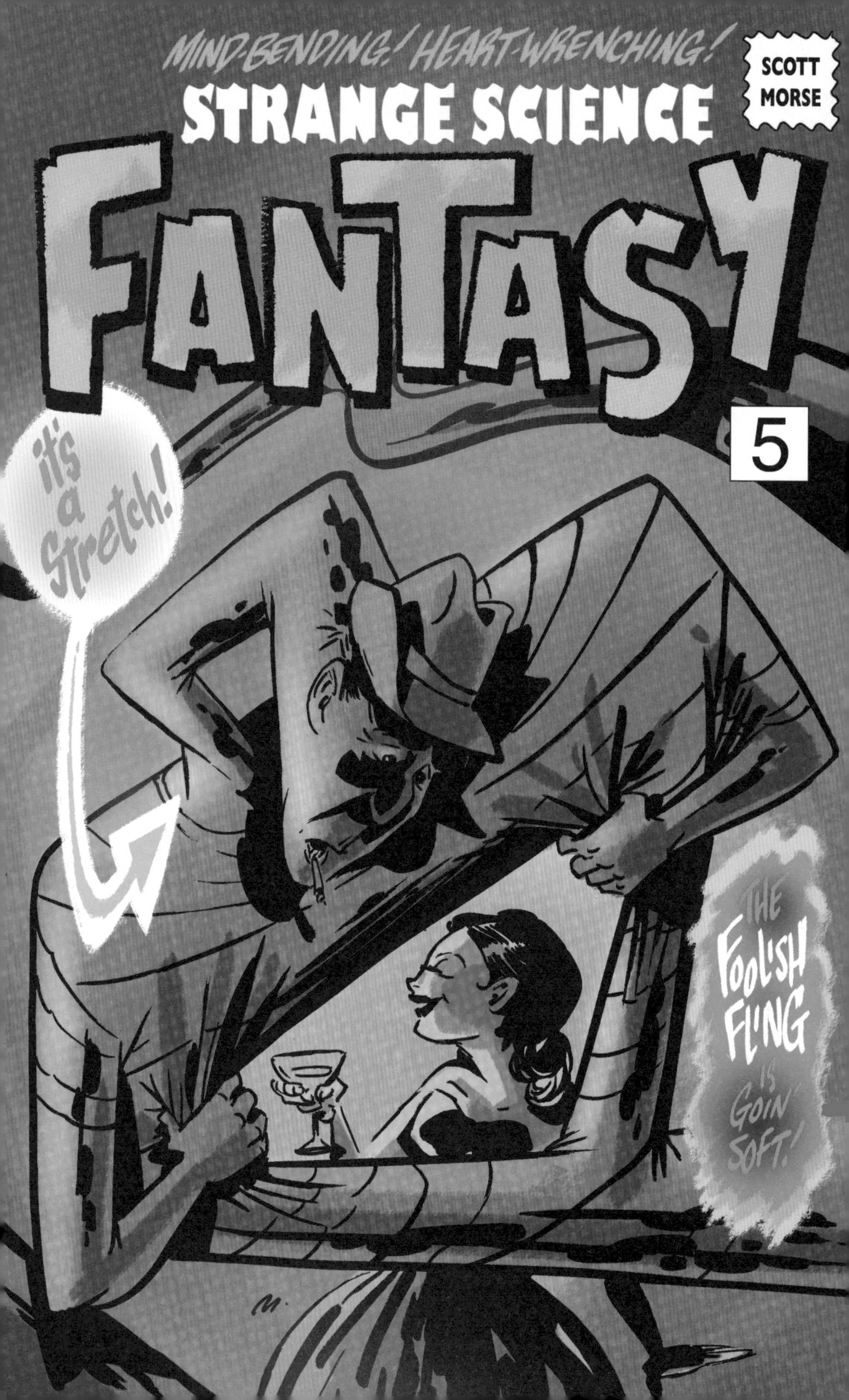
MIND-BENDING! HEART-WRENCHING!
STRANGE SCIENCE
SCOTT MORSE
FANTASY
5
it's a Stretch!
THE FOOLISH FLING IS GOIN' SOFT!

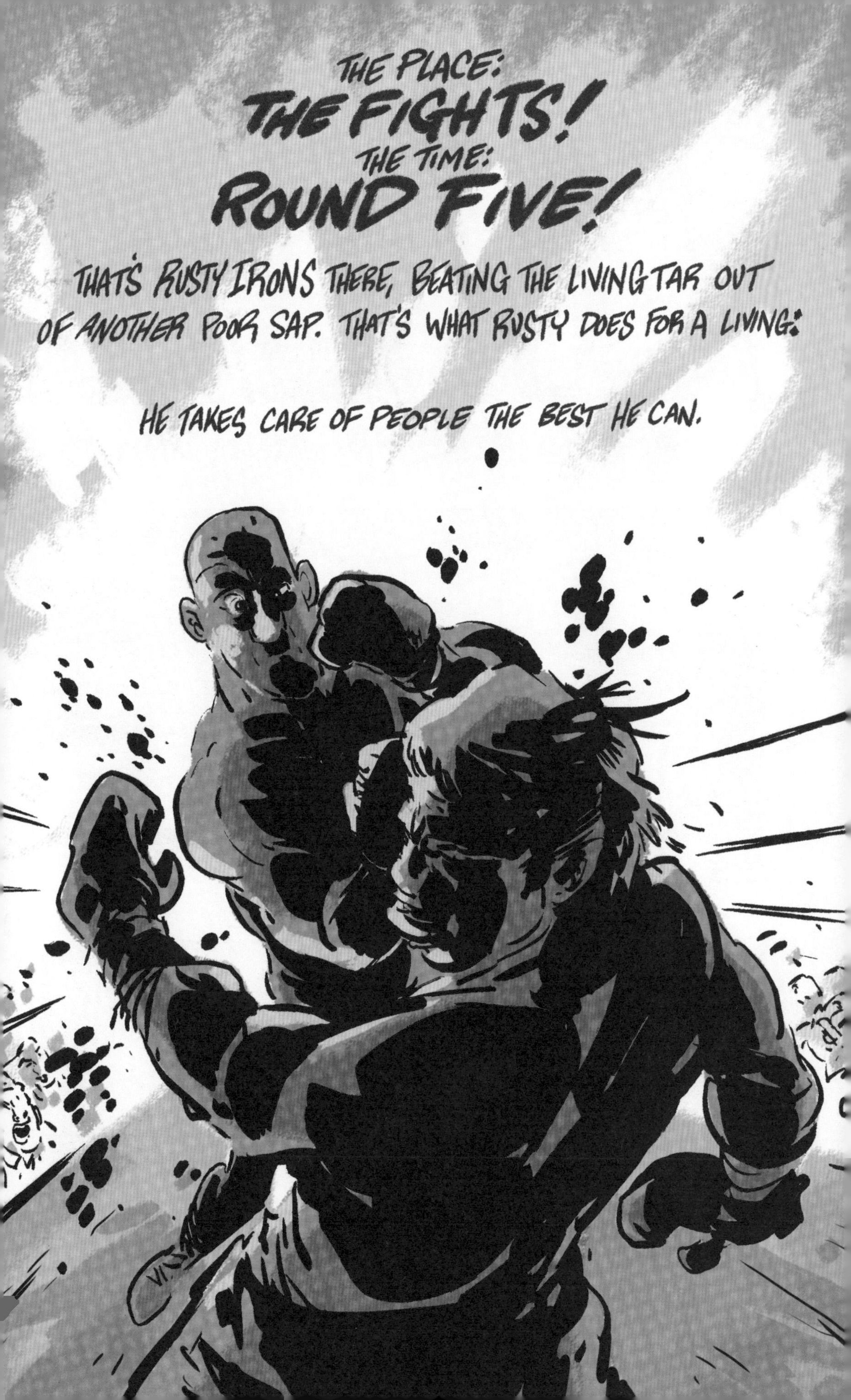
THE PLACE:
THE FIGHTS!
THE TIME:
ROUND FIVE!
THAT'S RUSTY IRONS THERE, BEATING THE LIVING TAR OUT OF ANOTHER POOR SAP. THAT'S WHAT RUSTY DOES FOR A LIVING.
HE TAKES CARE OF PEOPLE THE BEST HE CAN.

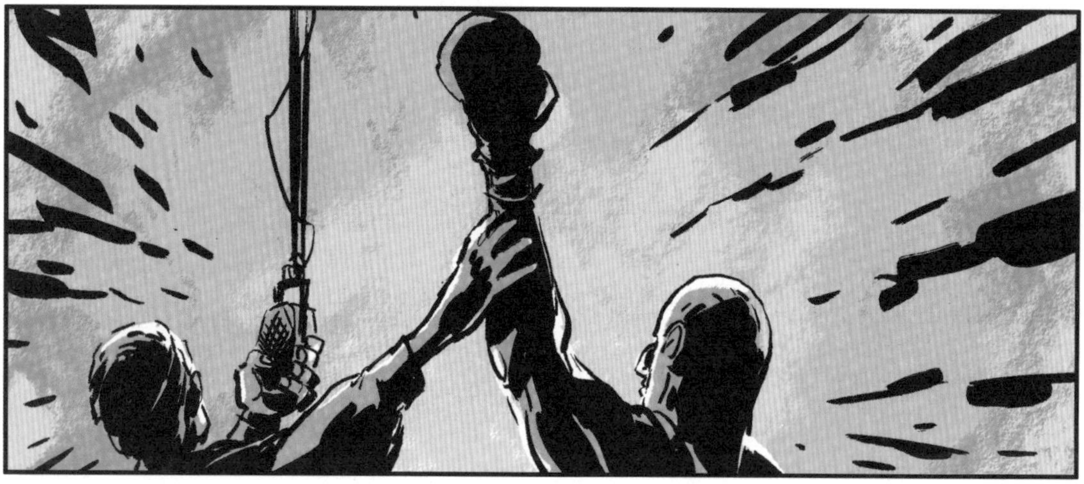

RUSTY IRONS GOT TO BE ON TOP BY WORKING HIS TAIL OFF.

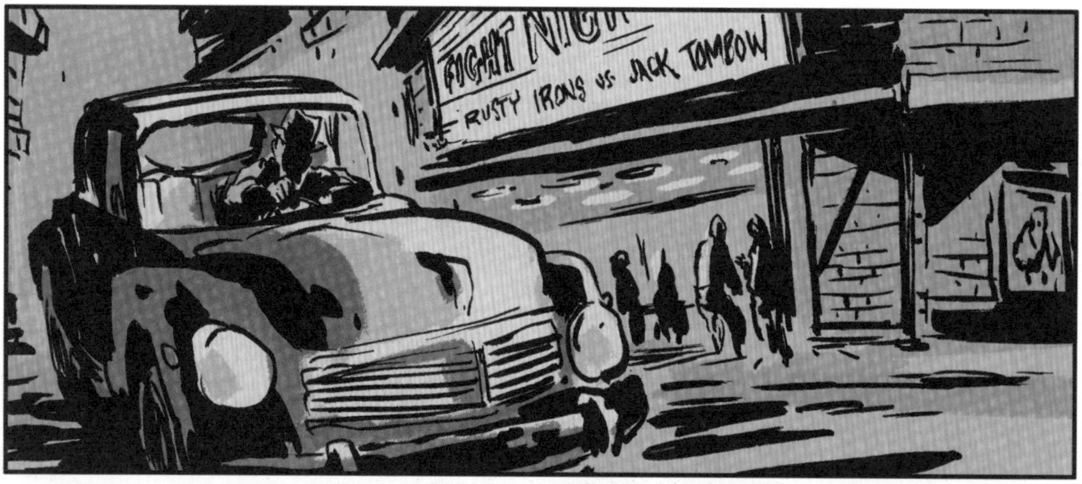
RUSTY IRONS VS. JACK TOMBOW

MORE IMPORTANTLY, RUSTY IRONS GOT TO BE ON TOP BY BEING A GOOD EGG.

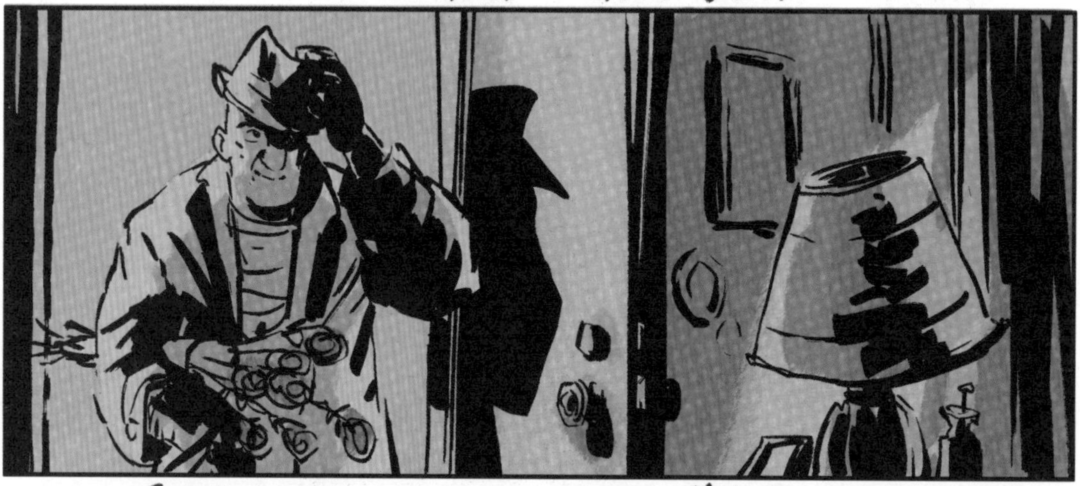

HIS FANS THREW HIM FLOWERS. HE BROUGHT 'EM SOMEPLACE SPECIAL AFTER EVERY FIGHT.

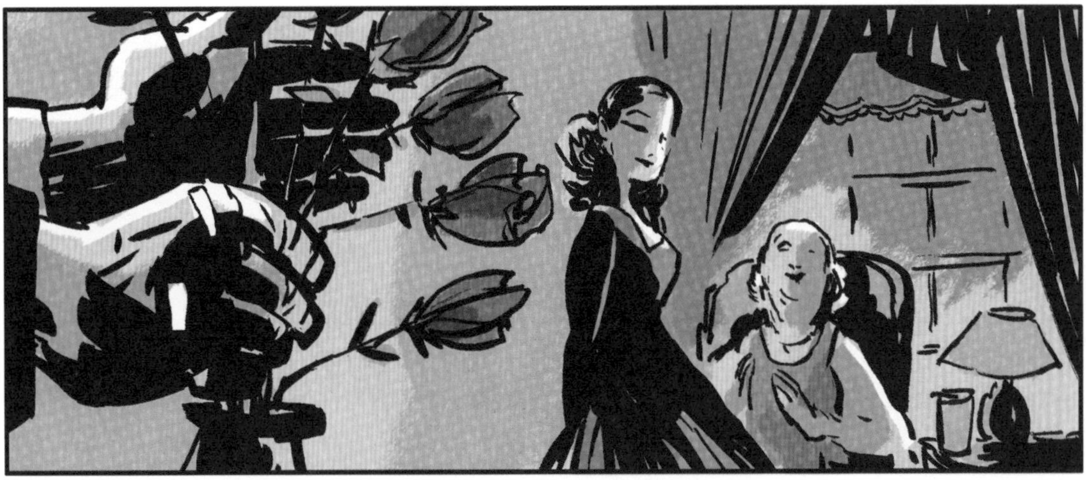

BETTER THAT THEIR BEAUTY GET SOME ATTENTION RATHER THAN JUST WILT AWAY.

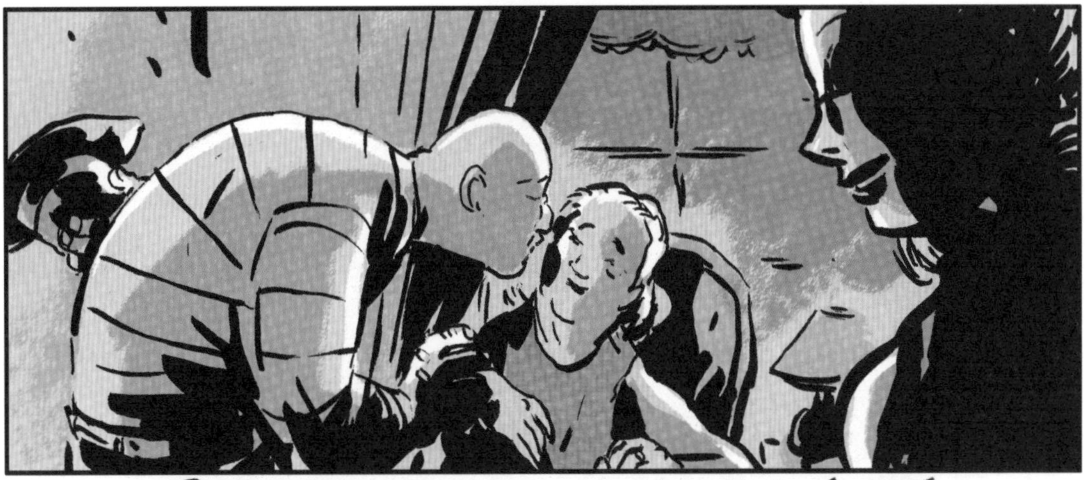

RUSTY HAD BEEN SEEING THIS GIRL, SUZIE, FOR MAYBE A YEAR NOW. SEEING HER OLD NANA, TOO.

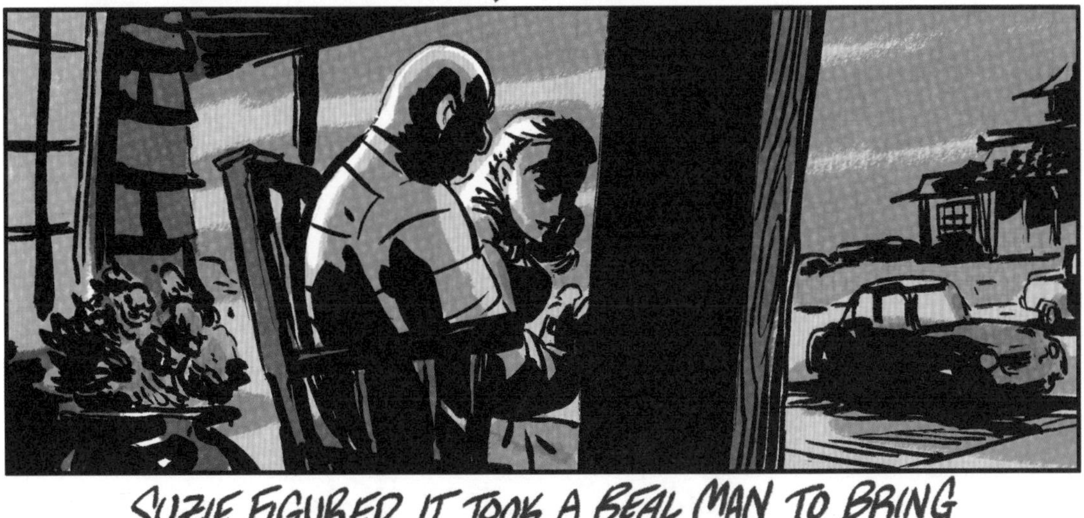

SUZIE FIGURED IT TOOK A REAL MAN TO BRING AN OLD LADY FLOWERS.

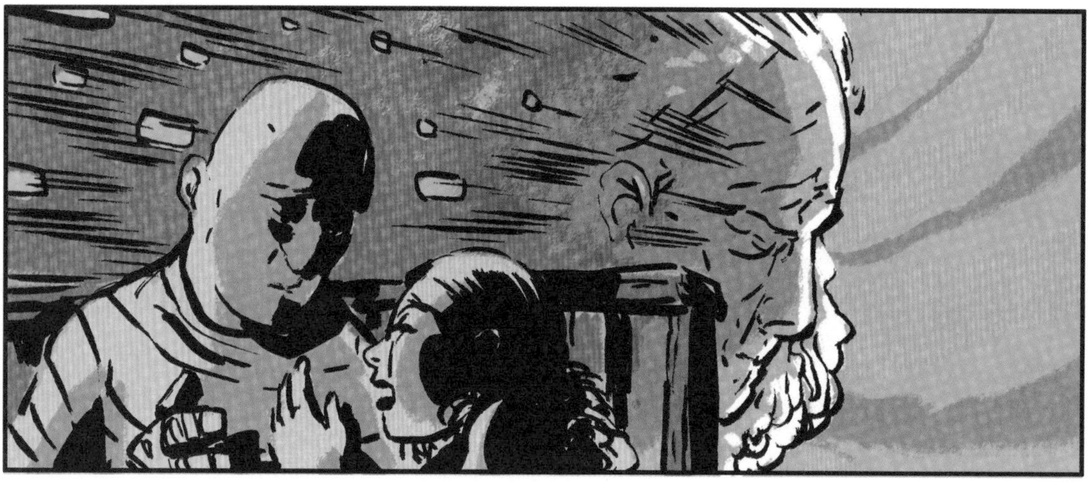

HER OLD NANA HAD GONE SOFT IN THE HEAD A WHILE BACK.
SOMETHING ABOUT NEURONS NOT BOUNCING RIGHT.

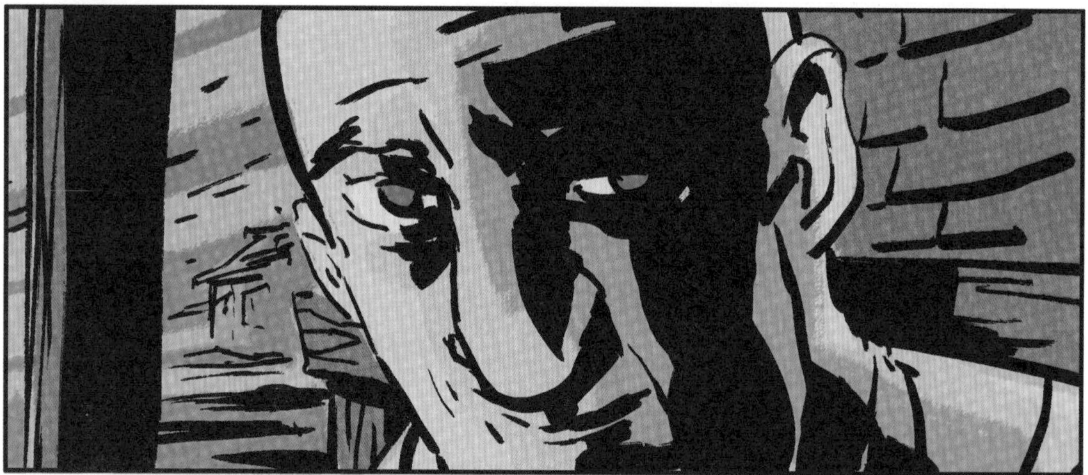

RUSTY, HE MIGHT JUST HAVE BEEN A PALOOKA,
BUT HIS CAULIFLOWER EARS WERE GOOD AT LISTENING.

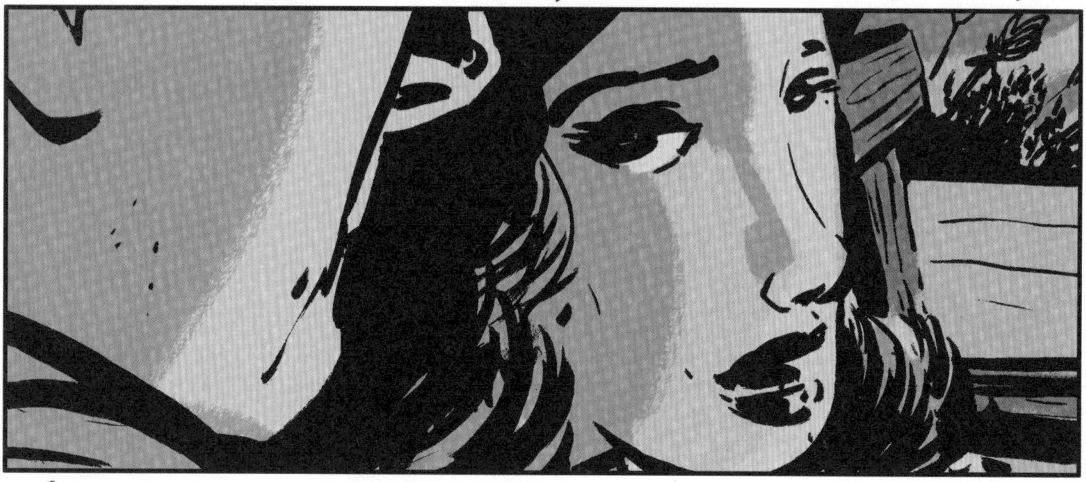

SUZIE SURE HAD SOME KINDA SOFT SPOT FOR RUSTY.

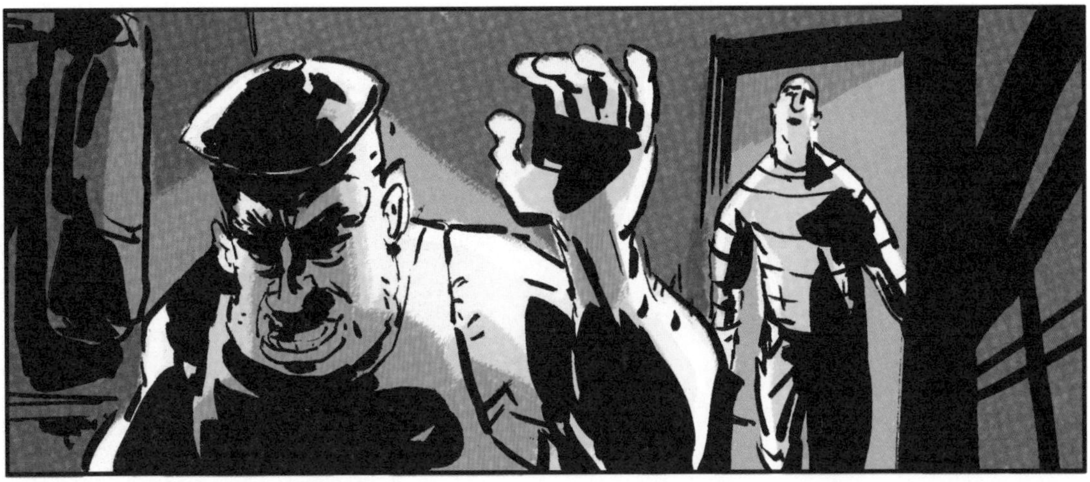

AND RUSTY, REMEMBER, HE KNEW HOW TO TAKE CARE OF PEOPLE.
HE JUST NEEDED A LITTLE EXTRA SCRATCH TO DO IT RIGHT.

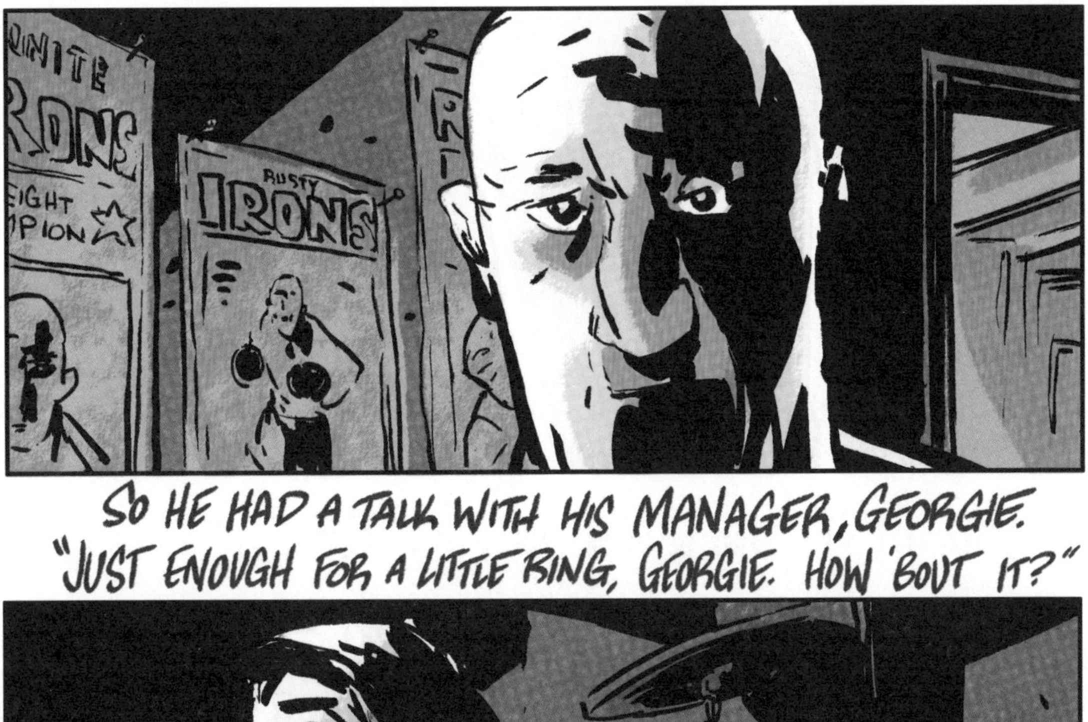
RUSTY
IRONS

SO HE HAD A TALK WITH HIS MANAGER, GEORGIE.
"JUST ENOUGH FOR A LITTLE RING, GEORGIE. HOW 'BOUT IT?"

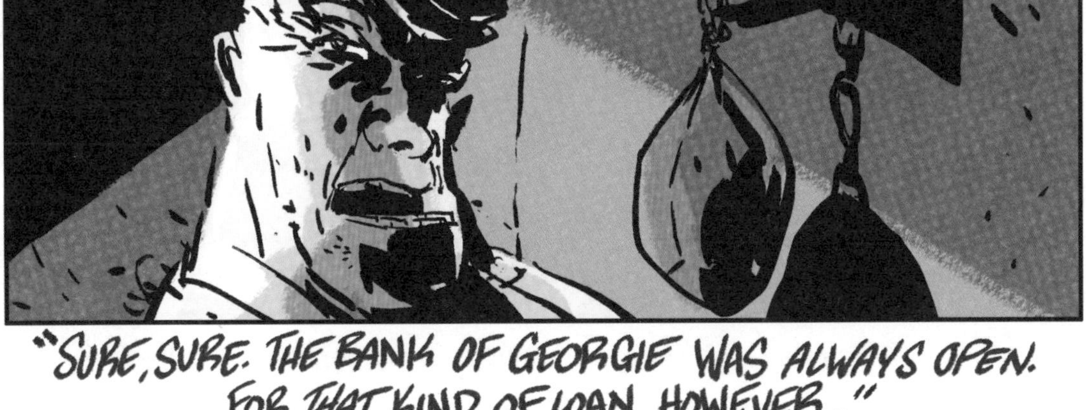

"SURE, SURE. THE BANK OF GEORGIE WAS ALWAYS OPEN.
FOR THAT KIND OF LOAN, HOWEVER..."

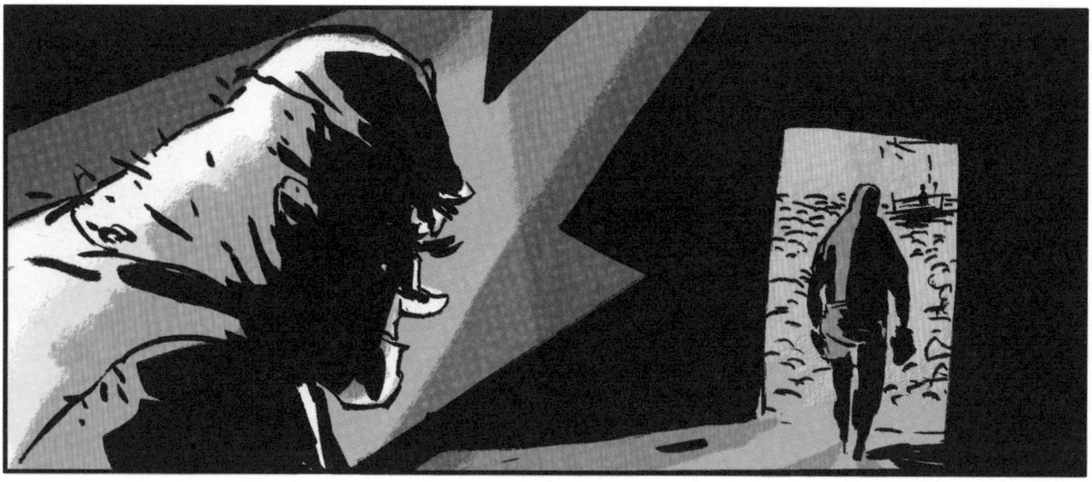

"...ONLY THE SORT OF FELLAS WILLING TO TAKE A *DIVE* NEED APPLY."
RUSTY NORMALLY WASN'T THAT SORT OF FELLA.

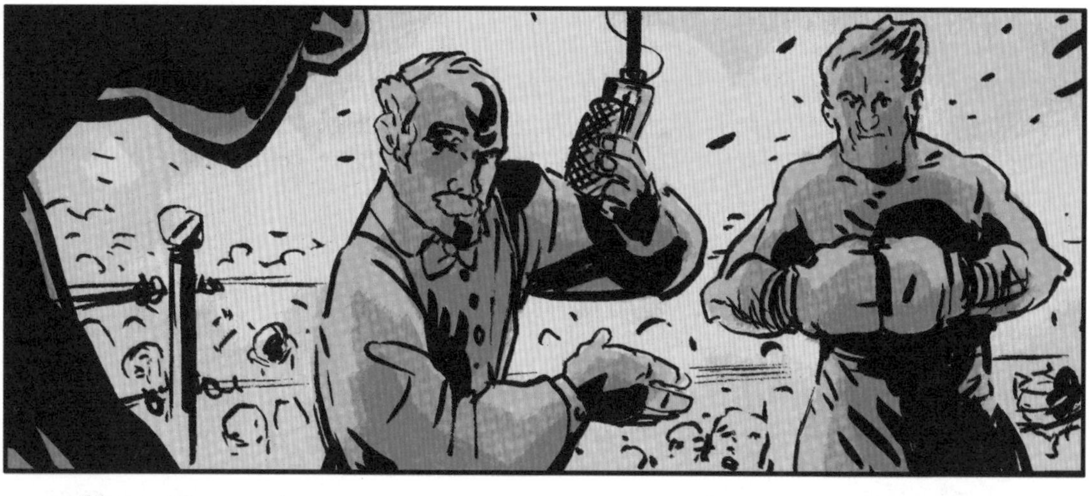

BUT RUSTY KNEW HOW TO TAKE CARE OF PEOPLE.

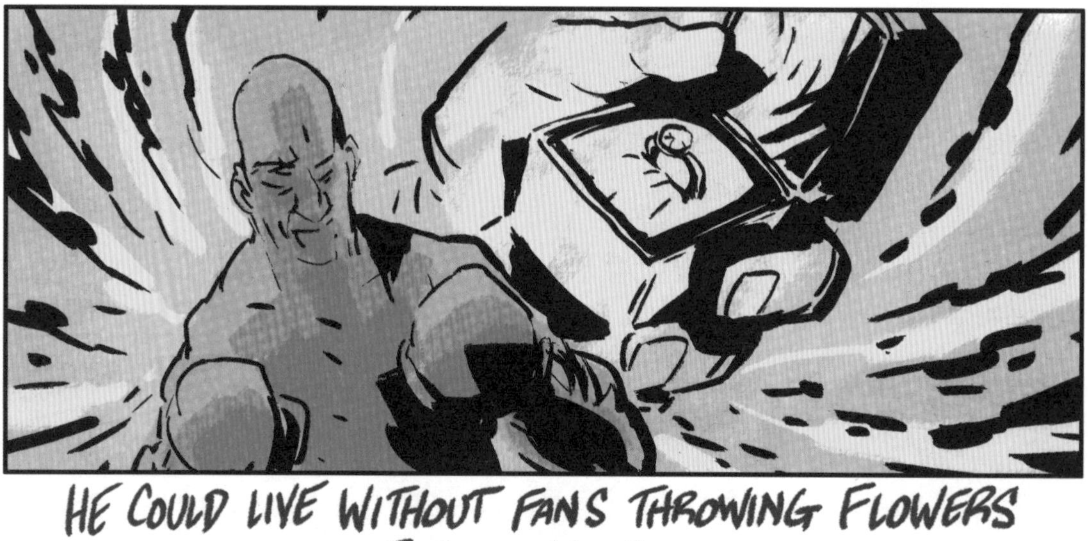

HE COULD LIVE WITHOUT FANS THROWING FLOWERS
FOR A WHILE.

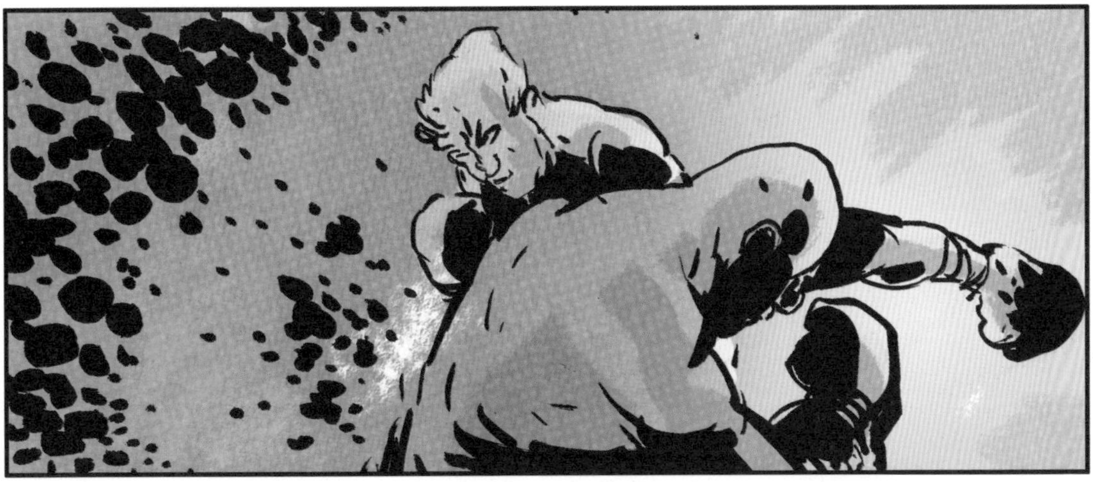

HE WANTED TO BRING SUZIE AN' HER NANA SOMETHING PRETTIER.

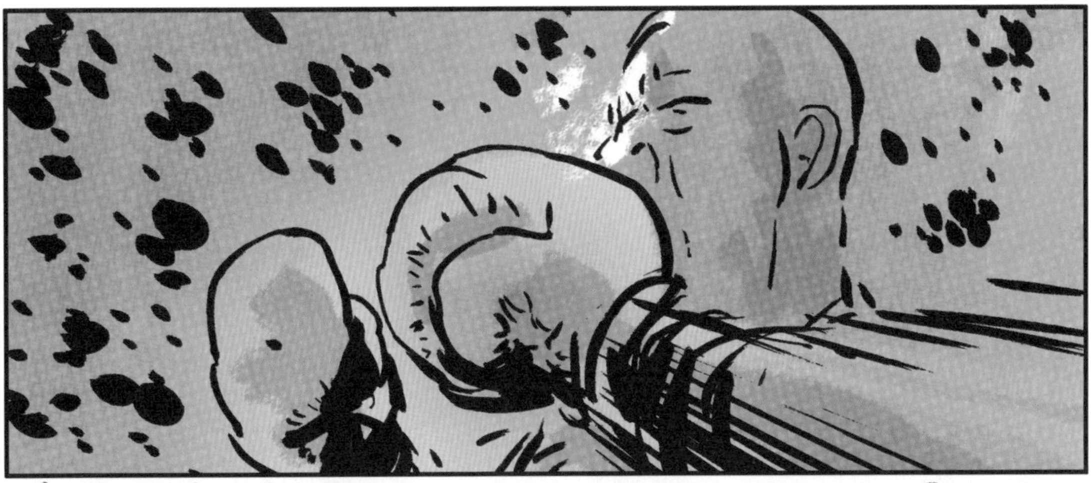

SO THROWN FLOWERS MADE WAY FOR THROWN PUNCHES THAT MADE WAY FOR THROWN FIGHTS,

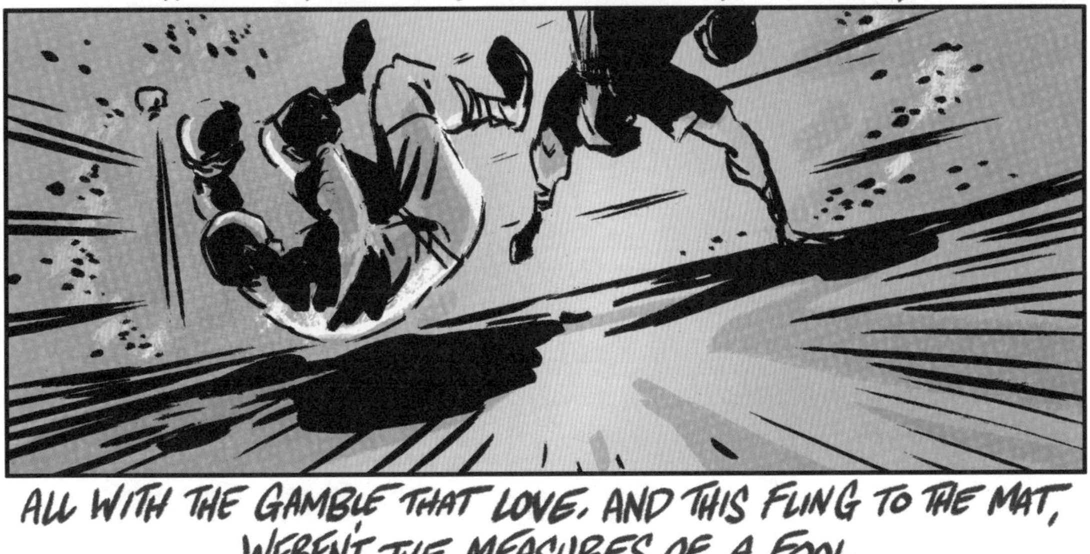

ALL WITH THE GAMBLE THAT LOVE, AND THIS FLING TO THE MAT, WEREN'T THE MEASURES OF A FOOL.

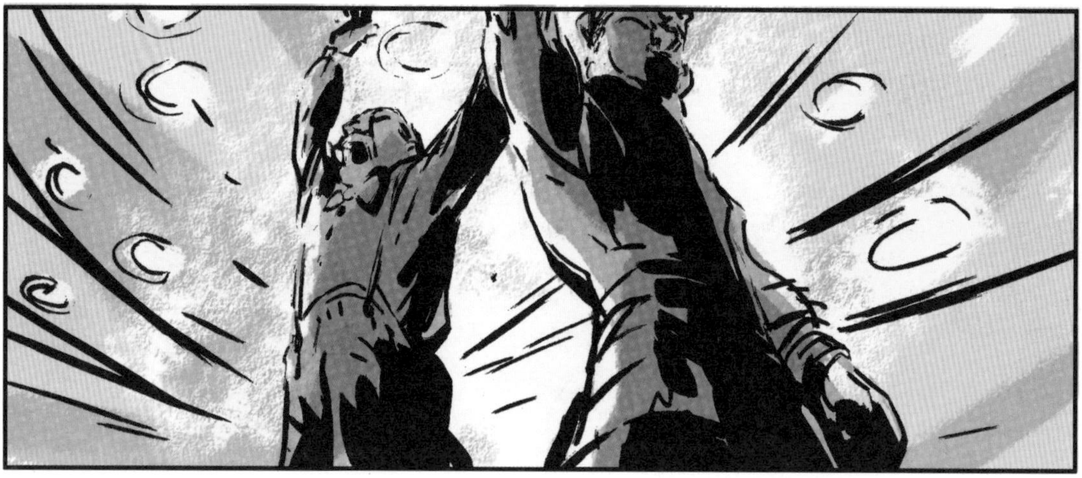

A FOOLISH FLING TO THE MAT?

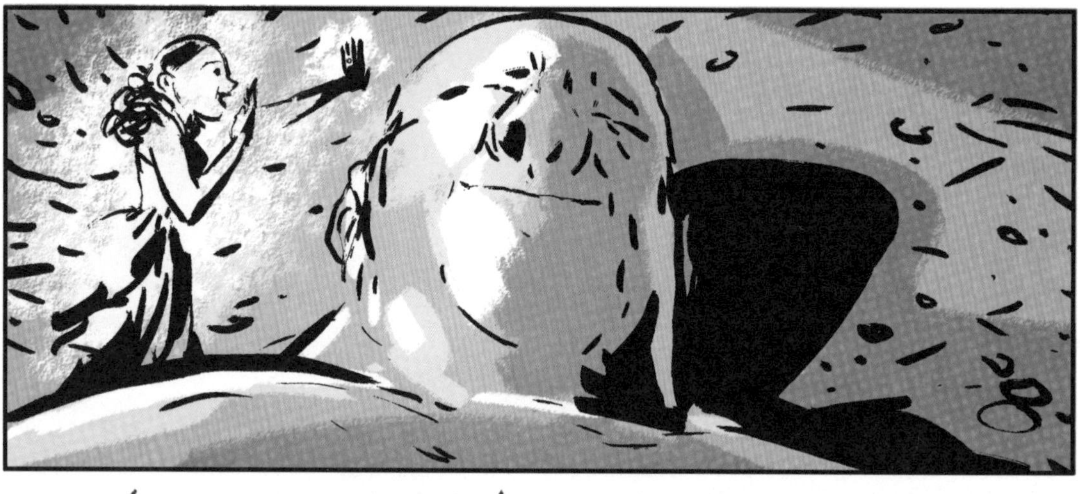

IT AIN'T SELLING OUT IF IT'S ALL FOR THE RIGHT REASONS.

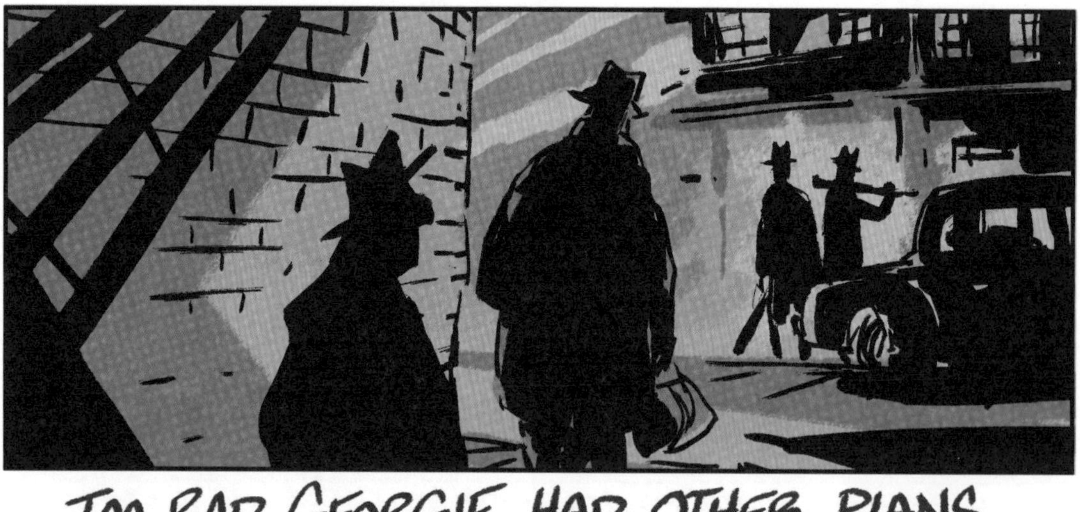

TOO BAD GEORGIE HAD OTHER PLANS.

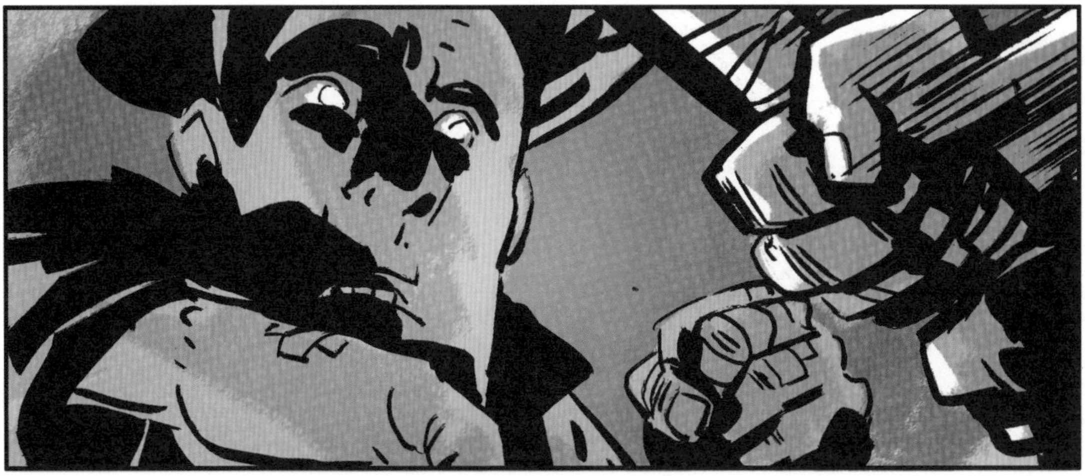

THE RESONANT CRACK OF A BAT WAS
THE ONLY "RING" THAT GEORGIE'S PLANS INVOLVED.

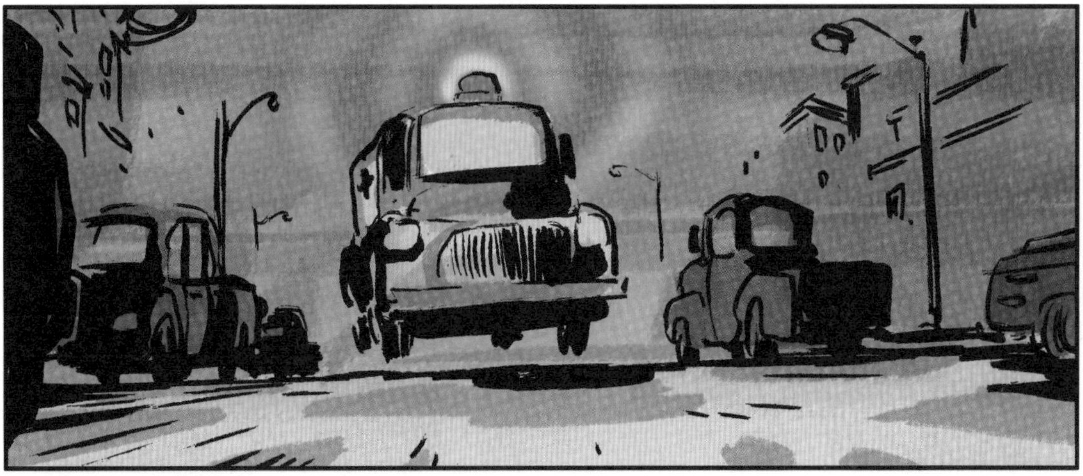

ALL RIGHT. MAYBE THE "RING" OF A SIREN, TOO.

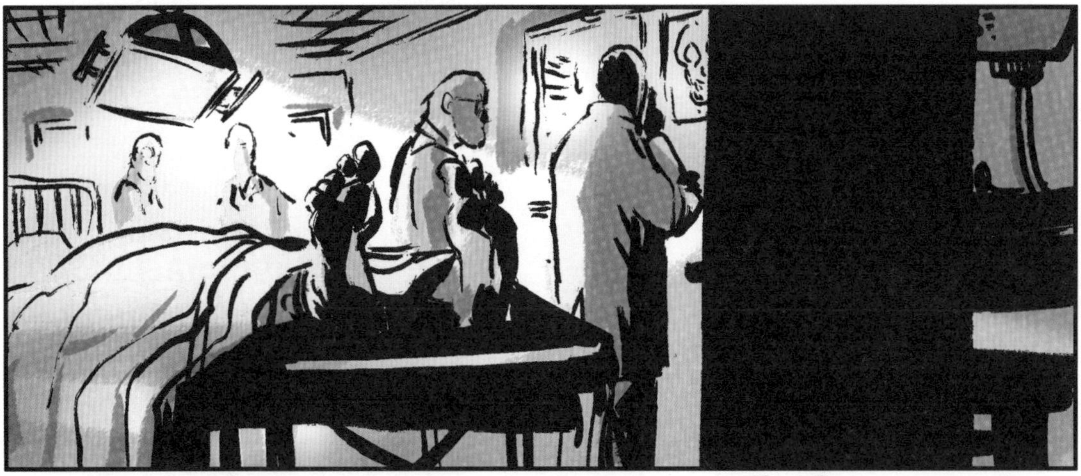

THE X-RAYS WERE A BUNCH OF BAD NEWS.
BROKEN BONES ALL OVER, INTERNAL LEAKS...

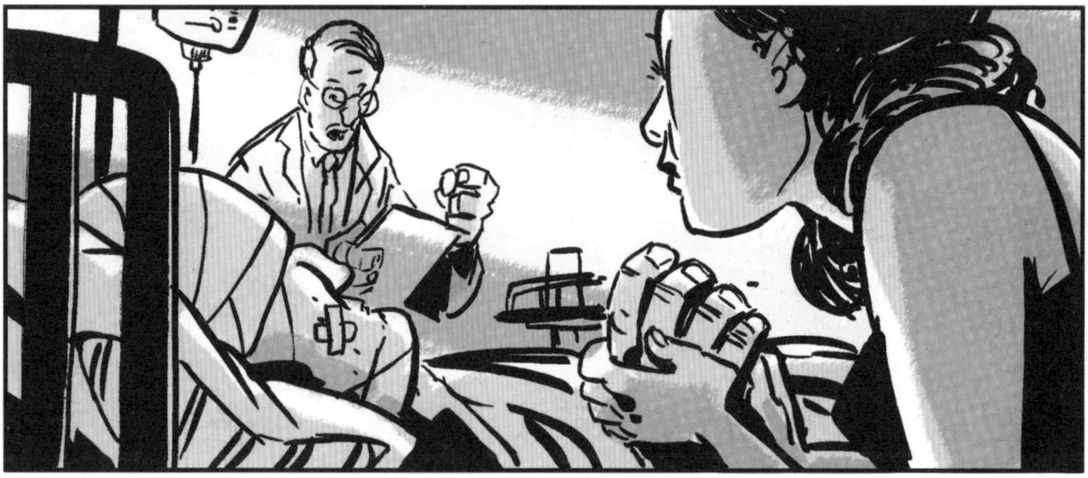

BUT STILL... HOPE...?
SOME BOOKSMART DOCTOR HAD A BRIGHT IDEA.

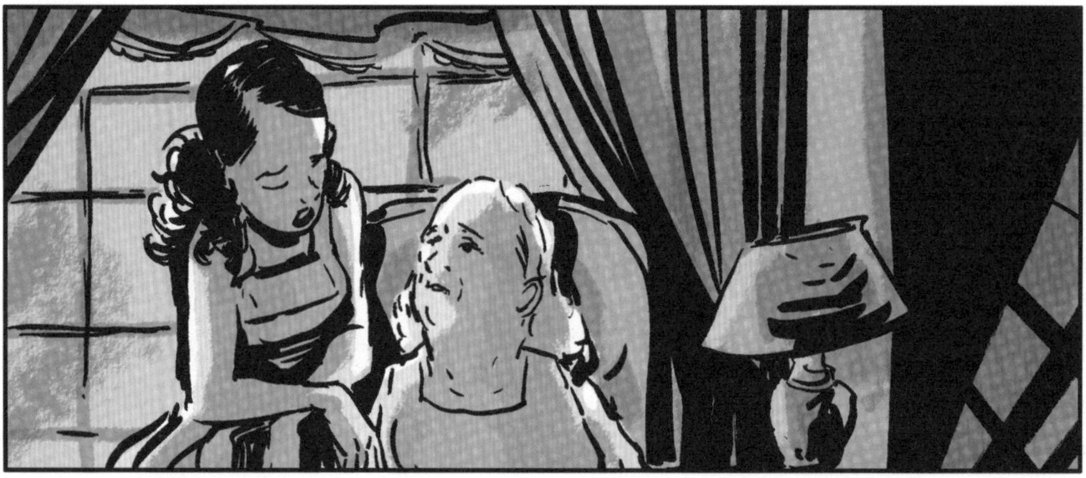

SOME KIND OF EXPERIMENTAL PROCEDURE. "NEW SCIENCE", HE SAID.
APPARENTLY IT WAS ONE SHOT. ALL OR NOTHING.

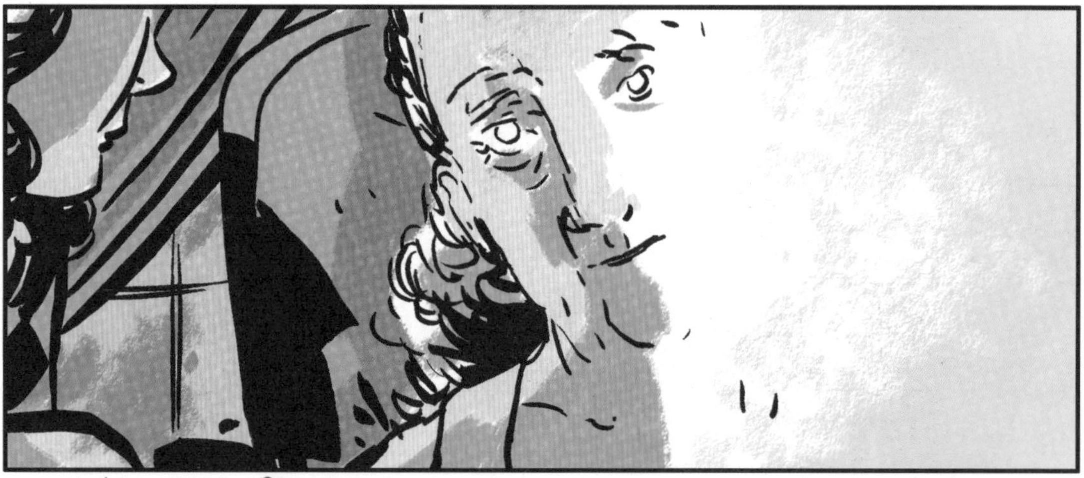

WHETHER SHE UNDERSTOOD OR NOT, NANA SIGHED.
THAT WAS ALL THE ANSWER SUZIE NEEDED.

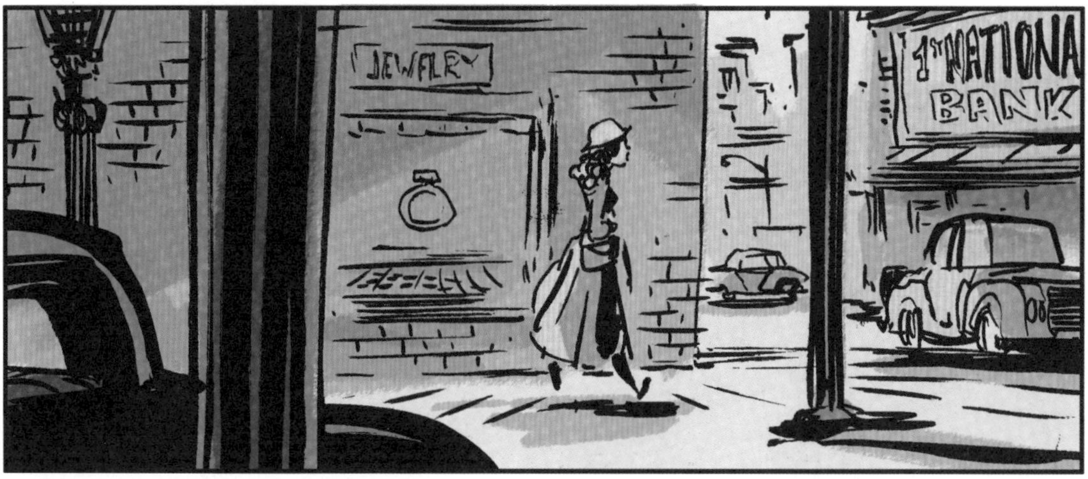
JEWELRY
1st NATIONA
BANK

NANA'S MIND COULDN'T BE SAVED, BUT NANA'S *SAVINGS*...
...SUZIE WAS SURE NANA WOULDN'T MIND.

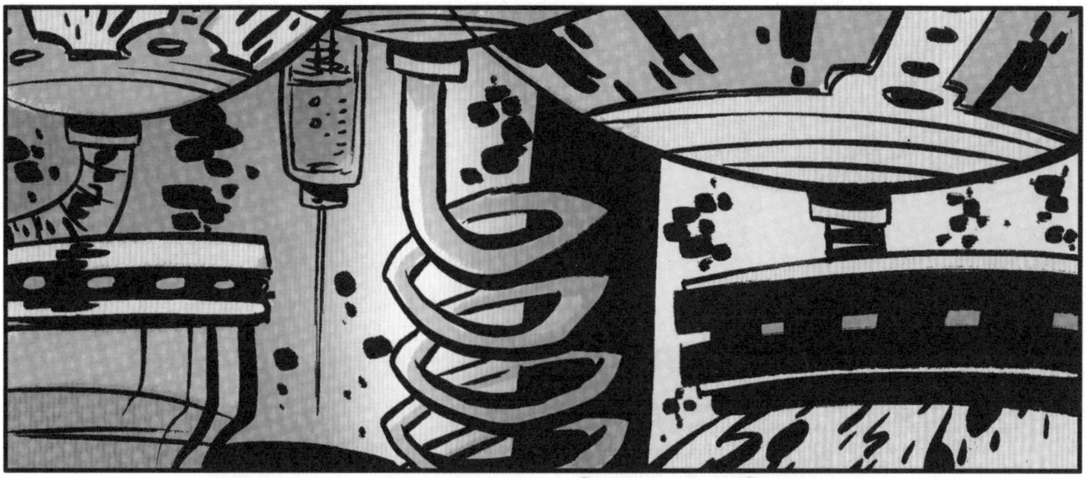

INTERNAPLASMIC REPAIR THERAPY.
IT HAD NEVER BEEN *DONE.* IT HAD NEVER BEEN *HEARD OF.*

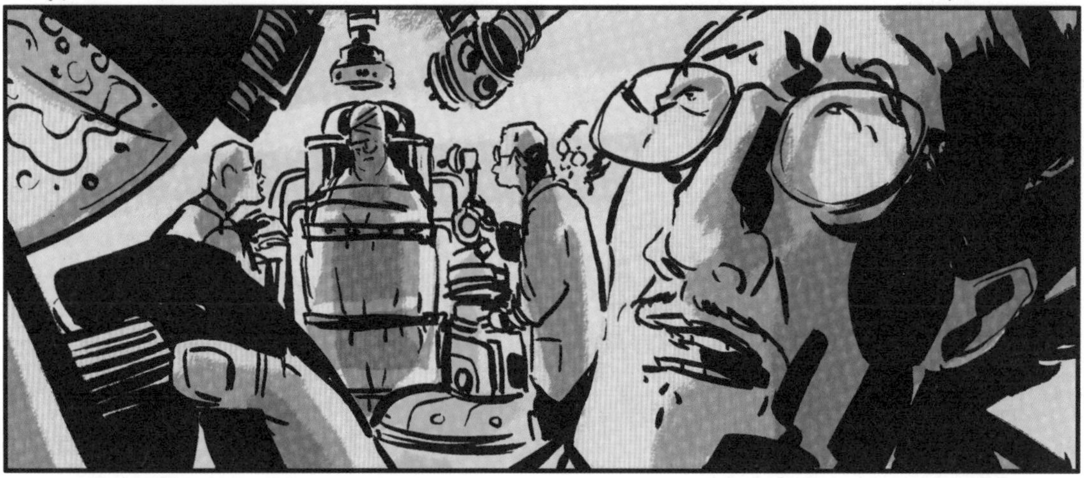

JUST ENOUGH CASH TO PRODUCE ONE DOSE OF *HOPE.*

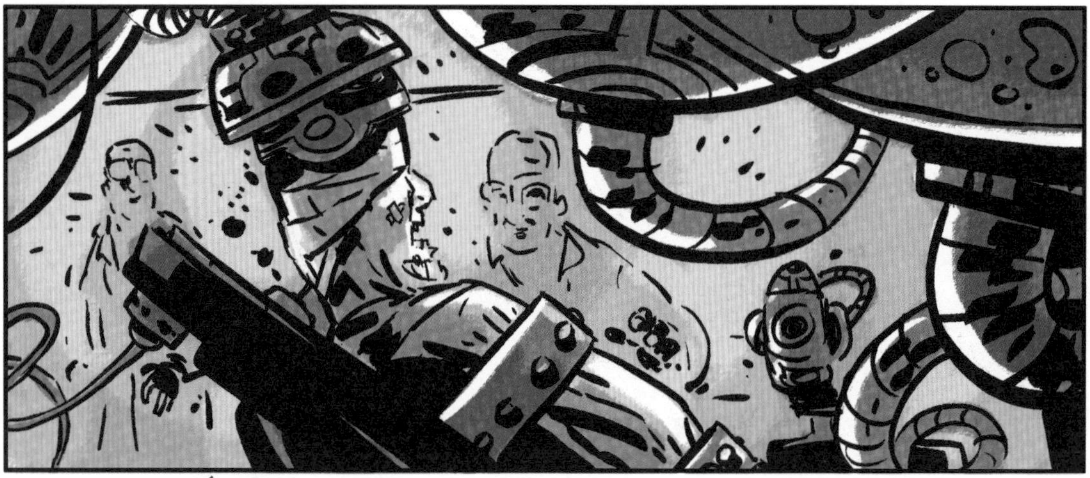

YEARS HAD GONE INTO THE RESEARCH.
ORGANIC MATTER ENHANCEMENT AND--

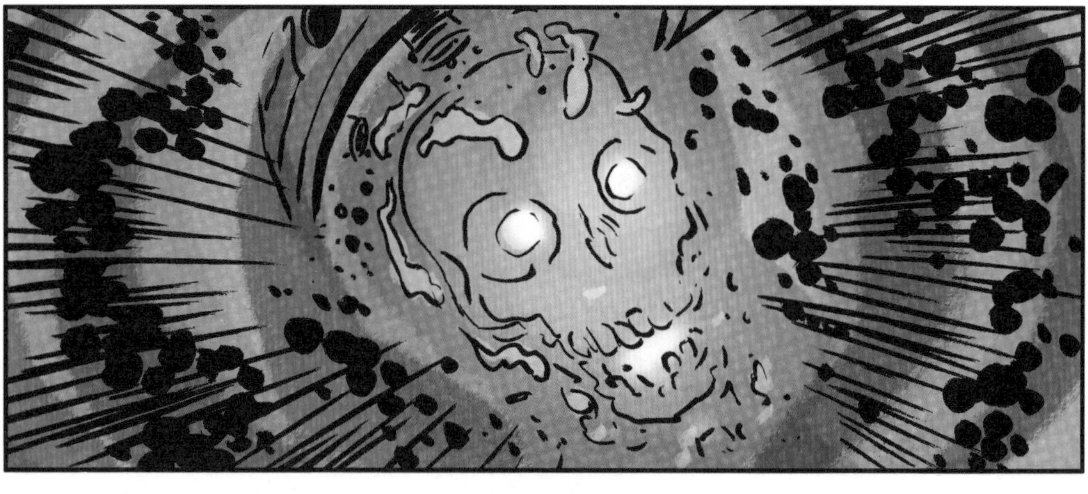

--WAIT--

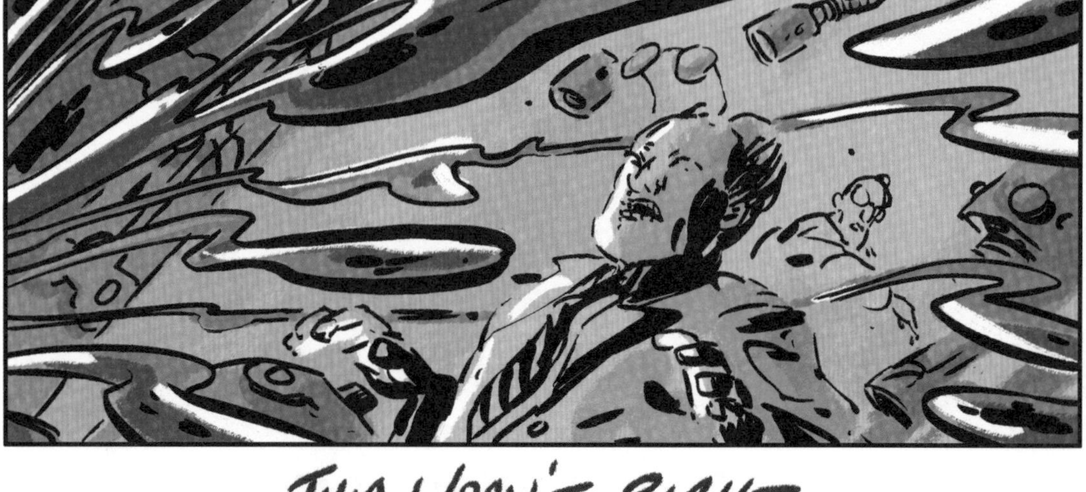

THIS WASN'T RIGHT.

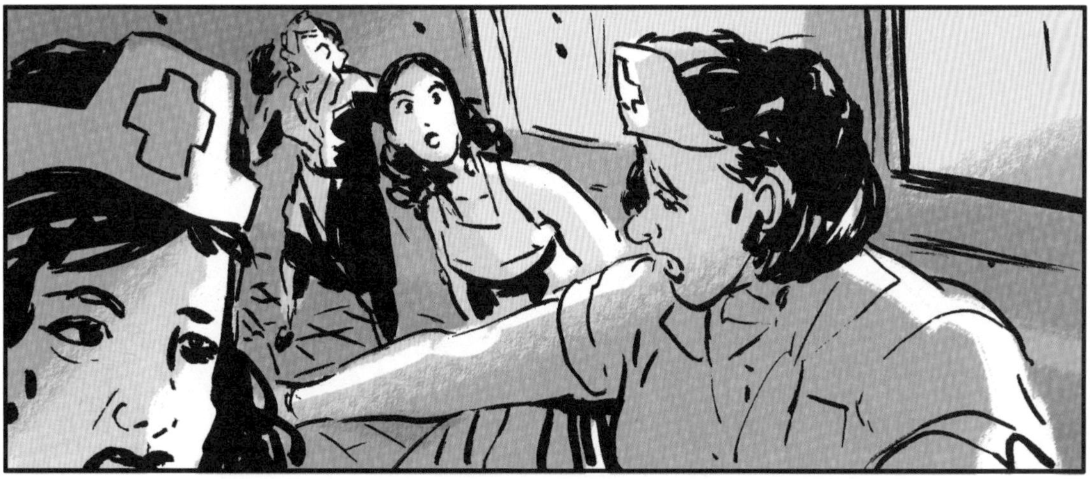

SUZIE COULD HEAR THE ONE-OF-A-KIND
EQUIPMENT BEING DESTROYED.

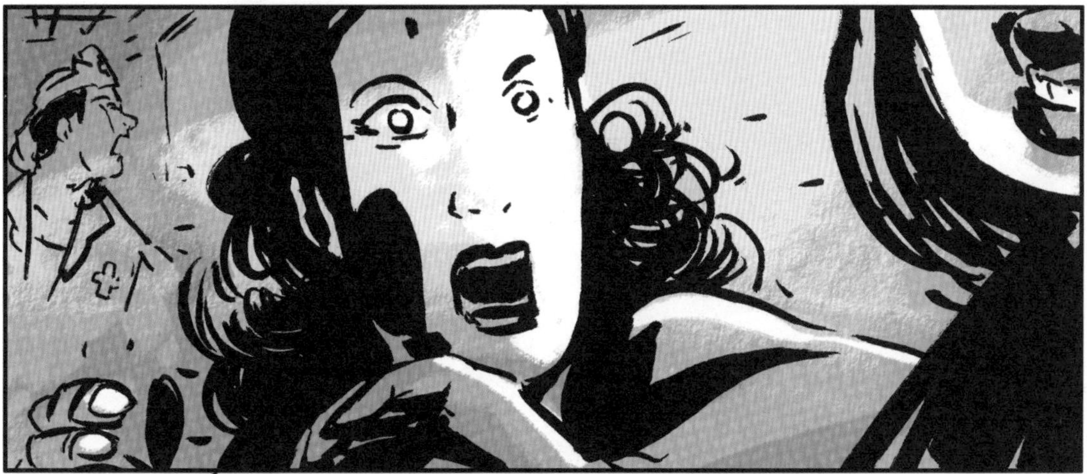

SUZIE COULD HEAR THE SCREAMS--
--BOTH HIS--AND HER OWN!

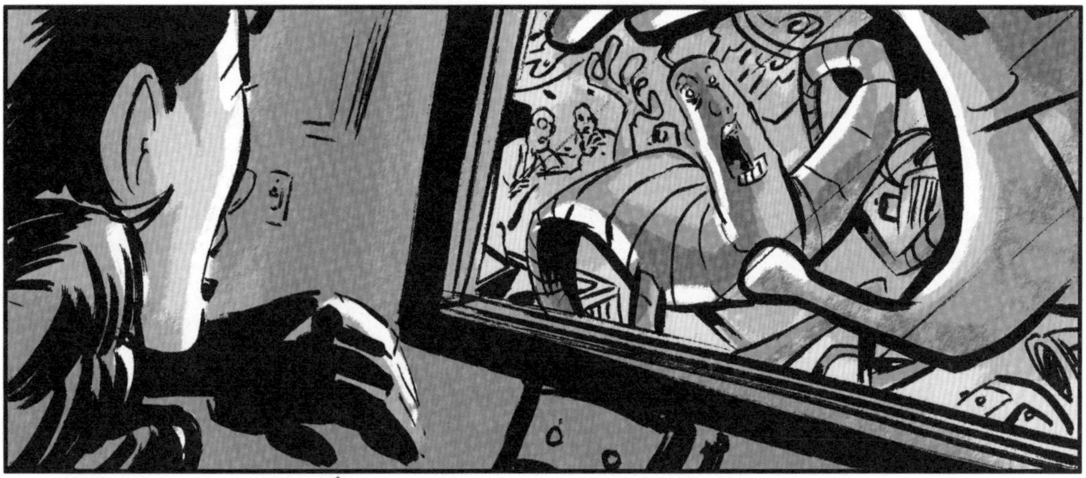

THIS WASN'T WHAT SHE'D PAID FOR.

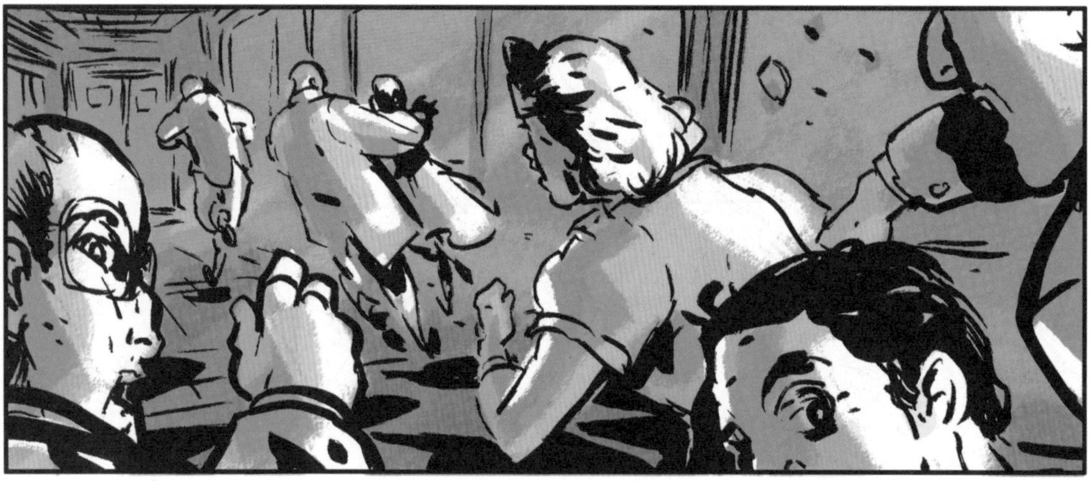

HOWLS OF CONFUSION BENT THEIR WAY DOWN
THE HALLS OF SCIENCE, HOT ON THE HEELS OF THE DO-GOODERS.

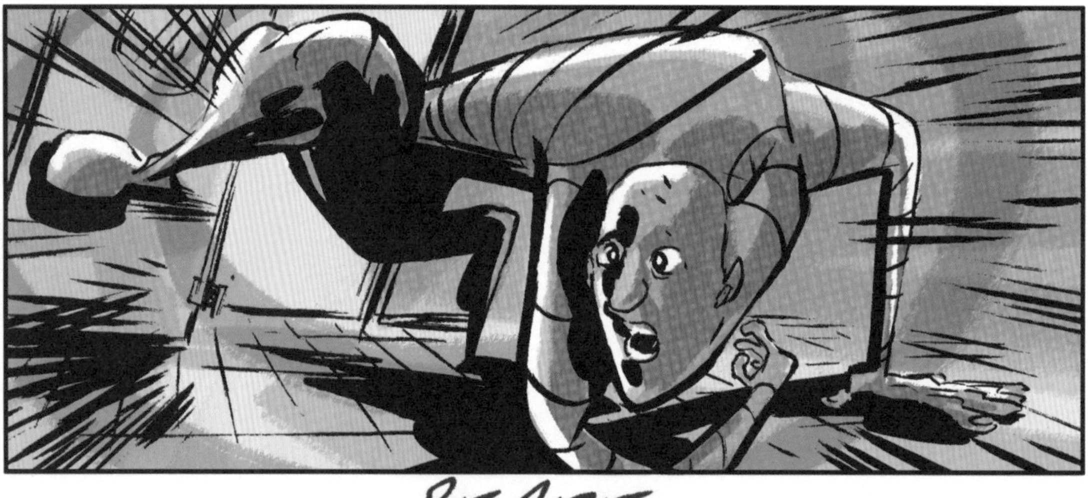

BUT SUZIE...
WHERE WAS SUZIE?

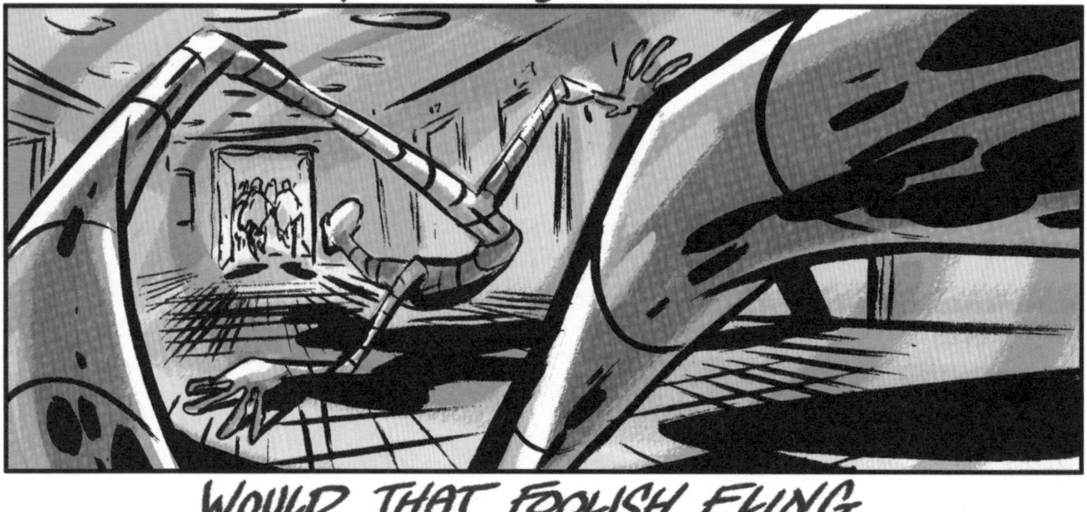

WOULD THAT FOOLISH FLING
IN NO WAY PAY OFF?

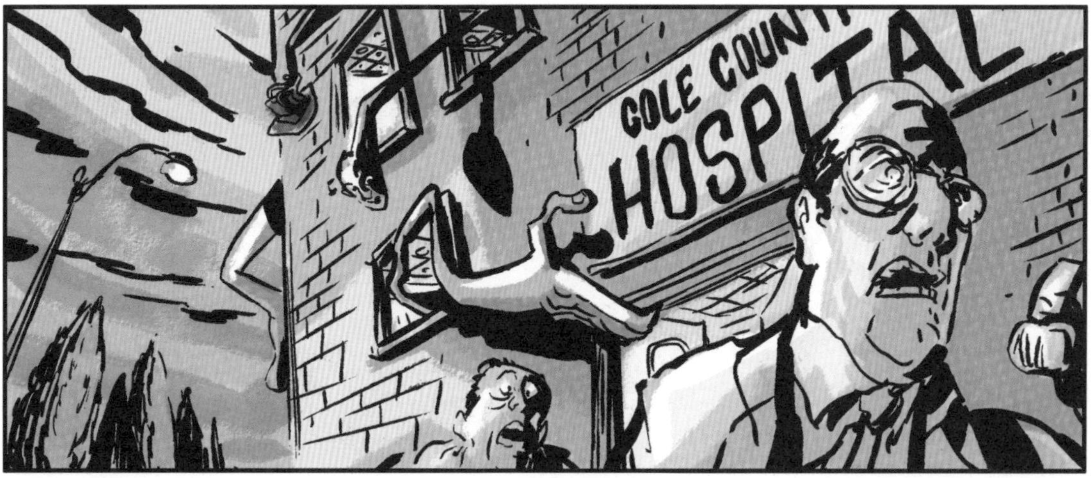
COLE COUNT
HOSPITAL

OH, CRUEL CIRCUMSTANCE! IT IS REALITY ITSELF THAT YOU STRETCH AND CONTORT TO YOUR HIDEOUS WILL!

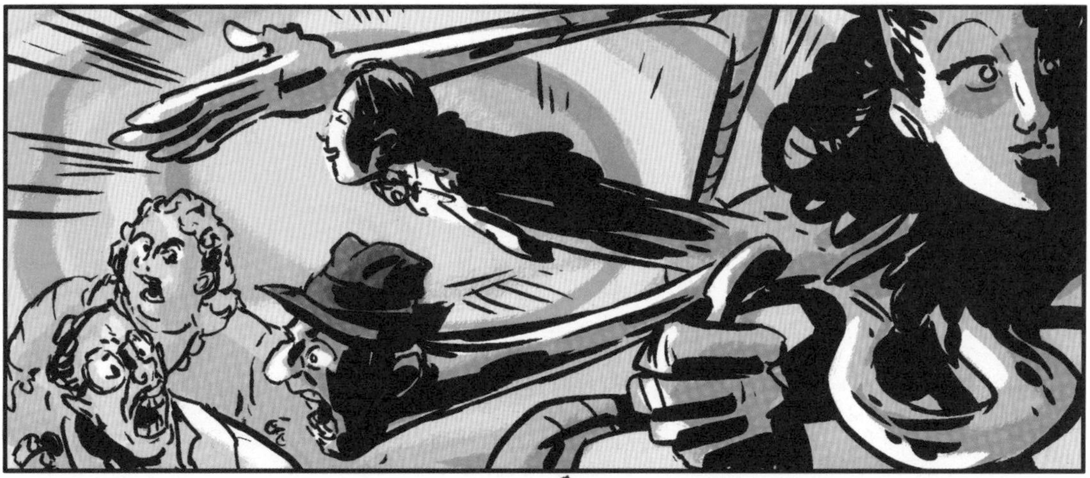

HE NEEDED TO FIND SUZIE! HAD ANYONE SEEN HIS GIRL? WITHOUT HER, HE WAS JUST ANOTHER--

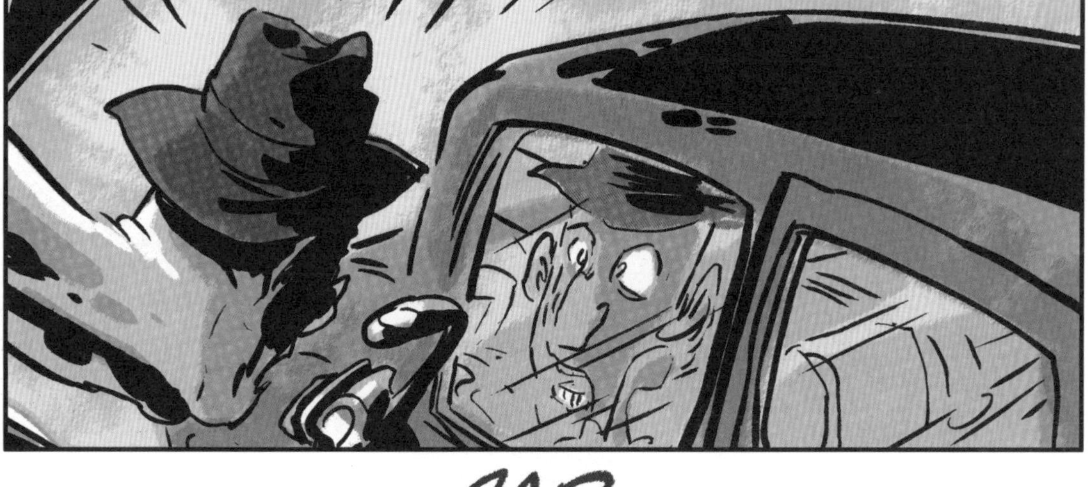

--SAP--

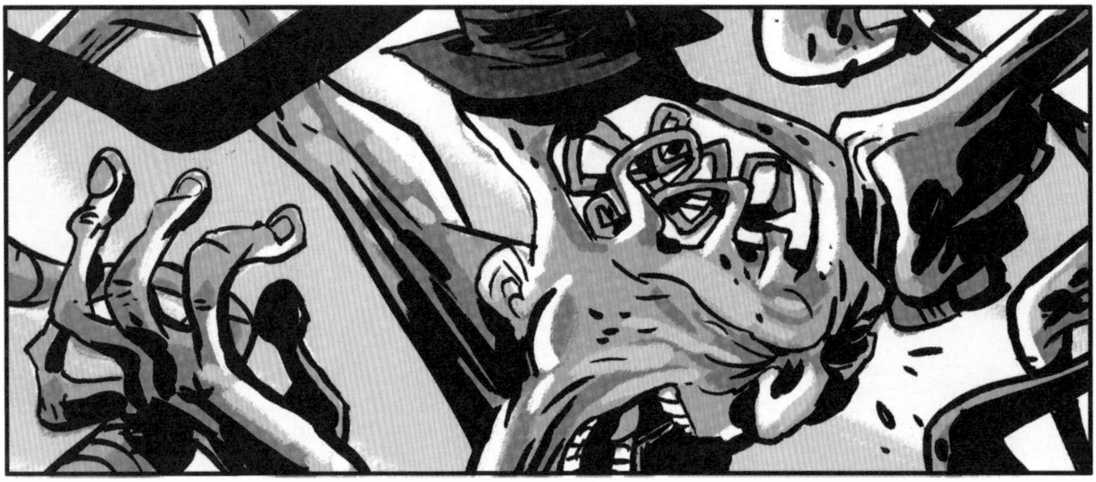

THE TRUTHS OF HIS HUMANITY--STRETCHED! THOUGHTS BOUNCED AROUND HIS BRAIN...

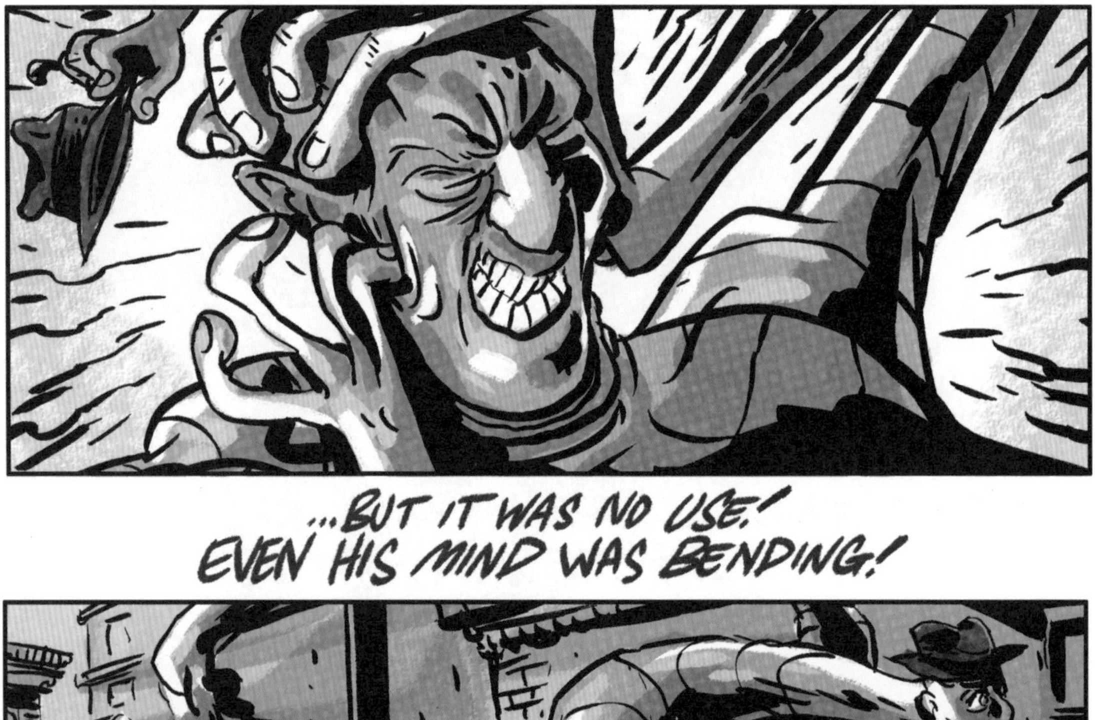

...BUT IT WAS NO USE! EVEN HIS MIND WAS BENDING!

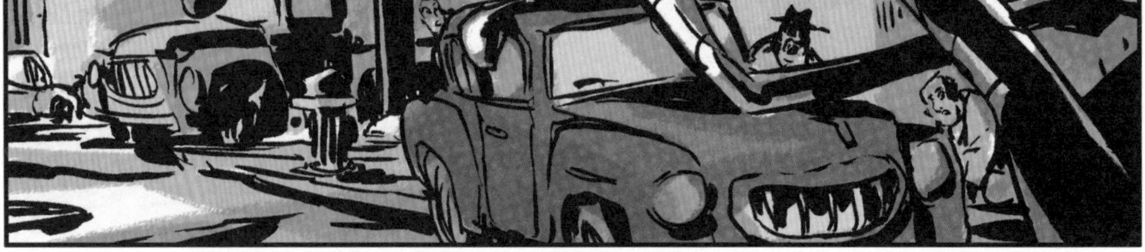

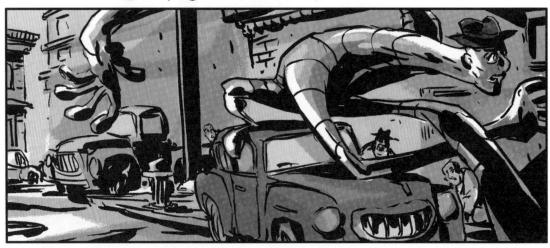

HIS PLOT HAD TAKEN THE TWIST OF A LIFETIME!

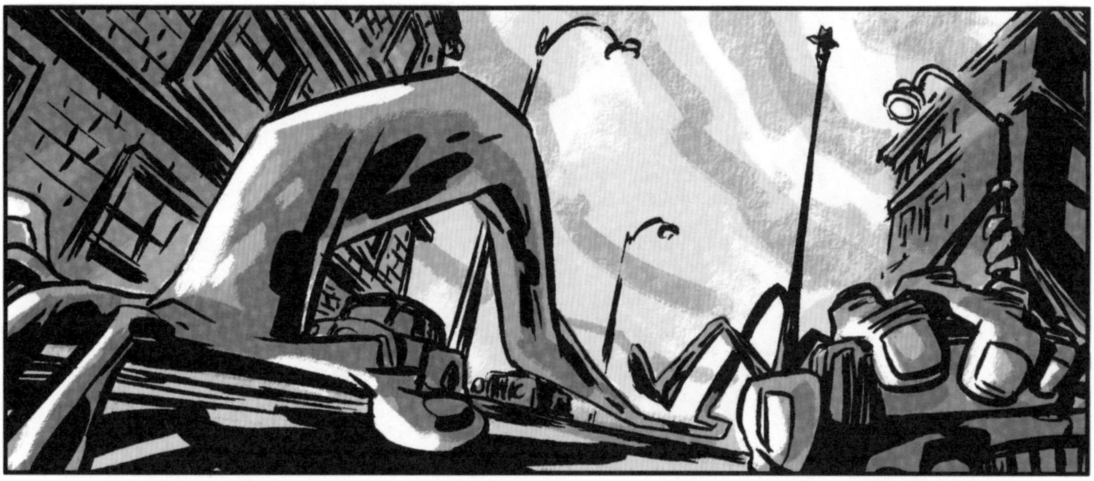

HIGH AND LOW, HE POURED THROUGH THE CITY LOOKING FOR ANSWERS... STRAIGHT ANSWERS.

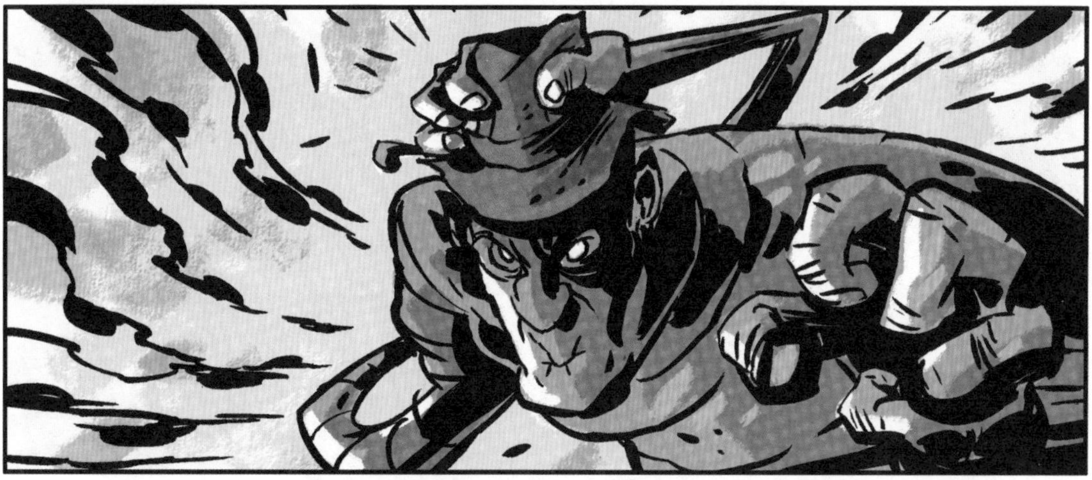

TWISTED THOUGHTS ONLY BOUNCED BACK INTO SOFT CONCLUSIONS.

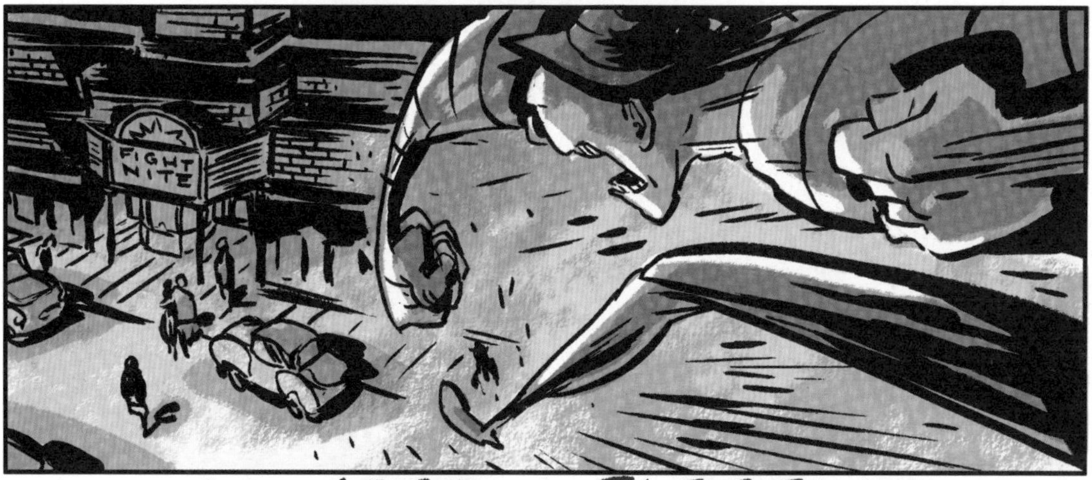
FIGHT NITE

IT ALL STARTED WITH THE FIGHTS...
...AND GOOD OL' TWO-FACED GEORGIE.

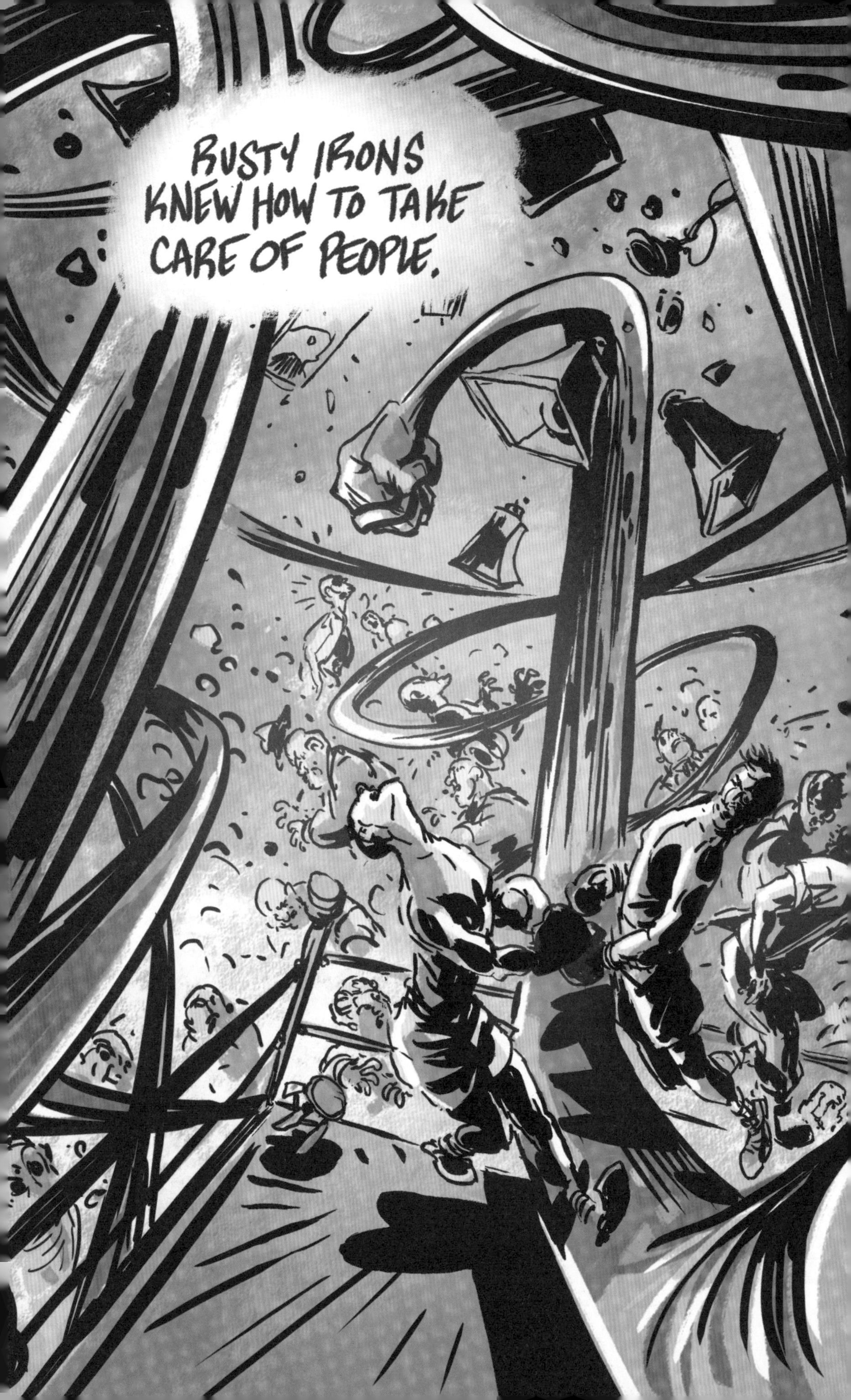
RUSTY IRONS
KNEW HOW TO TAKE
CARE OF PEOPLE.

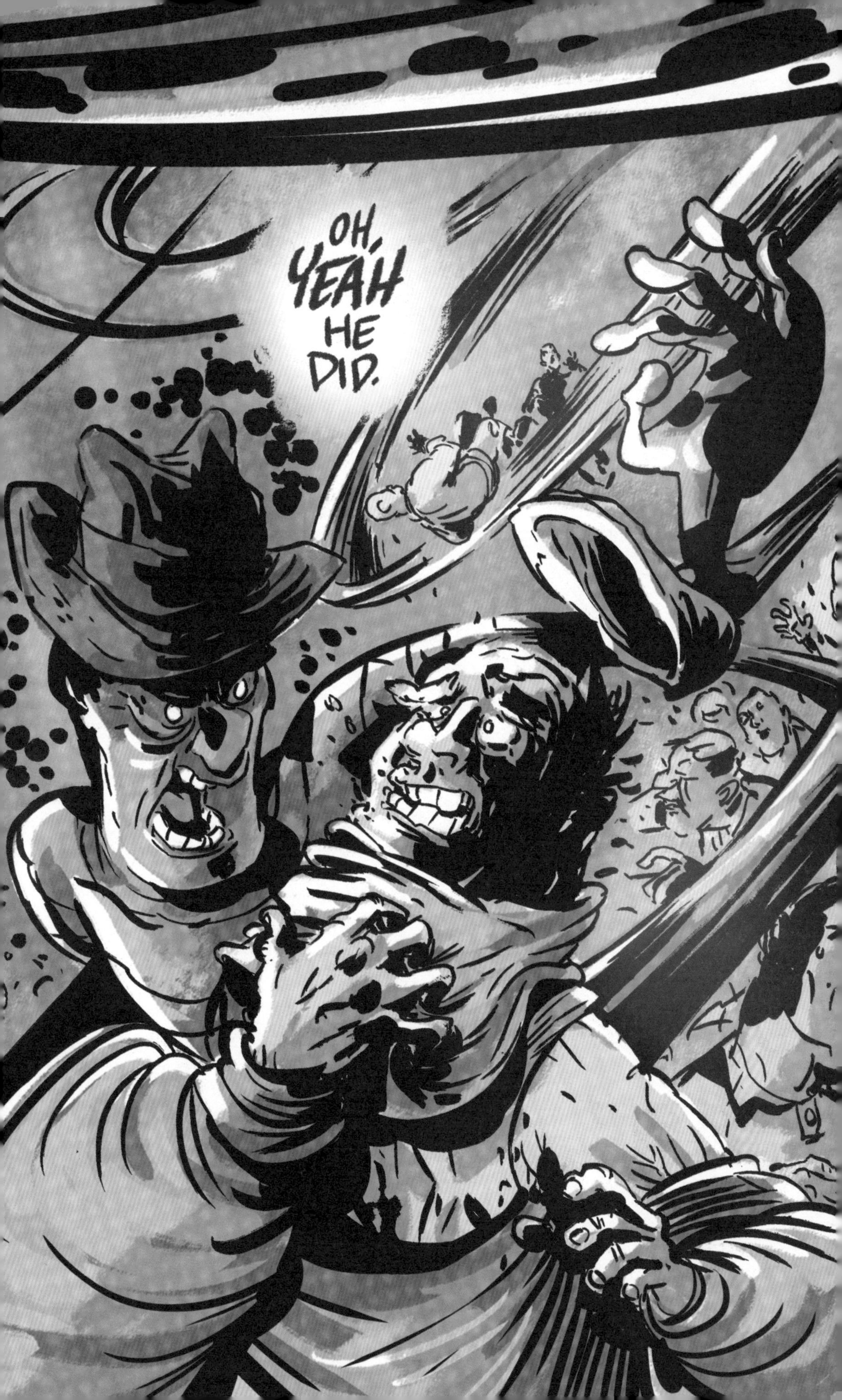
OH, YEAH HE DID.

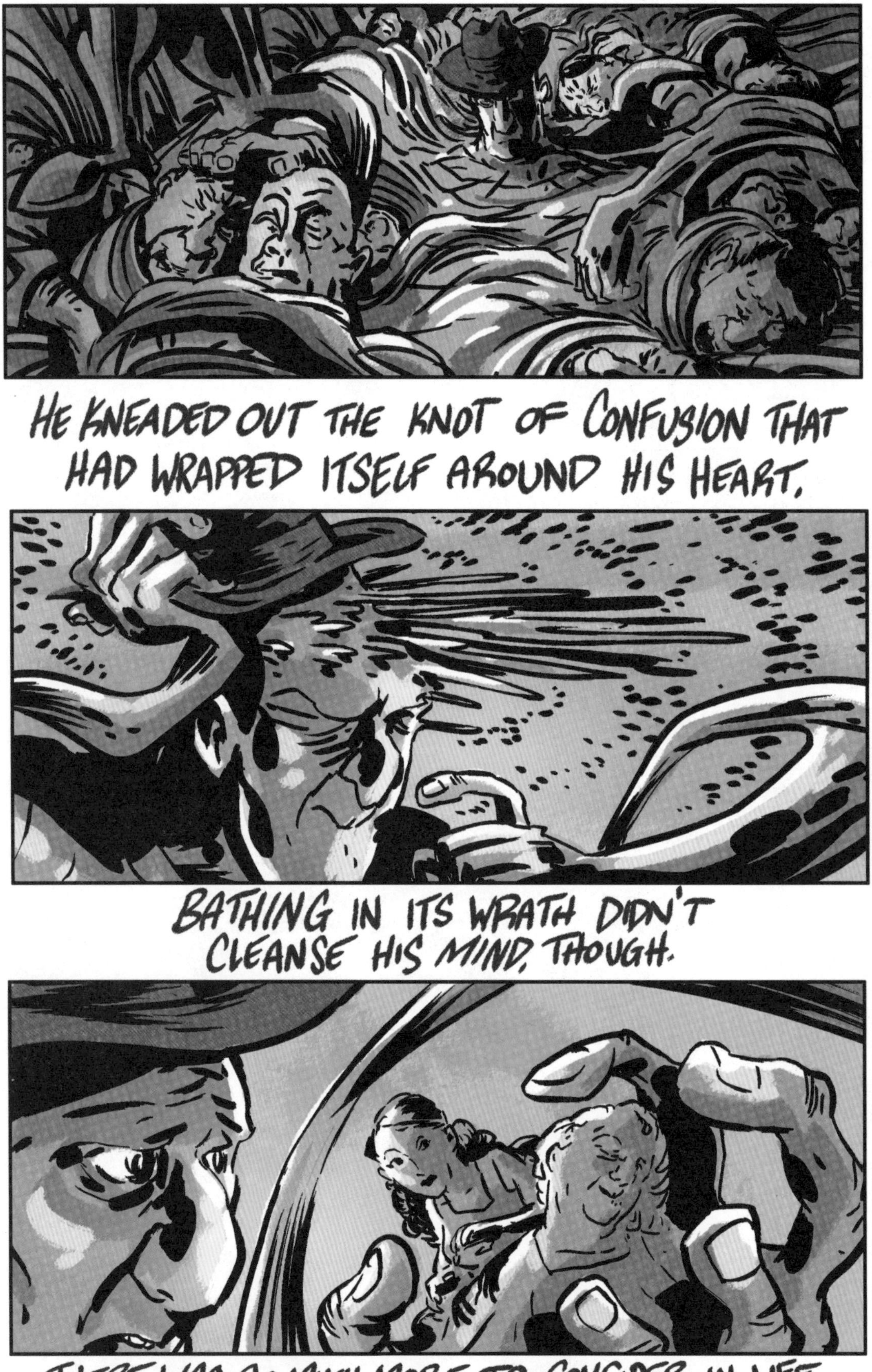
HE KNEADED OUT THE KNOT OF CONFUSION THAT HAD WRAPPED ITSELF AROUND HIS HEART.
BATHING IN ITS WRATH DIDN'T CLEANSE HIS MIND, THOUGH.
THERE WAS SO MUCH MORE TO CONSIDER IN LIFE. SO MUCH ENTWINED WITH HIS SOUL!

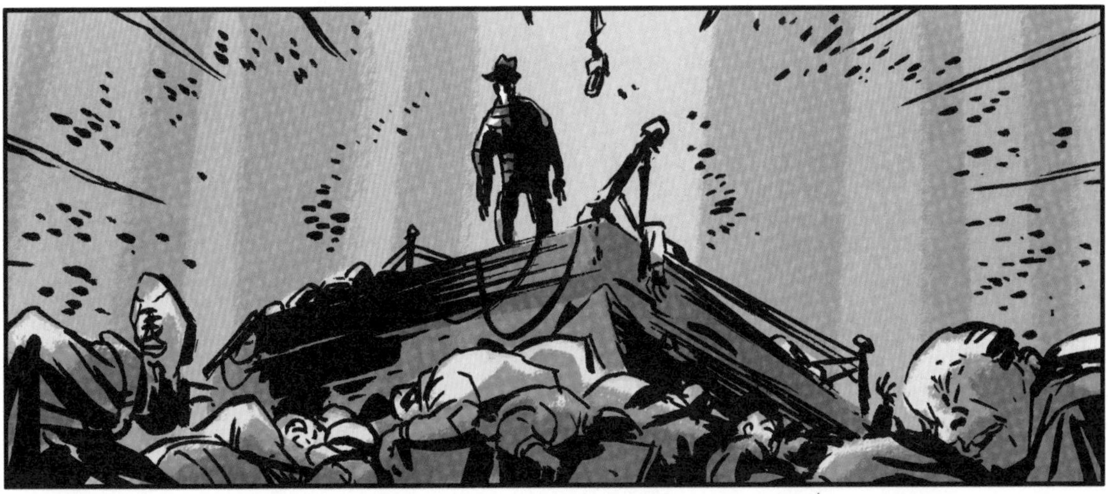

THE TWISTED TURN OF EVENTS AT HIS FEET WAS
THE DISTORTED MESS OF A MADMAN.

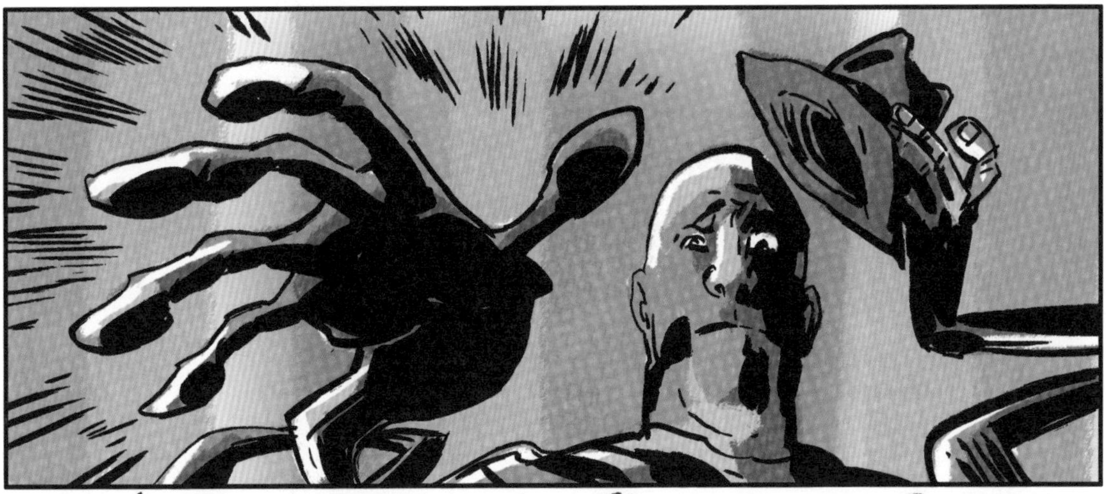

THEY'D BE AFTER HIM ...THE COPS... THE BOOKIES...
...REALLY AFTER HIM FOR A BENDER LIKE THIS.

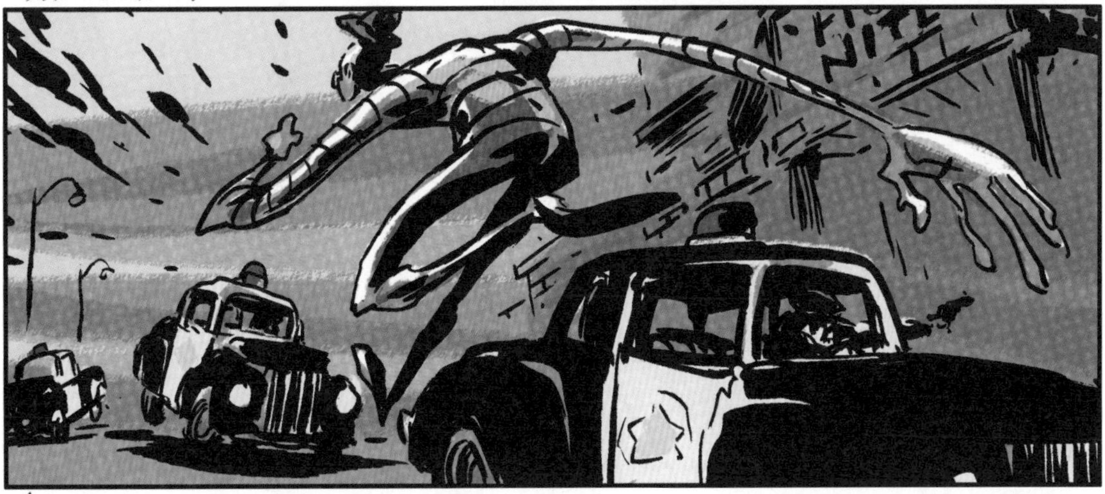

HE HAD TO FIND SUZIE... TRY TO PUSH IT ALL BACK INTO SHAPE!
PROBABLY AT HOME WITH NANA...

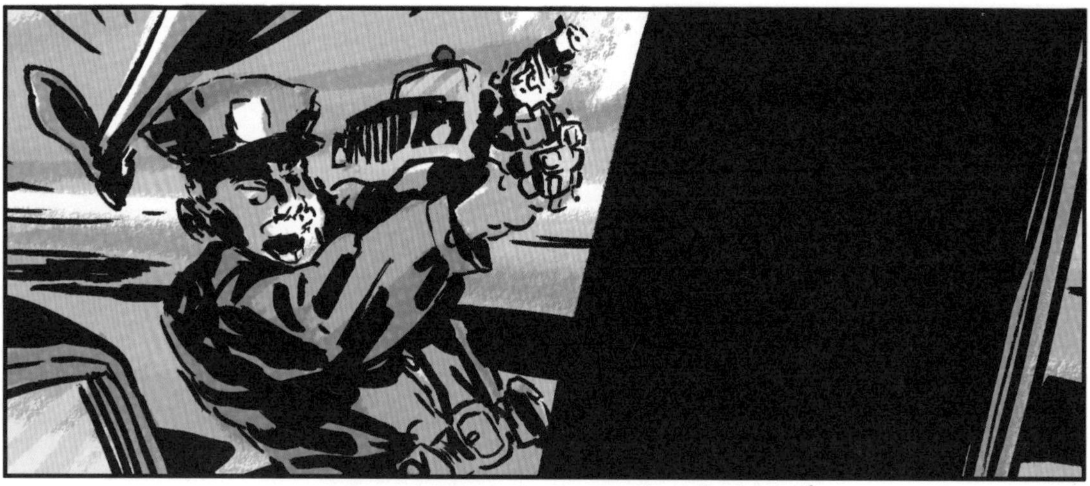

ALREADY WITH COPS!
THEY FLEW INTO THE FRAY LIKE BEES TO HONEY!

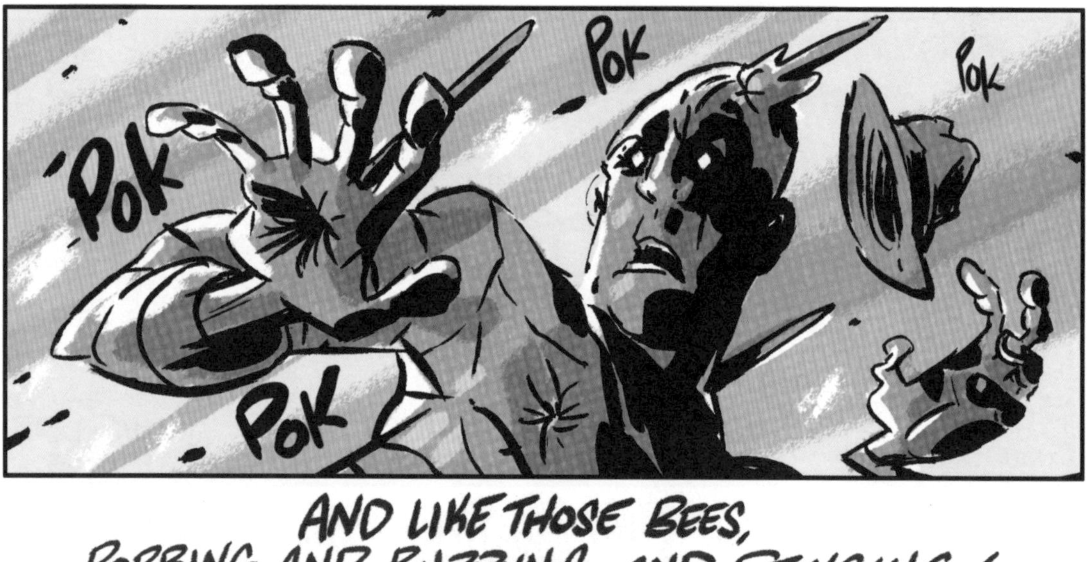
POK
POK
POK
POK

AND LIKE THOSE BEES,
BOBBING AND BUZZING AND STINGING!

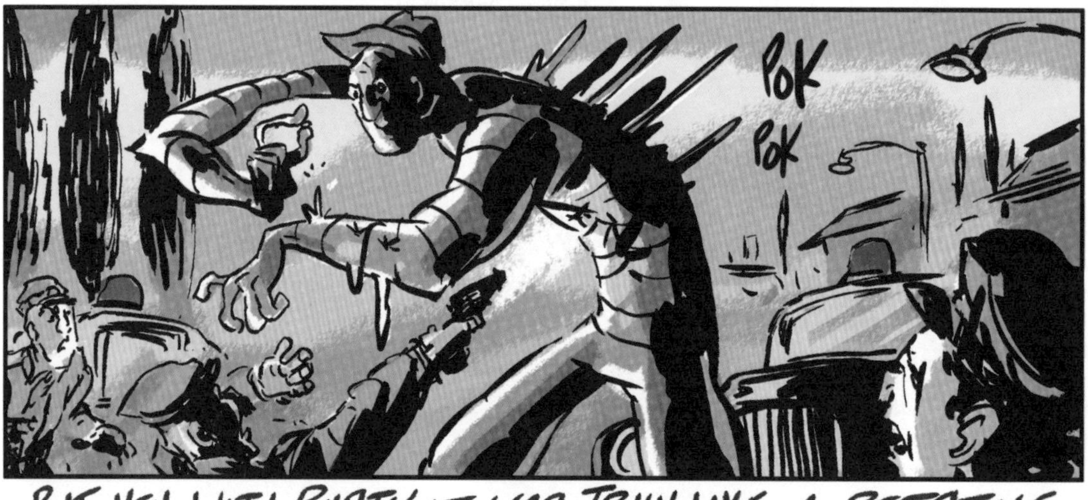
POK
POK

BUT HEY, WITH *RUSTY*, IT WAS TRULY LIKE A BEESTING.
JUST PLUCK OUT THE STINGER.

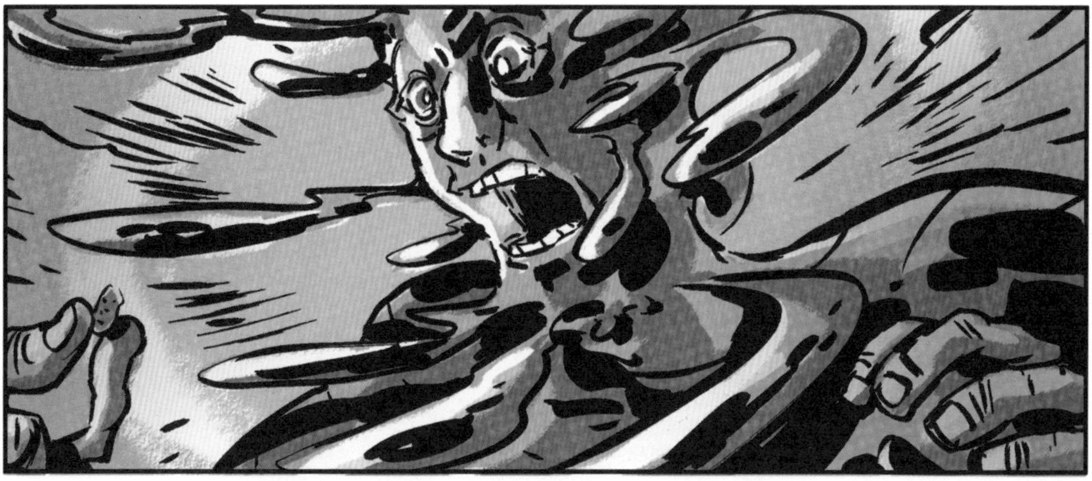

COULD HE EXPLAIN THIS SWARM OF STUFF TO SUZIE?
WOULD SHE UNDERSTAND?

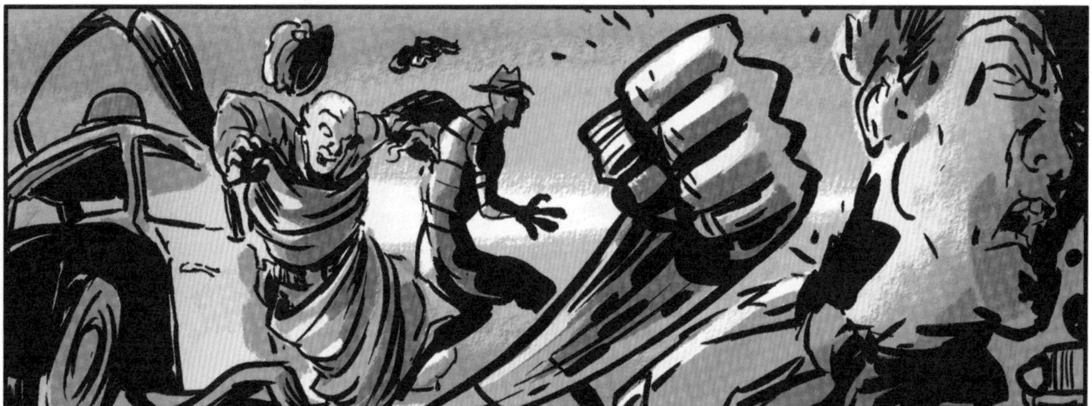

HE FRANTICALLY SWATTED AWAY THE DRONING
BUZZ OF THE FUZZ!

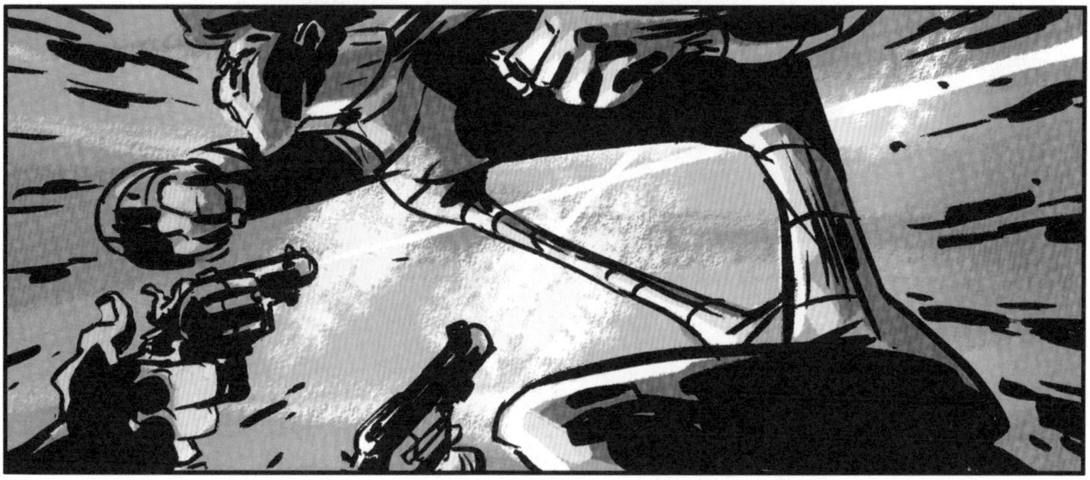

HE HAD TO GET TO HER HOUSE! SHE'D BE HOME... RIGHT?

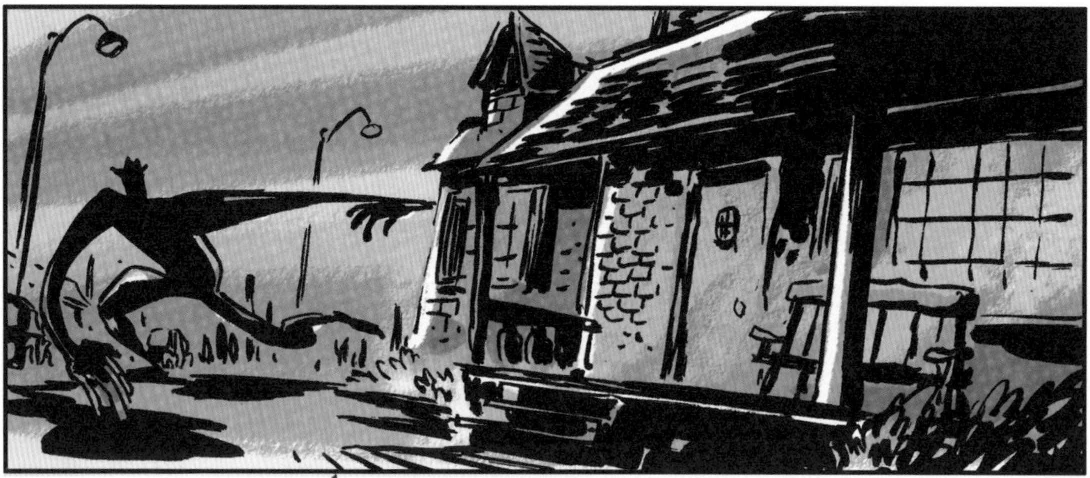

SHE'D BE WAITING FOR HIM...
...SHE ALWAYS DID, AFTER EVERY FIGHT!

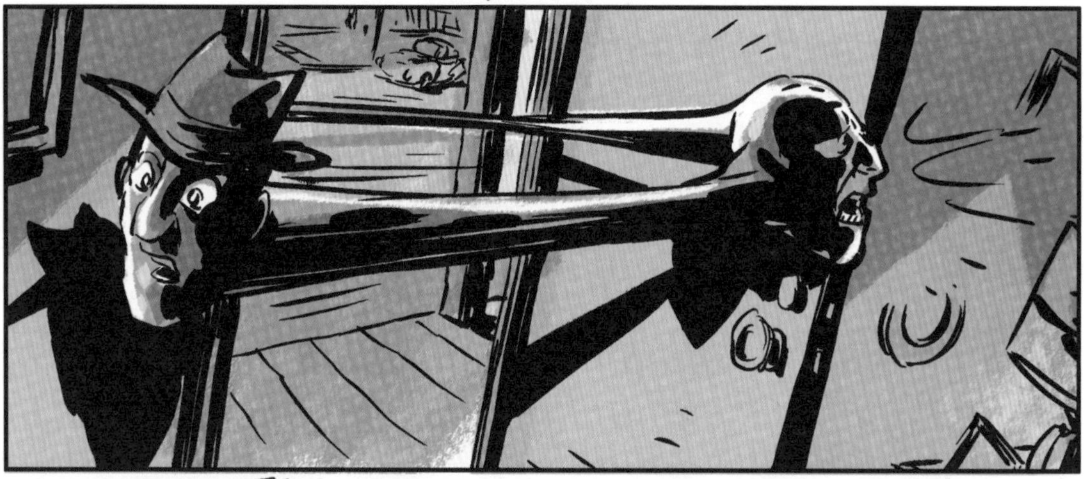

AND THIS FIGHT, IT WAS THE BIG ONE!
THE FIGHT OF HIS LIFE!

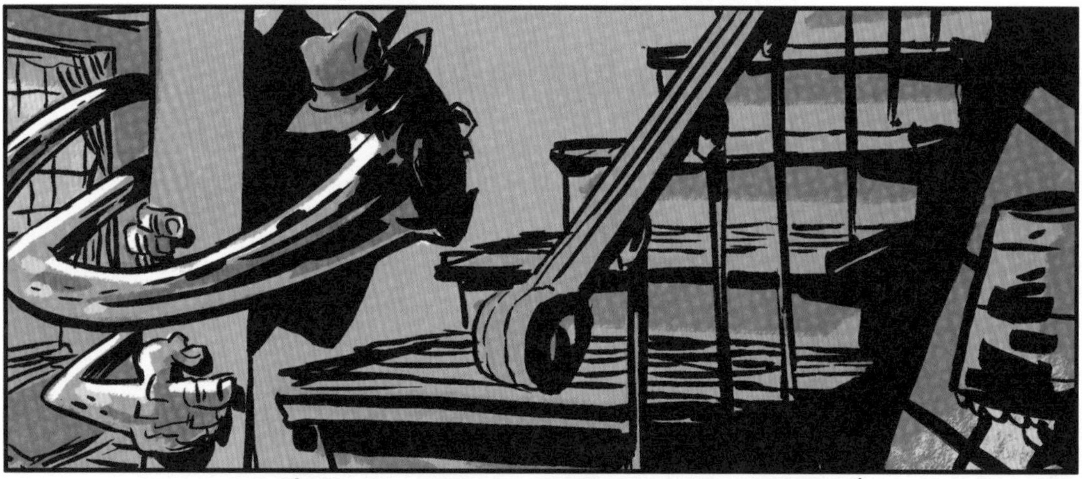

THE FIGHT FOR HIS LIFE!
FOR THEIR LIFE, TOGETHER! SUZIE!!!

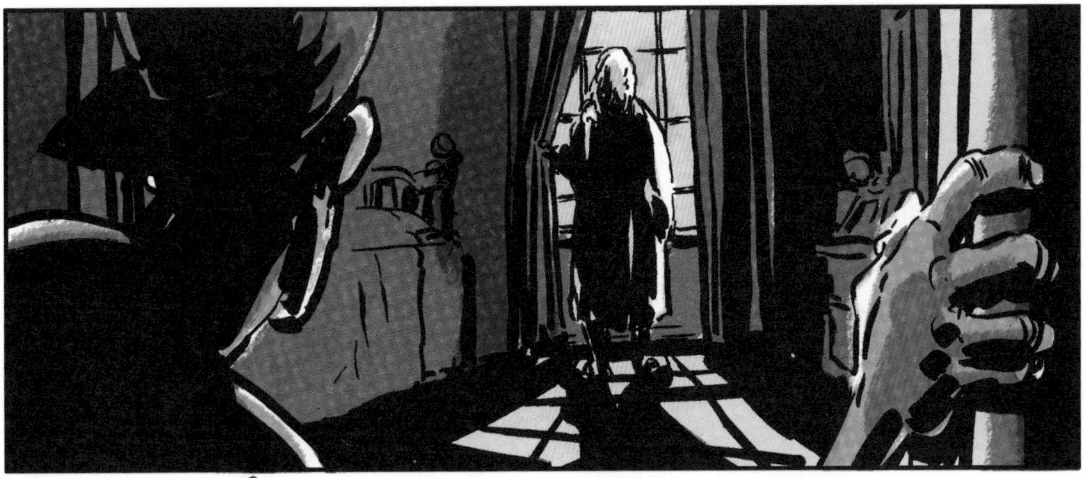

SUZIE...? NO... GOOD OL' NANA.
SHE MIGHT NOT UNDERSTAND, BUT SHE'D LISTEN...

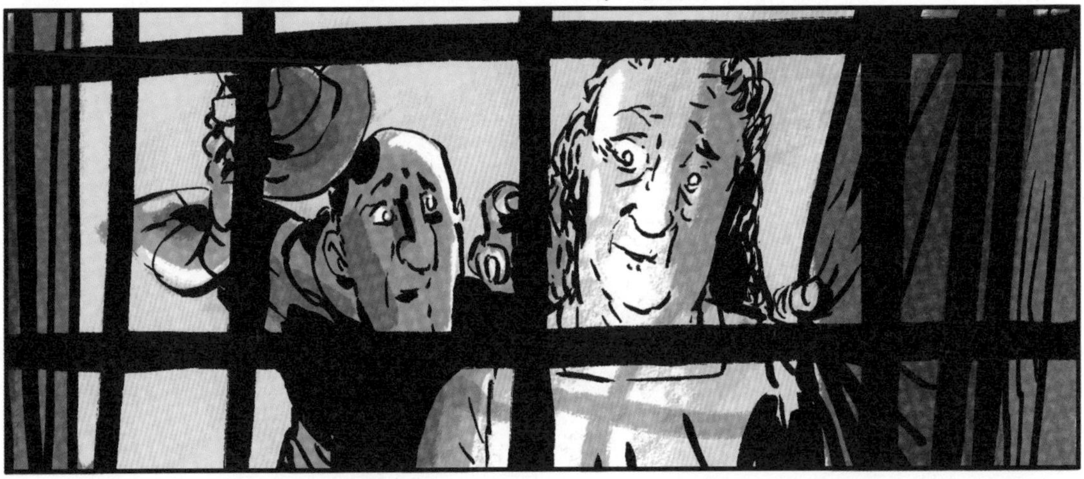

NANA... WHY WAS SHE AT THE WINDOW...?

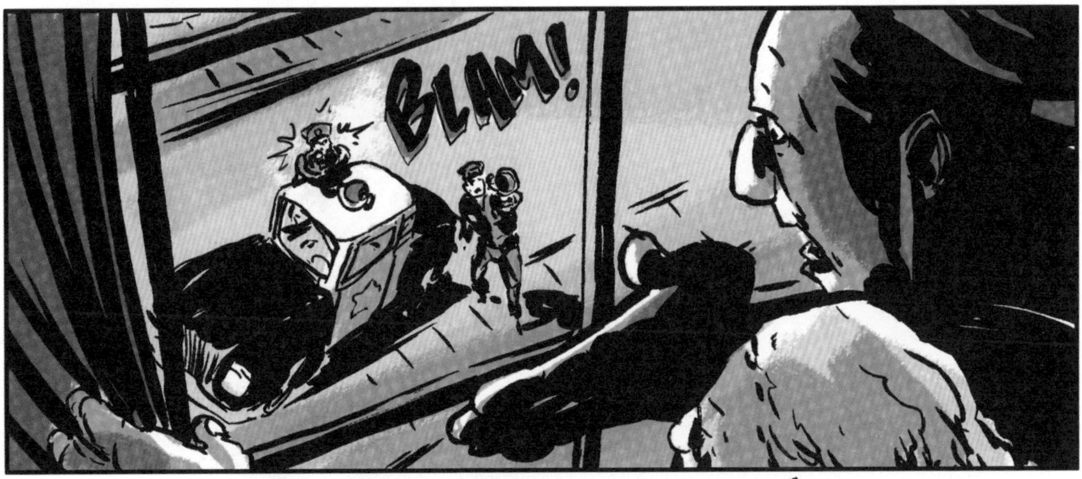
BLAM!

NOT THE COPS ALREADY!
NOT WITH THEIR STINGERS OUT! NO!!!

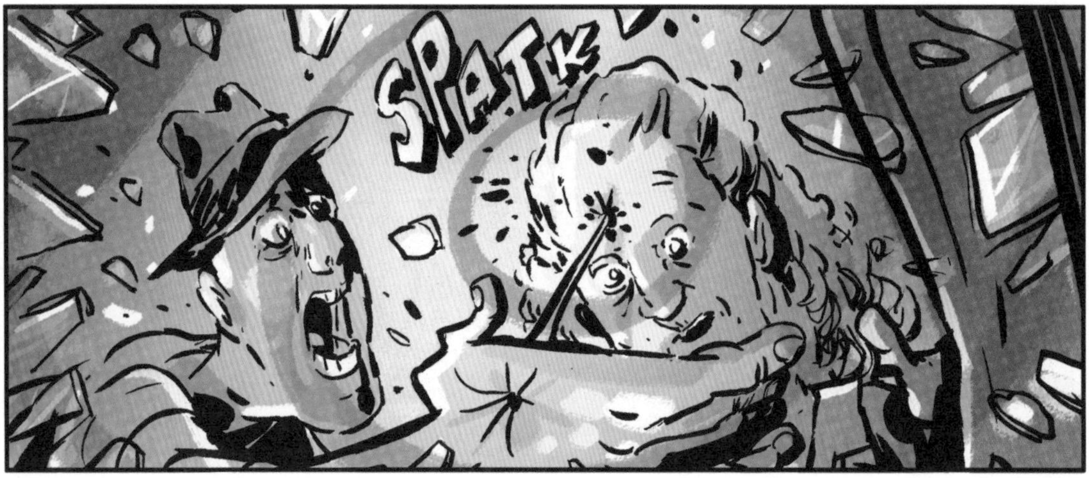
SPATK

OH, THAT TANGLED WEB OF SCIENCE... THAT SPIDER OF FATE!
WHILE SCIENCE MIGHT SAVE ONE PERSON...

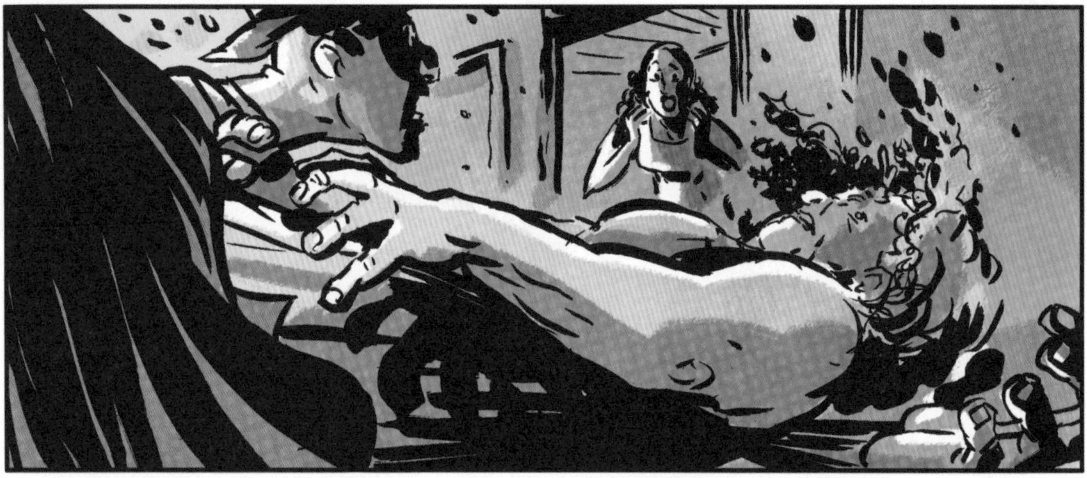

...THE HAND OF DOOM HAS A LONG REACH! THOSE EERIE
EIGHT LEGS OF FATE WILL WANDER WHERE THEY LIKE...

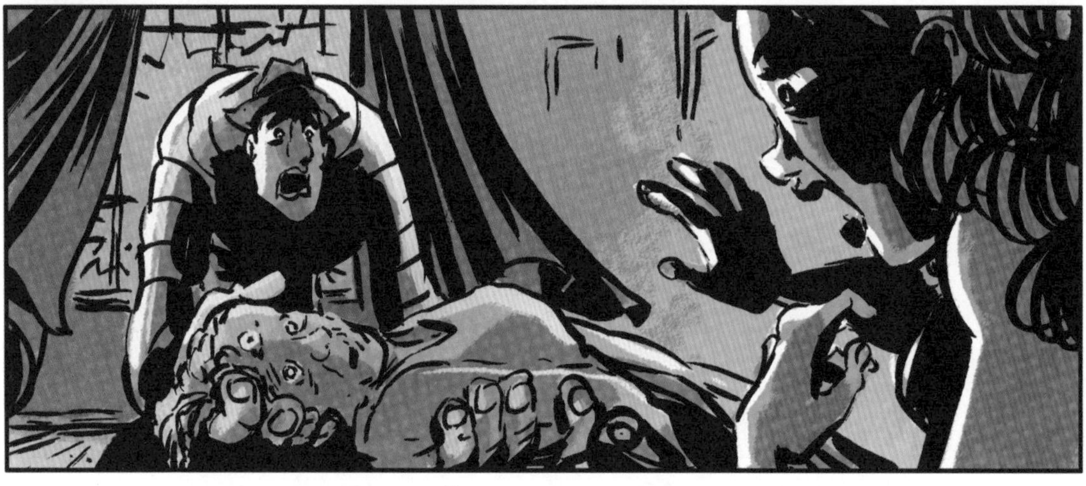

...EVEN TURNING MAN... INTO MONSTER!

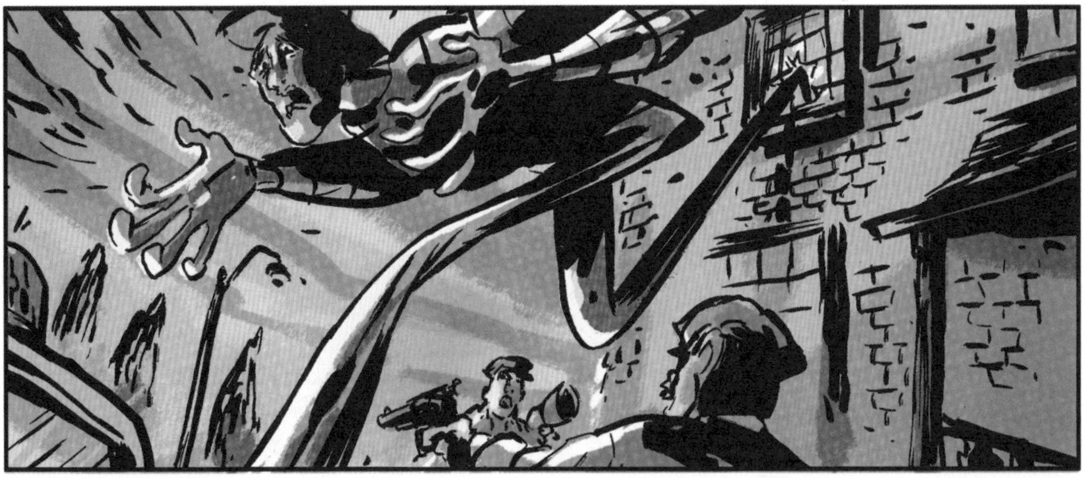

BUT REALLY... WHAT MAKES A MONSTER? PASSION? LOVE? THE MINDS OF SCIENCE? OR JUST THE TWISTED MIND?

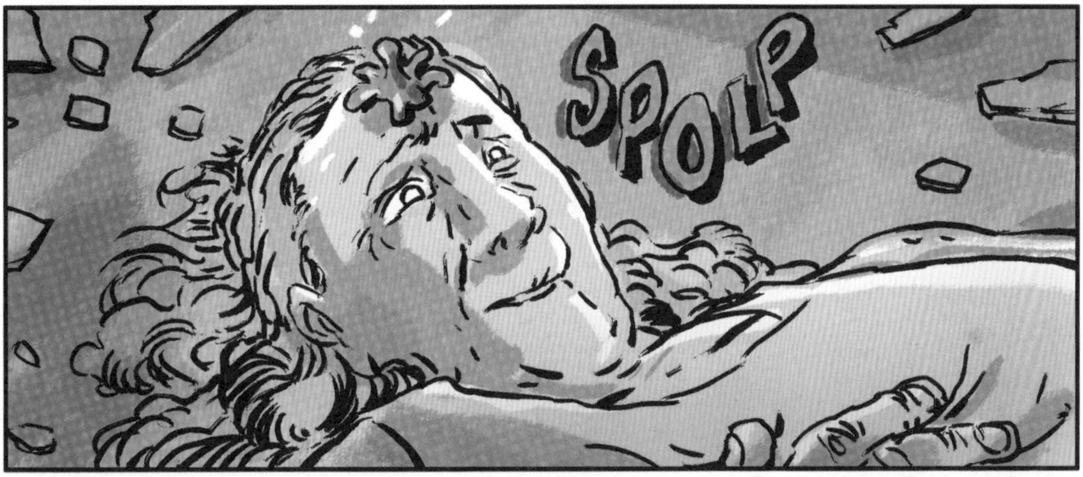
SPOLP

YOU PONDER THE ANSWER, BUT WRAP THIS AROUND YOUR BRAIN: NANA'S STINGER HAD A LITTLE EXTRA JUICE ON IT...

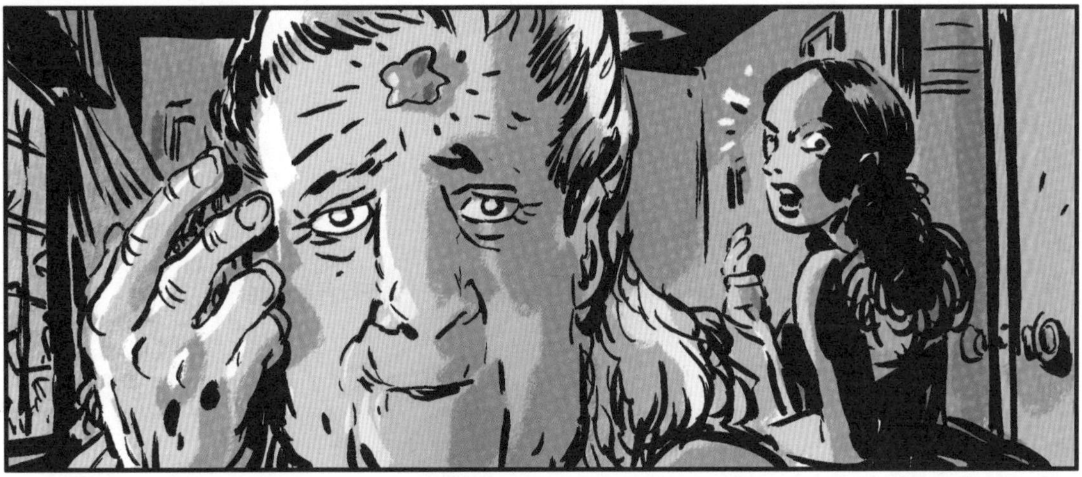

...JUICE FROM THAT MONSTER OF A MEDICAL MYSTERY. IT POPPED A CORK IN THAT OL' NOGGIN...

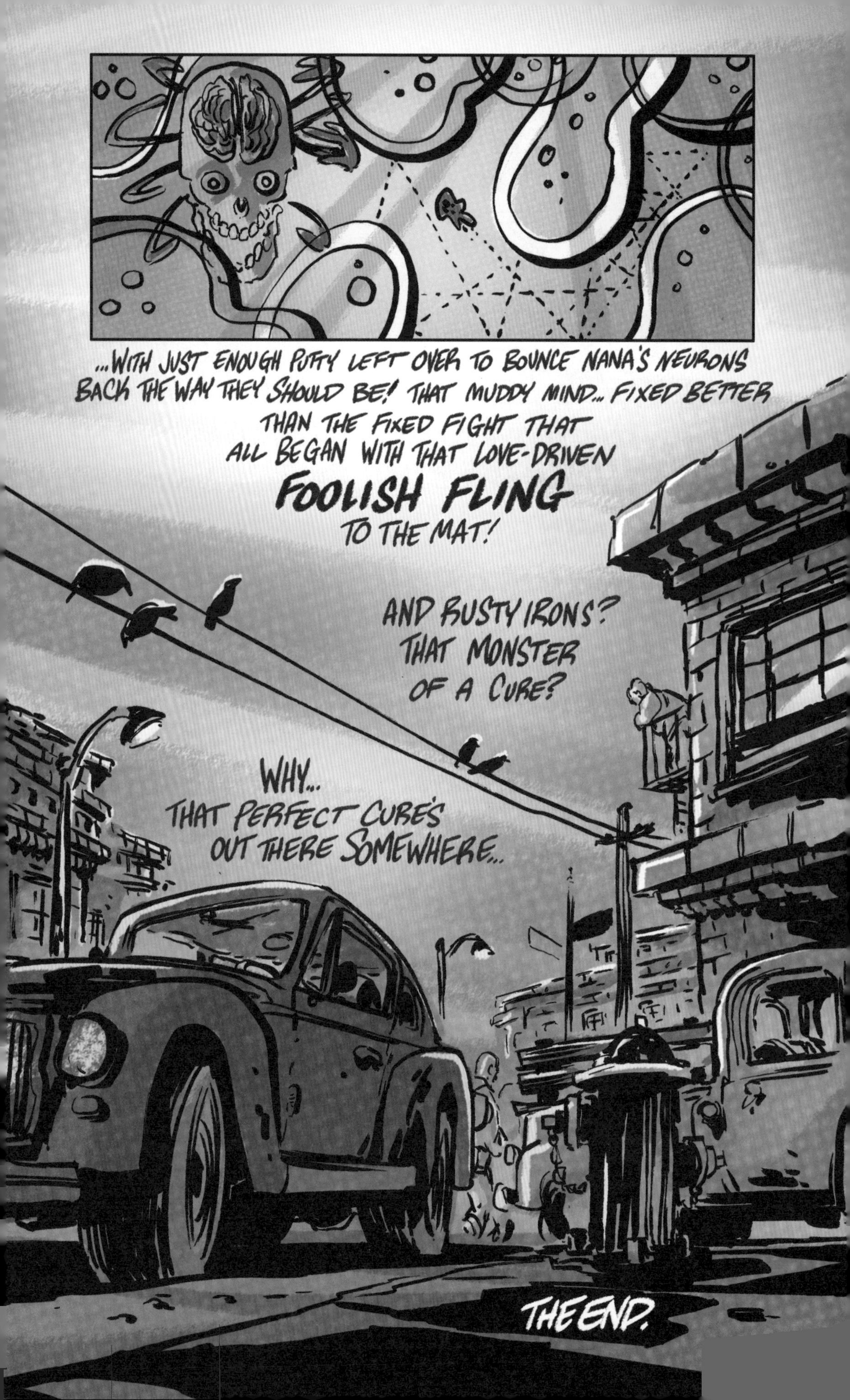
...WITH JUST ENOUGH PUTTY LEFT OVER TO BOUNCE NANA'S NEURONS BACK THE WAY THEY SHOULD BE! THAT MUDDY MIND... FIXED BETTER THAN THE FIXED FIGHT THAT ALL BEGAN WITH THAT LOVE-DRIVEN FOOLISH FLING TO THE MAT!
AND RUSTY IRONS? THAT MONSTER OF A CURE?
WHY... THAT PERFECT CURE'S OUT THERE SOMEWHERE...
THE END.

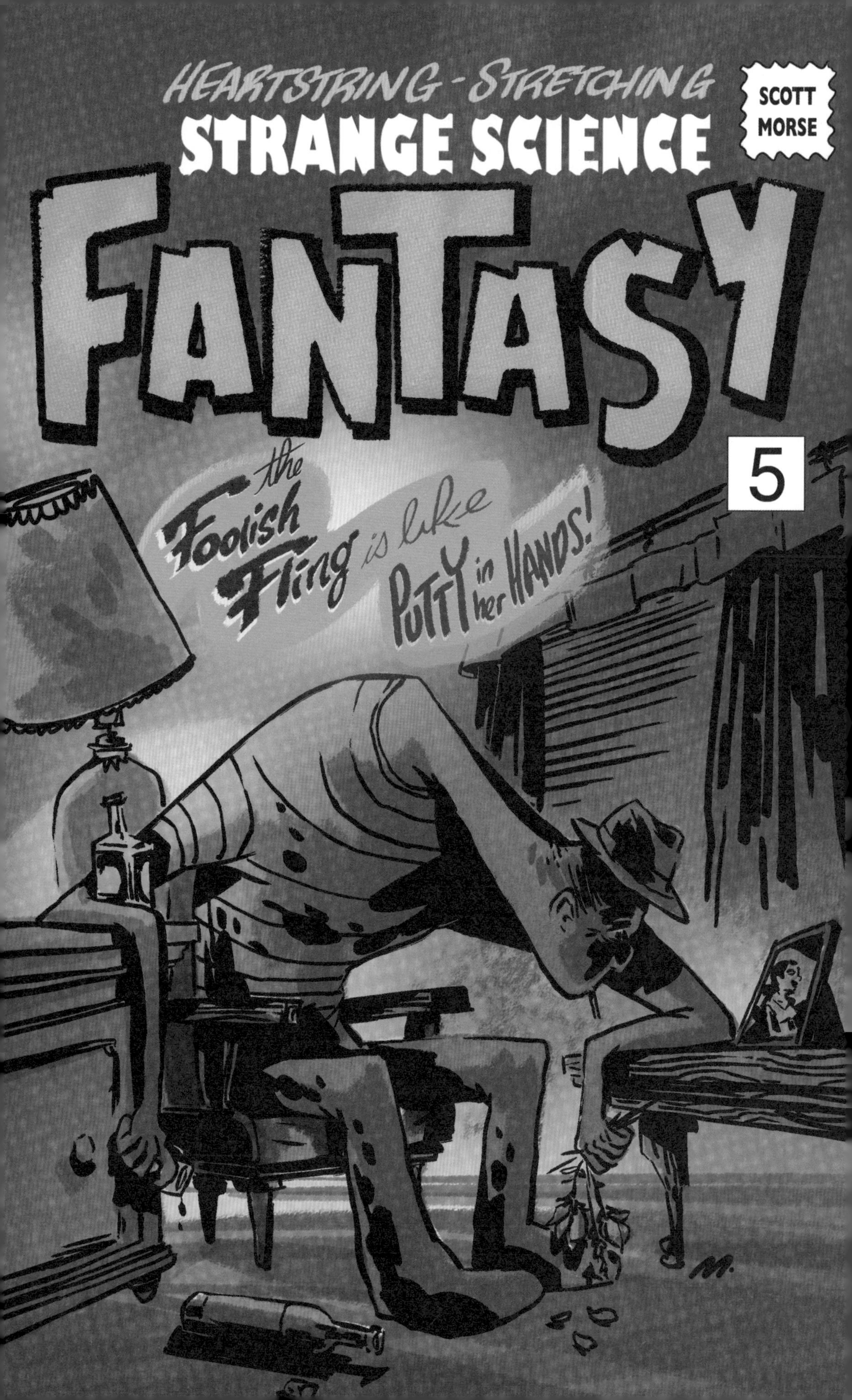

HEARTSTRING - STRETCHING
STRANGE SCIENCE
SCOTT MORSE
FANTASY
5
the Foolish Fling is like PUTTY in her HANDS!
M.

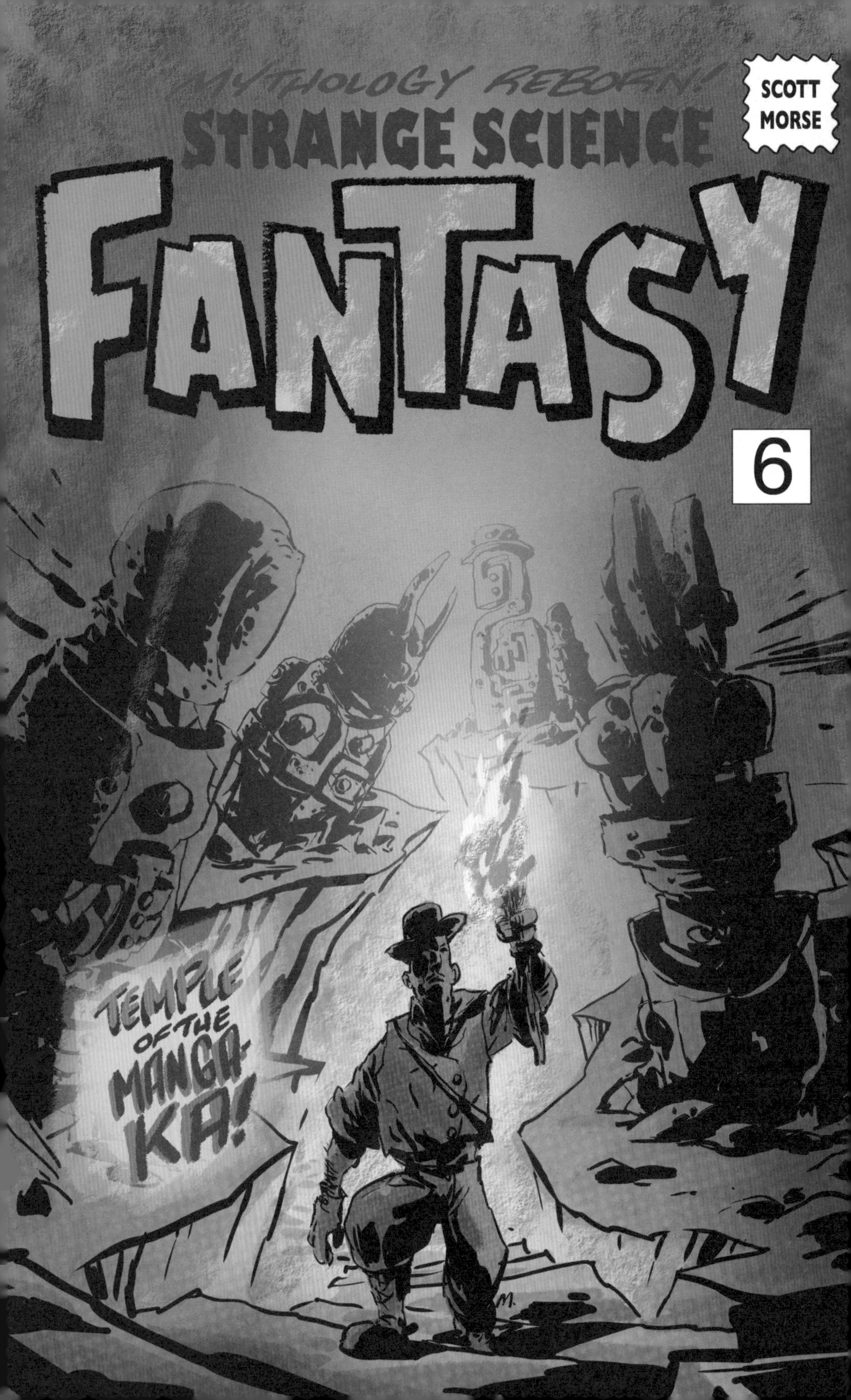

MYTHOLOGY REBORN!
STRANGE SCIENCE
FANTASY
SCOTT MORSE
6
TEMPLE OF THE MANGA-KA!
M.

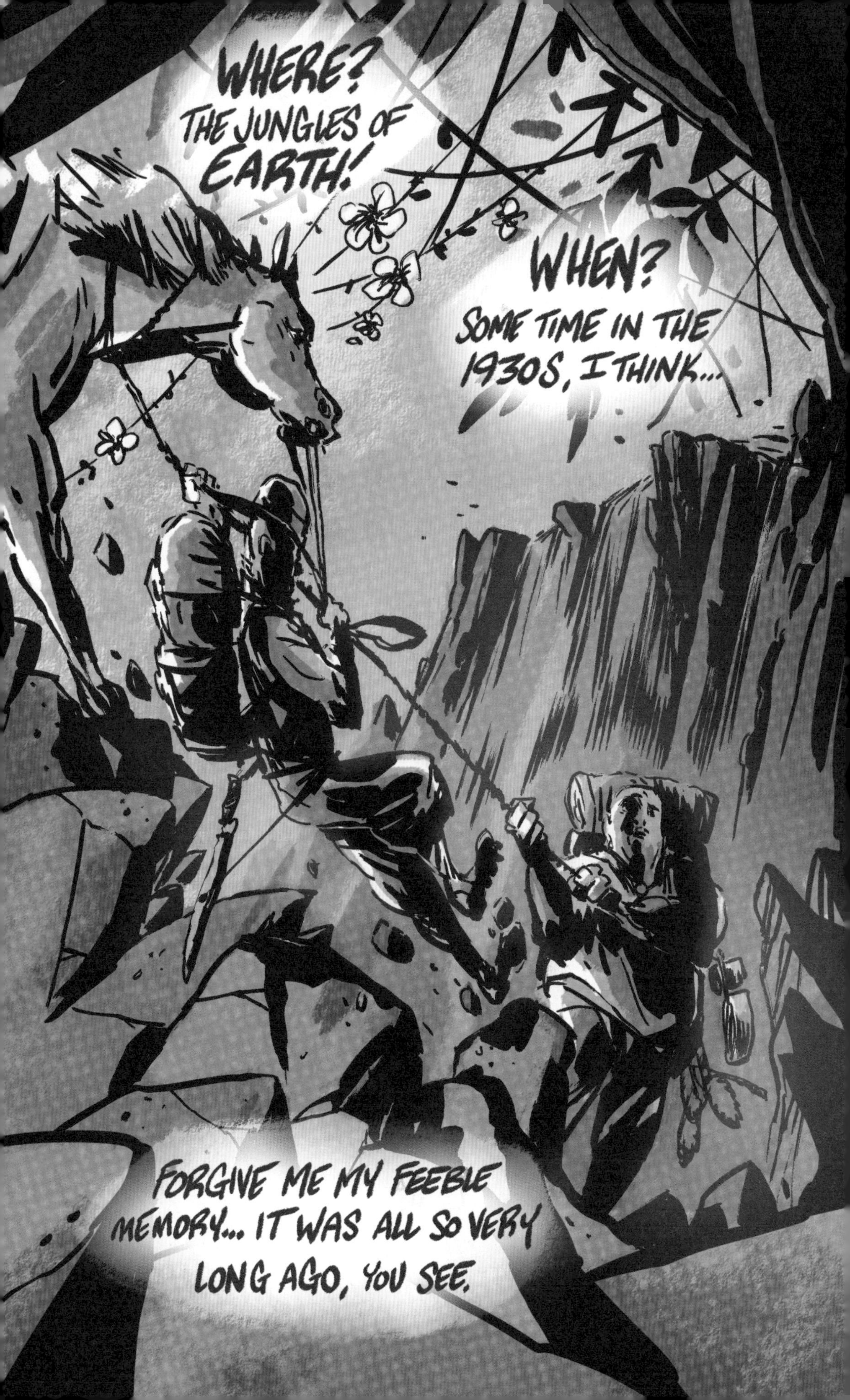
WHERE? THE JUNGLES OF EARTH!
WHEN? SOME TIME IN THE 1930S, I THINK...
FORGIVE ME MY FEEBLE MEMORY... IT WAS ALL SO VERY LONG AGO, YOU SEE.

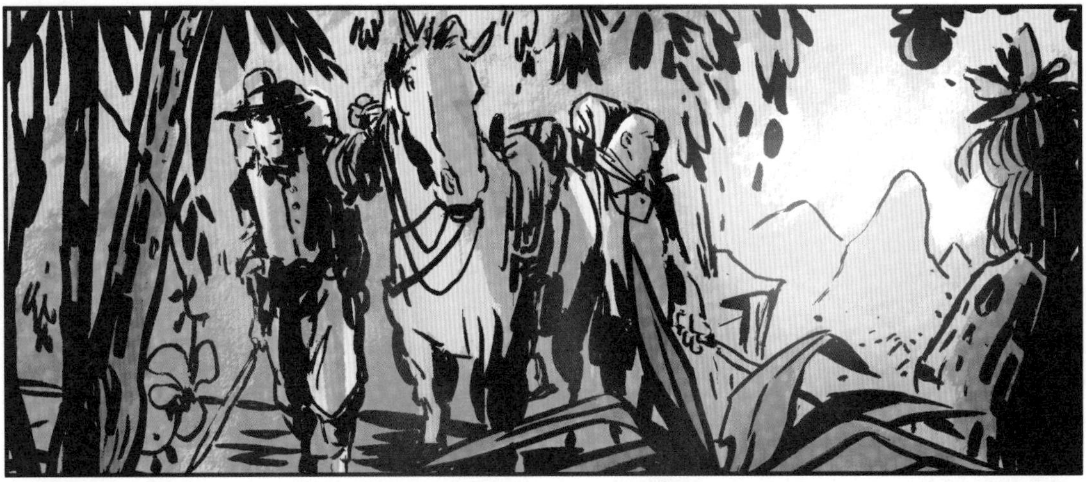

WE'D BEEN WANDERING A LAND THAT TIME HAD BOTTLED AND STORED FOR A SPECIAL OCCASION.

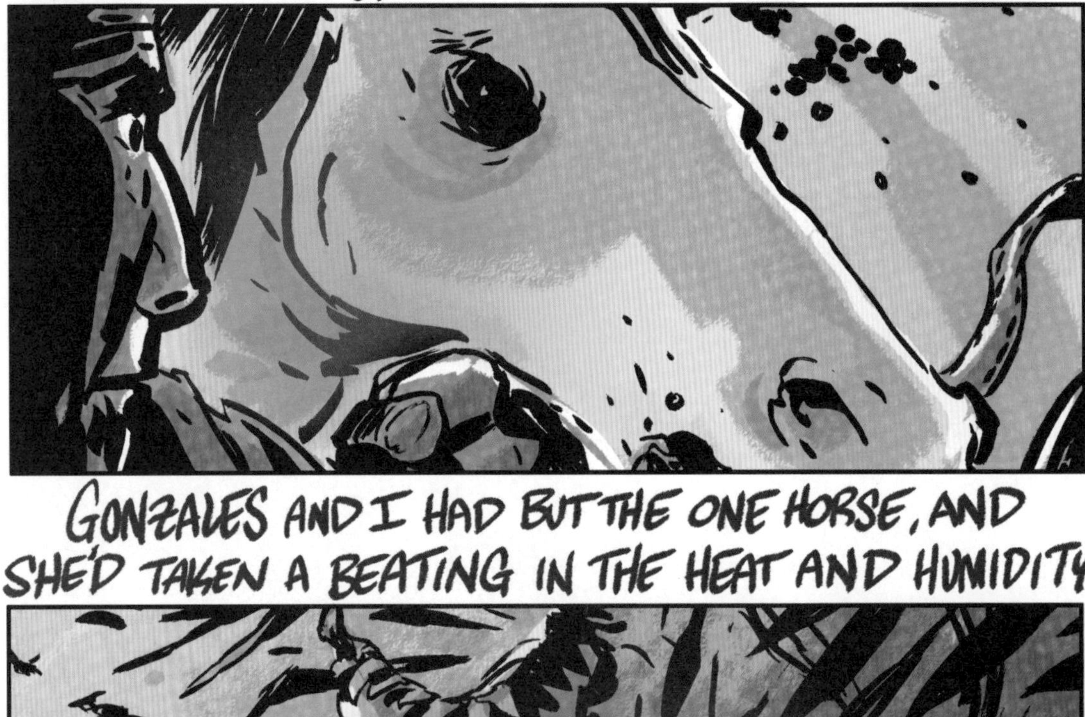

GONZALES AND I HAD BUT THE ONE HORSE, AND SHE'D TAKEN A BEATING IN THE HEAT AND HUMIDITY.

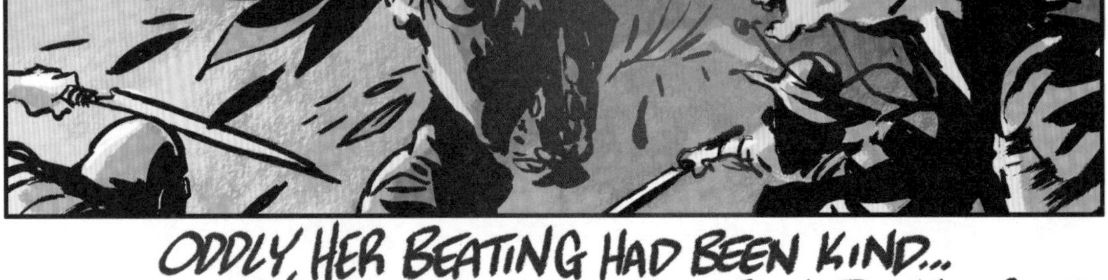

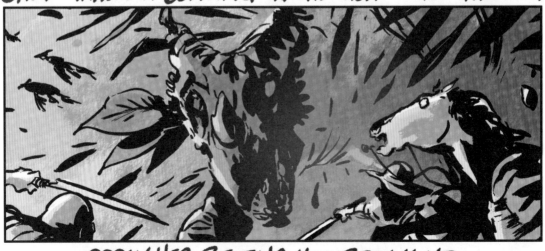

ODDLY, HER BEATING HAD BEEN KIND...
...UNTIL THE JUNGLE CAME ALIVE WITH *HUNGER*.

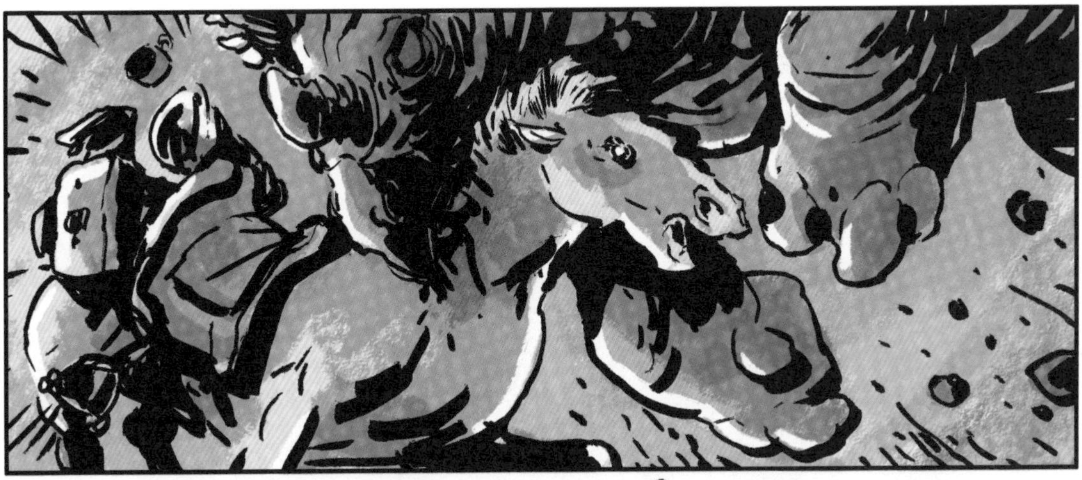

IT WAS OUR FIRST GLIMPSE OF
A THING OF LEGEND.

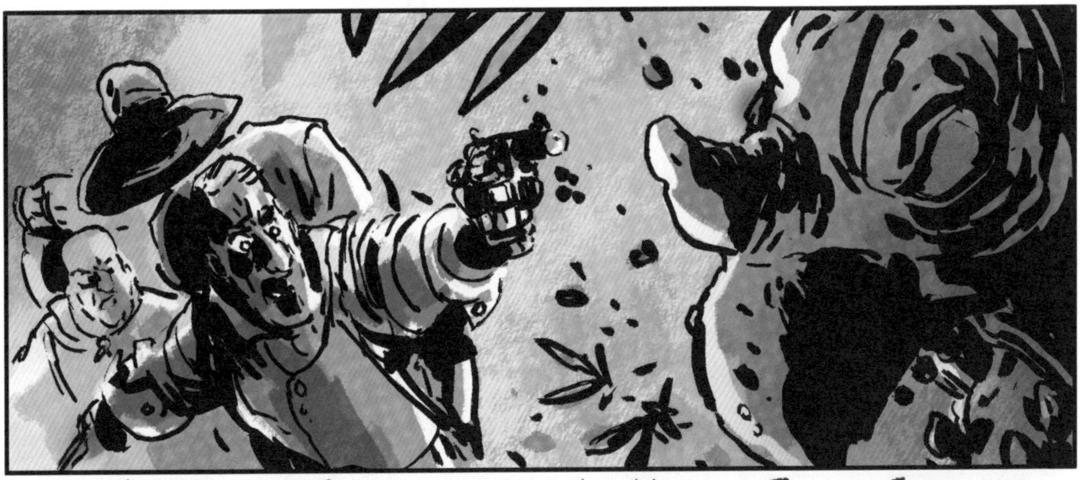

THE WHOLE JUNGLE-- AND MY WHOLE LIFE, IT SEEMED--
WOULD BECOME THE STORIED THINGS OF LEGEND.

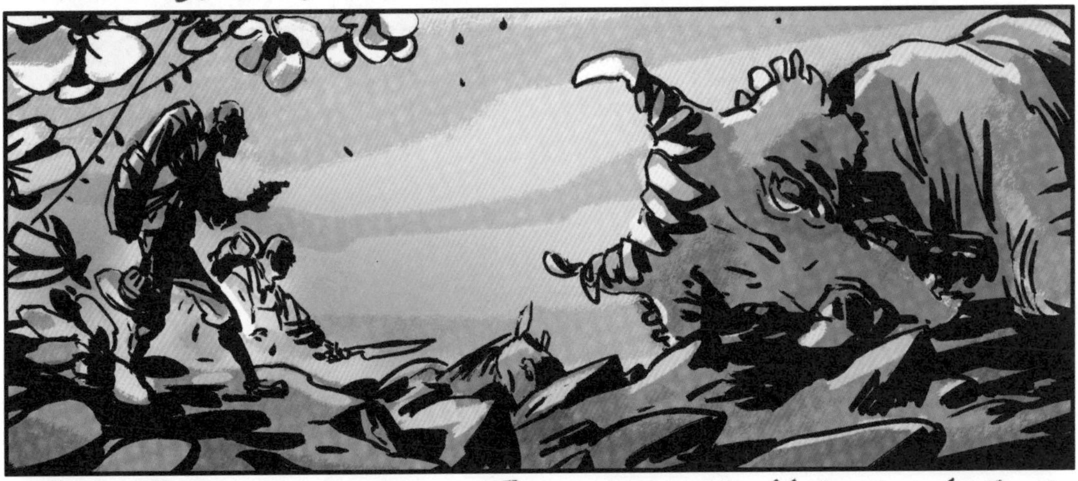

THIS FERTILE LAND, LITTLE DID I KNOW, WAS A
HOTBED OF FODDER FOR DREAMS GONE WILD.

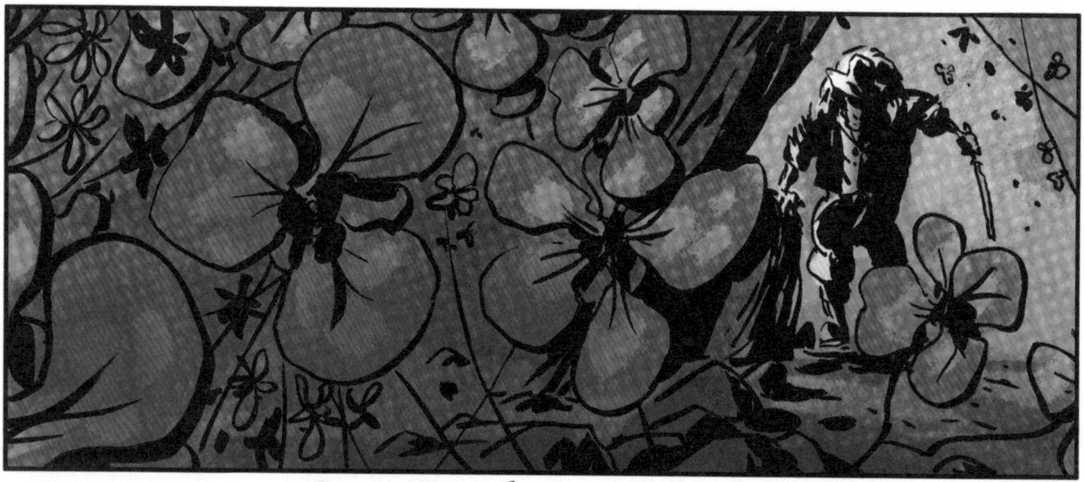

ONWARD, THEN. FRAGRANT BLOSSOMS ON SEVERED VINES FELL LIKE FLAMBOYANT ADJECTIVES...

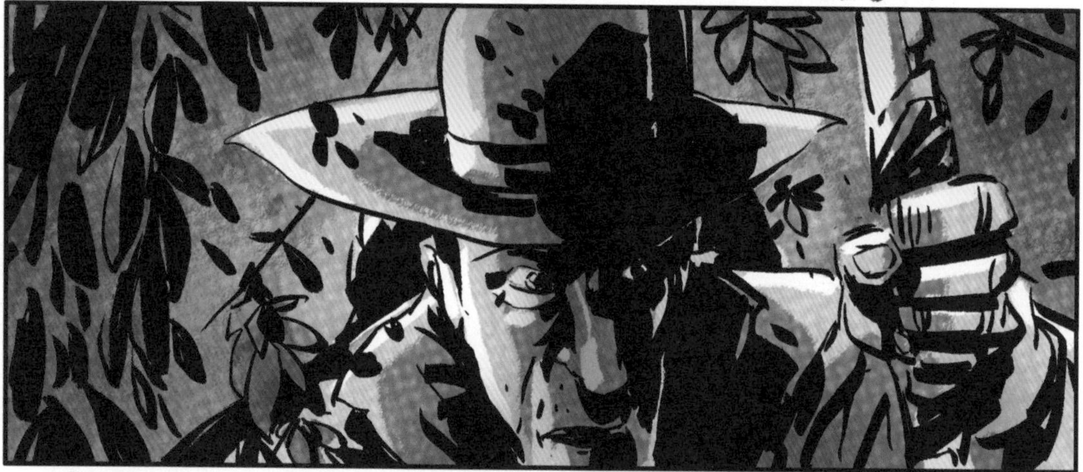

...DESCRIPTIVE, DECEPTIVE FLOURISHES TO A PLOT WRITTEN BY THE SOULS OF THE COSMOS.

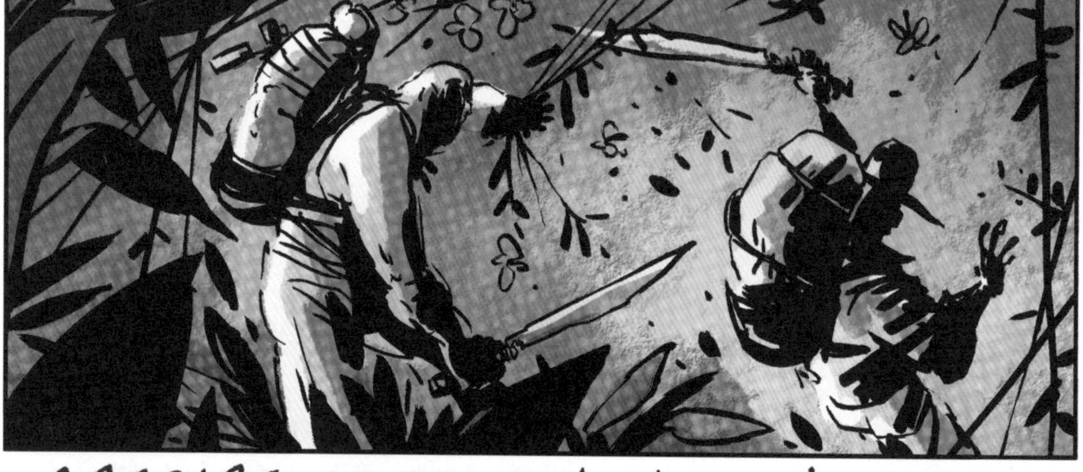

A STORY STRUCTURED ONLY BY HOW YOU, YOURSELF, COULD EMBELLISH IT WITH ADVENTURE.

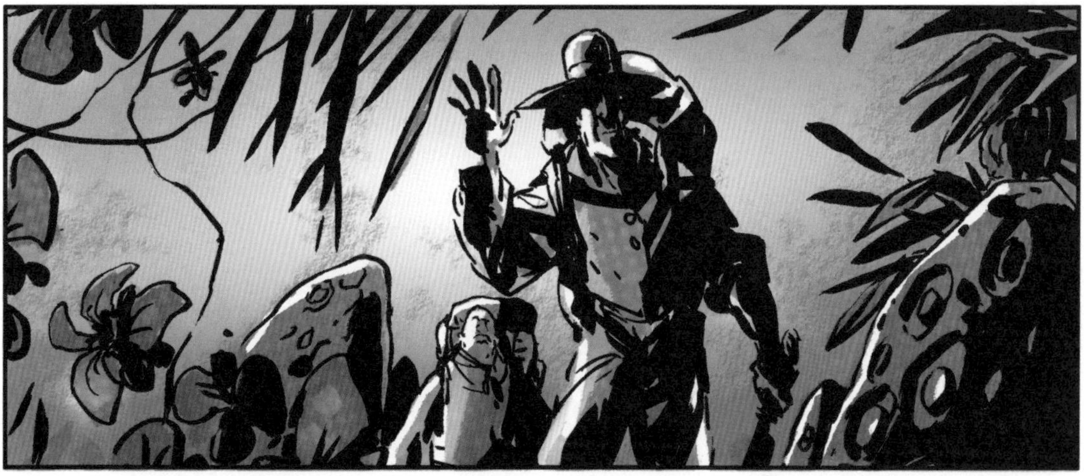

AND ADVENTURE IS WHAT WE DID, GONZALES AND I, AS WE STUMBLED UPON THIS SEAT OF MYTHOLOGY.

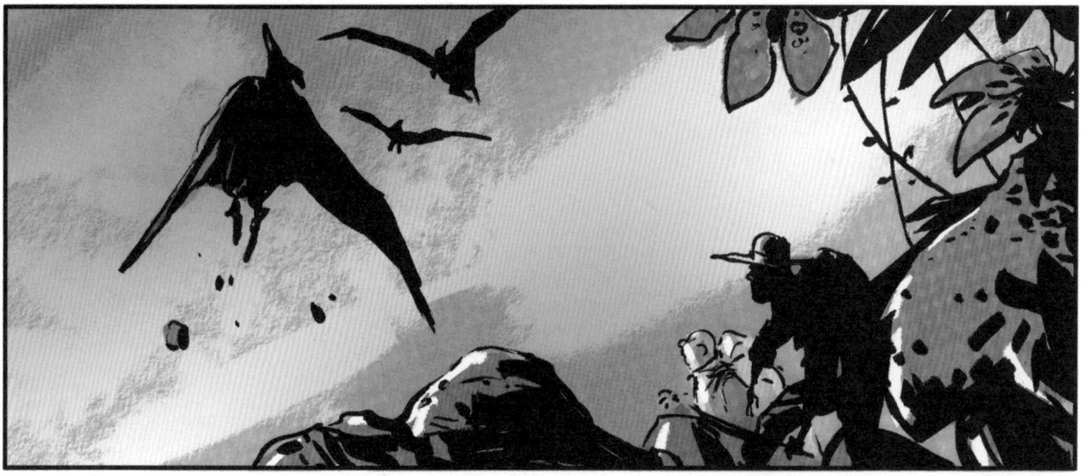

IT WAS ALL THAT WE'D ASKED FOR, ALL THAT WE'D SOUGHT: EACH LIVING MOMENT MORE ALIVE THAN THE LAST.

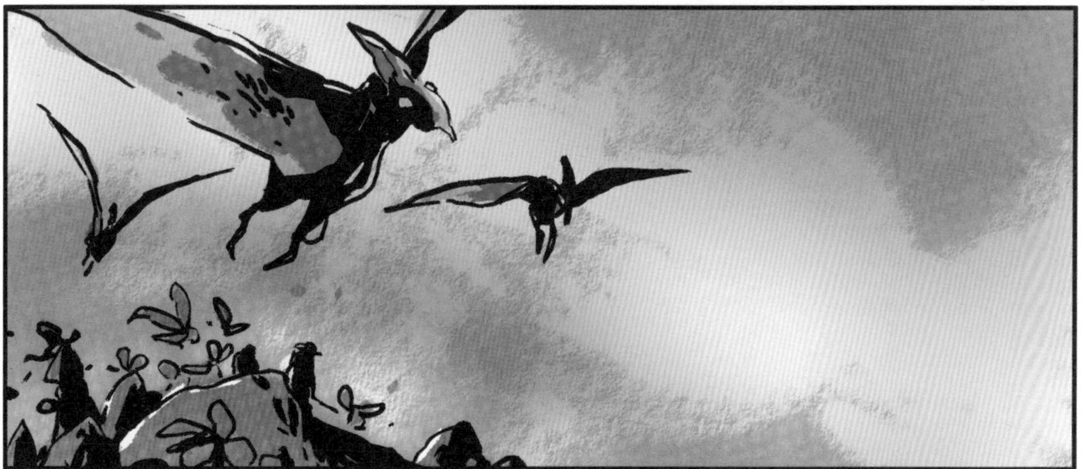

TWO MEN, HUFFING THIN OXYGEN, WHILE AROUND US THE LUNGS OF THE LAND SUCKED OUR IMAGINATIONS DRY.

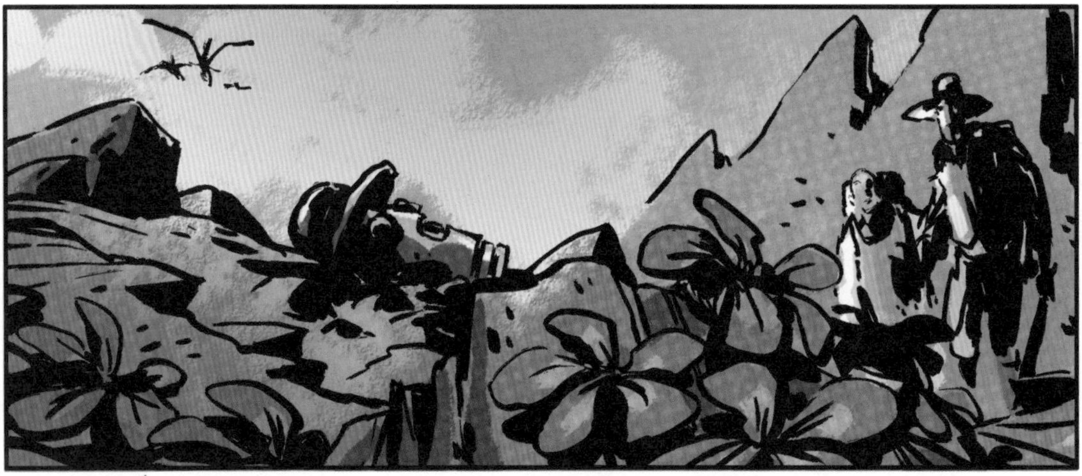

WE'D BEEN TOLD WE MIGHT VERY WELL FIND
THE HEART OF MANKIND'S SPIRIT...

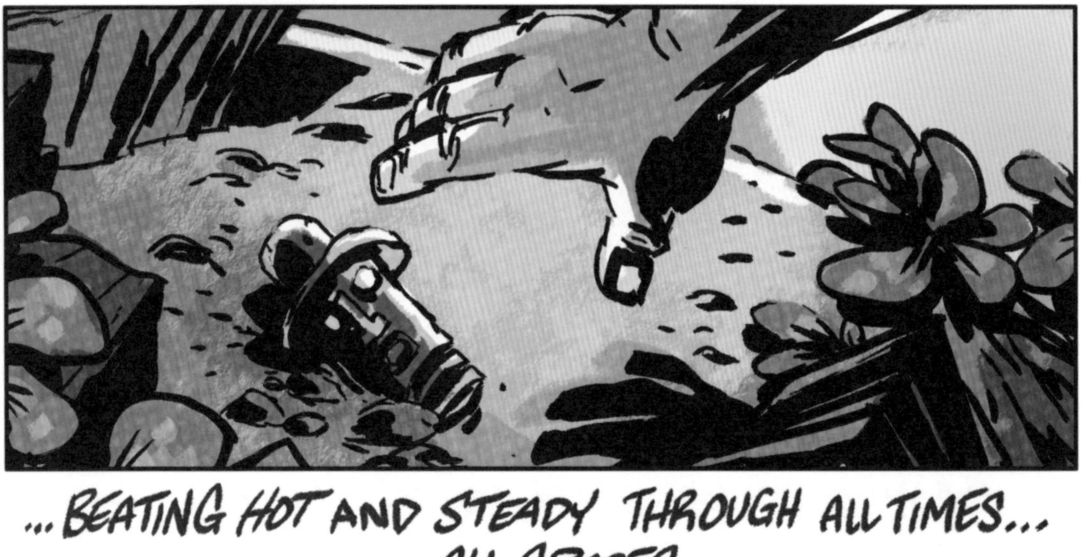

...BEATING HOT AND STEADY THROUGH ALL TIMES...
...ALL SPACES.

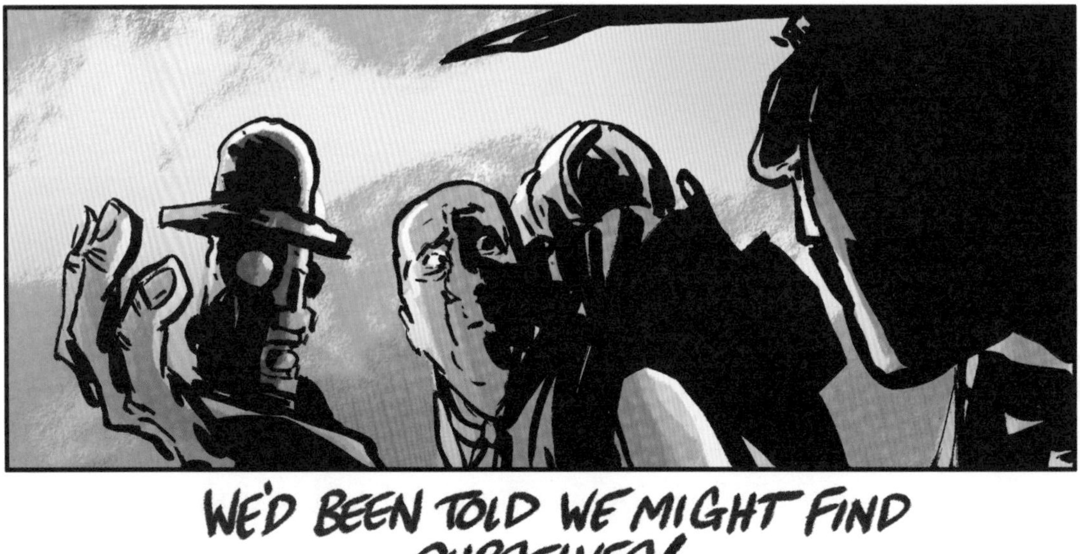

WE'D BEEN TOLD WE MIGHT FIND
OURSELVES!

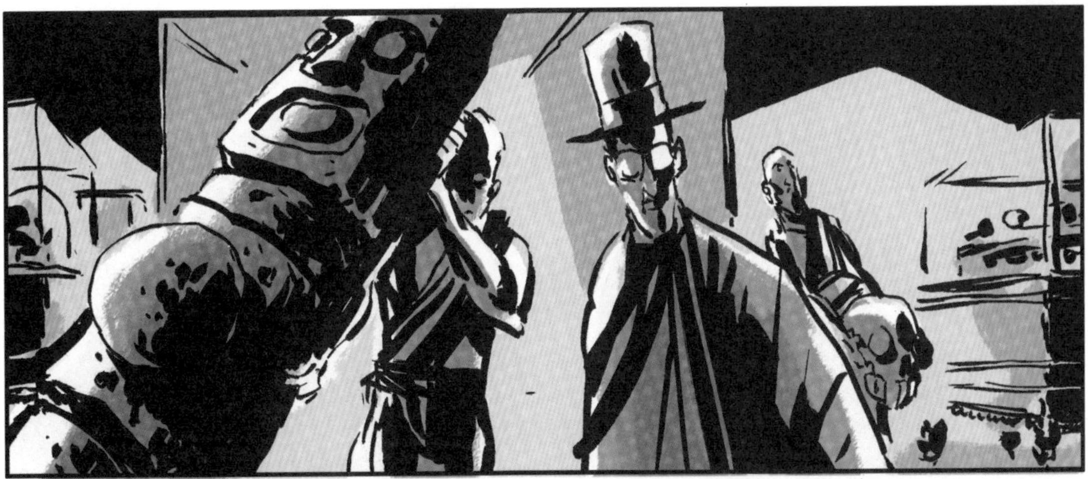

"BY WHOM?" YOU'RE PONDERING, I KNOW.
HIS NAME, WE'D COME TO UNDERSTAND, WAS *LEE PIERRE*.

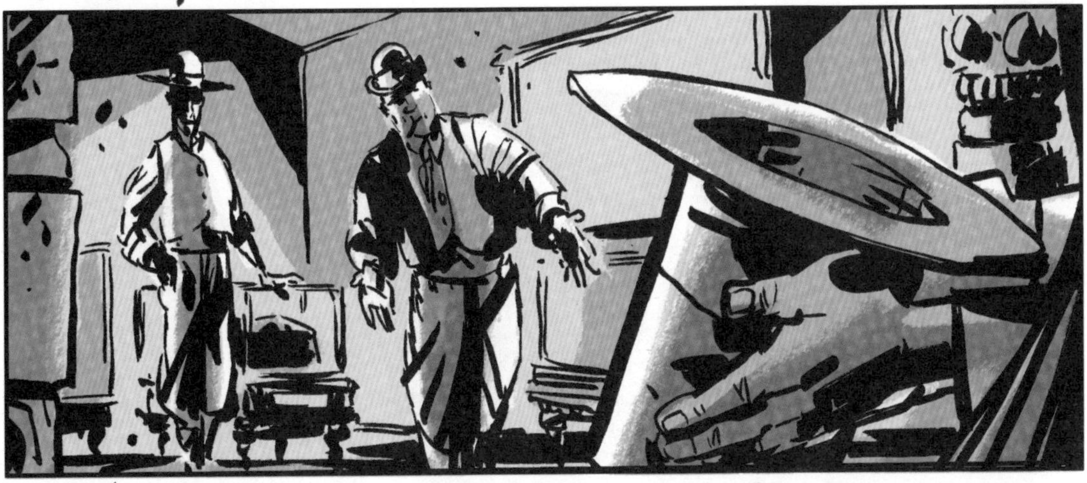

WE'D KNOWN HIM INTERMITTENTLY FOR SOME TIME.
BY "WE", I REFER TO MYSELF AND MY BROTHER.

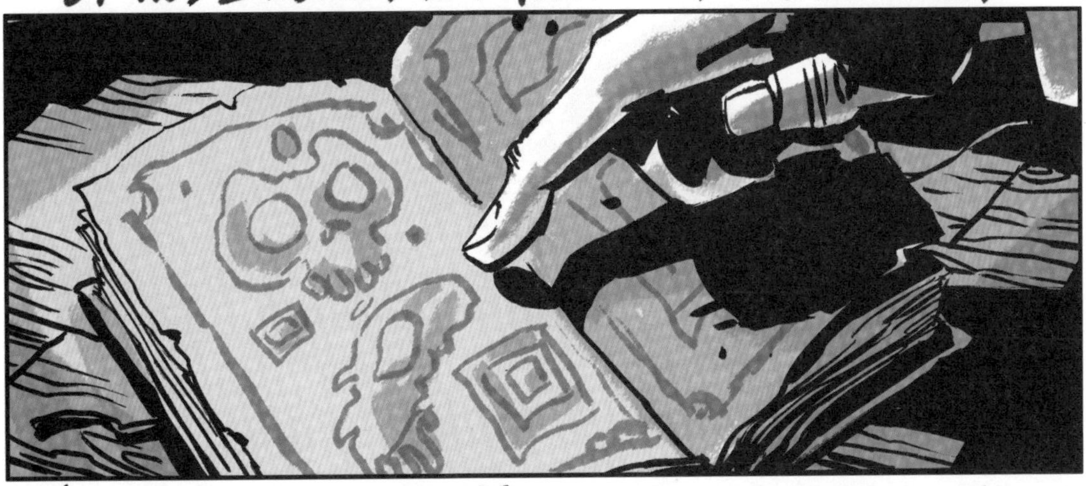

WE'D FORMED A BUSINESS VENTURE OF SORTS WITH LEE.
HE WAS AN ACQUIRER OF STRANGE ARTIFACTS.

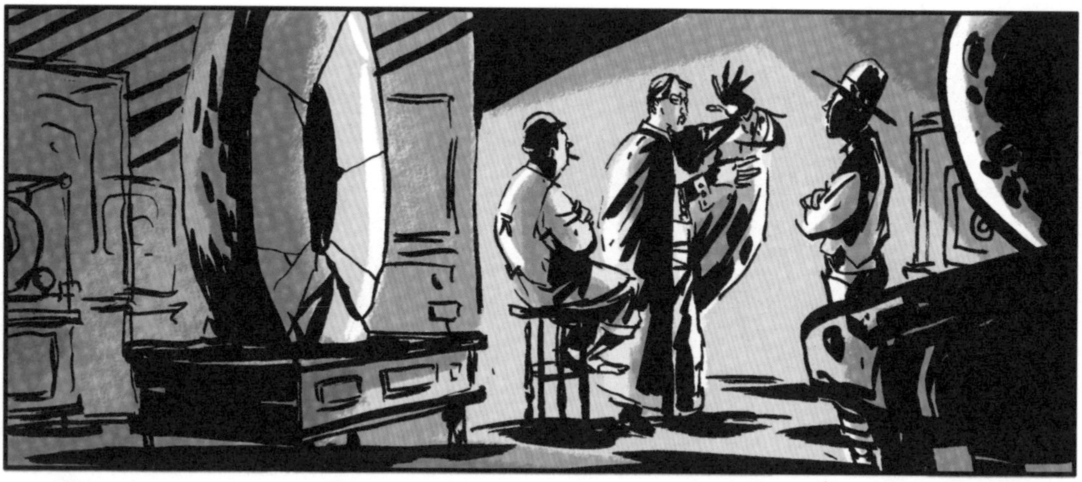

BY TRADE, WE WERE FABRICATORS OF "FACT." WE RAN A
CHARLATAN MUSEUM. "BELIEVE YOUR EYES, OR NOT," WE DARED.

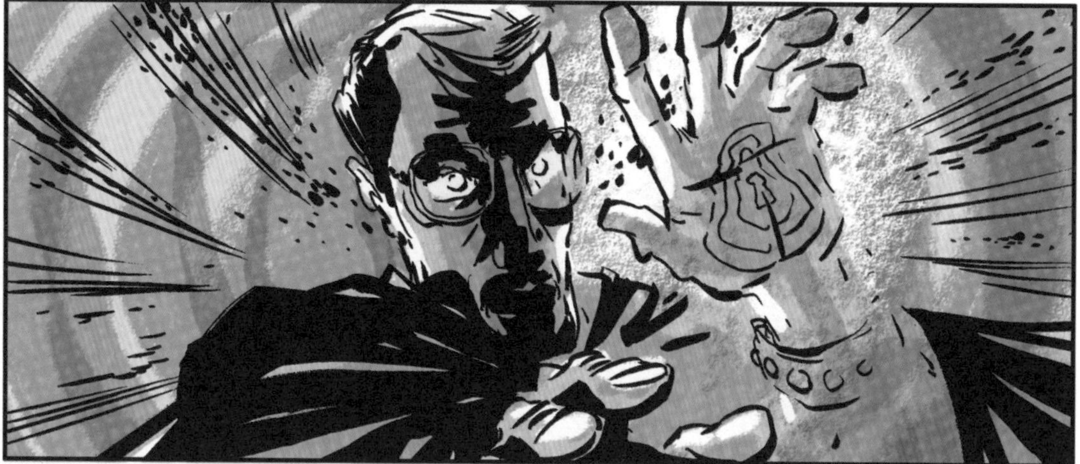

THEN, ONE DAY, LEE OPENED OUR EYES TO A LOST HORIZON.
HE'D VENTURED TO A FAR OFF LAND--

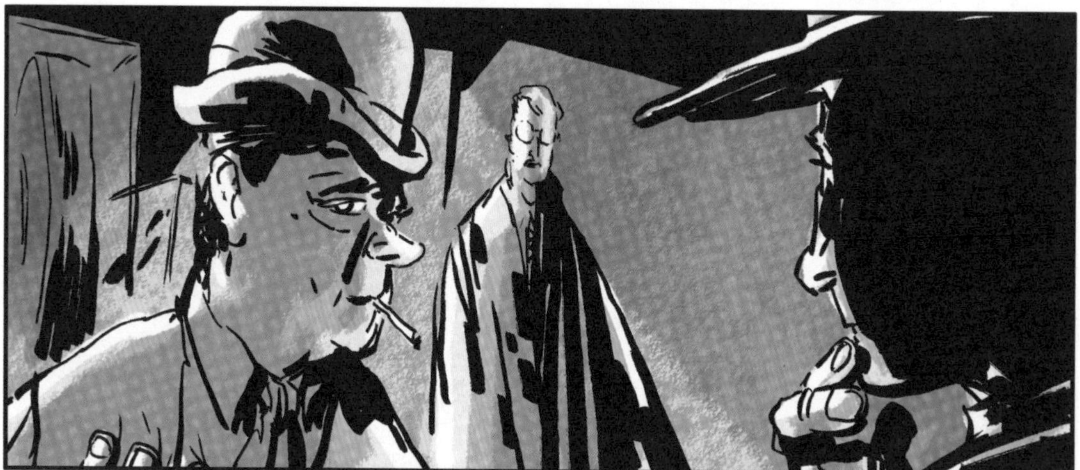

THE BIRTHPLACE OF ALL LEGENDS.
THE GRAVEYARD OF ALL RELIGIONS.

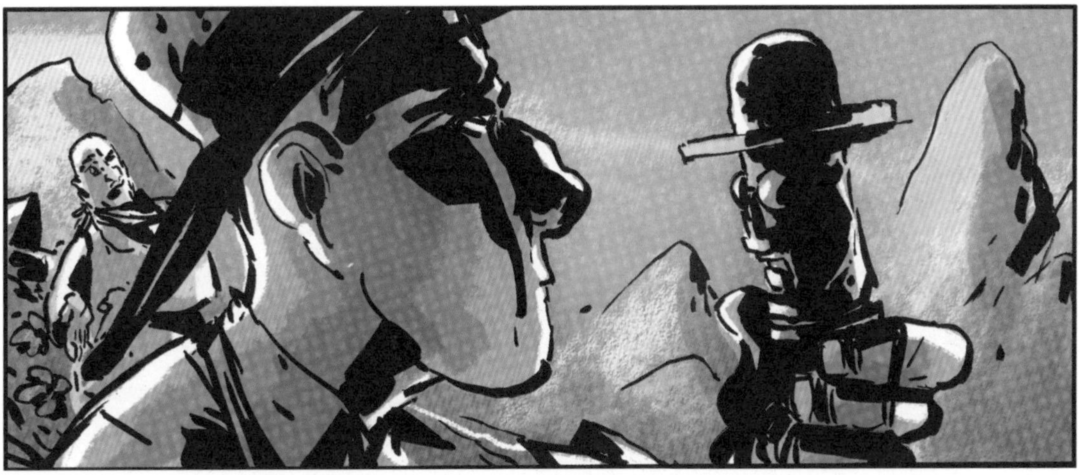

MY BROTHER FELT IT BEGGED A CLOSER LOOK.

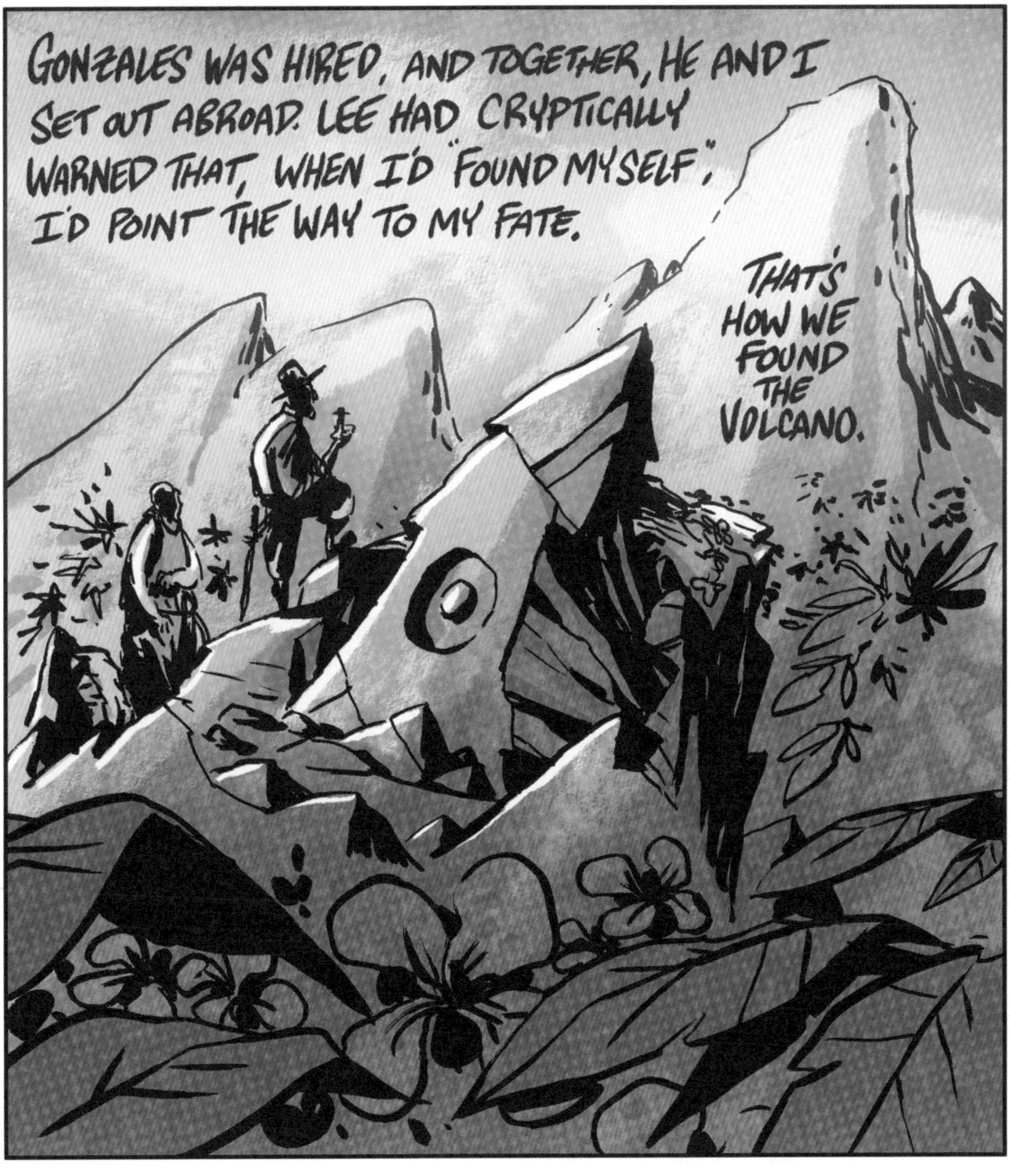
GONZALES WAS HIRED, AND TOGETHER, HE AND I SET OUT ABROAD. LEE HAD CRYPTICALLY WARNED THAT, WHEN I'D "FOUND MYSELF", I'D POINT THE WAY TO MY FATE.
THAT'S HOW WE FOUND THE VOLCANO.

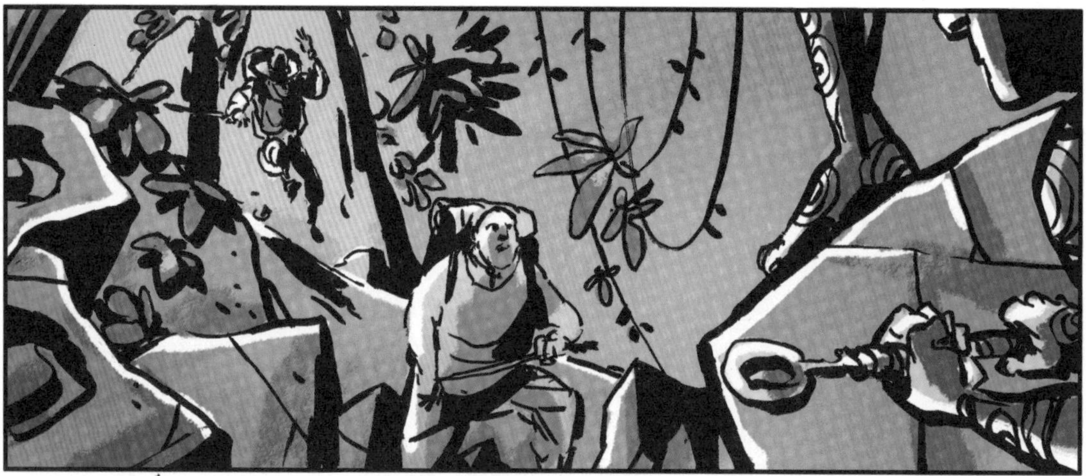

IT WASN'T FAR ALONG THAT PATH WHEN WE'D HAPPENED INTO THE GUARDIANS OF THE INCONCEIVABLE.

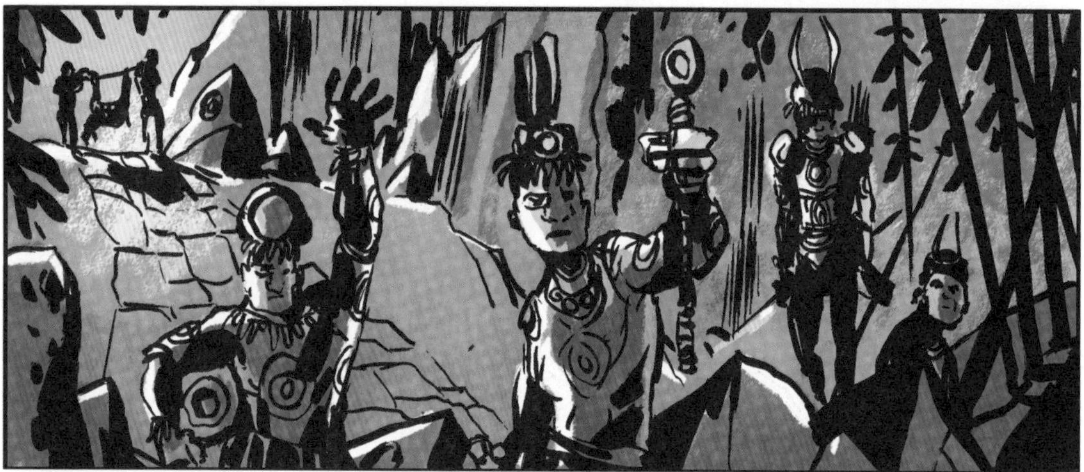

THEY'D BEEN EXPECTING US, AS IF THEY'D READ A FEW PAGES AHEAD IN OUR NOVEL QUEST.

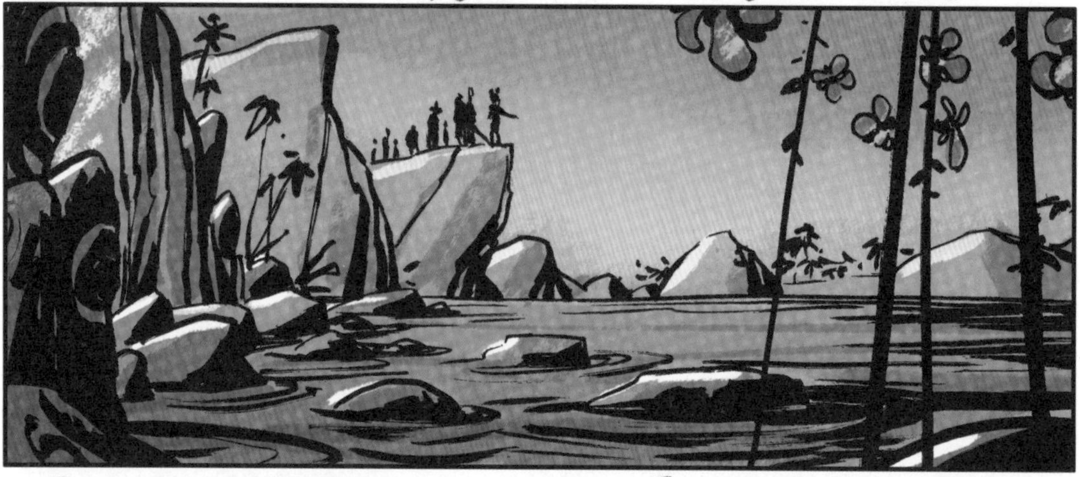

THEY SHOWED US TO THE LAKE-- THE COLLECTED TEARS OF A THOUSAND EVIL EYES, SOME MIGHT SAY.

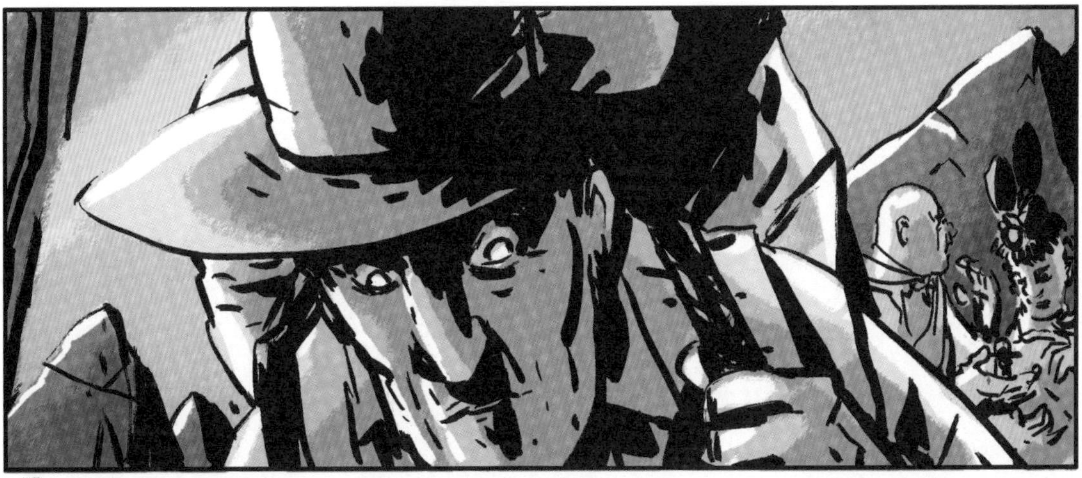

TO THE LAYMAN, IT APPEARED TO BE NOTHING MORE THAN THE DORMANT MOUTH OF A VOLCANO.

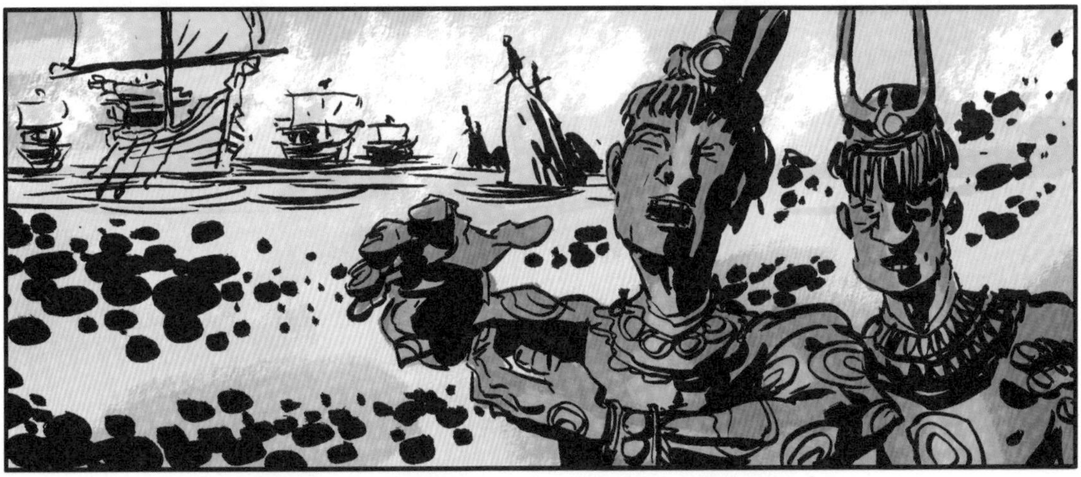

LOCAL CUSTOM CLAIMED MORE!
THIS WAS INSTEAD AN ANCIENT SEA PORT... ANTEDILUVIAN!

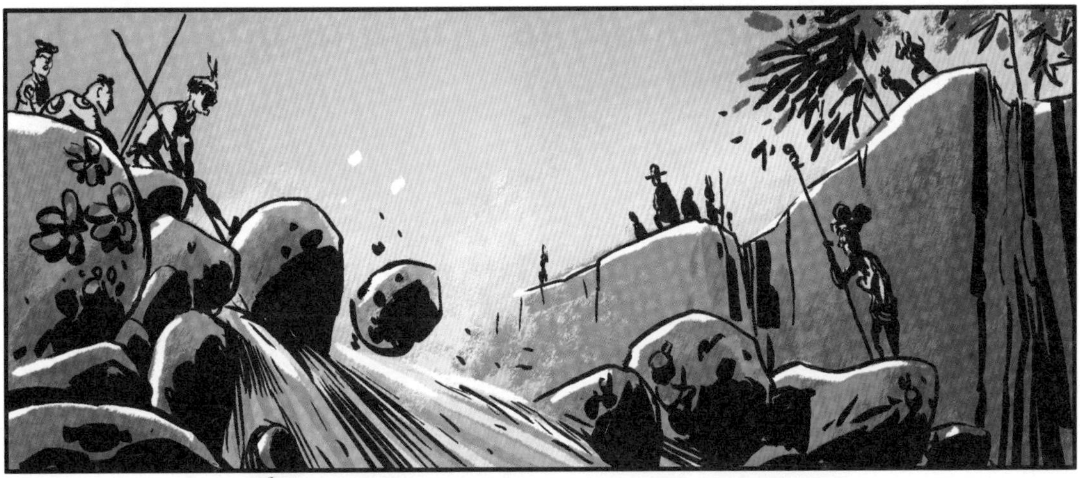

THAT DAY, A DUCT WAS OPENED,
SPILLING THE TEARS OF GODS... FOR US!

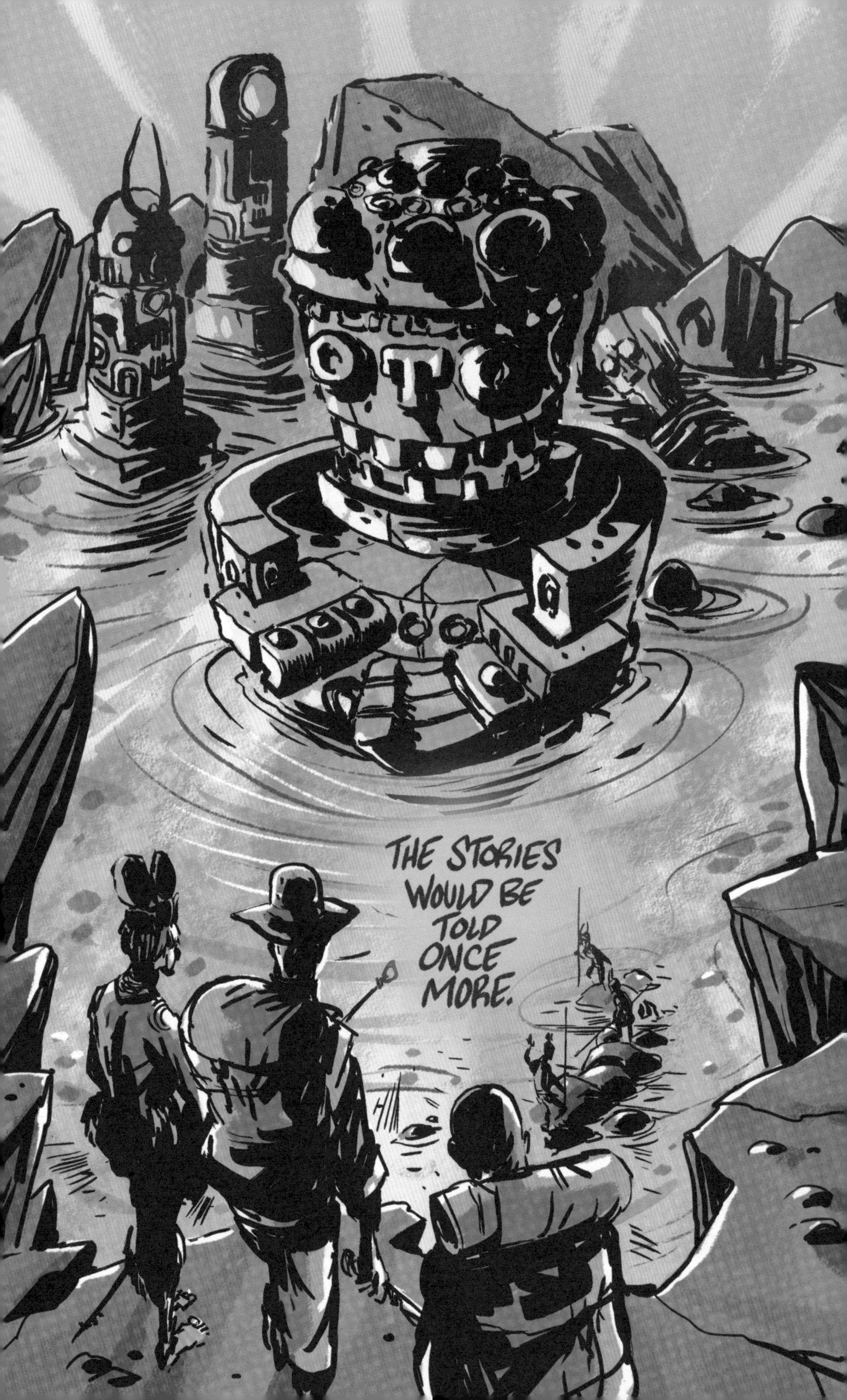
THE STORIES WOULD BE TOLD ONCE MORE.

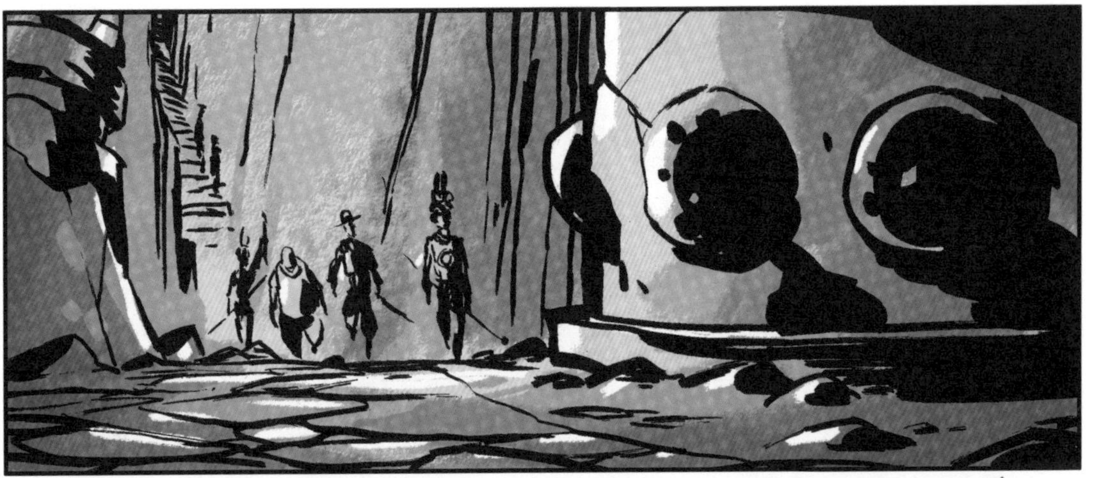

THIS WAS WHAT THEY CALLED "THE MANGA-KA".
"JAPANESE," GONZALES ASSURED ME, "FOR 'STORY MAKER.'"

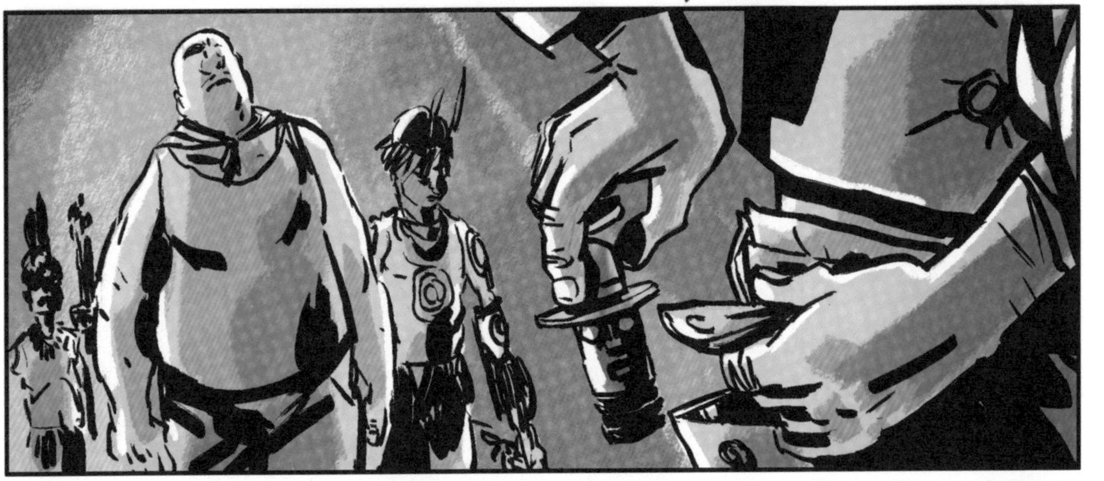

THESE NATIVES CLAIMED THAT, INDEED, ALL STORIES WERE
COLLECTED IN THIS VERY SPOT.

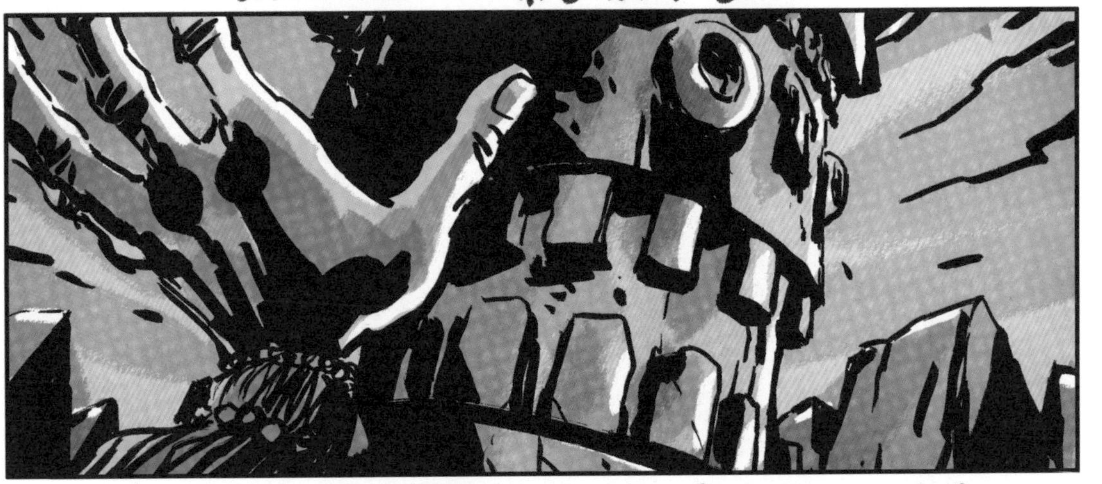

HEWN IN THIS VERY ROCK, SOMEHOW, WAS
THE SUMMIT OF IMAGINATION.

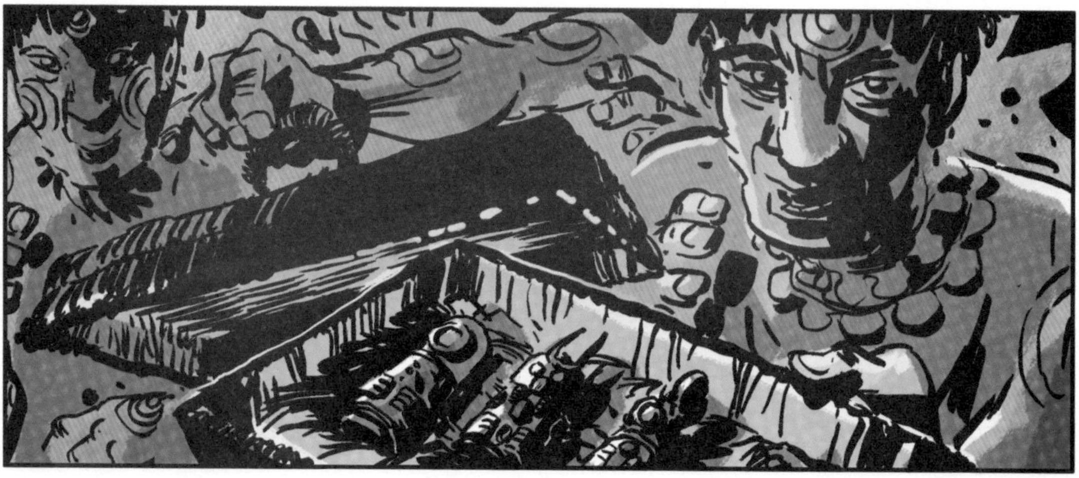

ON THIS PEAK, THE CULTURES OF A THOUSAND WORLDS, AND MORE, CONVERGED! THEIR TALES OF FAITH...

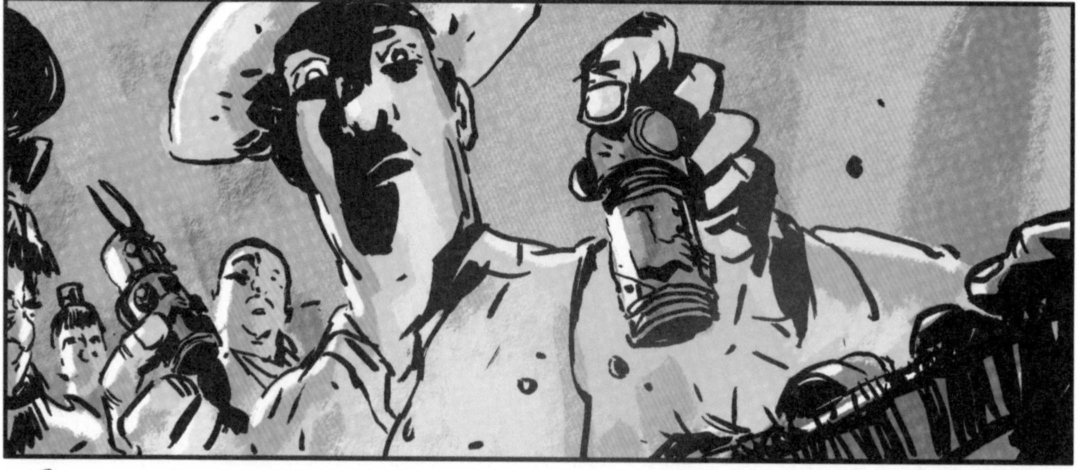

...FOREVER EMBODIED IN STONE EFFIGIES OF CHARACTER. TO HOLD THAT IDEA, IN YOUR HAND! AHH...

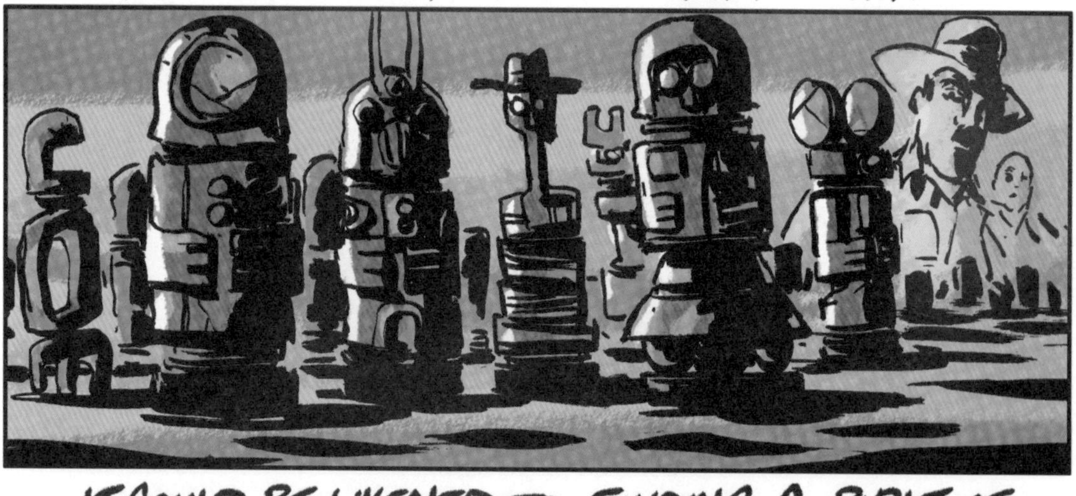

...IT COULD BE LIKENED TO FINDING A BIBLE OF ALL WORLDS! AN ARCHIVE TO THE SPIRIT OF ALL!

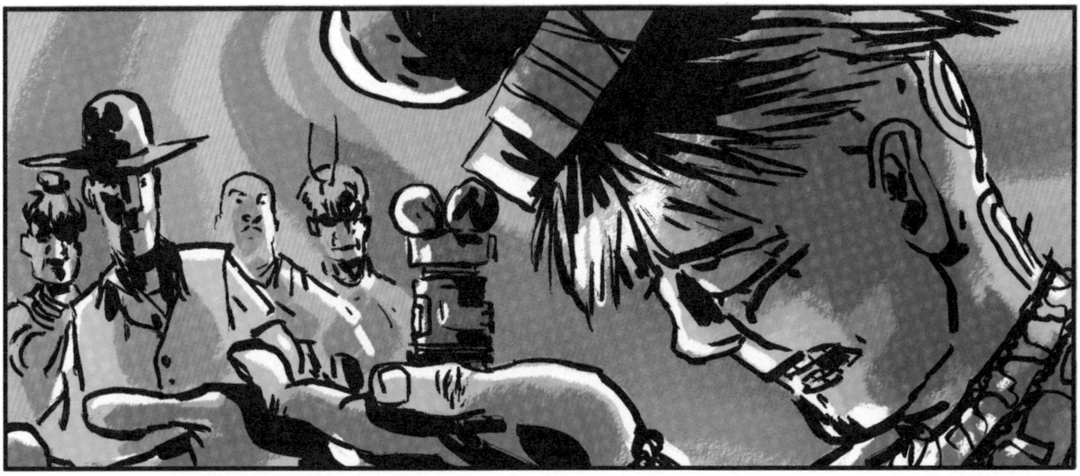

WE WERE PRESENTED WITH VERY FEW EXAMPLES,
AND WE COUNTED OURSELVES LUCKY TO SEE WHAT WE COULD.

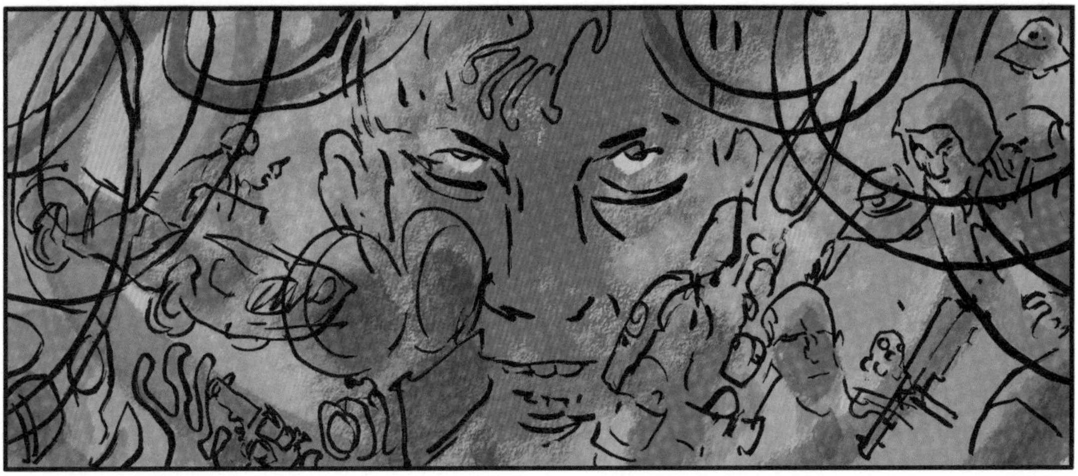

IT BOGGLED THE MIND! AS IF OUR FUTURES HAD EXISTED
LONG AGO, AND OUR PASTS WERE SOMEHOW YET TO COME!

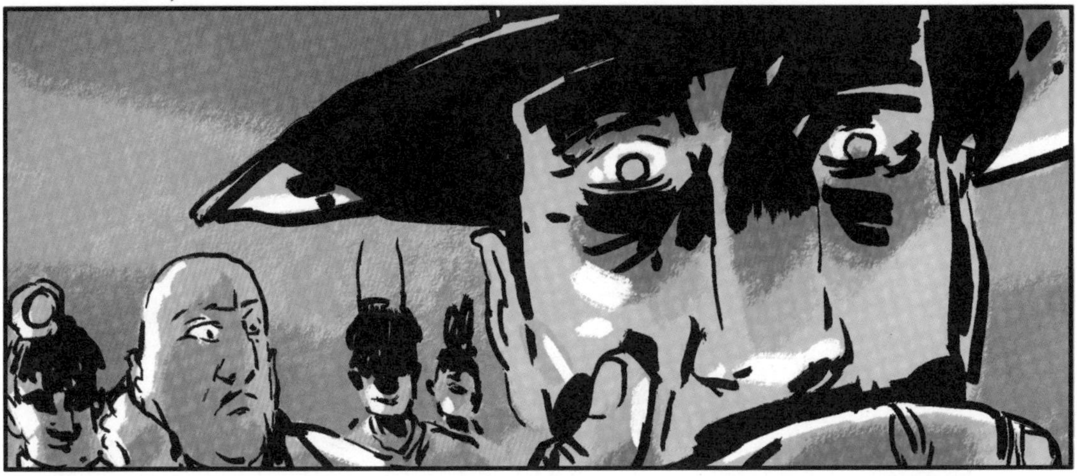

PARALLEL WORLDS, AND THE PARALLEL NEEDS OF MAN,
EXPLAINED THROUGH STORY FOR MAN TO COPE WITH HIMSELF!

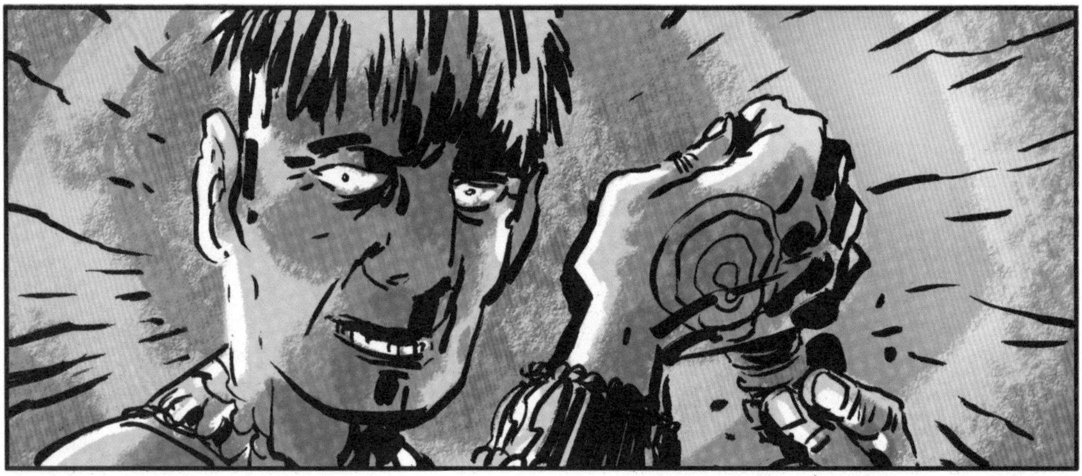

WE WERE WARNED TO CONTAIN OURSELVES! THESE WERE
SACRED IDEAS WE WERE FONDLING LIKE AWKWARD FOOLS!

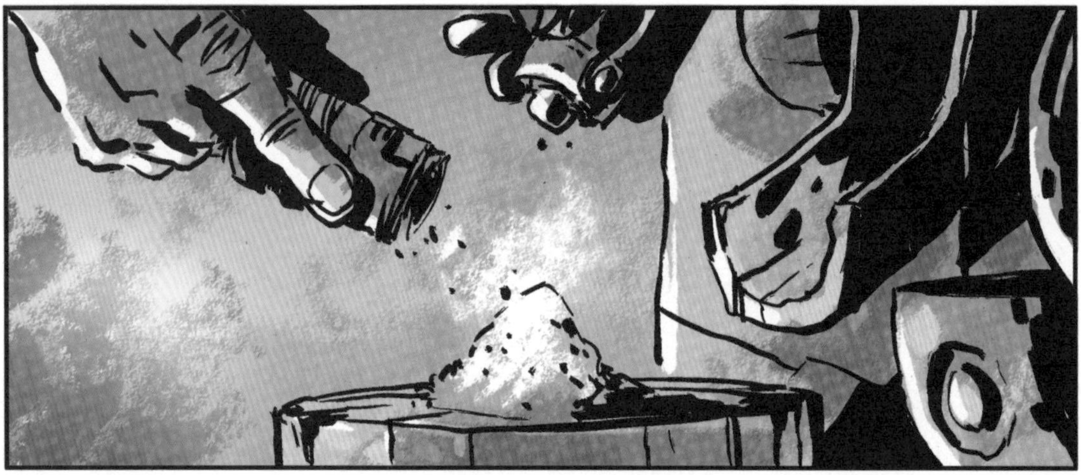

THE MANGA-KA COULD BREATHE THESE STORIES TO LIFE.
I'D ONCE SEEN AN AUTOMATON AT THE WORLD'S FAIR.

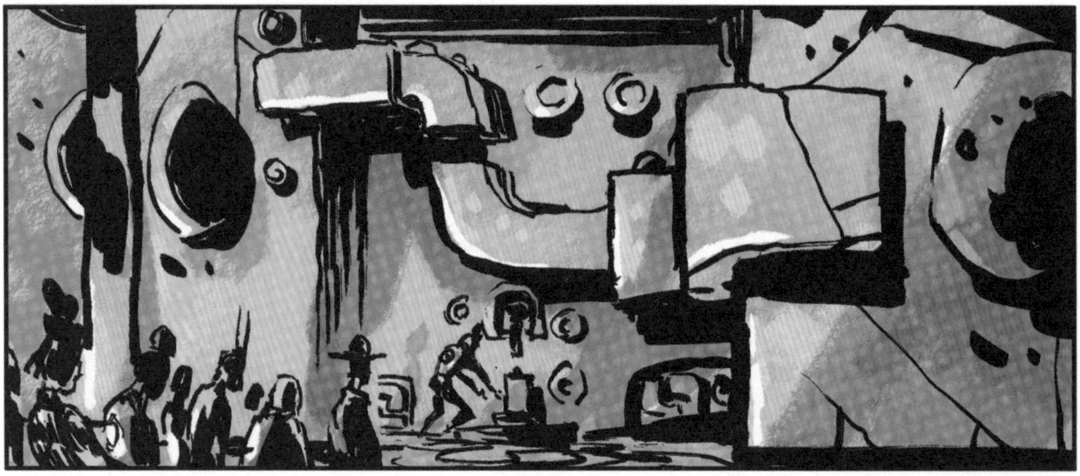

THIS WAS SIMILAR, BUT CHISELED OF AN ANCIENT STONE
NOT NATIVE TO THIS CONTINENT, I SUSPECTED.

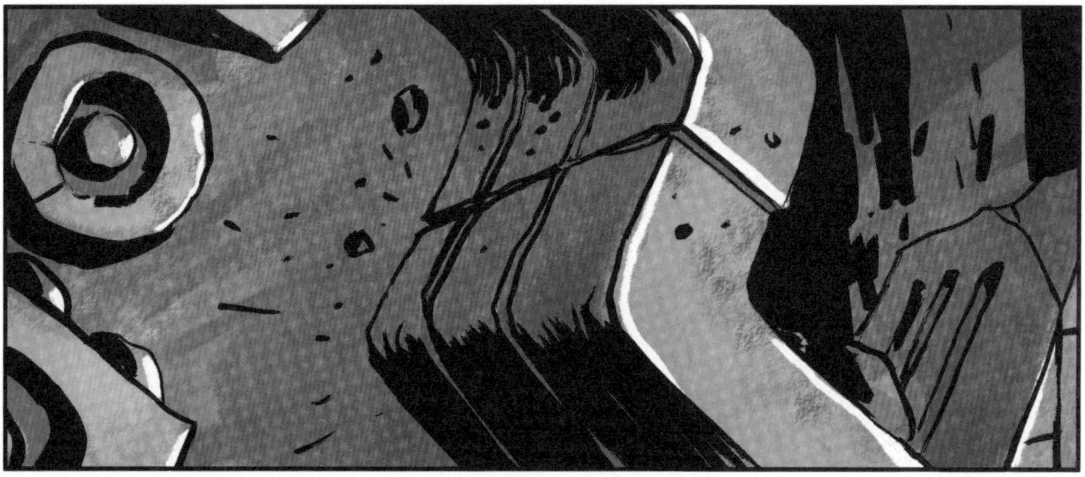

A HANDFUL OF IDOLS WERE EMPTIED OF THEIR DUST THAT DAY.

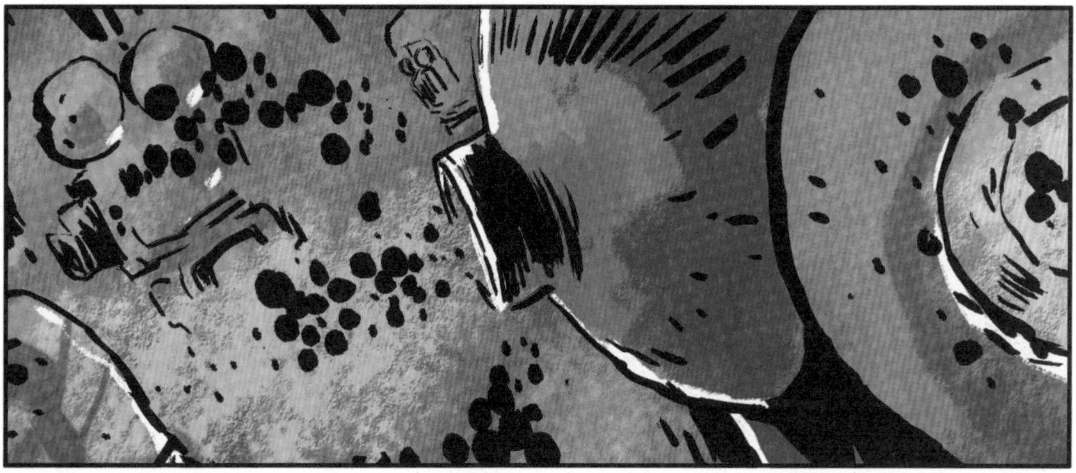

A HANDFUL OF STORIES CAME ALIVE AT ONCE.

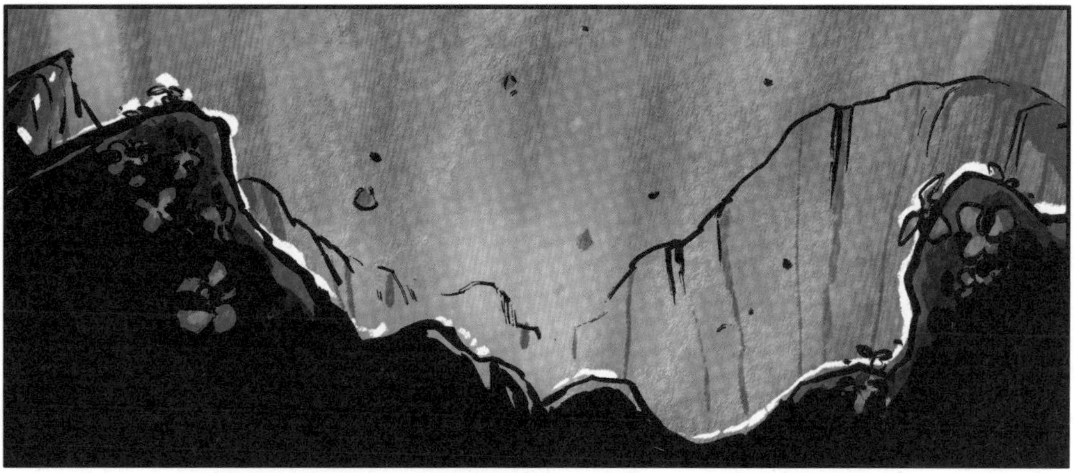

"ONCE UPON A TIME."

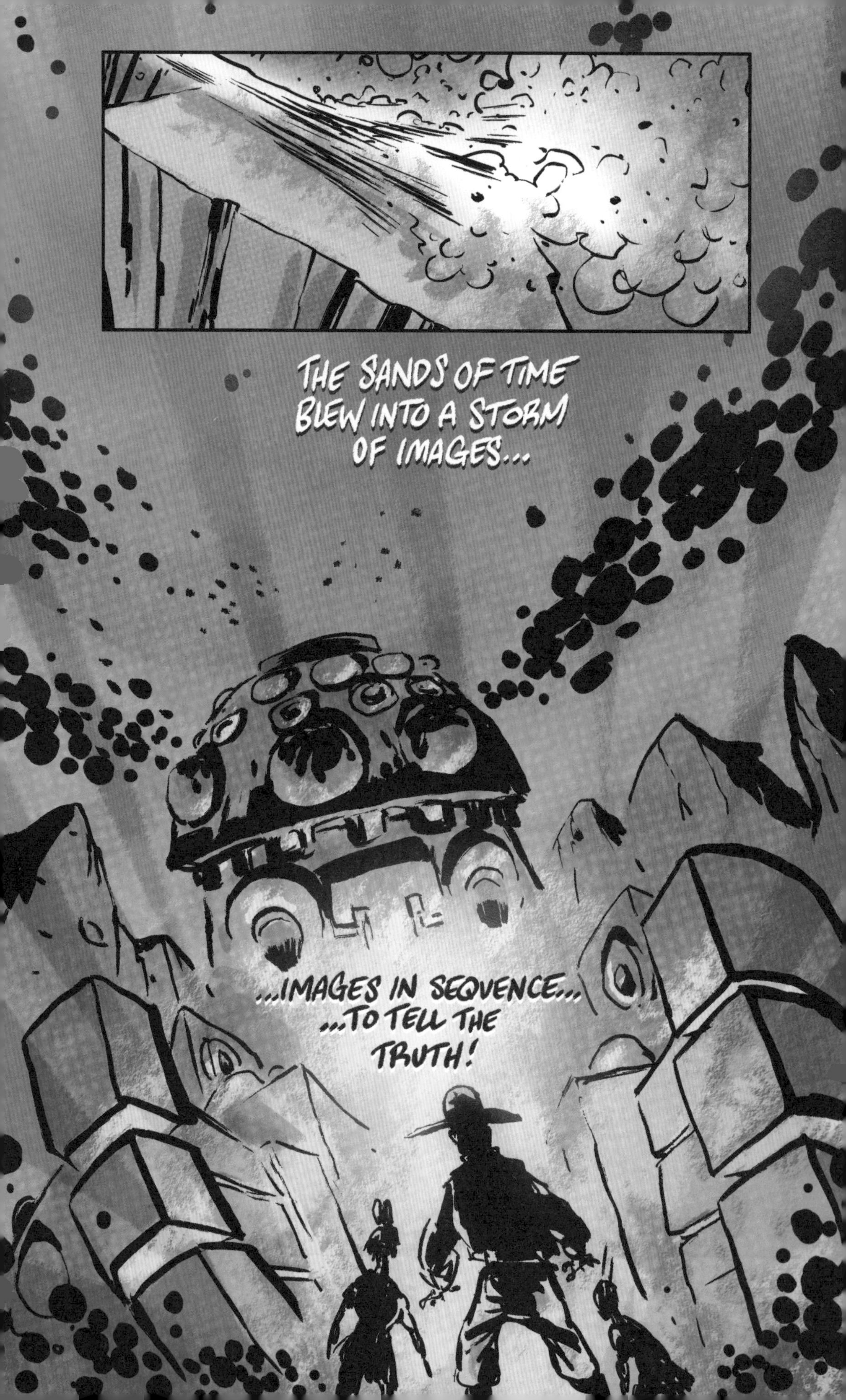
THE SANDS OF TIME BLEW INTO A STORM OF IMAGES...
...IMAGES IN SEQUENCE... ...TO TELL THE TRUTH!

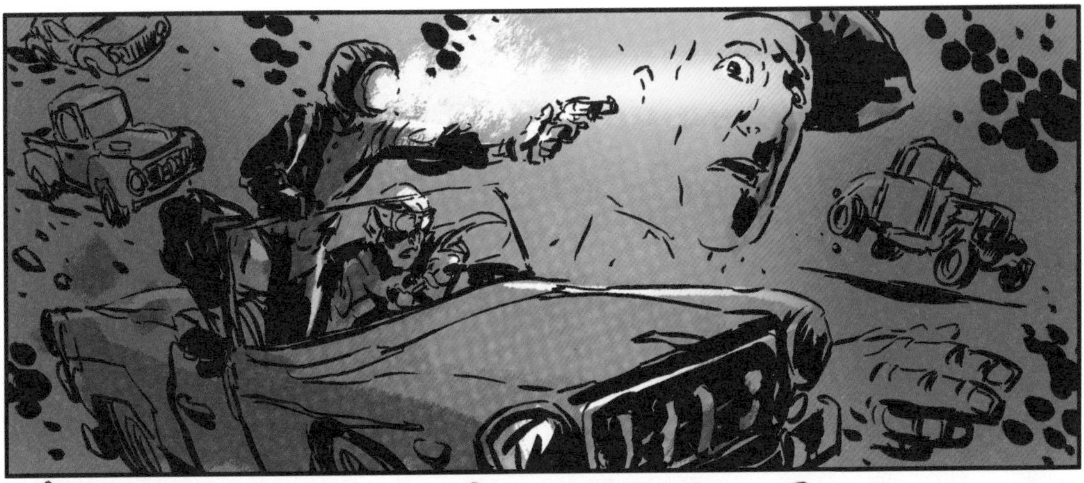

GLORIOUS LEGENDS OF REVOLUTIONARIES, BOUND ONLY BY A DESIRE TO BE TRUE TO THEMSELVES... AND TO HOPE!

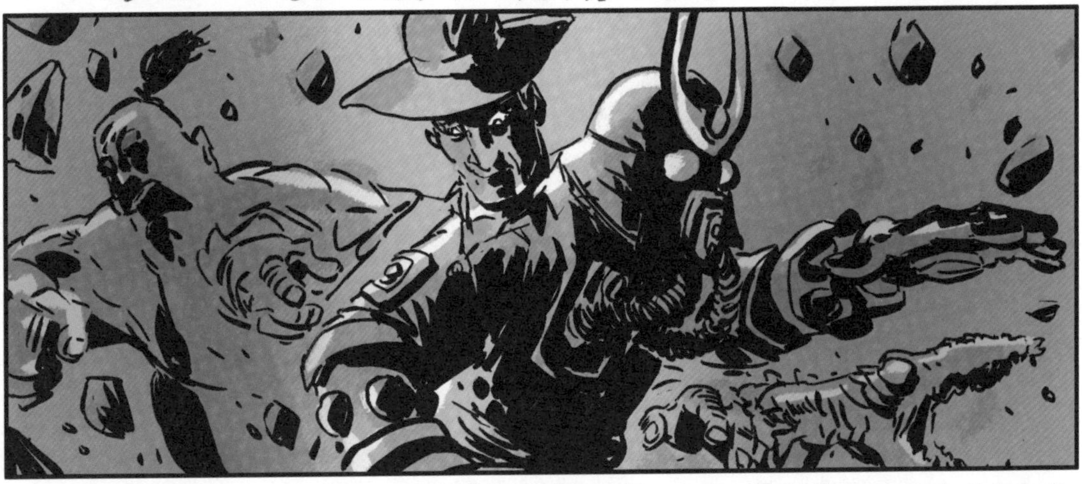

PARABLES OF COLLIDING WORLDS, OF FORBIDDEN LOVE... ...OF ENEMIES HEALING THE WOUNDS OF CIRCUMSTANCE!

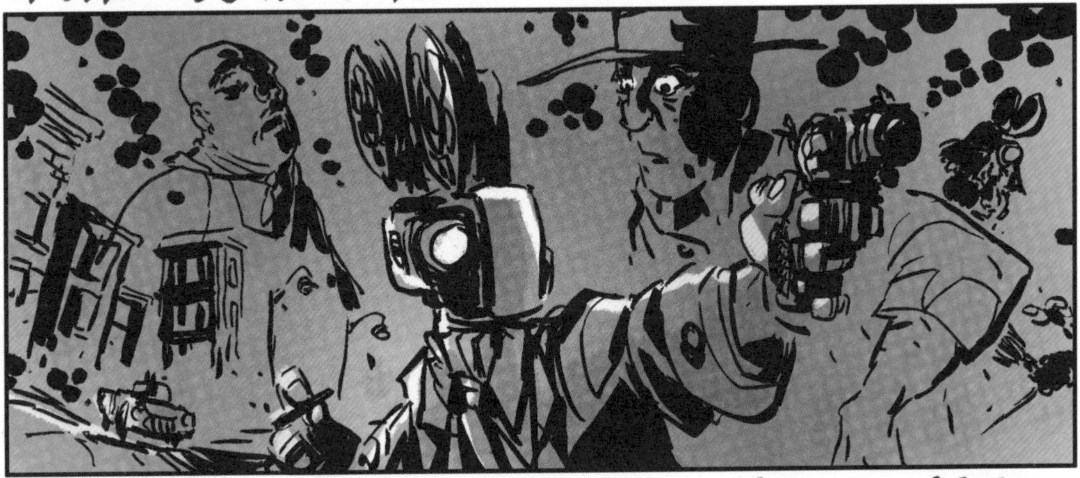

PROJECTED MYTHS OF PERSECUTION THROUGH GREED AND SELFISHNESS... AND THE WILL TO SURVIVE!

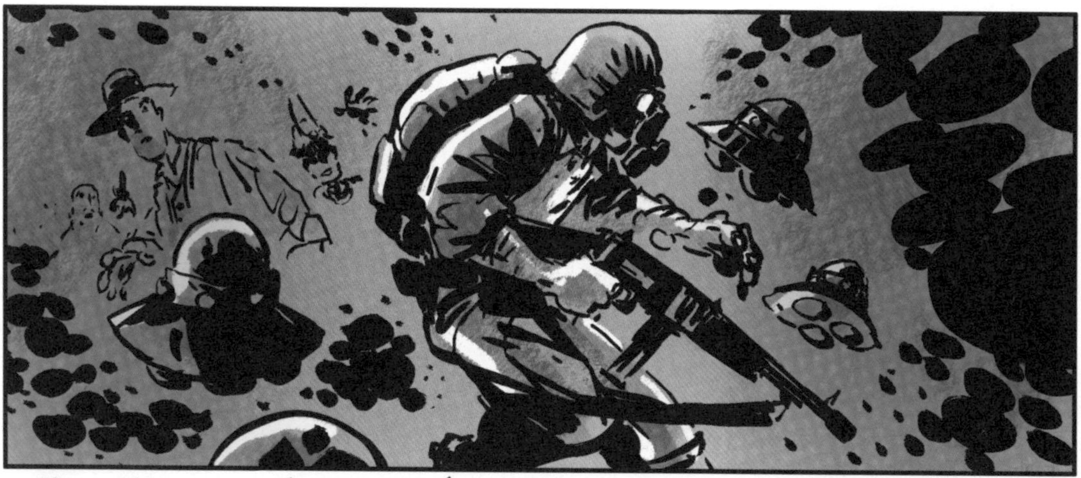

THE WILL TO *SURVIVE!* AND TO SURVIVE IN THE FACE OF THOSE WHO CLAIM CREDIT FOR YOUR VERY EXISTENCE!

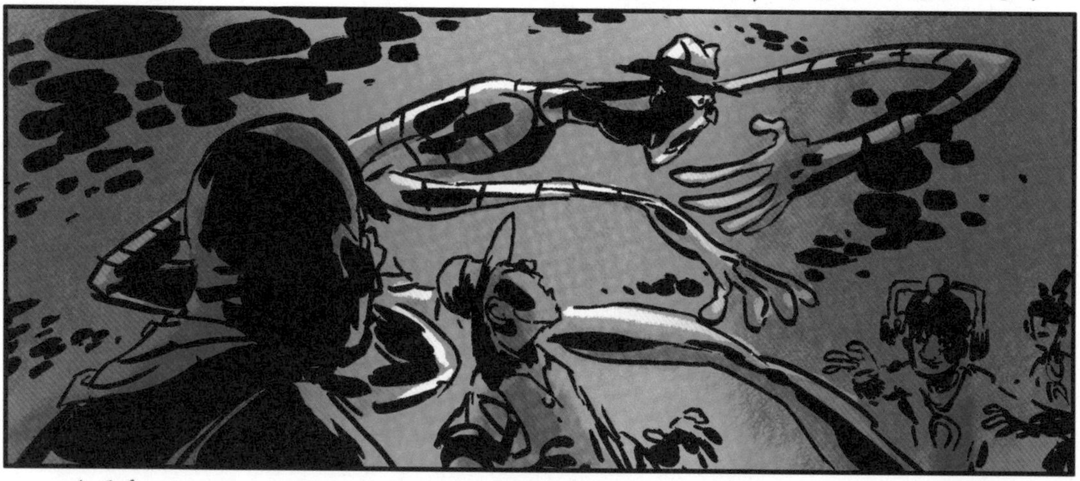

WE SURVIVE NOT AS *PAWNS*, BUT AS AGENTS OF *HOPE*... ...SOMETIMES MISUNDERSTOOD, BUT ALWAYS TRUE TO OUR STORY.

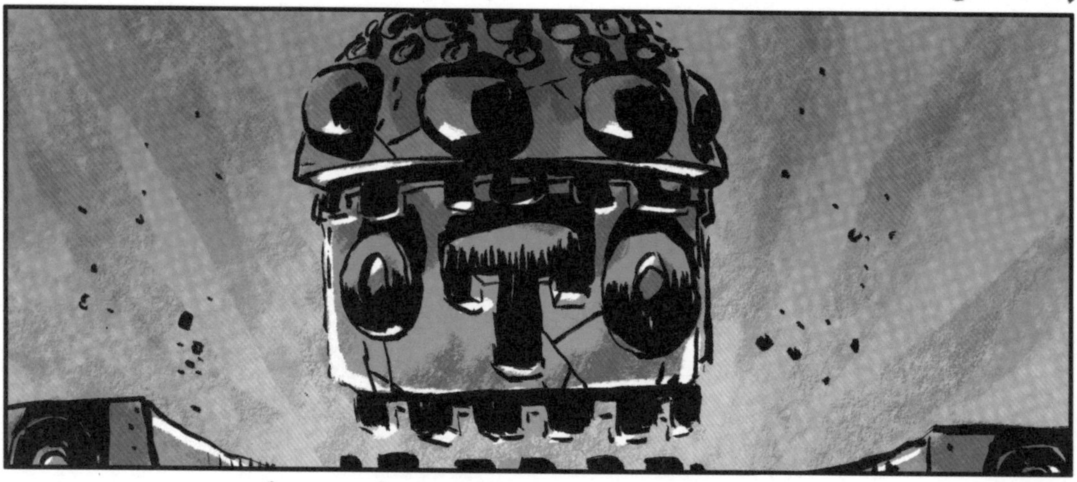

THE STORY OF MAN.

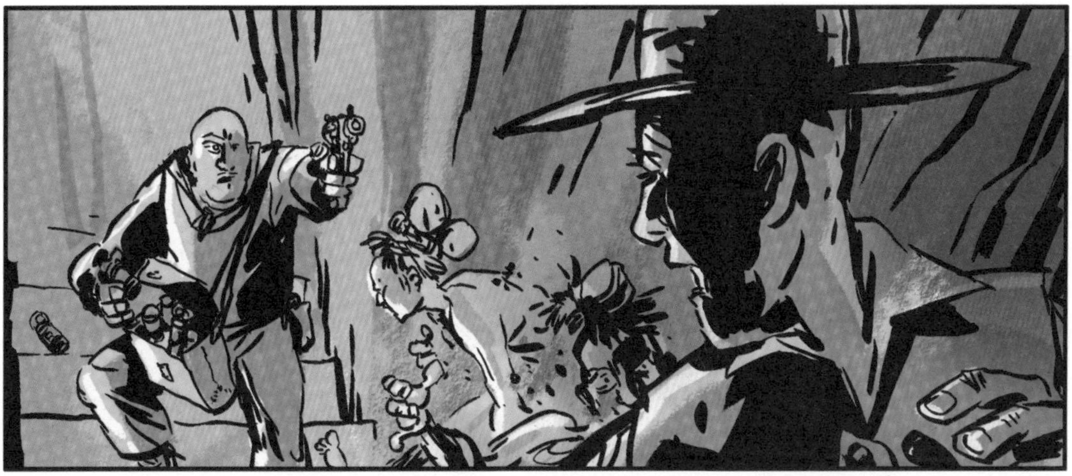

I'M FAIRLY CERTAIN THAT GONZALES WASN'T PAYING COMPLETE ATTENTION, THE TRAITOR.

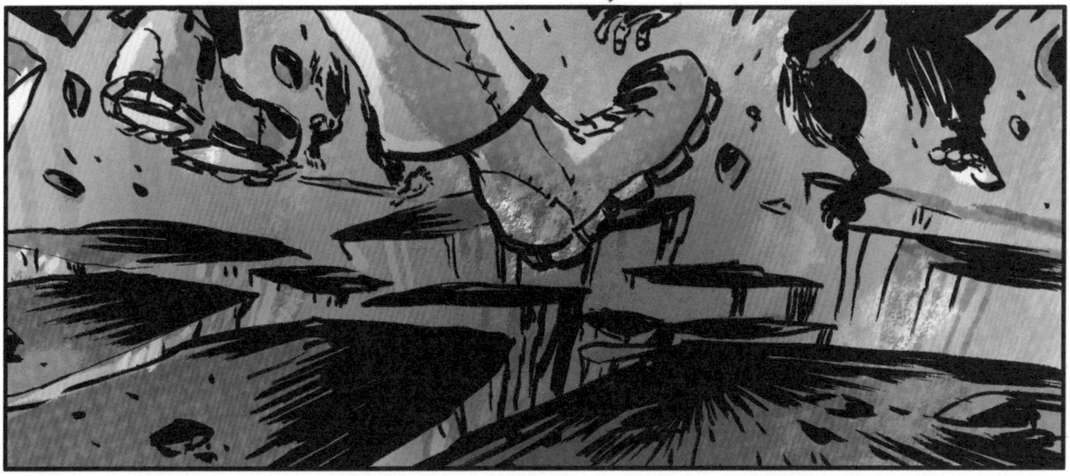

THEN AGAIN, I MYSELF MIGHT HAVE NEGLECTED THE DELICATE NATURE OF OUR SITUATION.

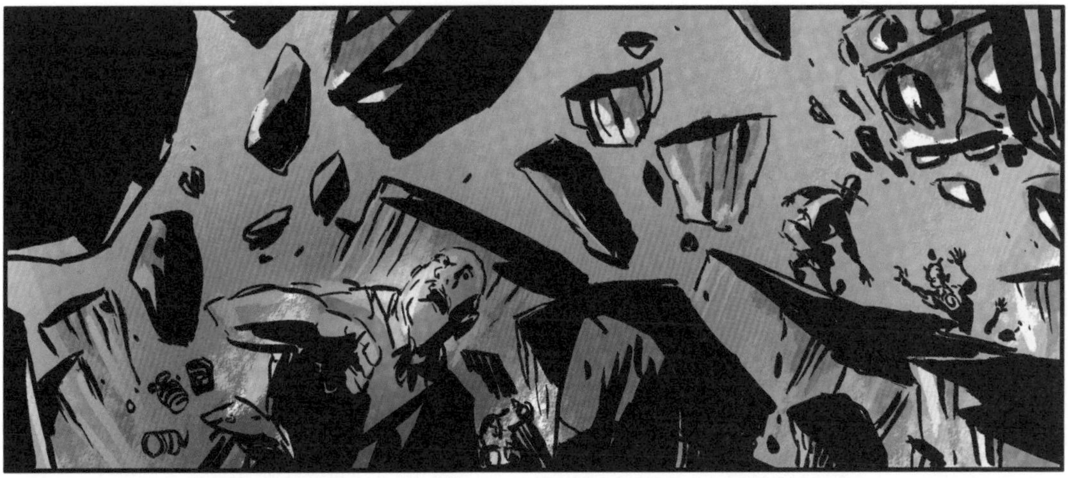

WE WERE STANDING IN THE MOUTH OF A VOLCANO, AFTER ALL, THE VERY SPIRIT OF HUMANITY DANCING HARD UPON ITS LIPS.

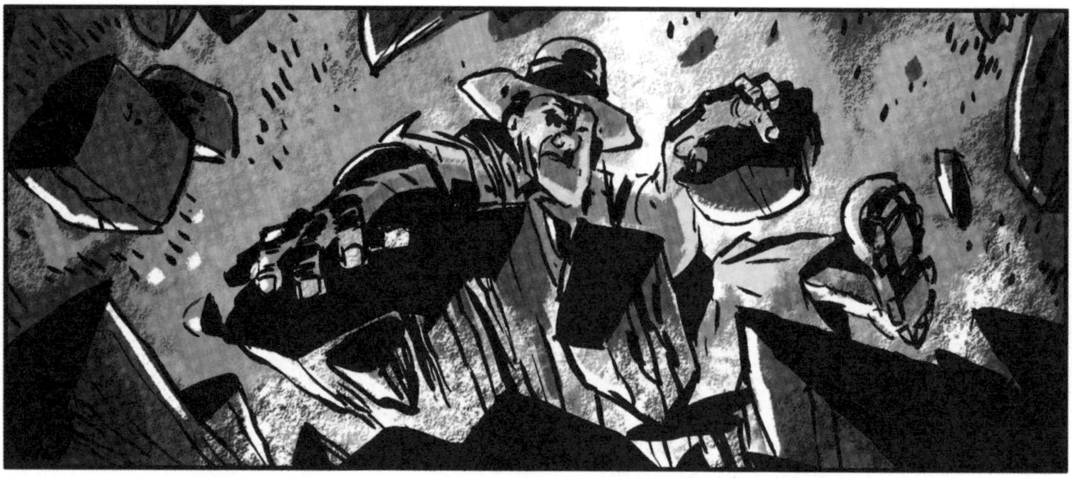

ALLUSION, POETRY, CONTRIVANCE...
THESE ARE PUZZLE PIECES TO THE MIND OF MAN.

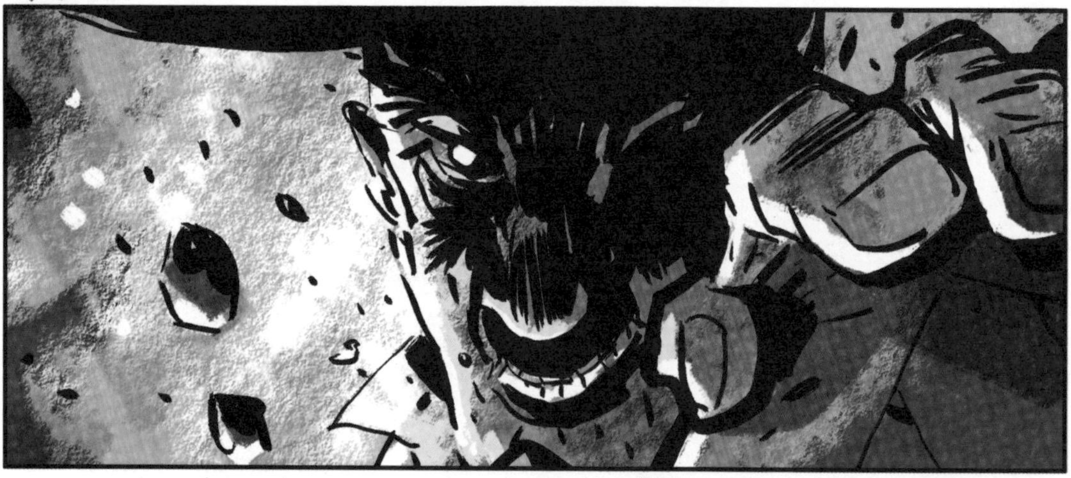

WE HAVE MORE THAN OUR OPPOSABLE THUMBS...
WE HAVE OPPOSING THOUGHTS. AGGESSIVE CURIOSITY.

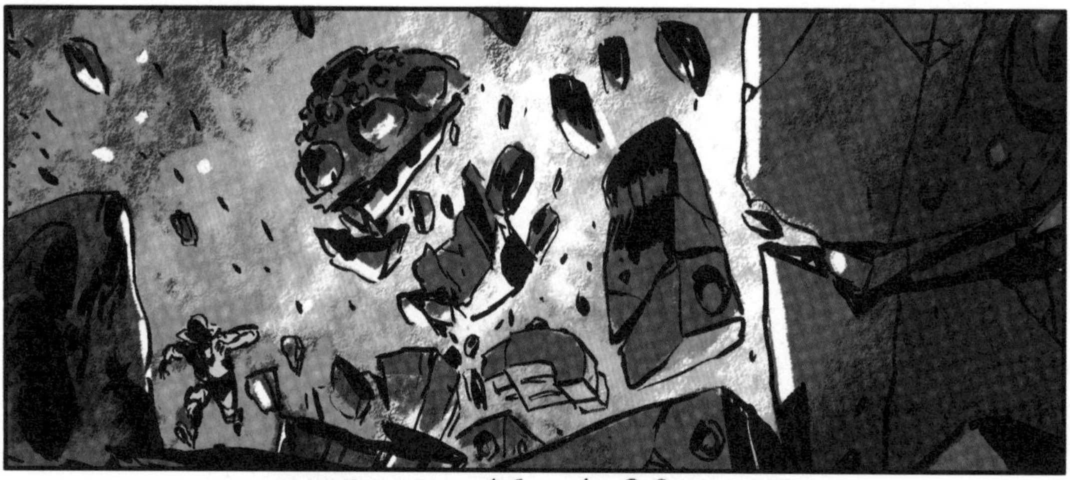

IMAGINATIVE NARRATIVE.
IT'S WHAT HELPS US DISCOVER: "WHAT'S NEXT?"

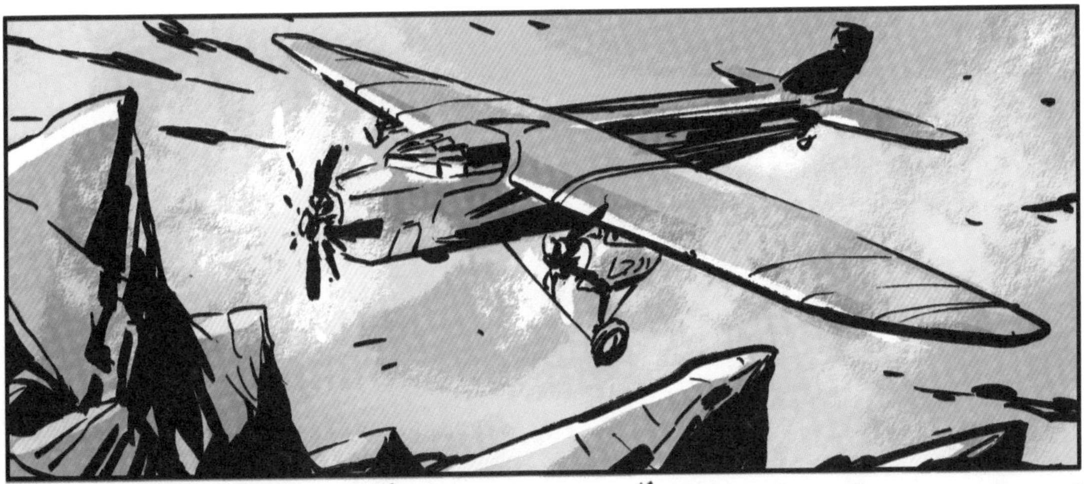

AT OUR MUSEUM OF "CURIOSITIES," MY BROTHER AND I LEFT BELIEVABILITY UP TO THE AUDIENCE.

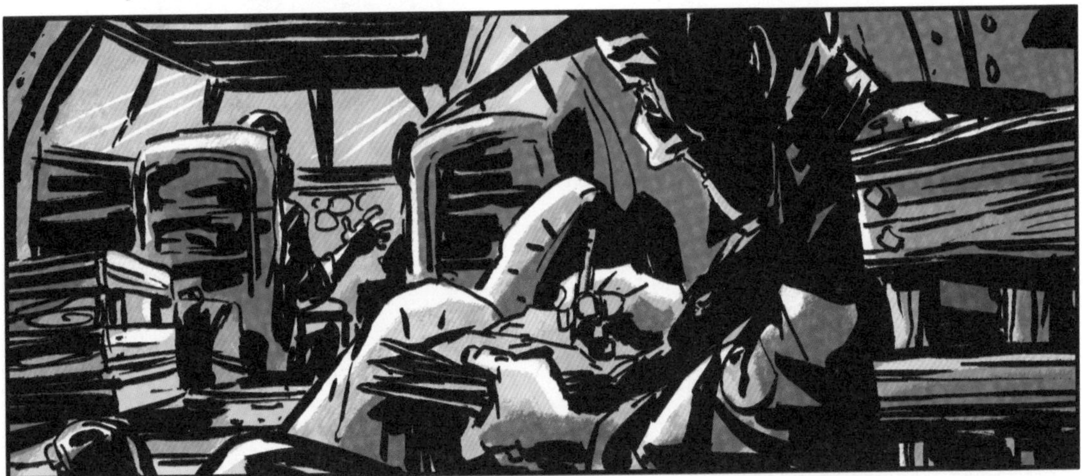

BUT IN THAT JUNGLE I'D LEARNED SOMETHING NEW: THE AUDIENCE VERY MUCH IS THE STORY...

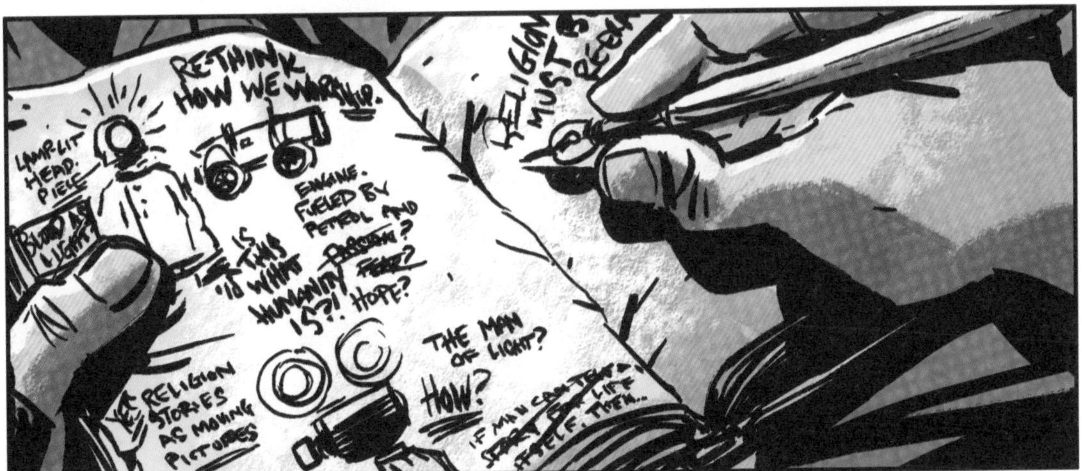
RE-THINK HOW WE WORSHIP.
LAMP-LIT HEAD. PIECE
ENGINE. FUELED BY PETROL AND
IS THIS WHAT HUMANITY IS?!
HOPE?
THE MAN OF LIGHT?
HOW?
RELIGION STORIES AS MOVING PICTURES
RELIGION MUST

...LEAVING BELIEF AS A MOOT POINT.

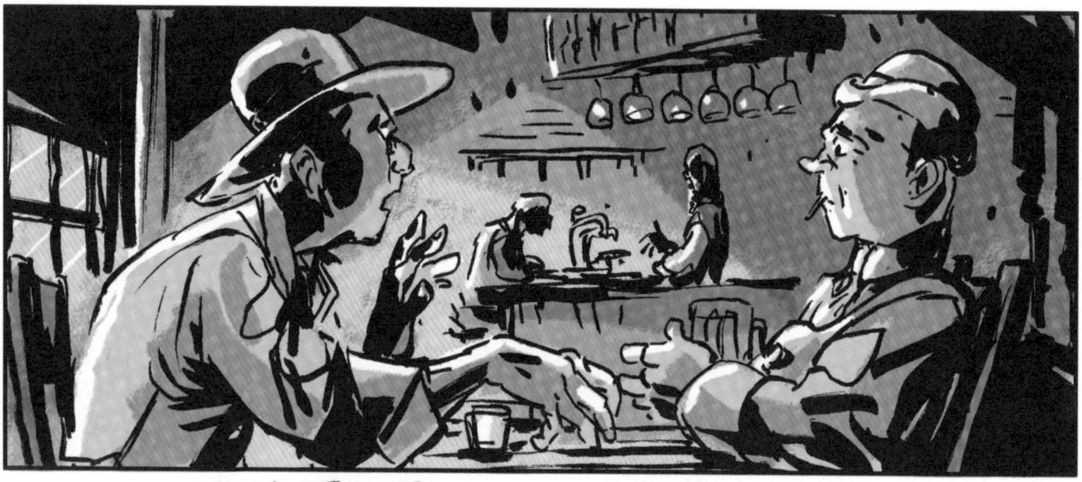

MY BROTHER LISTENED WELL,
A CAPTIVE AUDIENCE OF ONE.

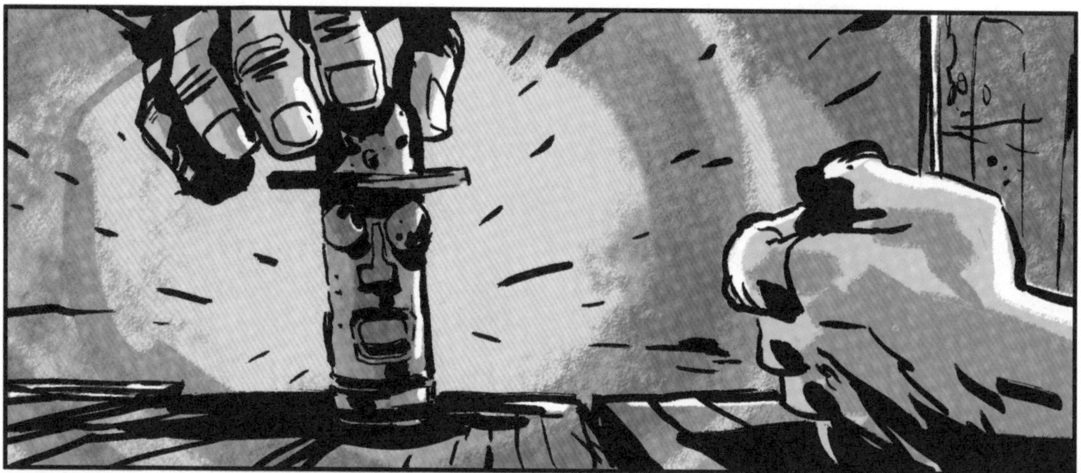

LEE PIERRE HAD LED US DOWN A PATH OF *SALVATION*. WE COULD SHED OUR CHARLATAN WAYS WITH STORIES OF GENUINE SOUL.

GENUINE GODS... FORGOTTEN BY MAN.
RESURRECTED BY US, GIVEN DIGNITY ONCE MORE!

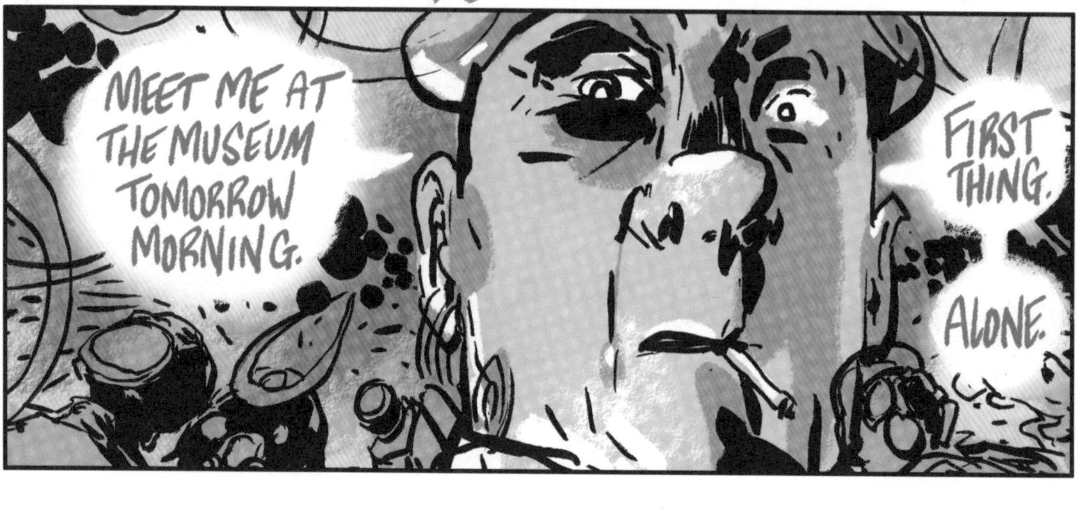
MEET ME AT THE MUSEUM TOMORROW MORNING.
FIRST THING.
ALONE.

THE NEXT MORNING, I SHOWED UP MORE EXCITED THAN WHEN MY HEAD HIT THE PILLOW.

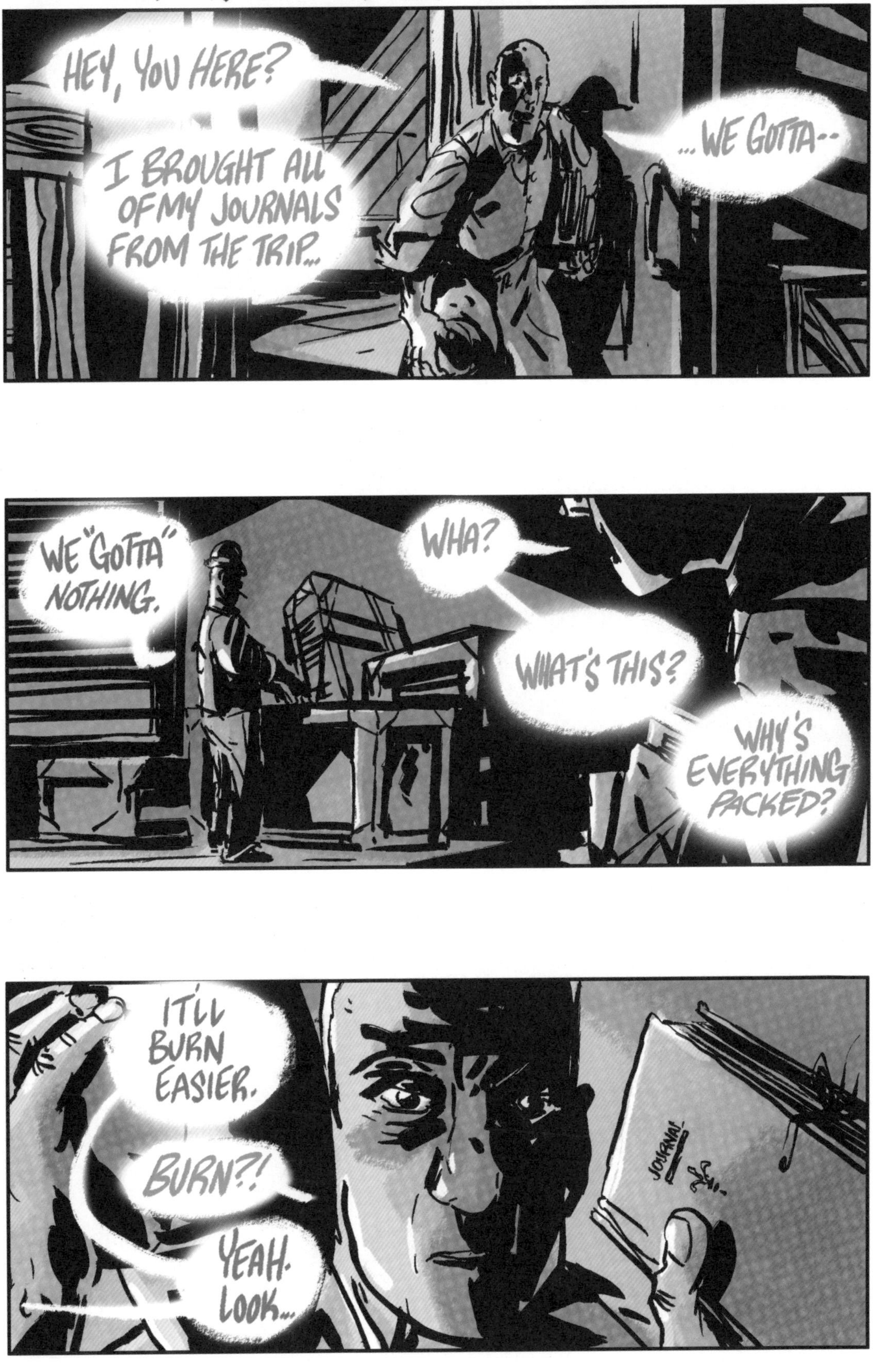
HEY, YOU HERE?
I BROUGHT ALL OF MY JOURNALS FROM THE TRIP...
...WE GOTTA--
WE "GOTTA" NOTHING.
WHA?
WHAT'S THIS?
WHY'S EVERYTHING PACKED?
IT'LL BURN EASIER.
BURN?!
YEAH. LOOK...
JOURNAL

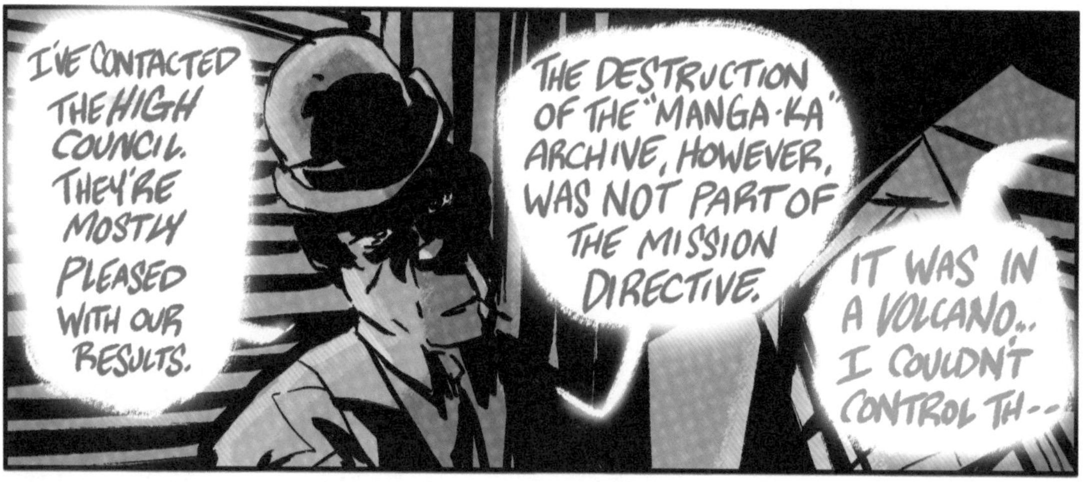
I'VE CONTACTED THE HIGH COUNCIL. THEY'RE MOSTLY PLEASED WITH OUR RESULTS.
THE DESTRUCTION OF THE "MANGA-KA" ARCHIVE, HOWEVER, WAS NOT PART OF THE MISSION DIRECTIVE.
IT WAS IN A VOLCANO.. I COULDN'T CONTROL TH--

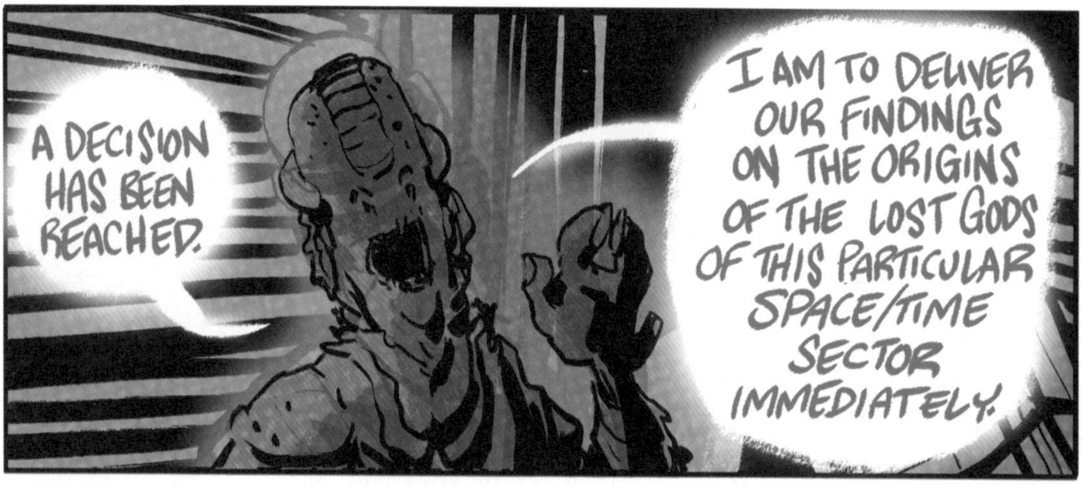
A DECISION HAS BEEN REACHED.
I AM TO DELIVER OUR FINDINGS ON THE ORIGINS OF THE LOST GODS OF THIS PARTICULAR SPACE/TIME SECTOR IMMEDIATELY.

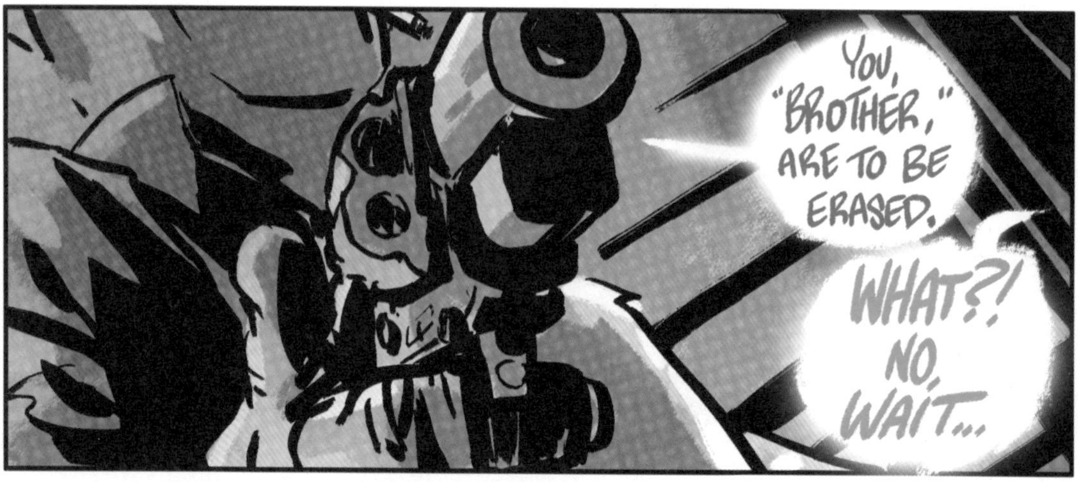
YOU, "BROTHER," ARE TO BE ERASED.
WHAT?! NO, WAIT...

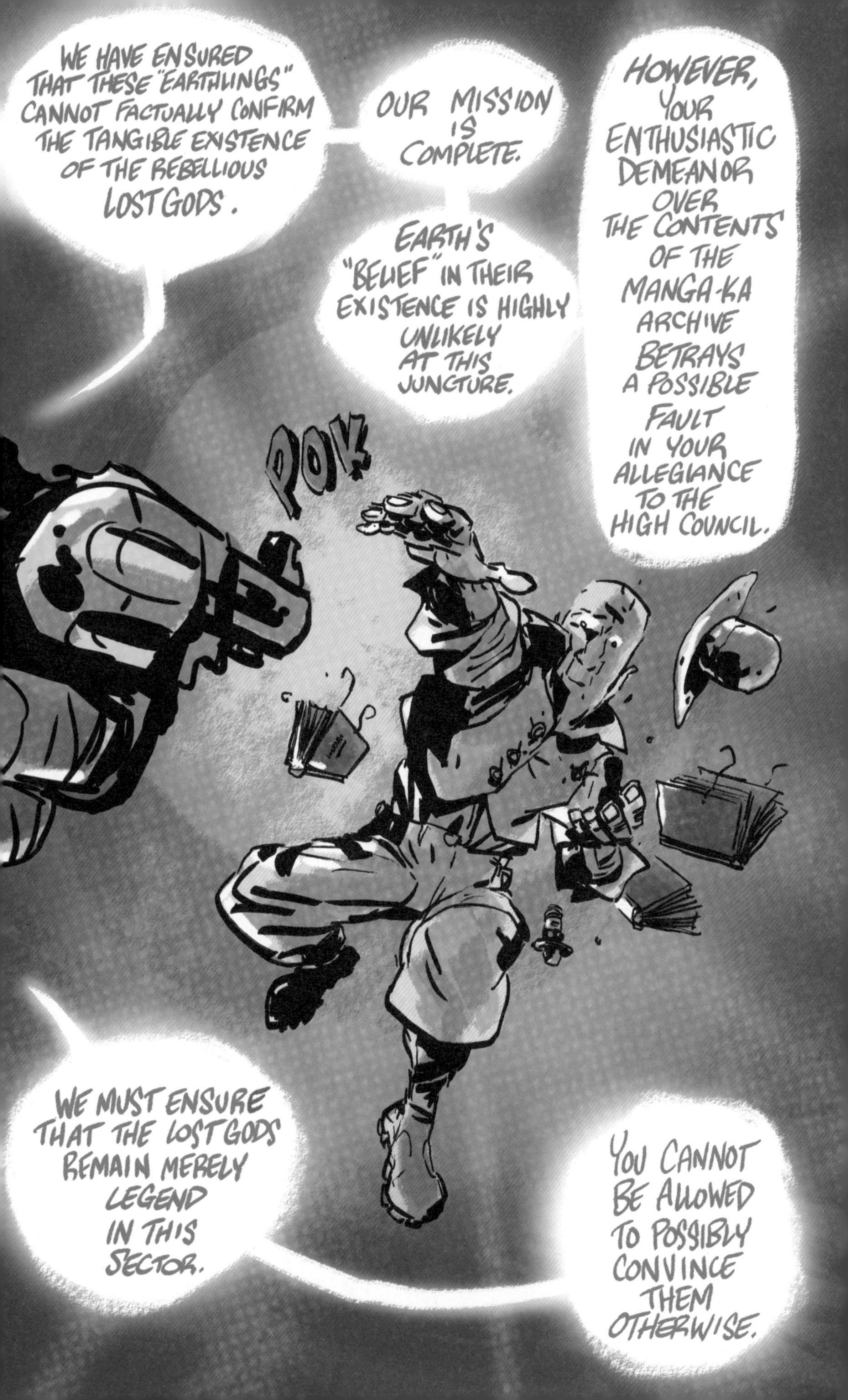
WE HAVE ENSURED THAT THESE "EARTHLINGS" CANNOT FACTUALLY CONFIRM THE TANGIBLE EXISTENCE OF THE REBELLIOUS LOST GODS.
OUR MISSION IS COMPLETE.
EARTH'S "BELIEF" IN THEIR EXISTENCE IS HIGHLY UNLIKELY AT THIS JUNCTURE.
HOWEVER, YOUR ENTHUSIASTIC DEMEANOR OVER THE CONTENTS OF THE MANGA-KA ARCHIVE BETRAYS A POSSIBLE FAULT IN YOUR ALLEGIANCE TO THE HIGH COUNCIL.
POK
WE MUST ENSURE THAT THE LOST GODS REMAIN MERELY LEGEND IN THIS SECTOR.
YOU CANNOT BE ALLOWED TO POSSIBLY CONVINCE THEM OTHERWISE.

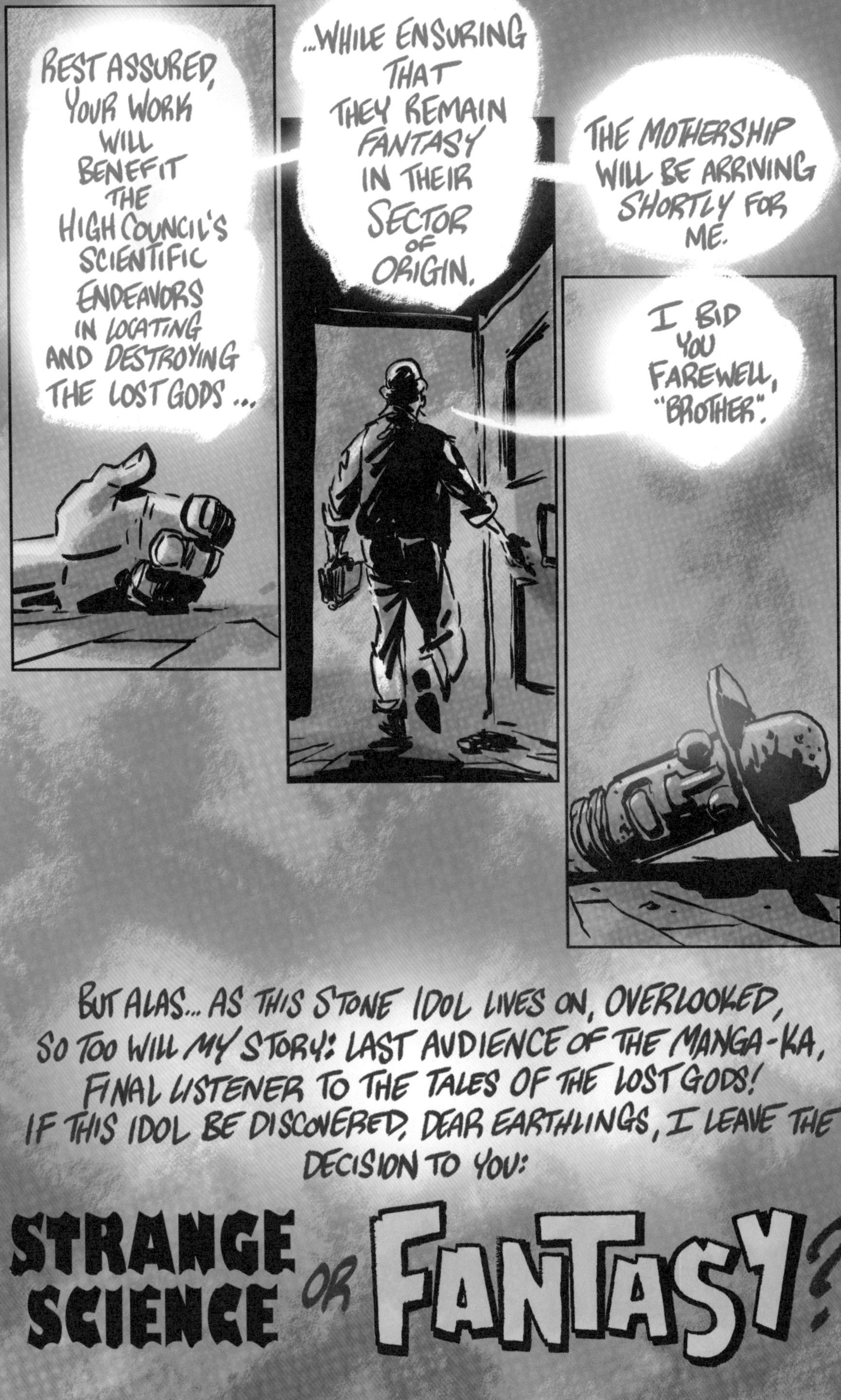
REST ASSURED, YOUR WORK WILL BENEFIT THE HIGH COUNCIL'S SCIENTIFIC ENDEAVORS IN LOCATING AND DESTROYING THE LOST GODS ...
...WHILE ENSURING THAT THEY REMAIN FANTASY IN THEIR SECTOR OF ORIGIN.
THE MOTHERSHIP WILL BE ARRIVING SHORTLY FOR ME.
I BID YOU FAREWELL, "BROTHER".
BUT ALAS... AS THIS STONE IDOL LIVES ON, OVERLOOKED, SO TOO WILL MY STORY: LAST AUDIENCE OF THE MANGA-KA, FINAL LISTENER TO THE TALES OF THE LOST GODS! IF THIS IDOL BE DISCOVERED, DEAR EARTHLINGS, I LEAVE THE DECISION TO YOU:
STRANGE SCIENCE OR FANTASY?

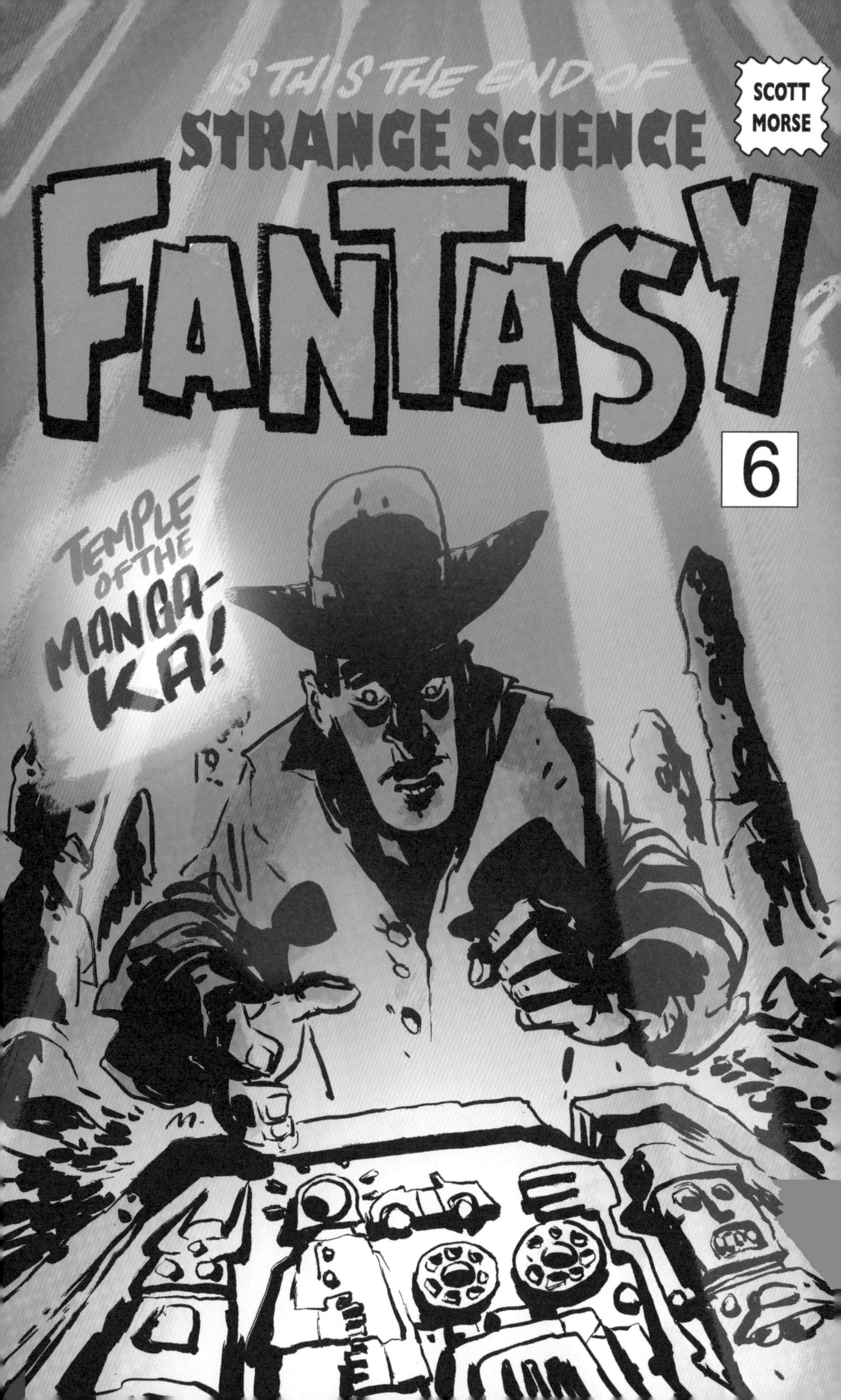
IS THIS THE END OF
STRANGE SCIENCE
FANTASY
SCOTT MORSE
6
TEMPLE OF THE MANGA-KA!

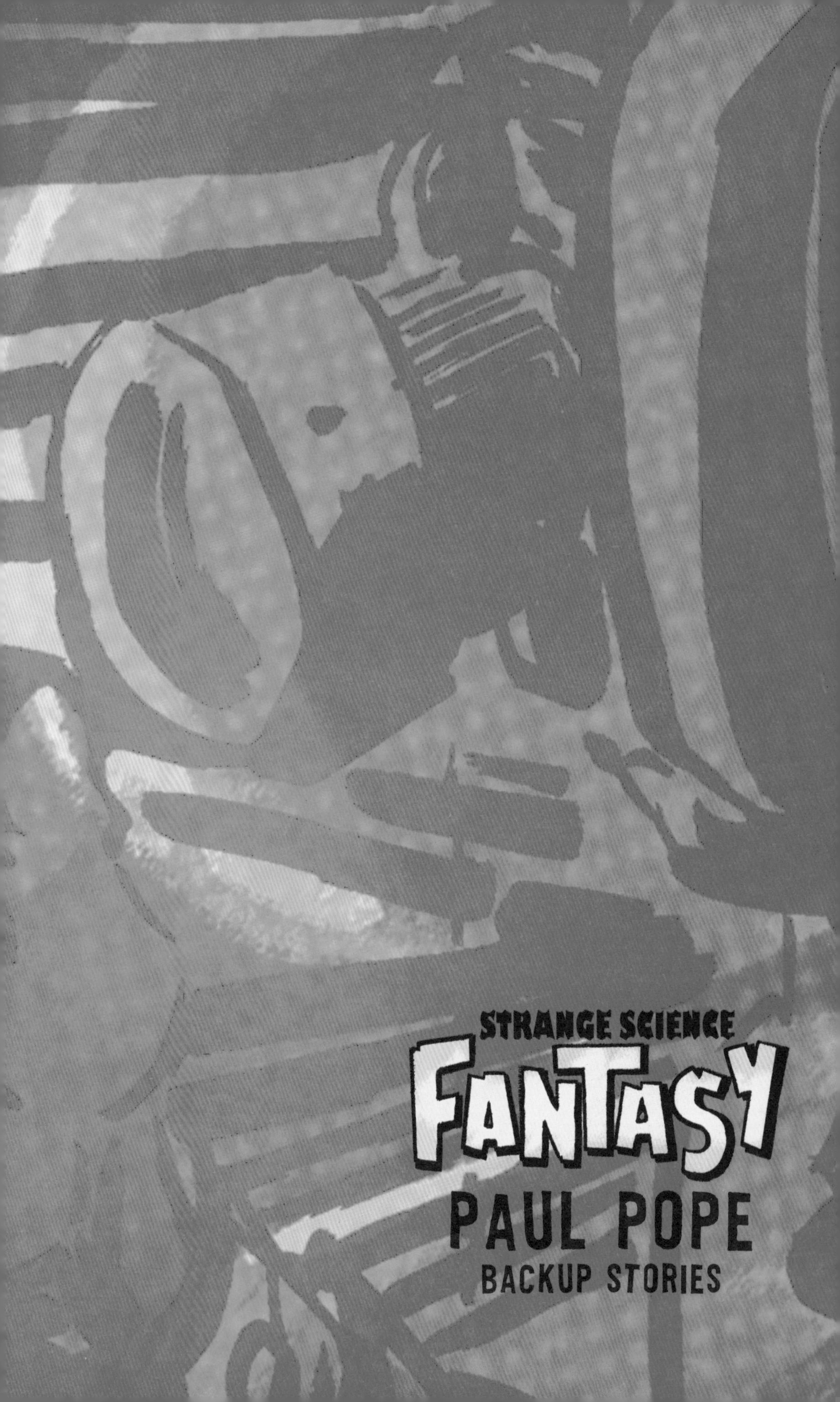
STRANGE SCIENCE
FANTASY
PAUL POPE
BACKUP STORIES

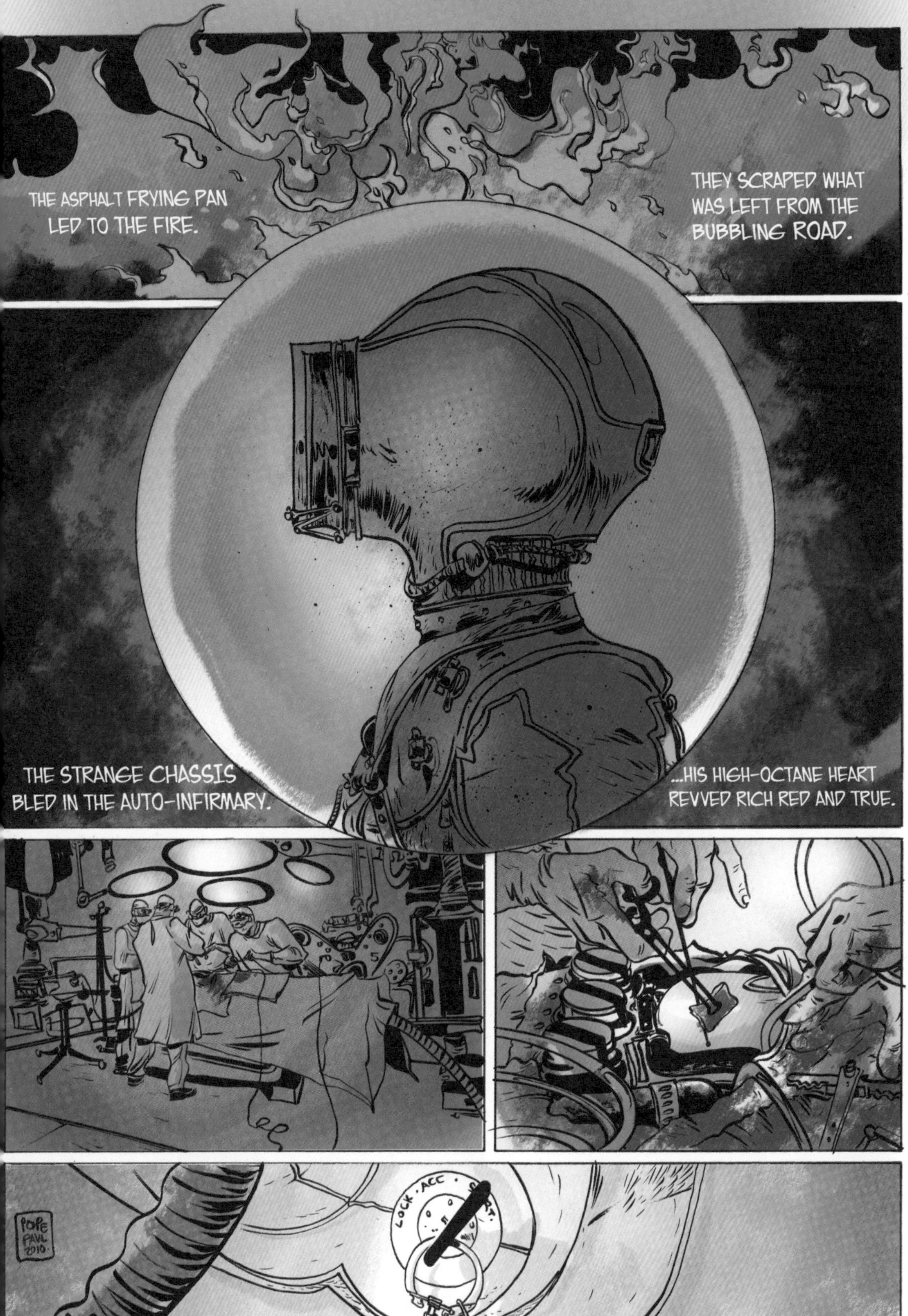
THE ASPHALT FRYING PAN
LED TO THE FIRE.
THEY SCRAPED WHAT
WAS LEFT FROM THE
BUBBLING ROAD.
THE STRANGE CHASSIS
BLED IN THE AUTO-INFIRMARY.
...HIS HIGH-OCTANE HEART
REVVED RICH RED AND TRUE.
POPE
PAUL
2010.

... A HAND CHARGED WITH CALCULATED JUDGEMENT...

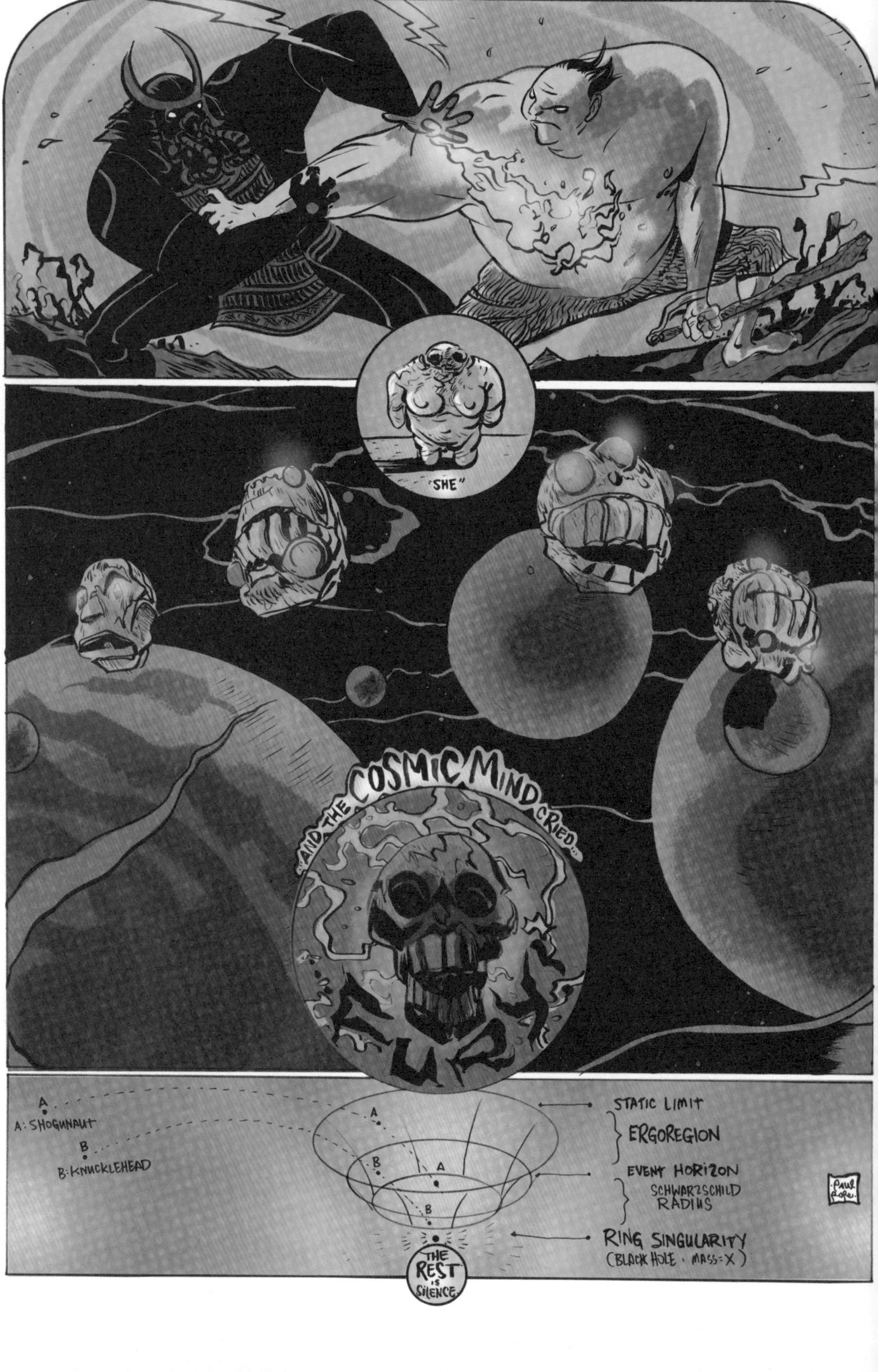
"SHE"
...AND THE COSMIC MIND CRIED...
A: SHOGUNAUT
B: KNUCKLEHEAD
STATIC LIMIT
ERGOREGION
EVENT HORIZON
SCHWARZSCHILD RADIUS
RING SINGULARITY
(BLACK HOLE · MASS=X)
THE REST IS SILENCE.
PAUL POPE

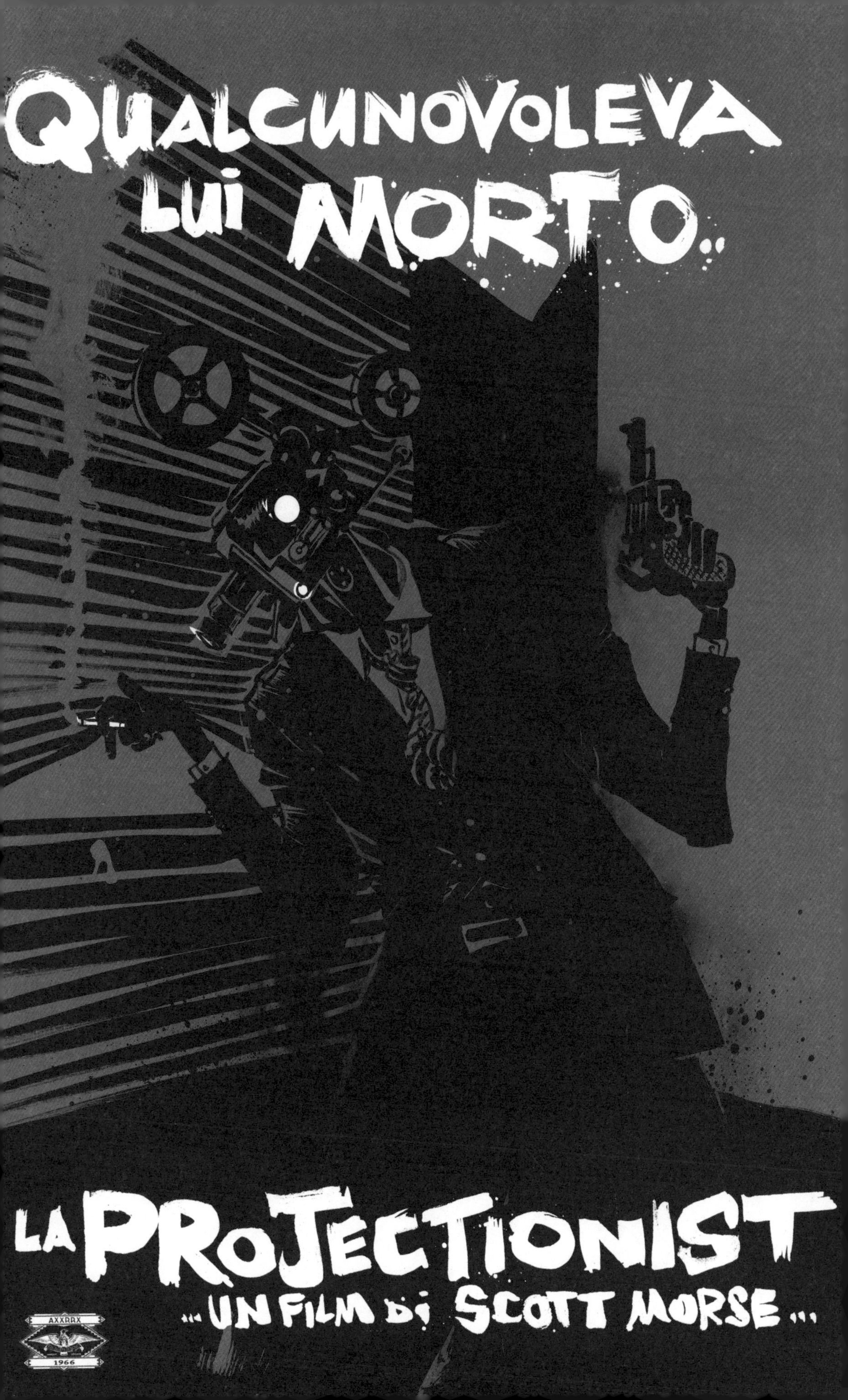
QUALCUNOVOLEVA
LUI MORTO...
LA PROJECTIONIST
...UN FILM DI SCOTT MORSE...
AXXRRX
1966

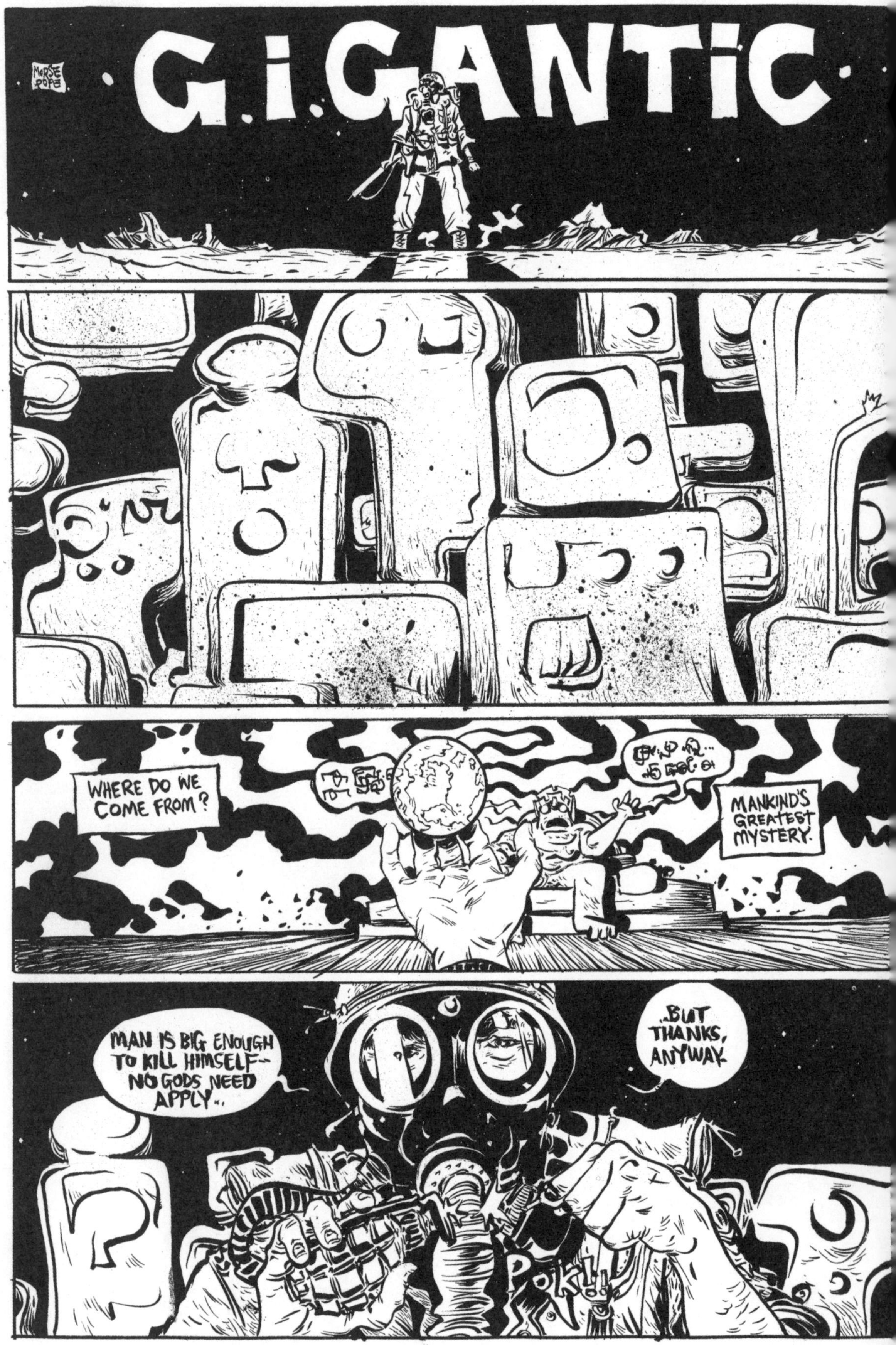

G.I.GANTIC
MORSE POPE
WHERE DO WE COME FROM?
MANKIND'S GREATEST MYSTERY.
MAN IS BIG ENOUGH TO KILL HIMSELF– NO GODS NEED APPLY...
..BUT THANKS, ANYWAY.
POK!!

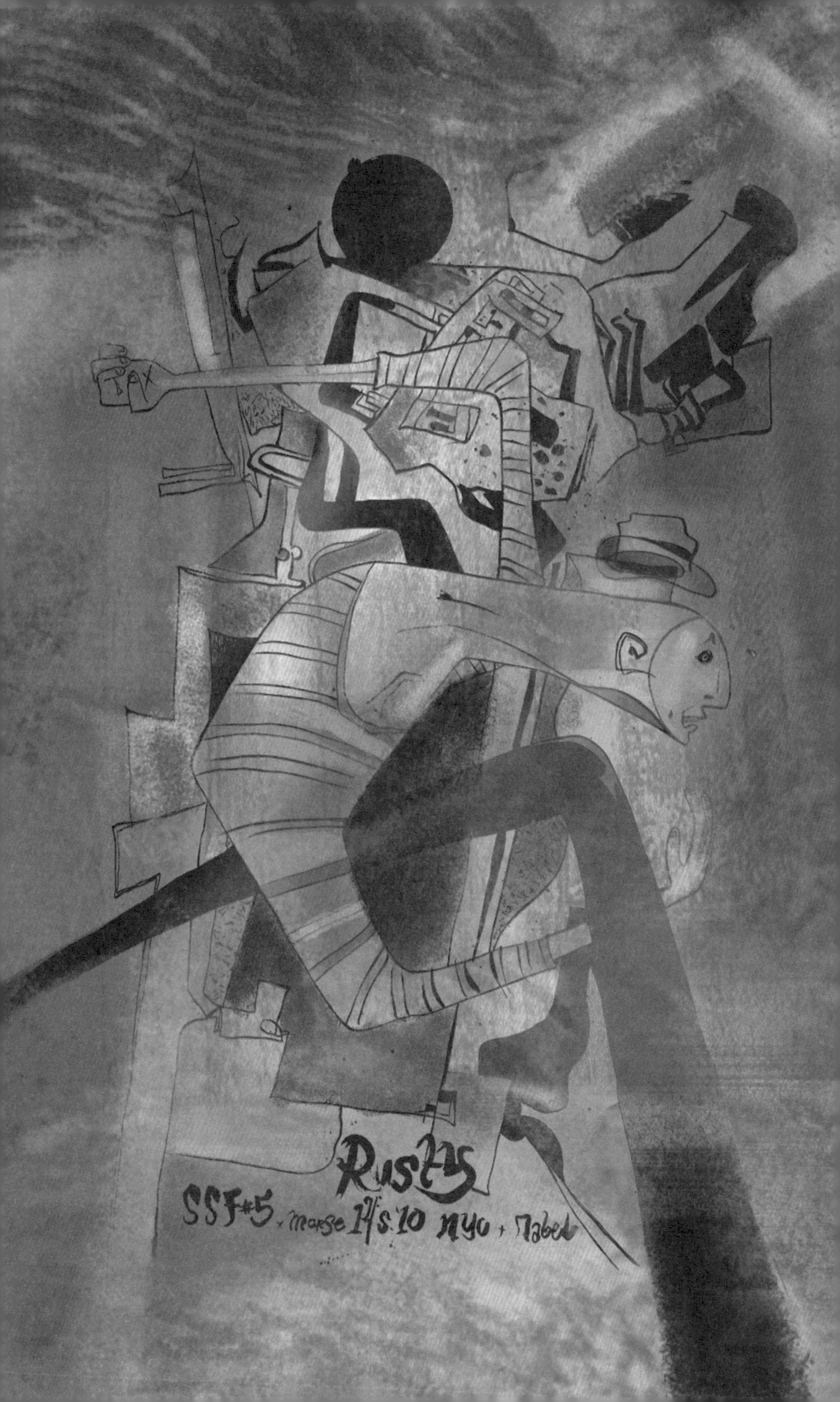
TAX
Rusty
SSF#5 × marse 14/s.10 nyc + Mabel

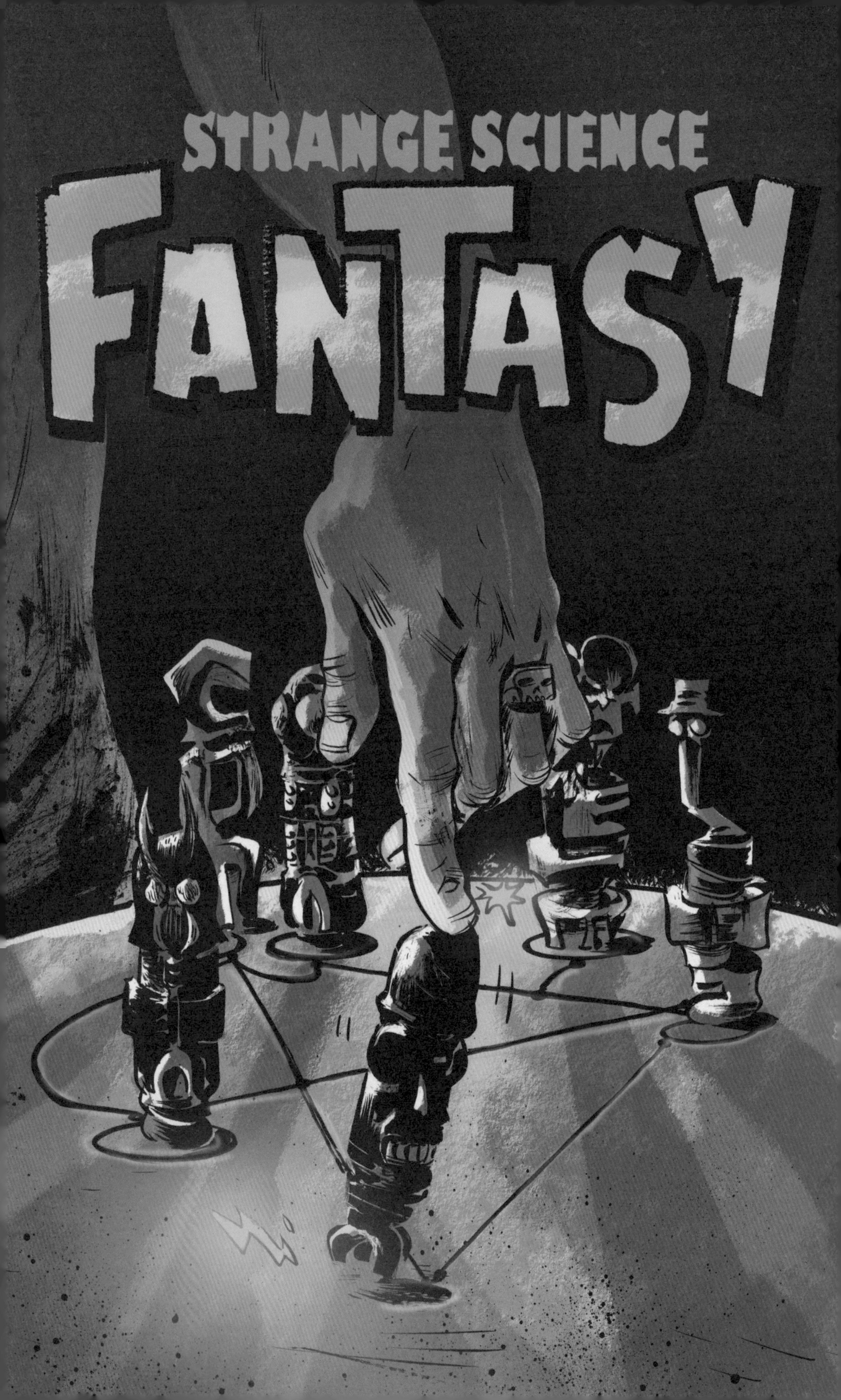
STRANGE SCIENCE
FANTASY

STRANGE SCIENCE
FANTASY

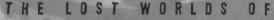

PURE COMICS. THAT'S WHAT I INTENDED TO DELIVER WITH STRANGE SCIENCE FANTASY, AND I HOPE IT FEELS TRUE TO ITS INSPIRATION: THE PURE COMICS VIBE GENERATED BY JACK KIRBY, STEVE DITKO, ALEX TOTH, JACK COLE, AND THE COUNTLESS OTHER CONJURERS OF PRE-HERO STORIES. I WANTED TO TRY TO TAP INTO THAT INSANE, BOLD, COURAGEOUS MINDSET MADE FAMOUS BY THESE HEROES OF MINE. THERE WAS AN AIR OF EXCITEMENT SURROUNDING THESE OLD STORIES, A NOTION OF MAKING CRAZY IDEAS VIABLE ON THE PAGE. POWER.

STRANGE SCIENCE FANTASY ENCOMPASSES ALL SORTS OF STORY "TYPES" UNDER ONE ROOF. INITIALLY, I THOUGHT ALMOST ANYTHING WOULD WORK IN THE OVER-ALL FRAMEWORK OF THE BOOK. HOWEVER, A FEW STORIES WERE MOVED OUT OF THE ROSTER FOR VARIOUS REASONS. WHAT FOLLOWS ARE INITIAL COVER CONCEPTS FOR "LOST" STRANGE SCIENCE FANTASY TALES. ASTUTE READERS MIGHT RECOGNIZE ONE OR TWO OF THE CHARACTERS OR IDEAS, AS I'VE HAD THEM IN THE DARK RECESSES OF MY SKULL FOR SOME TIME, WAITING FOR THE RIGHT OPPORTUNITY TO SPRING FORTH AND CONQUER. THEIR TIME HASN'T YET COME, I'M AFRAID, BUT THESE COVERS GIVE HINTS THAT THE WORLDS OF STRANGE SCIENCE FANTASY ARE FAR REACHING, INDEED, AND THERE'S EXPLORING YET TO DO...

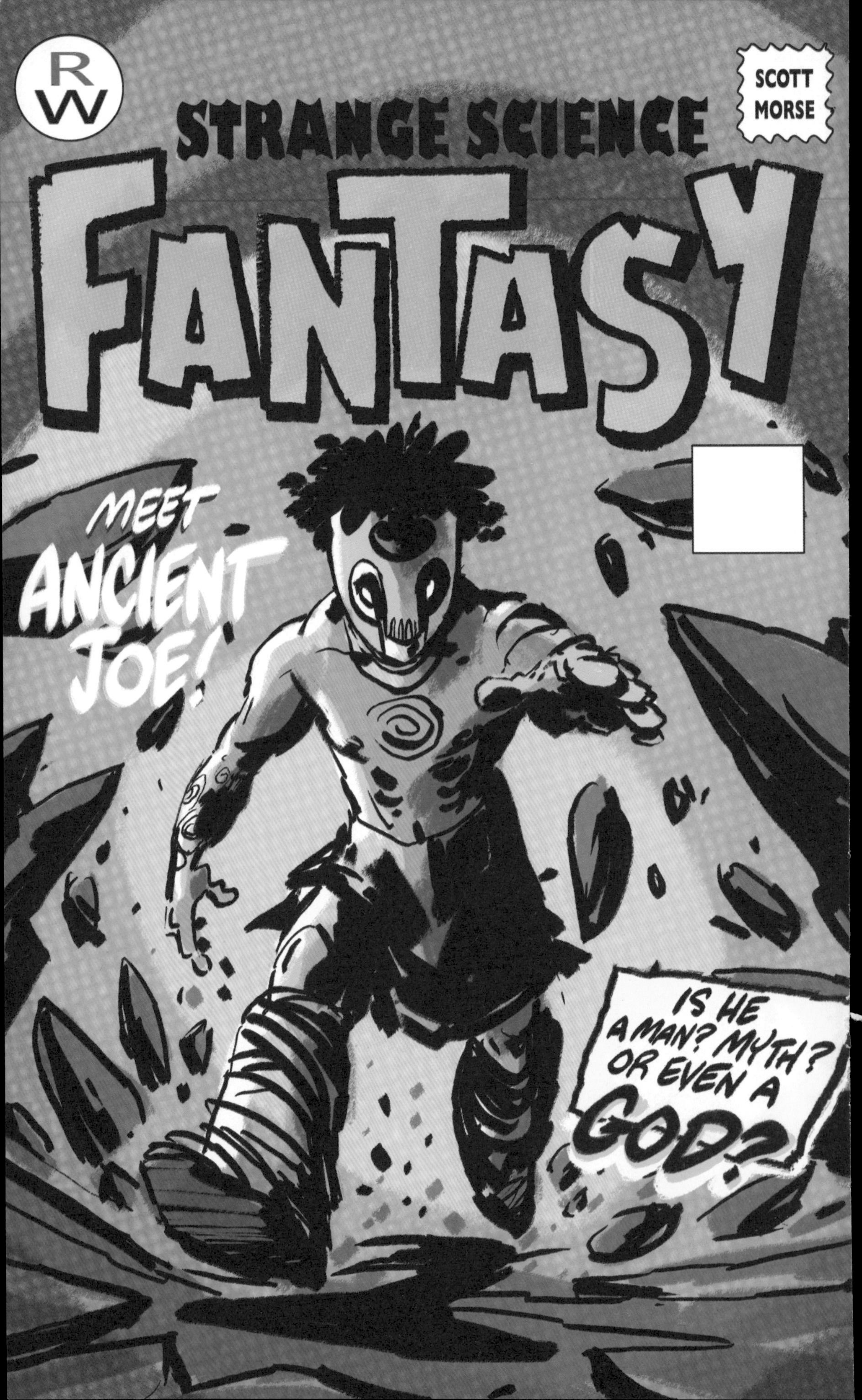
RW
SCOTT MORSE
STRANGE SCIENCE
FANTASY
MEET
ANCIENT
JOE!
IS HE
A MAN? MYTH?
OR EVEN A
GOD?

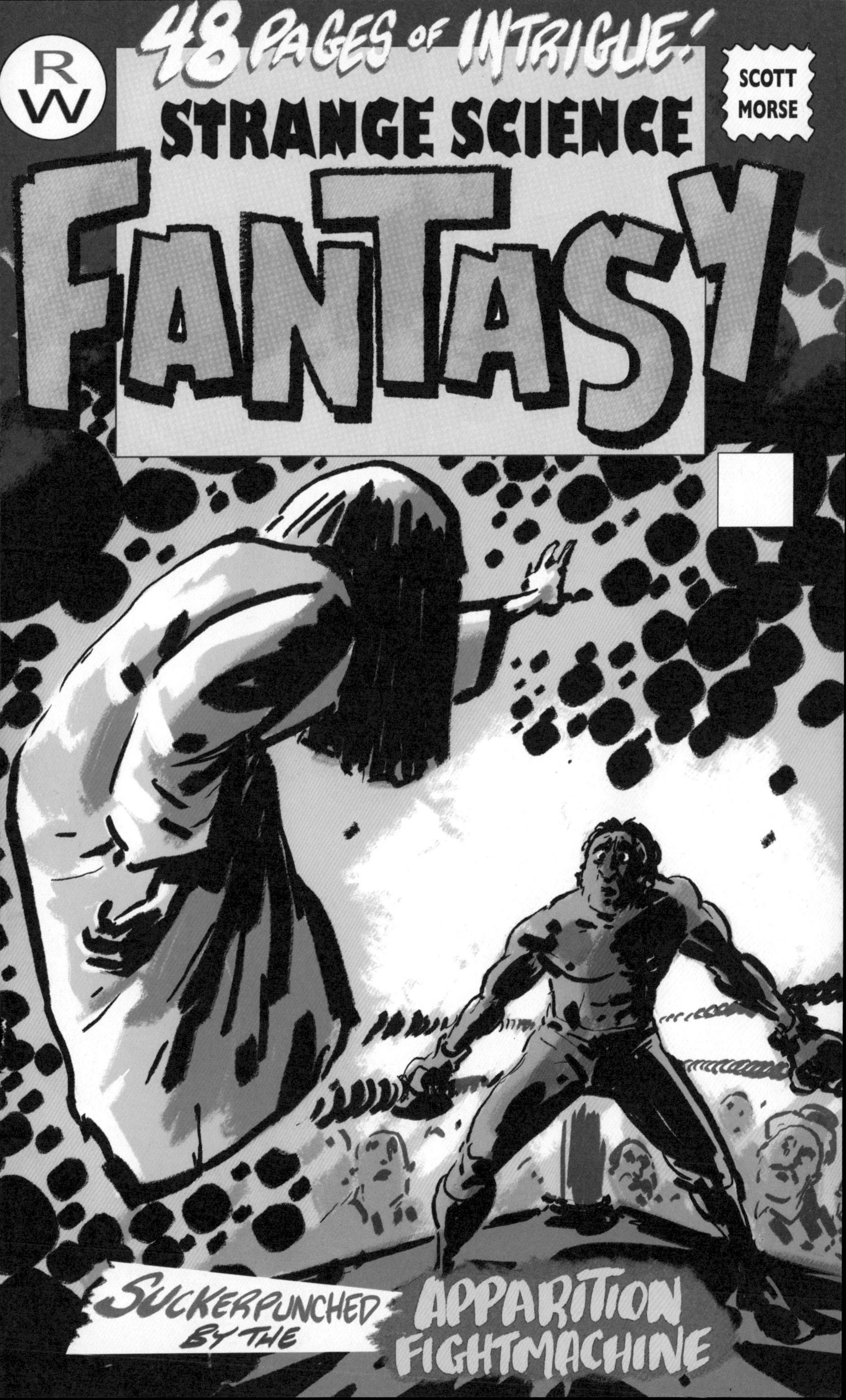

48 PAGES OF INTRIGUE!
RW
STRANGE SCIENCE
SCOTT MORSE
FANTASY
SUCKERPUNCHED BY THE
APPARITION FIGHTMACHINE

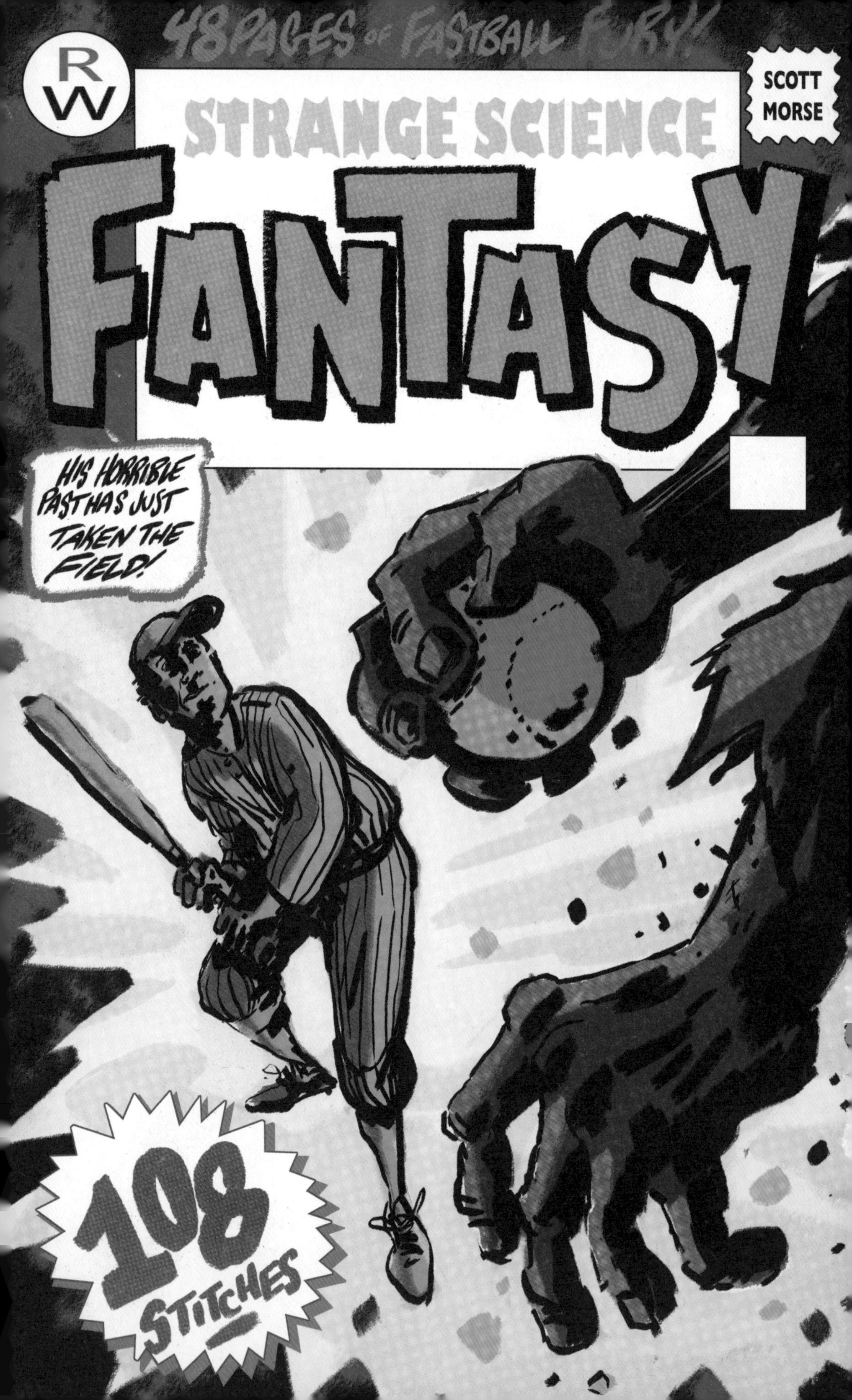
48 PAGES OF FASTBALL FURY!
RW
SCOTT MORSE
STRANGE SCIENCE
FANTASY!
HIS HORRIBLE PAST HAS JUST TAKEN THE FIELD!
108 STITCHES